Boyd's COMMENTARY

2022–2023

VOLUME 116

These commentaries are based on the International Sunday School Lessons and International Bible Lessons for Christian Teaching, copyrighted by the International Council of Religious Education, and is used by permission.

Entered according to Act of Congress in the Office of Librarian of Congress in the year 1903 at Washington, DC, by R. H. Boyd, DD, LLD

R. H. Boyd, DD, LLD, Founder (1896–1922)

H. A. Boyd, DD (1922–1959) • T. B. Boyd Jr., DD (1959–1979) • T. B. Boyd III, DD (1979–2017)

LaDonna Boyd, EdD
President/CEO (2017–Present)

LaDonna Boyd, EdD
President/CEO

David Groves, DMin, PhD
Director of Publications

EDITORIAL STAFF
Olivia M. Cloud, MRE
Associate Editor

Landon Dickerson, MTS; Monique Gooch, BA; Joseph Tribble, MDiv;
Brittany Batson, BA; Sinclaire Sparkman, BS; Freida Crawley, BS; Carla Davis, BA

Rev. Nikki Tolliver • Dr. Ricky Woods
Dr. Bernard Williams • Dr. Barry Johnson
Writers

Jasmine Cole
Cover Design

For Customer Service
and Toll-Free Ordering, Call
1-877-4RHBOYD (474-2693)
Monday–Friday
8 a.m.–5 p.m. Central Time or
Fax Toll-Free (800) 615-1815

R.H. BOYD
EST. 1896

www.rhboyd.com

R.H. Boyd Publishing Corporation
6717 Centennial Blvd.• Nashville, Tennessee 37209-1017

A WORD FROM THE PUBLISHER

To Our Readers,

Thank you for your patronage. We are elated you have chosen to share in the Gospel ministry of this commentary. For over a century, *Boyd's Commentary for the Sunday School* has been a mainstay in discipleship ministry. As you can expect of our brand, this commentary has been prepared and informed by prayerful and Spirit led scholarship.

Our hope is that you will encounter the Spirit as you work through this year's lessons. As you read, may these lessons give new you new vitality as a leader, minister, and lover of God. This past year undoubtedly has brought its own set of challenges, moments of grief, and times of celebration. We have not been able to eradicate COVID-19 from our midst and are having to learn flexibility as a part of our leadership tool bag. Now, possibly more than ever, building strong leaders with sound biblical knowledge and theological coping skills is vital. Our goal is to equip readers with a solid foundation for the world in which we live.

Again, thank you for your support. As you enjoy this resource, please visit our website, *www.rhboyd.com*, and follow us on social media @rhboydco to stay abreast of all the resources offered by R.H. Boyd.

Onward,

LaDonna Boyd, EdD
Fifth-generation *President/CEO*

A WORD FROM THE DIRECTOR

Greetings!

For well over a century, *Boyd's Commentary* has been an expositional resource for those who have a passion to study God's Word with depth and clarity. Be assured this commentary has been developed by people of faith who serve in all manner of leadership capacities within the Church. Our goal is to provide you with a commentary that will meet your needs as you apply biblical messages to guide, enlighten, and give voice to those for whom you are responsible. We pray that the carefully selected biblical texts will address your contemporary issues and needs in a way that brings you closer to God and grants the ability of discernment of His will. Our goal, hope, and prayer is that *Boyd's Commentary for the Sunday School* will serve your biblical and theological training needs. Thank you for your continued support of our products.

Yours in Christ,

Rev. David Groves, DMin, PhD

NOTES FROM THE EDITOR

The layout of the *2022–2023 Boyd's Commentary* has been formatted for easy use in the classroom. In keeping with our rich history of publishing quality Christian literature, we have added the Unifying Principle as a feature that will enhance our commentary. Listed below is an explanation of each feature and the intended use of each.

Lesson Setting: Gives the basic time line and place for the events in the lesson.

Lesson Outline: Provides the topics used in the exposition of the lesson.

Unifying Principle: States the main idea for the lesson across age groups. This feature allows the teacher to understand exactly what each lesson is about.

Introduction: Gives the thesis and any background information that will be useful in the study of the lesson.

Exposition: Provides the exegetical study done by the writer, breaking down the text for discussion.

The Lesson Applied: Provides possible life applications of the biblical text for today's learners.

Let's Talk About It: Highlights ideas from the text in a question-and-answer format.

Home Daily Devotional Readings: Located at the end of each lesson, the topics are designed to lead into the following lesson.

Know Your Writers

Rev. Nikki Harris Tolliver

Rev. Nikki Harris Tolliver is a native of Cleveland, Ohio currently residing in Nashville, TN. She is a graduate of Fisk University and received her Master of Arts in Theological Studies with emphasis in Black Church Studies from Vanderbilt University Divinity School. She has previously served full time in ministry as a Youth Pastor and later Pastor of Assimilation. Currently Nikki works as an Operations Associate for Faith Matters Network and Associate Minister at First Baptist South Inglewood Church.

• •

Dr. Ricky A. Woods

Dr. Ricky A. Woods was named senior minister of First Baptist Church-West in 1995, and has worked tirelessly, not only to serve as minister to the church's members, but also to help the church serve as a community beacon of social justice. He formerly served as the Samuel Dewitt Proctor Senior Mentor at United Theological Seminary in Dayton, Ohio. A graduate of North Carolina A&T State University in Greensboro with a Bachelor of Science degree in economics, Dr. Woods graduated cum laude with a Master of Divinity degree from the Samuel DeWitt Proctor School of Theology of Virginia Union University in Richmond, Virginia, and then earned the Doctor of Ministry degree from United Theological Seminary in Dayton. Dr. Woods is also a member of the World Baptist Alliance and the Academy of Homiletics. Dr. Woods is married to the former Laura Annette Hill and they are the proud parents of one daughter, Lauren Adelle.

• •

Dr. Bernard Williams

Dr. Bernard Williams is a native of Nashville, Tennessee. He has pastored churches in Tennessee and Florida. He is a graduate of the University of Tennessee Knoxville and The Southern Baptist Theological Seminary in Louisville, Kentucky. He also holds a Ph.D. in homiletics and church and society. Dr. Williams is a great proponent of small-group Bible study and serves as a teacher in Christian education. He holds numerous revivals, conferences, workshops, and seminars each year. He is a member of the American Academy of Religion and the Academy of Homiletics.

• •

Dr. Barry Johnson

Dr. Barry C. Johnson, a native of Louisville, serves as the Pastor of the Southern Star Baptist Church of Louisville, Kentucky. Dr. Johnson holds the Bachelor (BM) and Masters Degrees (MM) in Music Composition from the University of Louisville, Doctor of Musical Arts (DMA) degree in Music Composition from the University of Kentucky, Master of Divinity (M.Div) and Doctor of Ministry (D.Min) degrees in Black Church Studies from the Southern Baptist Theological Seminary, in addition to Post-Doctoral studies at Berklee College of Music. Previous teaching assignments were at Savannah State University, Western Kentucky University, and Kentucky State University, where he retired as a Full Professor of Music. An avid musician, scholar, and composer, Dr. Johnson is the owner of TNT Productions and Recording Studios and teaches part-time at the University of Louisville in the School of Music.

2022–2023 LESSON OVERVIEW

The Fall Quarter, God's Exceptional Choice, traces the arc of salvation history from Abraham to Jesus and on to the early church. Unit I, "God Calls Abraham's Family," is drawn from Genesis and chronicles the origin of the chosen people, Israel, from Abraham to Judah. Unit II journeys through Exodus, Deuteronomy, Judges, and 1 Samuel showing the move to nationhood. Finally, Unit III explores the theme of chosenness through the perspective of the book of Ephesians.

The Winter Quarter, From Darkness to Light, continues the theme "Chosen, Not Choice" and the peculiarity of God's calling, which is rooted in grace rather than humankind's merit. Unit I, "God Prepares the Way," concentrates on preparation for the coming Christ. Unit II, "God's Promises," reminds us to trust God's Word. Unit III, "God's Call and Its Responsibilities," teach that God's call is given without respect to a person's past.

The Spring Quarter, "Jesus Calls Us," connects Jesus' ministry on earth, as exhibited in passages from the Gospels, to the birth of the Church following Jesus' death, resurrection, and ascension as seen in passages from the Book of Acts. Unit I, "Called from the Margins of Society," highlights Jesus preference for those who from the margins of society. Unit II, "Experiencing the Resurrection," centers on Jesus' appearances to His followers. Unit III, "The Birth of the Church," dives in the Book of Acts and the growth of the early Church.

The Summer Quarter, "God's Kingdom Come," explores the broad sweep of biblical teaching about God's reign. Unit I, "The Prophets Proclaim God's Power," touches the depiction of God's reign according to the prophets. Unit II, "Jesus Envisions the Kingdom," uses the Jesus teachings in the Gospel of Matthew. Unit III, God's Eternal Reign," considers additional New Testament texts that elaborate on the theme of Jesus as King and what it means for believers to participate as joint heirs with Christ in God's eternal reign.

• •

Boyd's Commentary for the Sunday School (2022–2023)

Copyright © 2022 by R.H. Boyd Publishing Corporation
6717 Centennial Blvd., Nashville, TN 37209–1017
King James Version, the (KJV) *The King James Version* is in the public domain.

Scriptures taken from the Holy Bible, *New International Version*. Copyright © 1984 by International Bible Society. Used by permission of Zondervan Publishing House. All rights reserved worldwide. The NIV and *New International Version* trademarks are registered in the United States Patent and Trademark Office by International Bible Society. Use of either trademark requires the permission of the International Bible Society.

Scriptures taken from the *New Revised Standard Version* of the Bible © 1989 by the Division of Christian Education of the National Council of Churches of Christ in the United States of America. Used by permission. All rights reserved.

Scripture quotations are from The *Holy Bible, English Standard Version*® (ESV®), copyright © 2001 by Crossway, a publishing ministry of Good News Publishers. Used by permission. All rights reserved.

Printed in the United States of America.

The publisher, R.H. Boyd Publishing Corporation, bears no responsibility or liability for any claim, demand, action, or proceeding related to its content, including but not limited to claims of plagiarism, copyright infringement, defamation, obscenity, or the violation of the rights of privacy, publicity, or any other right of any person or party, and makes no warranties regarding the content.

PREFACE

The *2022–2023 Boyd's Commentary* has been formatted and written with you in mind. This format is to help you further your preparation and study of the Sunday school lessons.

We have presented a parallel Scripture lesson passage with the *New Revised Standard Version* alongside the *King James Version*. This allows you to have a clearer and more contemporary approach to the Scripture passages each week. This version is reliable and reputable. It will bless you as you rightly divide the word of truth (2 Tim. 2:15, KJV).

These lessons have a new look, but they still have the same accurate interpretation, concise Christian doctrine, and competent, skilled scholarship.

The abbreviations used throughout the commentary are as follows:

KJV — King James Version
NIV — New International Version
NKJV — New King James Version
NLT — New Living Translation
NRSV — New Revised Standard Version
RSV — Revised Standard Version
TLB — The Living Bible
NEB — New English Bible
JB — Jerusalem Bible
ESV — English Standard Version

To the pastor: Our hope is that this commentary will provide context and insight for your sermons. Also, we hope this commentary will serve as a preparatory aid for the message of God.

To the Bible teacher: This commentary also has you in mind. You can use it as a ready reference to the background of the text and difficult terms that are used in the Bible. To be sure, this commentary will provide your lesson study with the historical context that will enable you to interpret the text for your students more effectively.

This text is for anyone who wants to get a glimpse at the glory of God. This commentary seeks to highlight and lift the workings of God with His people and to make God's history with humanity ever present.

We hope and pray God will bless you and keep you as you diligently study His mighty and majestic Word. Remain ever steadfast to our one eternal God. Keep the faith, and pray always.

CONTENTS

FIRST QUARTER

CONTENTS

SECOND QUARTER

CONTENTS
THIRD QUARTER

CONTENTS

FOURTH QUARTER

FIRST QUARTER

September

October

November

THE CALL OF ABRAM

ADULT TOPIC:	BACKGROUND SCRIPTURE:
UNBROKEN PROMISES	GENESIS 12:1–7; 15:1–7

GENESIS 12:1–5, 7; 15:1–7

King James Version	New Revised Standard Version

King James Version

NOW the LORD had said unto Abram, Get thee out of thy country, and from thy kindred, and from thy father's house, unto a land that I will shew thee:

2 And I will make of thee a great nation, and I will bless thee, and make thy name great; and thou shalt be a blessing:

3 And I will bless them that bless thee, and curse him that curseth thee: and in thee shall all families of the earth be blessed.

4 So Abram departed, as the LORD had spoken unto him; and Lot went with him: and Abram was seventy and five years old when he departed out of Haran.

5 And Abram took Sarai his wife, and Lot his brother's son, and all their substance that they had gathered, and the souls that they had gotten in Haran; and they went forth to go into the land of Canaan; and into the land of Canaan they came.

• • • • • •

7 And the LORD appeared unto Abram, and said, Unto thy seed will I give this land: and there builded he an altar unto the LORD, who appeared unto him.

• • • Genesis 15:1-7 • • •

AFTER these things the word of the LORD came unto Abram in a vision, saying, Fear not, Abram: I am thy shield, and thy exceeding great reward.

2 And Abram said, LORD God, what wilt thou give me, seeing I go childless, and the steward of my house is this Eliezer of Damascus?

3 And Abram said, Behold, to me thou hast

New Revised Standard Version

NOW the LORD said to Abram, "Go from your country and your kindred and your father's house to the land that I will show you.

2 I will make of you a great nation, and I will bless you, and make your name great, so that you will be a blessing.

3 I will bless those who bless you, and the one who curses you I will curse; and in you all the families of the earth shall be blessed."

4 So Abram went, as the LORD had told him; and Lot went with him. Abram was seventy-five years old when he departed from Haran.

5 Abram took his wife Sarai and his brother's son Lot, and all the possessions that they had gathered, and the persons whom they had acquired in Haran; and they set forth to go to the land of Canaan. When they had come to the land of Canaan,

• • • • • •

7 Then the LORD appeared to Abram, and said, "To your offspring I will give this land." So he built there an altar to the LORD, who had appeared to him.

• • • Genesis 15:1-7 • • •

AFTER these things the word of the LORD came to Abram in a vision, "Do not be afraid, Abram, I am your shield; your reward shall be very great."

2 But Abram said, "O LORD God, what will you give me, for I continue childless, and the heir of my house is Eliezer of Damascus?"

3 And Abram said, "You have given me no

MAIN THOUGHT: And the LORD appeared unto Abram, and said, Unto thy seed will I give this land: and there builded he an altar unto the LORD, who appeared unto him. (Genesis 12:7, KJV)

King James Version	*New Revised Standard Version*
given no seed: and, lo, one born in my house is mine heir.	offspring, and so a slave born in my house is to be my heir."
4 And, behold, the word of the LORD came unto him, saying, This shall not be thine heir; but he that shall come forth out of thine own bowels shall be thine heir.	4 But the word of the LORD came to him, "This man shall not be your heir; no one but your very own issue shall be your heir."
5 And he brought him forth abroad, and said, Look now toward heaven, and tell the stars, if thou be able to number them: and he said unto him, So shall thy seed be.	5 He brought him outside and said, "Look toward heaven and count the stars, if you are able to count them." Then he said to him, "So shall your descendants be."
6 And he believed in the Lord; and he counted it to him for righteousness.	6 And he believed the LORD; and the LORD reckoned it to him as righteousness.
7 And he said unto him, I am the LORD that brought thee out of Ur of the Chaldees, to give thee this land to inherit it.	7 Then he said to him, "I am the LORD who brought you from Ur of the Chaldeans, to give you this land to possess."

LESSON SETTING
Time: Unknown
Place: Haran/Canaan

LESSON OUTLINE
I. **God's Call & Promise**
   (Genesis 12:1–5; 7)
II. **God's Confirmation**
   (Genesis 15:1)
III. **Abram's Objection & God's Response**
   (Genesis 15:2–17)

UNIFYING PRINCIPLE

The reality of our circumstances does not always match our expectations. How do we respond when circumstances and expectations conflict? Abram put his confidence in God, and God reassured him.

INTRODUCTION

Broken promises can sometimes cause years of resentment, hurt, and anguish. Some must deal with the disappointment of a significant other breaking their oath and promise always to love them. Broken promises can leave lasting scars that have far-reaching consequences and ramifications. The closer a person is to you, the more his or her broken promise hurts. Unfortunately, sometimes we have also been guilty of breaking promises. We may have had great intentions or even a great reason to break the promise, but it hurts none the less and trust has been lost. Thankfully God never breaks promises! No matter how outlandish the promise may seem, God is faithful to keep His promise.

In the first eleven chapters of Genesis, God struggled with humanity's repeated rebellious and violent insubordination, such as Adam, Eve, Cain, and the people during Noah's time. The struggle was so real that even God pressed the reset button by flooding the entire earth and destroying the bulk of humanity. God has now resolved to begin a new approach by using an unlikely couple Abram and Sarai. The promise to Abram and Sarai marks one of the most dramatic transitions in the entire Hebrew Bible. God initiated a promise to Abram. God took the first step and proved there is none like God. God's power and kindness in initiating this promise are only matched by His faithfulness in fulfilling it.

EXPOSITION

I. GOD'S CALL & PROMISE (GENESIS 12:1–5; 7)

In the opening verses of chapter 12, the writer describes God's call and promise to Abram. The divine call of Abram is central to the patriarchal narratives and the Pentateuch. This call of Abram is similar to the call later given to Jacob in Genesis chapter 31 to return to the land of his ancestors and birthplace. The calls have similar elements: land, family, name, and blessing In a real sense, Jacob's call is a continuation of his grandfather's call. Abram had been commissioned to leave his country, family, all the familiarity of his father's home and go to a land not yet revealed (vv.1–3). Abram is called to leave his father's house. God requested Abram to leave all that he had come to know and hold familiar. God never asks for a sacrifice He is unwilling to repay tenfold. Abram would receive more than he would have, had he remained in Haran. The land He promised is Canaan. It is this promise that is being referred to as Canaan is called the Promised Land. Those things that God promises at times take on their own kind of mystique. This is partly because God's promises will at times outlast those who receive the promise originally. This is certainly true in this case. As God makes the promise for land at this juncture, He does not fulfill that until hundreds of years later when the Israelites entered the land after having been slaves in Egypt for 440 years.

God calls Abram to loyalty and commitment that comes with a series of powerful promises. God's promises supersede Abram's all critically important family ties. God makes several promises to him that have both present and future implications. God promises to make Abram's offspring a great nation. Abram will have children, grandchildren, and enough descendants to populate a great nation. This is the most outrageous element of the promise. God called Abram, a man without children, to become the progenitor of a great nation. Not only would God bless Abram with offspring of his own, but God would make him the father of a nation. God's promise was beyond what Abram could even conceive in his mind because it is in direct tension with his wife Sara's infertility in Genesis 11:30. Yet, he trusts God!

God then promises to bless Abram. This blessing includes success, well-being, power, and riches. The word bless (*bārak*) is used here to indicate material wealth. In antiquity, wealth was not measured by currency but by livestock, servants, land, gold, and silver.

The third portion of the blessing is that God promises Abram to make his name great. Abram's influence would increase throughout nations, religions, and generations. Since God is the One who calls, then it is His business to fulfill the blessing as He determines. God certainly fulfilled the promise. There is probably no person's name more honored in history than the name of Abram, whose name is reverenced in Judaism, Christianity, and Islam. This promise to give Abram a great name was not solely for Abram but also for blessing others (v. 3). Interestingly, his name already means "exalted father". Imagine having a name like that with no children. However, his name in a very real sense portends what his future would entail in God. Abram's name would eventually be changed to Abraham by God Almighty. Abraham means, "father of a multitude." Thus his name becomes great as he is understood to be the ancestor of Israel and several of the neighboring nations.

The following promise, "I will bless those who bless you and curse them that curse you," shifts from being centered solely on Abram to Abram being a blessing to others. The blessing is so bountiful that God promises to bless Abram's family and friends, and his enemies would be cursed because they would also become God's enemies. Blessing is the highlight of the promise, while the curse is the protection of the promise. God promises to protect Abram. Those who treat Abram with no regard or disrespect would offend God, and their consequence would be a curse. God promised that all the families of the earth would be blessed in Abram. The fulfillment of this promise would come through Jesus Christ, who was a part of Abram's lineage. Abram's blessing was not just for him but all the families on earth. God's blessings are never intended to be solely for the person being blessed, but they are to be shared with the world.

Abram leaves as the Lord commanded as a sign of obedience and allegiance to God. Though God had given him a set of outlandish promises, Abram stepped out on faith. He took his wife Sarai, his nephew, Lot, and their possessions and went to Canaan. There were several obstacles that Abram would have to overcome to fulfill the promise. First, Abram was 75 years old, well beyond conventional childbearing age. Secondly, the land that he was promised was currently inhabited. Once Abram arrived in Canaan, the Lord reinforced his promise to him. He appears to Abram (v. 7) to reassure him of God's presence and the promise of children and land. Abram's response was to build an altar as a place to meet with God, offer sacrifices, and worship.

II. GOD'S CONFIRMATION (GENESIS 15:1)

God confirms His intentions toward Abram through a vision (v. 1). Abram is told not to be afraid. Abram has a right to be afraid; he had just fought a large army to rescue Lot (Genesis 14:14–16). He expected retribution. God then tells Abram that He is Abram's shield and reward. God's closeness to Abram is the reason for Abram to take courage. God was the answer to Abram's need. He anticipated a battle, and God would become his protection. God knows how to become precisely what is needed. God assures Abram that God would grant him victory and security in the face of hostilities. God would be his covering and defend him. God would block the enemy's attacks.

As Abram's shield, God promises to protect and defend Abram. Conceptually, this means that Abram would have battles in the future but no harm would come to him or his household. As a shield, God would go wherever Abram went. Even as Abram would wander with no place of permanence, God would travel with him and him from danger. As a shield, God would that which encountered danger first and also be that which Abram could hide behind.

God says He would be Abram's reward. While it may seem to the reader that God is indebted to Abram, that is not the meaning. To fully understand what God means, we must journey back to chapter 14. In chapter 14, Abram refused his rightful share of the victor's booty. Once a nation was defeated in ancient times, the victorious nation would raid their land for riches. Abram denounced his reward for being victorious in battle (Genesis 14:23), but the Lord confirmed that Abram would be compensated. The reward God promises is not the materials secured from the raid; instead, it looks ahead to fulfill His promises. God has a way of paying back believers who are obedient in ways that far outweigh worldly paydays. God can reward you with things money cannot buy. God can give you peace during a storm. God will reward you with grace to cover your mistakes. God will reward you with a song in sorrow. God knows how to reward those who trust Him.

III. ABRAM'S OBJECTION & GOD'S RESPONSE (GENESIS 15:2–7)

Abram had already seen elements of God's fulfillment come to pass. God had increased Abram's assets, showed him Canaan, and helped him battle. Abram complains because he does not have an heir (v. 2). Abram's real desire was a son, and while God was a shield and reward, God was not any assistance for the couple's infertility. Abram wants his promised son. God had promised to give Abram an heir and then increase his descendants. Abram recognized that God had increased his assets, but he saw little to no value in it because his servant would be the recipient of his estate if he died without an heir. Abram's servant Eliezer would be Abram's designated heir (v. 3). Eliezer of Damascus was Abram's chief assistant and domestic servant. Eliezer was a close companion and confidant to Abram, but he was no replacement for a son. Abram was boldly honest with God in this passage about his disappointment. This is an example of an intimate relationship between God and Abram. Abram felt comfortable and secure in his relationship enough to discuss his frustrations. Abram was honest with God sharing what troubled him and why his heart was heavy. Sometimes believers do not feel comfortable sharing their honest feelings with God. God desires to hear believers' genuine feelings, and God can handle disappointment. Believers should share their honest feelings with God in prayer instead of denying or attempting to withhold their feelings. Abram certainly had doubts about God's promise.

God responds to Abram's doubt by ensuring that Eliezer would not be his heir. God tells Abram that he would have a natural heir. God had not forgotten His promise. God repeats the promise to Abram with clarity. God explained to Abram what He meant. There would be a natural blood relative that would fulfill God's promise to Abram. This time the confirmation would be more clairvoyant because God used an illustration (v. 5). He tells Abram that his descendants would outnumber the stars in the sky. Not only would he father a child, but he would also be the patriarch of multitudes.

Verse 6 describes Abram's response of faith to God's promise. Abram believed/trusted in God with confidence. Genesis 12 informs that Abram has previously trusted God. Remember Abram left his home and went to Canaan in obedience to God. Verse 6 literally reads that Abram continued his trust in God. When Abram chose to trust God again, God rewarded his belief and counted him righteous. The term "credited" means to assign value. The assigned value for Abram's faith is righteousness. Righteousness can only be achieved in two ways: by works or a gift from God. Since no one is good enough to accomplish righteousness on their own, God must account for us. God grants believers righteousness when like Abram, they are obedient and believe in God. Faith alone caused God to count Abram as righteous. God speaks in verse 7. God reminds Abram that just as he brought him to Canaan, He would also keep His word, regarding His promise for a son. God reminds Abram as He had been faithful, He would continue to be faithful to His covenant.

THE LESSON APPLIED

God chose Abram and decided to initiate his plan for salvation by blessing him and his descendants so they would be a blessing to the world. This parallels believers' experiences. Believers are chosen to be children of God. Like Abram, believers must have faith and trust God to be credited as righteous. God wants His children to be like Abram and place

their trust in His promises. Like Abram, we are also called at various times to any number of adventures. God will call us to trust Him as He seeks to move us from places of comfort to promise, destiny, and purpose. One of the lessons that we should take from this passage is that in order to access our potential in God, we must trust Him and move beyond home places to uncertainty and struggle. It is beyond the uncertainty and struggle that lies our ultimate destiny and blessing. Walk in faith and not by sight to reach God's promises!

LET'S TALK ABOUT IT

1. Can you imagine what Abram felt when he heard these promises? When the promises were made, nothing in his life had changed. He had to decide if he would trust the promises.
2. Should he pick up his family and go to an unfamiliar land that he did not know anything about? Abram had to make a decision on whether or not to trust God.
3. How do Christians respond when God's promises seem afar?

God calls Abram and promises him blessing beyond his imagination. God promised to make a great nation from Abram, give him a land, and use his life and his lineage to bless the families of the earth. These are such amazing promises.

HOME DAILY DEVOTIONAL READINGS						
SEPTEMBER 5–11, 2022						
MONDAY	**TUESDAY**	**WEDNESDAY**	**THURSDAY**	**FRIDAY**	**SATURDAY**	**SUNDAY**
The First Will Be Last	God Is Great and Gracious	God Judges Rightly	God's Word Does Not Fail	Who Can Argue with God?	God Blesses Jacob	God Is Free to Choose
Luke 13:23–30	Psalm 147:1–6, 12–20	Psalm 75	Romans 9:6–16	Romans 9:17–29	Genesis 28:10–22	Genesis 25:19–34

GOD CHOOSES THE YOUNGER TWIN

GENESIS 25:19—34

King James Version

AND these are the generations of Isaac, Abraham's son: Abraham begat Isaac:

20 And Isaac was forty years old when he took Rebekah to wife, the daughter of Bethuel the Syrian of Padanaram, the sister to Laban the Syrian.

21 And Isaac intreated the LORD for his wife, because she was barren: and the LORD was intreated of him, and Rebekah his wife conceived.

22 And the children struggled together within her; and she said, If it be so, why am I thus? And she went to enquire of the LORD.

23 And the LORD said unto her, Two nations are in thy womb, and two manner of people shall be separated from thy bowels; and the one people shall be stronger than the other people; and the elder shall serve the younger.

24 And when her days to be delivered were fulfilled, behold, there were twins in her womb.

25 And the first came out red, all over like an hairy garment; and they called his name Esau.

26 And after that came his brother out, and his hand took hold on Esau's heel; and his name was called Jacob: and Isaac was threescore years old when she bare them.

27 And the boys grew: and Esau was a cunning hunter, a man of the field; and Jacob was a plain man, dwelling in tents.

28 And Isaac loved Esau, because he did eat of his venison: but Rebekah loved Jacob.

New Revised Standard Version

THESE are the descendants of Isaac, Abraham's son: Abraham was the father of Isaac,

20 and Isaac was forty years old when he married Rebekah, daughter of Bethuel the Aramean of Paddan-aram, sister of Laban the Aramean.

21 Isaac prayed to the LORD for his wife, because she was barren; and the LORD granted his prayer, and his wife Rebekah conceived.

22 The children struggled together within her; and she said, "If it is to be this way, why do I live?" So she went to inquire of the LORD.

23 And the LORD said to her, "Two nations are in your womb, and two peoples born of you shall be divided; the one shall be stronger than the other, the elder shall serve the younger."

24 When her time to give birth was at hand, there were twins in her womb.

25 The first came out red, all his body like a hairy mantle; so they named him Esau.

26 Afterward his brother came out, with his hand gripping Esau's heel; so he was named Jacob. Isaac was sixty years old when she bore them.

27 When the boys grew up, Esau was a skillful hunter, a man of the field, while Jacob was a quiet man, living in tents.

28 Isaac loved Esau, because he was fond of game; but Rebekah loved Jacob.

MAIN THOUGHT: And the LORD said unto her, Two nations are in thy womb, and two manner of people shall be separated from thy bowels; and the one people shall be stronger than the other people; and the elder shall serve the younger. (Genesis 25:23, KJV)

GENESIS 25:19–34

King James Version	New Revised Standard Version
29 And Jacob sod pottage: and Esau came from the field, and he was faint:	29 Once when Jacob was cooking a stew, Esau came in from the field, and he was famished.
30 And Esau said to Jacob, Feed me, I pray thee, with that same red pottage; for I am faint: therefore was his name called Edom.	30 Esau said to Jacob, "Let me eat some of that red stuff, for I am famished!" (Therefore he was called Edom.)
31 And Jacob said, Sell me this day thy birthright.	31 Jacob said, "First sell me your birthright."
32 And Esau said, Behold, I am at the point to die: and what profit shall this birthright do to me?	32 Esau said, "I am about to die; of what use is a birthright to me?"
33 And Jacob said, Swear to me this day; and he sware unto him: and he sold his birthright unto Jacob.	33 Jacob said, "Swear to me first." So he swore to him, and sold his birthright to Jacob.
34 Then Jacob gave Esau bread and pottage of lentiles; and he did eat and drink, and rose up, and went his way: thus Esau despised his birthright.	34 Then Jacob gave Esau bread and lentil stew, and he ate and drank, and rose and went his way. Thus Esau despised his birthright.

LESSON SETTING
Time: Unknown
Place: Beer-lahai-roi

LESSON OUTLINE
  I. Pedigree (Genesis 25:19–21)
 II. God's Ultrasound (Genesis 25:22–28)
III. Esau's Rash Decision (Genesis 25:29–34)

UNIFYING PRINCIPLE
We sometimes make rash decisions that are not in our best long-term interest. How do we respond when life doesn't go the way we think it should? God's plans supersede ours.

INTRODUCTION
In football, in a broken play the quarterback scrambles and sometimes makes a touchdown out of what could have been a loss of yards. There are times when quarterbacks and their teams can make amazing highlight plays. There are other times when a broken play does not fare as well. The quarterback must make quick decisions to give his team the best chance to score. The lesson below is full of metaphorical broken plays. Thankfully, God intervenes and makes touchdowns out of broken plays. God knows how to make miracles out of the messes of our rash decisions.

Both Christianity and Judaism recognize the story in our lesson as God's unmerited grace and love. Jacob deliberately wrongs and takes advantage of his brother's indifference to his birthright. God still chooses to bless Jacob's lineage to be an essential part of God's salvific plan. God did not renege on His appointment of Jacob even after his selfish, disastrous, and scandalous attempts to claim the birthright for himself. This passage describes a dysfunctional family dealing with extreme favoritism and competition. Badly misaligned priorities, and deliberate manipulation for selfish gain replaced cooperation and ideal family values and interactions. The ethical lessons to be learned from Jacob's family are really in the negative. However, when we remember that this is the family God chose to carry out his plan of salvation, God's unconditional love, patience, and grace emerge as the true ethical highlights of this passage.

EXPOSITION

I. PEDIGREE
(GENESIS 25:19–21)

The narrative is introduced as the account of Abraham's son, Isaac, and then quickly shifts to the sons of Isaac probably because of the similarities in Genesis' patriarchal narratives. Isaac was like Abram, Isaac married a barren woman, Rebekah, and prayed to God for the blessing of a male heir, and the Lord answered his prayer. The Lord blessed him with two sons. The similarity in the narratives enables the writer to reinforce that the blessing through Abram's seed could not be accomplished without God's power and intervention. Neither Sarah nor Rebekah could have conceived without the assistance of God. The text reinforces the notion that when God makes a promise, the fulfilling of the promise is God's responsibility. The fulfillment of God's promises can only be achieved solely with the partnership of God. Isaac and his descendants are part of the promise God had given to Abram earlier in Genesis. God promised Abraham to make his lineage a great nation and that He would bless all the families of the earth through him (Genesis 12:1–3). Isaac and Rebecka pray, knowing that life is a gift given by God and that

they are heirs to God's promise. This is a reminder to us, who are also children of God's promise, that God's promises cannot be achieved with human capabilities. God has the power to make promises and keep them despite any human expectation or obstacle. Sometimes God's fulfillment of promises is less about us as much as it is about the promise God has made to our ancestors. Many Christians today are reaping the blessings from promises God made to their ancestors many years ago.

II. GOD'S ULTRASOUND
(GENESIS 25:22–28)

The story of the twins, Jacob and Esau, is filled with conflict like other brothers and relatives throughout Genesis. Genesis has already highlighted the conflict between Cain and Abel, Abram and Lot (13:7–12), and Isaac and Ishmael (21:9). The struggle between Jacob and Esau was already forecast while in the womb of their mother (25:22). The twins are gifts of God and the fulfillment of God's pact made with Abraham. However, conflict will follow Jacob throughout his life. This is evident to Rebekah even before their birth (v. 22). The text says that the twins, while in the womb, caused their mother discomfort and pain. Sometimes our blessings, those miracles we prayed for, can cause discomfort. Take note that Rebekah sought counsel from the Lord about her discomfort. It was only in speaking with God that she was able to understand the predicament of her unborn children. The writer wants the reader to know immediately that Jacob's life is filled with unrest and inquietude. As a result he struggles to attempt to take, and exploit others' weaknesses. He grapples with himself and those around him.

Verse 23 is a foreshadowing of a life filled with struggles for Jacob and his heirs. The writer again makes the emphasis that struggles are not always malevolent, and they are necessary for the accomplishment of the will of God.

Many Biblical figures had to struggle like David, Esther, Jesus, Job, Peter, John, Tamar, and Paul. There are many ancestors that have struggled as well. Struggling is a part of the Christian journey. It is through struggle that Christians are able to see God in ways that otherwise they would not have known.

Another significant part of the text is the proclamation in verse 23, "the older will serve the younger." In the Bible, the "younger one" means to be the lesser one. Obviously, one would not choose to be the "younger one." God chooses to defy human and cultural norms by blessing the "younger one." God has a way of blessing and choosing what others ignore and dismiss. Throughout Genesis, there are examples of God choosing and esteeming the younger sibling to accomplish His plan and keep His promise. The blessing of God is not a right given solely to the firstborn son, but God's blessing can be given to those who would normally have no claim to it. We should all be glad because we are not the firstborn children of God, yet we still are eligible to receive the promise of God. We can receive what we did not earn (Romans 9:10–13).

Although Jacob had wrestled his brother in the womb (v. 22), been promised to be stronger and preeminent brother (v. 23), he was born second (v. 24–26). Jacob and Esau's names explanation were then given with clever wordplay. Esau is named so because his complexion was red and hairy. Jacob, though his name's origin is unclear, is ascribed to "heel," meaning the one who kicks his way out, or "supplanter," the one who would displace this twin. Both meanings are fitting for his narrative. From his birth Jacob, according to Genesis' writer, will dishonor God and his family. Scripture tells us that Esau was a skilled hunter and loved the outdoors and that he was the favorite of Isaac. Jacob, to the contrast, was a homebody; he liked to stay around the tents, and he was the favorite of their mother Rebekah, probably because of the Lord's promise that the older would serve the younger (v. 27–28).

III. Esau's Rash Decision (Genesis 25:29–34)

The next verses share the negotiation of the brothers over Esau's birthright. Traditionally in ancient Jewish culture, birthrights are general and the right of children to inherit from the father. The birthright was an official signifier of the son's rightful place in the lineage, legacy, and inheritance of his father's ancestors. Typically, the oldest son would receive double the inheritance of other siblings. Although in modern times, we ascribe this inheritance to monetary and material wealth, in ancient times, the father's name and reputation were also a part of the inheritance and equally as valuable. At the father's death, the oldest son would become the patriarch of the family, holding both the name and responsibility of continuing the family legacy and increasing the family's reputation.

The text begins with Esau coming in from the country on a hunting trip, stating he is famished and requesting that Jacob give him some of the pottage he had been cooking (v. 29–30). Being a homebody, Jacob learned to cook, and the passage tells that he made a stew, or pottage, that is red in color. "Pottage" transliterates to ʽnāzîd in Hebrew. It is modified by the adjective "red," ʽādôm. The latter is the same word used to describe the redness of Esau at birth (v. 27). Derivatives of both words, "pottage" and "red," consist in the Hebrew letters ʽdm, the same letters in "Edom," the people embodied in Esau (cf. Gen. 36:16–43). Thus, the wordplay of "Edom/red/pottage" cleverly asserts that Esau is a man (and the Edomites a people) peculiarly destined for pottage and not more. The implicit contrast is the claim that Jacob/Israel, though younger, is destined for birthright. The remainder of the Jacob narrative is the suspenseful account of the way in which this claim becomes a reality.

Esau came from the fields apparently hunting but had not caught anything. He is hungry and famished. In Hebrew, famished is translated to mean, tired, and faint from a lack of food and or drink. When Esau comes in from the field, he smells Jacob's pottage and asks for some because he is too famished to make his own food.

In return for the pottage, Jacob senses an opportunity and requests that Esau sell him his birthright (v. 31). Esau trades his future, security, prosperity, and wealth for an immediate fulfillment for pottage (v. 32–33). Esau is hungry and could not deny himself instant satisfaction; he could not wait. Sometimes immediate gratification can hinder our judgment in making wise decisions concerning the future. Esau trades his future to subdue his hunger

pains. What's worse is that Esau is willing to trade in his birthright for a meatless stew, and he, by nature, is a hunter. He was capable of being his own solution to his dilemma if only he could look beyond the immediate. At that moment, his birthright looked far off, and his immediate desire was food.

Jacob sees this as an opportunity to get something that he believes would assure his rule over his brother. For Jacob, a bowl of pottage is a small price to pay to receive a birthright, the leadership of the family, and a double portion of the inheritance. Jacob requested that Esau swear by an oath that he was indeed selling his birthright to him.

Did Jacob believe in God's prophecy and power over life? Certainly, at this point, Jacob had been taught about God from his father, learned his heritage and family history about how God called his grandfather Abraham out of Ur, and promised to make his family great and bless them (Genesis 12:1–3). No doubt he had heard from his father how God commanded Abraham to take Isaac up on Mount Moriah and offered him as a sacrificial lamb and how God provided a ram as a substitute to die in his place (Genesis 22:1–19). It is quite possible that Jacob believed in God but was not willing to wait on God to fulfill the promise of the older serving, the younger. His faith reminds me of his grandparents when they also became impatient in waiting on God to fulfill His promise (Genesis 16). Patience is a requirement for God's blessings. The prophecy in Genesis 25:23 demonstrates that Jacob's manipulation of Esau was unnecessary. God had already prophesied that Jacob would receive the birthright. Unfortunately, Jacob decided to force God's hand; Jacob ended up creating a tragedy that had ripple effects that had him later escape to distant relatives.

Jacob gave Esau the lentil stew and some bread. Esau ate and drank and then got up and left with little thought about what he had done and despised his birthright (v. 34). In a very few cases in Genesis, do we find such a blunt statement of the understanding. The writer emphasizes that Esau, though he had the right of the firstborn, did not value it more than a bowl of lentil soup. Although Jacob's manipulation of Esau is clearly wrong, it is equally clear that Esau is judged harshly for his actions as well. Imagine trading away your future for such meager momentary fulfillment. Esau threw away God's blessing for passing satisfaction. By treating his birthright so carelessly, he did not appreciate his heritage.

THE LESSON APPLIED

There are multiple lessons to be gathered from this passage. Parents must be careful in the kind of favoritism that they put forth with their children. Much of the conflict between Esau and Jacob was fueled by their parents who chose which son each one preferred. Healthy sibling relationships develop in part through healthy parental relationships.

It is of the utmost importance to consider the value of family blessings, inheritances, and gifts. Esau is not the only one in history who sold that which was to be his blessing for little to nothing because he got a little too anxious and hungry. There are many stories of people selling their ancestral property because a developer flashed a little money. We should consider the true value of anything before allowing it to be sold.

LET'S TALK ABOUT IT

1. Have you ever made a hasty decision based on immediate gratification? If so, what consequences, good or bad, did you face? If given another chance, would you make a different choice?
2. What influenced you to make that hasty choice? Was it time, money, pressure from family or friends, a deadline, etc.?

The passage describes a dysfunctional family: extreme favoritism, competition, the lack of self-control, inability to see beyond the immediate future and misguided priorities, and manipulation for selfish gain. Instead of making hasty decisions, we should make decisions based upon our faith in our almighty and all-powerful God.

HOME DAILY DEVOTIONAL READINGS
SEPTEMBER 12–18, 2022

MONDAY	TUESDAY	WEDNESDAY	THURSDAY	FRIDAY	SATURDAY	SUNDAY
Don't Reject God's Grace	A Blessing Bestowed	A Blessing Forsaken	God Will Be Merciful to All	Praise for God's Wonderful Works	Seeking Favor in God's Sight	Wrestling for a Blessing
Hebrews 12:7–17	Genesis 27:18–29	Genesis 27:30–41	Romans 11:25–32	Psalm 105:1–11	Genesis 32:3–12	Genesis 32:22–32

JACOB CALLED ISRAEL

ADULT TOPIC:	BACKGROUND SCRIPTURE:
PERSEVERE IN TIMES OF DIFFICULTY	GENESIS 32:22–32

GENESIS 32:22–32

King James Version

AND he rose up that night, and took his two wives, and his two womenservants, and his eleven sons, and passed over the ford Jabbok.

23 And he took them, and sent them over the brook, and sent over that he had.

24 And Jacob was left alone; and there wrestled a man with him until the breaking of the day.

25 And when he saw that he prevailed not against him, he touched the hollow of his thigh; and the hollow of Jacob's thigh was out of joint, as he wrestled with him.

26 And he said, Let me go, for the day breaketh. And he said, I will not let thee go, except thou bless me.

27 And he said unto him, What is thy name? And he said, Jacob.

28 And he said, Thy name shall be called no more Jacob, but Israel: for as a prince hast thou power with God and with men, and hast prevailed.

29 And Jacob asked him, and said, Tell me, I pray thee, thy name. And he said, Wherefore is it that thou dost ask after my name? And he blessed him there.

30 And Jacob called the name of the place Peniel: for I have seen God face to face, and my life is preserved.

31 And as he passed over Penuel the sun rose upon him, and he halted upon his thigh.

32 Therefore the children of Israel eat not of the sinew which shrank, which is upon the

New Revised Standard Version

THE same night he got up and took his two wives, his two maids, and his eleven children, and crossed the ford of the Jabbok.

23 He took them and sent them across the stream, and likewise everything that he had.

24 Jacob was left alone; and a man wrestled with him until daybreak.

25 When the man saw that he did not prevail against Jacob, he struck him on the hip socket; and Jacob's hip was put out of joint as he wrestled with him.

26 Then he said, "Let me go, for the day is breaking." But Jacob said, "I will not let you go, unless you bless me."

27 So he said to him, "What is your name?" And he said, "Jacob."

28 Then the man said, "You shall no longer be called Jacob, but Israel, for you have striven with God and with humans, and have prevailed."

29 Then Jacob asked him, "Please tell me your name." But he said, "Why is it that you ask my name?" And there he blessed him.

30 So Jacob called the place Peniel, saying, "For I have seen God face to face, and yet my life is preserved."

31 The sun rose upon him as he passed Penuel, limping because of his hip.

32 Therefore to this day the Israelites do not eat the thigh muscle that is on the hip socket,

MAIN THOUGHT: And he said, Thy name shall be called no more Jacob, but Israel: for as a prince hast thou power with God and with men, and hast prevailed. (Genesis 32:28, KJV)

King James Version	*New Revised Standard Version*
hollow of the thigh, unto this day: because he touched the hollow of Jacob's thigh in the sinew that shrank.	because he struck Jacob on the hip socket at the thigh muscle.

LESSON SETTING
   Time: Unknown
   Place: Peniel

LESSON OUTLINE
   I. Jacob Prepared to Meet Esau (Genesis 32:22–23)
   II. Jacob's Wrestling Match (Genesis 32:24–26)
   III. A New Name & A New Day (Genesis 32:27–32)

UNIFYING PRINCIPLE

We often feel alone in our struggles. How do we persist in time of struggle? Jacob persevered in his struggle and experienced blessing.

INTRODUCTION

Have you ever been in a situation where you did not know where to turn? You've analyzed and struggled, thought about all the options, sought advice from wise counsel, and still, you had no idea what to do. Perhaps you've struggled with your faith or a mystifying theological issue. You may have read your Bible, searched the Internet, reached out to Sunday school teachers, and pastors seeking answers. You have sought the Lord, and are exhausted from praying. You may have even wondered if anybody even up there is still listening to you. Maybe you've even felt God gently tugging at you, wanting you to do something. Perhaps you felt like you were being beaten over the head with a bat as God insists that you go somewhere, take some action, do something, and you're just not interested in doing so. If any of this sounds familiar, you're in good company; you've been wrestling with God.

Today's lesson is another story about Jacob. Jacob is the younger son and his mother's favorite, while his dad favored his twin brother Esau. Jacob has been in trouble since birth. In our last lesson, he tricks his brother into giving him his birthright and then runs away. He struggles with his father-in-law Laban because he is in love with Rachel, and later marries her sister Leah. When Jacob is older, he decides to return to his homeland, full of anxiety and apprehension. He is fearful because his brother Esau lives there, and he is unsure what to expect upon their first meeting. On his way to meet his brother, he has a theophanic moment and must wrestle with God.

EXPOSITION

I. JACOB PREPARED TO MEET ESAU (GENESIS 32:22–23)

The lesson begins with Jacob preparing and anticipating a meeting with his older brother Esau. Jacob envisioned that this meeting could be unfavorable for him. He approaches the meeting with extreme deference, undoubtedly resulting from his fear of Esau's revenge. There is a lot of suspense and anxiety surrounding this meeting of brothers. Jacob is unsure of how Esau will receive him or Esau's intentions. After all the last we read of Esau, he intends to murder Jacob as revenge for stealing his birthright (Genesis 27:41). Jacob's fear results in him praying that God would save him from his brother, and he reminds God of the promise God had made "You have said. I will surely make you prosper and make your descendants like the sand of the sea" (Genesis 32:9–12). Jacob presents himself to God as heir to God's promise and is insistent that his actions are representative of that.

The lesson's printed text picks up with Jacob putting his cunning plan into action. Jacob is faithful to his prior scheming He plans to save himself and his family by pacifying Esau with extravagant gifts. Jacob again conspires when all he had to do was follow God's plan because God had prepared his way. Jacob has prepared for his reunion. Jacob carefully planned to appeal to his brother's sympathy and he has prayed to God for protection.

II. JACOB'S WRESTLING MATCH (GENESIS 32:24–26)

Jacob anticipates his meeting with Esau, but to his surprise, God ordains another meeting first. Jacob encounters a stranger in the night. Scholars have debated the interpretation of this text extensively mainly because it lacks clarity, and like great pieces of art, it leaves room for many interpretations. For example, Jacob has an encounter with an unnamed entity with supernatural abilities. Some argue that the man was a demon, Esau, or a Canaanite deity. In any case, the Scripture is not clear. The writer is not explicit in the portrayal of the man. It is conceivable that the unknown person is God. It is ironic that Jacob must also face his God on his way to make peace with his brother. This epitomizes Jacob's life story. Jacob's life has been filled with the struggle to gain blessing, and now he must wrestle the Giver of gifts. Jacob struggled with Esau (Genesis 25 & 27), his father (Genesis 27), his father-in-law (Genesis 29–31), and now in Genesis 32, he is wrestling with God.

Verse 23 states that Jacob has sent his possessions and family across the stream and is now alone. It is in his isolation that God initiated this wrestling match with Jacob (v. 24). Jacob was alone without distractions, without facades, and unable to evade his controversies. This indicates that God is both accepting of our struggles, encourages us to face them, and is able to handle our wrestling. God waited until Jacob was alone and away from his distractions to wrestle with him. Maybe God is waiting on us to remove our distractions before God faces us head-on. What keeps us distracted from our one-on-one with God, perhaps our social media, friends, wealth? None of these are immoral pursuits, but we must adequately prioritize them. Traditionally, Christian teaching has encouraged followers not to question God. Still, the text reminds us that God is more than capable of handling our questions, wrestling, and confusion about God, faith, or theological understanding without being offended. The text does not describe much about the wrestling match other than it lasted all night. Wrestling all night would be an intense struggle regardless of the opponent by any measure.

Jacob must have been a worthy opponent or at least evenly matched with the man because of the lengthiness of the match. Jacob is more potent than he knew; he was able to wrestle with both his brother Esau and with The Divine and hold his own. This serves as a reminder that Jacob possessed everything he desired within himself already and that God was faithful to the prophecy that he revealed to Rebecca while Esau and Jacob were still in her womb (Genesis 25:22–23). Jacob gives the match his everything and holds his own against his opponent until the man realizes he could not overpower Jacob, so he injures him by pulling Jacob's hip out of the joint. We must also note Jacob's perseverance and stamina to wrestle until daybreak. We, too, should pursue God with the same vigor. Sometimes we are frustrated when God does not immediately answer our prayers and request, or our blessings seem delayed, and we quit, but we should continue to seek God through prayer, study, and worship no matter how long the answer takes.

III. A New Name & A New Day (Genesis 32:27–32)

Versus 26 through 29 gives a glimpse of the first and only dialogue between Jacob and The Divine. At daybreak, the man wants to leave, but Jacob Would not allow the man to leave. The man pleads to be discharged from Jacob's grip. Jacob senses that he now has the upper hand. He tells the man that he won't let him go until he blesses him (v. 26). Jacob is once again exploiting a situation and opponent for his gain. Scripture records that since chapter 27 of Genesis, Jacob will do anything to receive a blessing no matter who he must swindle scheme, undercut, or trick. But something is different this time

with Jacob's request. Jacob's grandfather Abraham received God's first covenantal blessing, and Jacob tricked his brother Esau out of their family blessing and heritage. Jacob's demand for blessing indicates that he still does not understands that God's blessing cannot be demanded but only given freely and comes only through a personal relationship with God.

The man asked Jacob what his name is seemingly ignoring Jacob's request and changing the subject. We are unsure of what type of blessing Jacob was requesting from the man. Perhaps he was looking for protection, security, wealth, more land, more sons but what he got was a new name, a new identity, a new beginning through a wrestling match with God. Sometimes what we desire is not what we need. Thankfully, God knows what we need and denies our request through prayer and only to bless us with what we need. In the ancient Near East, fathers and occasionally kings renamed individuals; these new names were always descriptive of the person's newly emerging quality. God renames Jacob, simultaneously expressing a new relationship with Jacob and highlighting a significant change in Jacob's character from deception to engaging with God. He had been named Jacob, synonymous with trickster and an exploiter; though each of these were facts about him, God desired to rename him and give him a life-changing blessing. Jacob would now be called Israel. Many believers like Jacob had different names as well before God changed their names. Some have been called liars, cheaters, drug-addicted, orphan, promiscuous, drunk, mean until the believer wrestles with God and God changes his/her name to son or daughter Christian or follower. It is amazing how God can write over your past and who you were, rename you, and give you a clean slate. Sometimes others who knew you before your name change will continually remind you of your past wrongdoings without room for your growth, but God can write over your past to blot out your past and to bring about a fresh start.

Many scholars debate the etymology of Israel. It is difficult to trace where and how this name develops. Jacob's new name reflects his new future and new self. He is now named Israel because he has struggled with both humanity and divinity. Jacob/Israel is interpreted to mean the one who striven with God and with humans. Naming Jacob "Israel" foreshadows the nation of Israel, telling the reader that Jacob is now a recipient, with Abraham, of God's blessing that his descendants will be a great nation (Genesis 12:1–5). Jacob/Israel is now a new man who knows God as both as the night nemesis and the promise-keeping God of the day. Jacob/Israel has wrestled God, been touched by God, victoriously gained a blessing from God, and now renamed by God. Now that Jacob/Israel has been given a new name, he requests to know the stranger's name. Like Adam and Eve, Jacob desires knowledge that he cannot comprehend, and God is not yet ready to reveal. It is not until Exodus 3:14 the God decides to reveal God's name to Moses. The man blesses Israel, which he so desperately desired, and then departs with his name still unknown, but Jacob's forever changed to Israel. As a new day emerges, the stranger is gone, and so is Jacob; now, he is Israel. He was emerging from an assault by God as a new being.

As Israel reflects upon the recent events of the night, he names the site Peniel because he had seen God face to face, and yet his life was spared. Peniel was one of the first capitals of the Northern Kingdom (1 Kings 12:25). Israel names the site as a reminder for himself and future generations that this is the place where his life and name changed because he wrestled with God. Believers should note and remember the place where they received a new beginning with God for their children and future generations to come. Do you remember where you were when God changed your name and life? Have you told your dependents, friends, and others that you encounter that there has been a change in your life? While some components of our current worship services have needfully evolved, it is essential that we do not diminish the importance of testimonies and sharing our conversion stories. These stories give evidence like Israel that one has wrestled with and been blessed by God and given a new beginning. Nonbelievers and believers alike need to hear our testimonies because we overcome with the help and power of God and the gift of our testimonies.

Israel passed Peniel changed with a new name and a new walk. He now has a limp from his wrestling match with The Almighty (v. 25). Meeting God led to his crippling. Typically, we ascribe healing to God, but in this instance God crippled. Consider this Jacob/Israel was blessed to be able to see God face to face and to live a feat that few have been able were able to do throughout the entire Bible, yet he was crippled with the blessing. Big blessings come at a high cost..As believers we must consider that blessing and pain are often present in the same spaces. Jacob was at once crippled and blessed but his blessing would not have been possible without his crippling. Believers must consider what price they are willing to pay for their blessing? Note that God's gift only came when Jacob/Israel was finally ready to acknowledge God's authority and superiority and submit to God. Still, it came at a cost, his hip dislocation. It was a reminder of God's ultimate power and strength, and though Israel was strong and intelligent, he was still no match for God.

THE LESSON APPLIED

Like Jacob, sometimes we may have to wrestle God for some blessings, not because God is reluctant to bless us but because there are blessings and lessons in wrestling with God. What do you need from God right now? What blessing are you in search of? God has promised to meet you in your moments of uncertainty and fear, but God will not always show up the way you expect or desire. Sometimes God will show up like your adversary and entice you into a wrestling match. So when God calls you to wrestle in prayer or wrestle with your faith or even wrestle with your doubts, consider it an invitation to receive a blessing. So do not give up during your wrestling with God; there is a blessing on the other side. Don't let God go, be persistent until you get your blessing. God loves His children and blesses that kind of determined and resilient faith.

LET'S TALK ABOUT IT

1. Are there ever times you wrestled with your faith during a tragedy, a loss, or by increasing your theological knowledge?

2. What was the outcome of the struggle? During the struggle, did you find it difficult to persevere? What was the residue or mark left by the battle?

From the lesson, we can conclude that there can be a blessing in wrestling and struggling with God. Healthy conflict resolution is essential in any relationship. The Bible is full of examples of people who wrestled with God like Jacob, David, Mary, Jesus, John, etc. Yet many believers avoid wrestling, struggling, and conflict with God. It can be beneficial during a struggle to remind oneself of Jacob. God is accepting of our struggles with Him and encourages us to face them and Him head-on, rewarding our struggle for understanding, blessings, and faith with God's blessings of relationship and commission to play a part in God's greater mission.

HOME DAILY DEVOTIONAL READINGS
SEPTEMBER 19–25, 2022

MONDAY	TUESDAY	WEDNESDAY	THURSDAY	FRIDAY	SATURDAY	SUNDAY
Tamar Asserts Her Rights	Ruth Gives Birth to Obed	God's Blessings for Israel	A Scepter Shall Rise from Israel	The Heavenly Throne	The Conquering Lion of Judah	Judah Destined to Reign
Genesis 38:12–19, 24–26	Ruth 4:9–17	Numbers 23:18–26	Numbers 24:2–9, 15–17	Revelation 4	Revelation 5	Genesis 49:8–12

THE SCEPTER GIVEN TO JUDAH

ADULT TOPIC: DYNAMICS OF FAMILY LEADERSHIP	BACKGROUND SCRIPTURE: GENESIS 35:22–26; 38:12–19, 24–26; 49:8–12

GENESIS 35:22–26; 38:24–26; 49:10–12

King James Version

AND it came to pass, when Israel dwelt in that land, that Reuben went and lay with Bilhah his father's concubine: and Israel heard it. Now the sons of Jacob were twelve:

23 The sons of Leah; Reuben, Jacob's firstborn, and Simeon, and Levi, and Judah, and Issachar, and Zebulun:

24 The sons of Rachel; Joseph, and Benjamin:

25 And the sons of Bilhah, Rachel's handmaid; Dan, and Naphtali:

26 And the sons of Zilpah, Leah's handmaid: Gad, and Asher: these are the sons of Jacob, which were born to him in Padanaram.

• • • Genesis 38:24–26 • • •

AND it came to pass about three months after, that it was told Judah, saying, Tamar thy daughter in law hath played the harlot; and also, behold, she is with child by whoredom. And Judah said, Bring her forth, and let her be burnt.

25 When she was brought forth, she sent to her father in law, saying, By the man, whose these are, am I with child: and she said, Discern, I pray thee, whose are these, the signet, and bracelets, and staff.

26 And Judah acknowledged them, and said, She hath been more righteous than I; because that I gave her not to Shelah my son. And he knew her again no more.

New Revised Standard Version

WHILE Israel lived in that land, Reuben went and lay with Bilhah his father's concubine; and Israel heard of it. Now the sons of Jacob were twelve.

23 The sons of Leah: Reuben (Jacob's firstborn), Simeon, Levi, Judah, Issachar, and Zebulun.

24 The sons of Rachel: Joseph and Benjamin.

25 The sons of Bilhah, Rachel's maid: Dan and Naphtali.

26 The sons of Zilpah, Leah's maid: Gad and Asher. These were the sons of Jacob who were born to him in Paddan-aram.

• • • Genesis 38:24–26 • • •

ABOUT three months later Judah was told, "Your daughter-in-law Tamar has played the whore; moreover she is pregnant as a result of whoredom." And Judah said, "Bring her out, and let her be burned."

25 As she was being brought out, she sent word to her father-in-law, "It was the owner of these who made me pregnant." And she said, "Take note, please, whose these are, the signet and the cord and the staff."

26 Then Judah acknowledged them and said, "She is more in the right than I, since I did not give her to my son Shelah." And he did not lie with her again.

MAIN THOUGHT: The sceptre shall not depart from Judah, nor a lawgiver from between his feet, until Shiloh come; and unto him shall the gathering of the people be. (Genesis 49:10, KJV)

Genesis 35:22–26; 38:24–26; 49:10–12

King James Version	New Revised Standard Version
• • • Genesis 49:10–12 • • •	• • • Genesis 49:10–12 • • •
THE sceptre shall not depart from Judah, nor a lawgiver from between his feet, until Shiloh come; and unto him shall the gathering of the people be.	THE scepter shall not depart from Judah, nor the ruler's staff from between his feet, until tribute comes to him; and the obedience of the peoples is his.
11 Binding his foal unto the vine, and his ass's colt unto the choice vine; he washed his garments in wine, and his clothes in the blood of grapes:	11 Binding his foal to the vine and his donkey's colt to the choice vine, he washes his garments in wine and his robe in the blood of grapes;
12 His eyes shall be red with wine, and his teeth white with milk.	12 his eyes are darker than wine, and his teeth whiter than milk.

LESSON SETTING
Time: Unknown
Place: Canaan

LESSON OUTLINE
**I. Reuben's Violation
(Genesis 35:22–26)**
**II. Judah & Tamar
(Genesis 38:24–26)**
**III. Jacob Blesses Judah
(Genesis 49:10–12)**

UNIFYING PRINCIPLE

People often link the family challenges they face in the present to the challenges faced in previous generations. How do we overcome the problems we inherited from our families of origin? God called Jacob's fourth son, Judah, to lead a dysfunctional family from whose family would emerge the nation of Israel and, one day, God's chosen Messiah.

INTRODUCTION

No person has ever chosen their birth family. In many instances, we are about as healthy as the families from which we come. Scripture has a spiritual dynamic of "family blessings" and "family influences" and the streams that flow from generation to generation. This is in part why we are invited to become a part of God's family. The pollution of our emotional and physical health can sometimes be tied to the soul pollution that has never been healed.

The Bible is full of stories about dysfunctional families and family drama. Genesis has the record of the first family in the Bible. Adam and Eve and their sons are an example of a family full of flaws. King David, a man who the Bible dubs as "a man after God's heart (1 Samuel 13:14)," suffered from his fair share of toxic familial relationships. No one is exempt from family drama. The lesson to follow is an excellent example of how God can make a miracle out of a domestic mess. God is willing to forgive and forget mistakes as soon as a person repents of their deeds. The preceding verses of this chapter discuss the death of Jacob, the death of his wife, the birth of the son, followed by the son's disobedience, which all lead up to our lesson.

EXPOSITION

I. REUBEN'S VIOLATION (GENESIS 35:22–26)

The preceding verses of this chapter discuss the death of Jacob's wife, Rachel (Genesis 35:16–21), the birth of the son (Genesis 35:16–18), followed by Reuben's disobedience and violation of his father's honor, by sleeping with Jacob's concubine (v. 22). Bilhah was the handmaid of Rachel, the wife who Jacob loved the most. Bilhah was given to Rachel by her father Laban as a wedding present when she married Jacob. Reuben's action was more than just a moral failure but also had political repercussions. Bilhah was more than just a concubine; she was also the mother of Jacob's sons, Dan and Naphtali (v. 25). When Rachel realized that she could not give Jacob a son, she gave her handmaid to her husband so that she might obtain children through her servant (Genesis 30:3–8). Reuben's lack of respect, transgressions, and discretion made his actions even more reprehensible.

Consequently, Reuben lost the privileges afforded to the firstborn son (Genesis 49:3–4). While it has been speculated that Reuben's action was his way to ensure his mother, Leah secured the position of being Jacob's preferred wife now that Rachel was dead. Others believe that Reuben was attempting to quench his thirst for power. The text is not clear on Reuben's motive; however, his actions were driven by selfishness and a desire for power.

In ancient culture, taking of the father's concubines is an attack upon the father. It is an effort to seize the patriarch's power and announce to the world that your father is dead. In those days, when a son inherited leadership from his father due to his father's death, the son would customarily inherit the father's property, including his concubines. The possession of the father's concubines affirms his new leadership position and power within the family. Reuben attempted to dethrone his father as leader of their family and Israel. Reuben's action is an indication of abrasion and disarray in Jacob's family. Jacob is made aware of the incident but does not mention it until about forty years later in Genesis 49:3–4. Jacob's life was so filled with controversy and struggle that there was a struggle involving his sons even in the latter years of his life. The four oldest sons of Leah and heirs to God's promise made to Abraham (v. 23): Reuben, Simeon, Levi (Genesis 34), and Judah (Genesis 38) have all violated their family's honor and name. His sons had clearly fallen prey to Canaanite culture and have led aside their devotion and commitment to God. Thankfully, God's promises are not assured or dependent upon the attributes and virtues of its agents. When God makes a promise, He is the guarantor of the promise, and the delivery of the promise is solely up to God and not humanity's frailties. Reuben's assault of Jacob's concubine, Bilhah, is a tragic event within Jacob's family, which experienced many tragedies.

II. JUDAH & TAMAR (GENESIS 38:24–26)

To fully understand the text, one must be aware of the practice of levirate marriage and the backstory of the text. Deuteronomy 25:5–10 states that if a married man dies without a son, his brother or next male kin should marry the widow so that she can provide the dead man with an heir. As a widow, Tamar had the legal right and responsibility in the ancient Near East to continue her husband's bloodline and provide him with an heir to ensure her place in his family (see also Genesis 19:30–38). While some writers find fault in Tamar's actions, Scripture shows that she was simply attempting to fulfill her commitment to her dead husband and provide security for herself. Culturally, a widow without a son to take care of her would be left without family protection and wealth and forced to be destitute or prostitution. The verses leading up to the lesson's text provide insight.

Er marries Tamar, and before she can bore him an heir, he dies. According to the custom of Levirate marriage, Er's next of kin should marry his widow. Onan was Er's next of kin and refused to obey Judah and the cultural customs of the day. Onan's death was attributed to his refusal to perform this duty of impregnating Er's widow. Having now two dead sons who have been married to Tamar, Judah is fearful and refuses to give his younger son Shelah to him and send her back to her father's house.

Tamar takes matters into her own hands. Tamar tricks Judah into impregnating her by disguising herself as a sex worker and allowing him to hire her for sex. Judah gives Tamar his signet as collateral until he can come back with her payment. The signet was a seal, often suspended from the neck with a cord, used similarly as a signature on documents. Just as signatures are unique to each individual, so were signets unique to each individual.

Three months later, Judah is confronted by the report that his daughter-in-law Tamar is pregnant. After hearing the initial reports, Judah is filled with anger and orders her execution, which was a normal consequence of her actions. According to culture, Tamar had engaged in deception, which included violating her betrothed Shelah and Judah, the father of the betrothed. Judah being a man of status and good standing in his community he would have been justified and supported by his decision to execute Tamar. Tamar, on the other hand, as a widow, would be defenseless and without recourse by cultural and legal standards.

The story could have ended there if Judah had let his pride overshadow his participation in the narrative and ordered Tamar's indictment to only protect his interest. Tamar sends word and evidence to Judah that the person whose signet, cord, and staff she possessed is the father of her unborn child (v. 25). Judah is now aware that he is the father of his daughter-in-law's unborn child. Judah shows a vast amount of integrity. He could have been dishonest and denied the truth because a man's word outweighed a woman's.

In contrast, Judah vindicates Tamar and indicts himself (v. 26). Judah holds himself to a responsible standard, and in doing so, he provides a new standard because up to this point in the narrative, women were held to a higher or double standard than men. Judah has the power in this dynamic series of events. He is a man; he has wealth, security, sons and is in good standing within his community. Tamar's safety and honor can only be affiliated with her husband or father.

Judah acknowledges his sin failing to comply with Tamar's legal right to his last son, and being more concerned about his preference at the expense and determent of his community. Judah preferred not to risk his last son for the sake of the solidarity and future of the community. Many believers and churches fall prey to this same sin of choosing comfort over community and preference over purpose. We are cozy within our churches, and we prefer to stay in our comfort levels with the same annual outreach methods, the same type of music, attracting people we deem acceptable because it makes us comfortable and never assess if our preferences are costing the church it's future in the community or if we are forsaken the purpose of the church. Moreover, Judah realizes she has violated Tamar's right to dignity and her ability to flourish in the community. In verse 26, he confesses that Tamar acted as a response to his sinfulness. Thus, Judah states that she is more righteous than he because she cares more about the continuation of community than he did. Therefore, the continuation of the lineage of Judah was not due to the righteous actions of the patriarch Judah but rather to the honest widow woman Tamar.

III. Jacob Blesses Judah (Genesis 49:10–12)

Jacob is old and near death; he called together his sons and handed out blessings and prophesies to them. Many Jews and Christians believe that the prophetic utterance was focused upon the coming Messiah. Orthodox Jews believe that the Messiah has not yet arrived. Christian believers contend that Jacob's prophecy was fulfilled through Jesus Christ.

Jacob has eliminated the older brothers as the heirs of his blessing. Jacob foretold a future for the tribe of Judah that located the eponymous Judah as the preeminent son. Judah had not been given the rights of the firstborn but had been chosen as a royal tribe. Jacob uses poetic imagery to describe Judah as a warrior returning home victoriously and is saluted by his brothers. In verse 10, the imagery of the young warrior transforms to the king. He is now the one who holds the scepter and the ruler's staff. The scepter is the symbol of rule, authority, and royalty. The imagery of domination supports Judah's preeminence among his brothers and his new role in the future Davidic line and God's plan of salvation. Judah would be the dominant and the ruling tribe. It also states that those who reign from the house of Judah will only do so temporarily in anticipation of the one who is truly king and whose rule will never end. He promises that the king will come from his household. We know that we can trace King David and Jesus, the King of King's lineage, to Judah. In verse 10, the writer states that the obedience of the nation is his. The writer uses the plural version of nations ('ammîm) rather than the singular version of nation ('am). This version of nations suggests that Jacob was speaking not just of Israel but of many other nations. God used the same word ('ammîm) previously to promise Jacob to make his heirs so numerous that they become a "company of peoples" (Genesis 28:3). Jacob remembered God's promise as he blessed Judah.

In verse 11, the writer's imagery suggests that vines were in great abundance in the land of Judah's. The quantity was so great that a donkey could be tied to them almost anywhere. The imagery highlights the immense productivity and fruitfulness of the land where Judah would dwell. Some scholars suggest that "washing" one's garments in wine hint at the cleansing of garments by the blood of Jesus (Revelation 7:14). While other scholars believe that in Judah, wine would be so ordinary and plentiful that it could be used as water for the most common purpose, even washing clothes.

THE LESSON APPLIED

Integrity is a characteristic that many people lack. Integrity, according to Webster's dictionary, is the quality of being honest and fair. Like Judah, believers should act with integrity even when facing undesirable consequences. Integrity is also the quality of being the same throughout. In other words, to be a person of integrity means that one is the same wherever they go and whatever they do. It is not unlike the song, this little light of mine, "This little light of mine, I'm going to let it shine. All in my home, I'm going to let it shine. All at my job, I'm going to let it shine." The point is wherever and whatever one is doing, his/her light is going to shine.

For us in a modern context, Judah acts with integrity because he recognizes his own faults and failures in applying the law and customs of the day. If one is to be about law and customs then one must be about law and customs.

In some ways, this is why Judah is chosen over his older brothers. He had acted in integrity, as opposed to Reuben, and it was for his integrity that he was elevated and now has a name that is remembered. Remember God calls us to act with and in integrity.

LET'S TALK ABOUT IT

1. Why do you think Reuben showed no remorse while Judah did?
2. What are some take always about leadership and accountability that may be gleaned from each brother's response?
3. What characteristics are you hoping to apply to your leadership style?

Each person is a leader in some aspect of their life. Whether in church, work, community, home, social groups, or just our own lives, God has called each person to be a leader. God desires for His leaders to involve the submissive spirits and repentant hearts. The lesson highlights two different types of leaders by two brothers Reuben and Judah. Reuben shows little remorse for his sexual misconduct. Judah, on the other hand, acknowledges his sins, and attempts to act with integrity. Each brother fell prey to sin, but their responses to sin differed.

HOME DAILY DEVOTIONAL READINGS
SEPTEMBER 26–OCTOBER 2, 2022

MONDAY	TUESDAY	WEDNESDAY	THURSDAY	FRIDAY	SATURDAY	SUNDAY
God Preserves the People	From Lack to Abundance	Thriving in Spite of Adversity	God Prepares Moses	Challenges of Heeding God's Call	Awaiting a Heavenly Reward by Faith	God Raises Up a Deliverer
Psalm 105:12–25	Genesis 47:1–12	Exodus 1:8–22	Acts 7:17–29	Acts 7:30–41	Hebrews 11:23–29	Exodus 2:1–15

THE BIRTH OF MOSES

ADULT TOPIC:	BACKGROUND SCRIPTURE:
A PROTECTIVE FAMILY	EXODUS 2:1–10, 15–22 (SEE ALSO EXODUS 1:15–22)

EXODUS 2:1–10

King James Version

AND there went a man of the house of Levi, and took to wife a daughter of Levi.

2 And the woman conceived, and bare a son: and when she saw him that he was a goodly child, she hid him three months.

3 And when she could not longer hide him, she took for him an ark of bulrushes, and daubed it with slime and with pitch, and put the child therein; and she laid it in the flags by the river's brink.

4 And his sister stood afar off, to wit what would be done to him.

5 And the daughter of Pharaoh came down to wash herself at the river; and her maidens walked along by the river's side; and when she saw the ark among the flags, she sent her maid to fetch it.

6 And when she had opened it, she saw the child: and, behold, the babe wept. And she had compassion on him, and said, This is one of the Hebrews' children.

7 Then said his sister to Pharaoh's daughter, Shall I go and call to thee a nurse of the Hebrew women, that she may nurse the child for thee?

8 And Pharaoh's daughter said to her, Go. And the maid went and called the child's mother.

9 And Pharaoh's daughter said unto her, Take this child away, and nurse it for me, and I will give thee thy wages. And the women took the child, and nursed it.

New Revised Standard Version

NOW a man from the house of Levi went and married a Levite woman.

2 The woman conceived and bore a son; and when she saw that he was a fine baby, she hid him three months.

3 When she could hide him no longer she got a papyrus basket for him, and plastered it with bitumen and pitch; she put the child in it and placed it among the reeds on the bank of the river.

4 His sister stood at a distance, to see what would happen to him.

5 The daughter of Pharaoh came down to bathe at the river, while her attendants walked beside the river. She saw the basket among the reeds and sent her maid to bring it.

6 When she opened it, she saw the child. He was crying, and she took pity on him. "This must be one of the Hebrews' children," she said.

7 Then his sister said to Pharaoh's daughter, "Shall I go and get you a nurse from the Hebrew women to nurse the child for you?"

8 Pharaoh's daughter said to her, "Yes." So the girl went and called the child's mother.

9 Pharaoh's daughter said to her, "Take this child and nurse it for me, and I will give you your wages." So the woman took the child and nursed it.

MAIN THOUGHT: And the woman conceived, and bare a son: and when she saw him that he was a goodly child, she hid him three months. (Exodus 2:2, KJV)

Exodus 2:1—10

King James Version	*New Revised Standard Version*
10 And the child grew, and she brought him unto Pharaoh's daughter, and he became her son. And she called his name Moses: and she said, Because I drew him out of the water.	10 When the child grew up, she brought him to Pharaoh's daughter, and she took him as her son. She named him Moses, "because," she said, "I drew him out of the water."

LESSON SETTING
 Time: Unknown
 Place: Egypt

LESSON OUTLINE
 I. **Civil Disobedience**
  (Exodus 2:1–4)
 II. **A Compassionate Princess**
  (Exodus 2:5–8)
 III. **The Contract**
  (Exodus 2:9–10)

UNIFYING PRINCIPLE

The tumultuous world can endanger our well-being in many ways. How do we survive in a chaotic world? Moses' family went to great lengths to save him.

INTRODUCTION

Moses' story centers around his family's clever and creative response to the injustices the imperiled Moses's life. Many families find themselves in similar predicaments. Families are struggling to raise their children while simultaneously battling brokenness, systems of capitalism, racism, classism, sexism, ageism, and other injustices. America has systems like the cradle to prison pipeline and unjust laws that too often lead to the arrest, conviction, incarceration, and in some cases, death of African-American youth. Many African-American parents are tasked with teaching their young children how to interact with law enforcement because law enforcement has already determined the child to be a threat. Protecting African-American children from state-sanction violence has been an arduous task that parents have had since the first Africans arrived in the United States of America. Unfortunately, being African American, while conducting everyday actions, is dangerous. Consider: jogging (Ahmaud Arbery), walking home from the store (Trayvon Martin), sleeping in your own home (Breonna Taylor).

Trying to protect children from the viciousness of oppression seems like an impossible task for many African Americans. Parents want to provide the best for their children, and unfortunately, too many parents struggle to keep their children safe.

The lesson reminds Christians to continue addressing injustice on behalf of endangered young people; your labors are not in vain. While parents and other loved ones cannot see into the future of the youth, they can trust God and find hope in Miriam, Jochebed, and Pharaoh's daughter, who make creative, quick-witted, and selfless decisions that protect Moses. In the lesson, God uses these three women who love Moses to save an entire nation. God's plan looked unknown, small, and insignificant, as parenting can sometimes feel, but God was engineering a miracle.

EXPOSITION

I. CIVIL DISOBEDIENCE (EXODUS 2:1–4)

The story of Moses's birth is one of the most well-known in the Bible. The birth of Moses is a story of God preparing a leader to deliver Israel. It is also a story of a protective family. Moses' parents, Amram and Jochebed (Genesis 6:20), were both from the priestly tribe of Levi. Moses's heritage as a Levite, on both maternal and paternal sides, demonstrates God's provision and care for him: although the Law has not been given yet, Moses is born into the right tribe because he will become a prophet, mediator, priest, and intercessor for God's people. Of course, the line of priest will come from Aaron, his older brother, but he was born to the right family. Moses was not the firstborn of this union; he had an older brother Aaron and his sister Miriam. As much as this narrative is about Moses, it is also about the three women who do their part, not even aware of what their role is, who have become united as a family through baby Moses. Three women of different ages, nationalities, social standings worked together and fulfilled God's great plan of redemption.

Moses was born against the brutality and cruelty of the times. Pharaoh issued a decree to murder Hebrew boys. At the end of Exodus 1, state-sanctioned violence was circulated to cast all Hebrew baby boys into the Nile. Pharaoh attempted to stop the Hebrews from multiplying and overpowering the Egyptians. Pharaoh made them slaves and he could extort them to build his wealth.

Moses' family enacts a tense drama of protection and care against a much larger backdrop of God's own security and care: He rewards their hope and trust with protection that transcends the injustice of their own family situation. Moses is born to his parents, and they hide him until they can no longer hide him anymore. They hide him for three months in their home against the law. Imagine the creativity it must have taken to hide a newborn for months hushing the baby's whimpering, muffling the baby's hunger cries, hiding the baby from neighbors, friends, and family, so that the baby has a chance to survive. It worked for three months, but then he got older, his cries louder and more assertive.

When they can no longer hide baby Moses, his mother designs a basket to become a boat for Moses's escape. There is irony in the story as well. Moses's mother puts him in a basket and floats him down the Nile in order to save his life. She seeks an alternative for her son other than death by drowning in the Nile. The Nile, Pharaoh's chosen instrument of destruction, becomes the escape mechanism and the means for saving Moses. Throughout the narrative, there is an overlapping theme of civil disobedience.

She does what she thinks is fair, hoping that someone will find him and save him. Look at the creativity that this Hebrew woman had to weave together a basket and place her son in it, hoping that he would drift into someone's life who would care for him in the same manner. The basket was made from papyrus reeds and caulked with pitch, a tar-like substance to make it watertight (v. 3). The Hebrew word for basket appears elsewhere in the Bible only as a destination or designation for Noah's ark in Genesis 6:14, in which Noah and his family in the animals were saved. The basket in this text is used for rescuing the person who will save the Israelites, Moses. The overt link points to God's care and provision for His people and His plans in the midst of catastrophic destruction. Moses's mother took every precaution for safety. There are all kinds of threats against Moses's safety, like Pharaoh's decree; he could have fallen prey to animals who inhabited the Nile, or a person lacking compassion could have discovered him. Imagine the courage it took to put her baby unassisted and unprotected into the Nile River. The courage she had to trust her three-month-old baby's safety to the makings of your own hand. It took courageousness and faith for civil disobedience.

The narrative of Moses shows us that civil disobedience against an unjust edict is not only the right thing, but by doing so also you will be on God's side and help to bring God's justice into the world. This story is full of courageous women who act with faith instead of fear. We should all be grateful for the daring and faith-filled women in our own lives. Moses's mother knew that this edict/law was unjust, yet she is determined to buck this unfair male-dominated system. She risked their lives for the sake of life, and as a result, she saves Moses's life and, ultimately, Israel's life. What a strong woman she was. Her courageousness breeds defiance, she defies the law of the land, and God honors her defiance.

While as Christians, we should aim to be a model citizens but not to the point of disobedience to God's Word and love.

Sometimes that may call us to be defiant to the law of the land. God was sovereign over Pharaoh, and God was worthy to be obeyed. When a law does not honor God, Christians should feel free to glorify God through their own acts of defiance against the law. God is the ultimate judge, who we ultimately must answer to; not presidents, nor kings, or queens, but it is God who we answer. Believers should not be afraid to defy an unjust law because defiance is God's work too. Freedom Fighters, abolitionists, Black Lives Matter activists, and Civil Rights Movement protesters all practiced civil disobedience. There were times in the United States when laws discriminated against people of color, denying them the right to vote, obtain employment, attend certain schools, live in specific neighborhoods, or even patronize certain restaurants or retail stores. Thank God for those who defied unjust laws like Harriett Tubman, Nat Turner, Fannie Lou Hammer, Rev. Dr. Martin L. King Jr., Angela Davis, John Lewis, Diane Nash, and so many others who stood up against unjust laws regardless of the consequences. Believers are called to be like Moses's mother and obey God rather than the law. After all, you never know your defiance might be saving a child's life and ultimately the nation Israel.

Moses's mother could have sat in despair. She could have cried or been passive in her dependence for the divine to dive into position to do all work. However instead of doing so, she used her human agency and acted in faith. Miriam, Moses's sister, was tasked with watching her brother float along the Nile to see what would become of the baby boy in the basket.

II. A Compassionate Princess (Exodus 2:5–8)

As Pharaoh's daughter, the princess went down to the Nile to bathe with her attendants. Walking around the riverbank, she saw the basket among the reeds and sent one of her servants to go get it (v. 5). The princess discovered the reed basket and opened it to find a Hebrew baby boy crying. The Bible says the sight of the baby moves her to compassion (v. 6). When was the last time you have looked upon a person who has been othered by the world and was moved to compassion? When did you look at those who are addicted to an illegal substance, a homeless person, an immigrant, or an orphan and were moved to compassion?

Verse 4 states that Miriam stood at a distance to see what would be done to the baby. She's not just standing, but she's looking very intently and wondering what's going to happen to her younger brother. Miriam notices the princess's discovery of the baby and acts as the middle person between the princess and her mother. If Moses's mother was courageous and creative, his sister was persistent and resourceful. Miriam, as she watched, could not make a neutral observation; she intercedes. She appears from her hiding place and volunteers to get one of the Hebrew women to nurse the child for her. At such a young age, Miriam was able to avail herself to God and ultimately play an essential role in the salvation of her brother and of her people. This is evidence that age does not defy who God can or will use for the accomplishment of His will. Age or gender is not a deterrent for God. God used this young woman to help bring about the exodus of His people. Imagine what would have happened if Miriam stayed in hiding and remained silent? Who would have been charged with raising and rearing Moses if Miriam had not spoken up? We should encourage young people in our church, communities, and homes, people, to step up and act, for they too can play pivotal roles in the deliverance of our people. Young people do not have to wait until they are older; there is no age requirement to be on God's team. The only requirements are willingness and obedience. Miriam was indeed willing to be a part of God's great plan. She suggests that the princess hire a Hebrew wet nurse. Hiring a wet nurse was a usual practice of elites in the ancient Near East.

III. The Contract (Exodus 2:9–10)

Moses is returned to his mother, Jochebed, and she was paid to nurse him (v. 9). Amazingly God orchestrated that the baby would be returned to her to raise, even though she initially thought she might never see her child again. Now Jochebed is afforded the opportunity to love on, nurture, and teach him all she knew about God for the first three years of his life. We hear nothing else about Moses's dad. Throughout the text, he fades to the back and disappears, yet the women continue to play an important part in leadership in the text.

Mesopotamian tablets note a legal adoption of an abandoned baby: the wet nurse acted as a legal guardian, and the formal adoption occurred once the child was weaned. This story appears to reflect the same situation. Moses grew and was weaned from his birth mother's comfort and care. Moses is then taken to Pharaoh's daughter, who adopts him and names him "Moses", because she drew him out of the water. Moses now grows up in Pharaoh's palace, being fed, clothed, educated, and raised in the same home as the man who ordered his death. Pharaoh had ordered the new born males of Israel to be killed, but God worked miraculously to bring up the greatest Old Testament prophet in Pharaoh's household. He delivered Moses so that he could deliver the Israelites. God always has a plan, and He can use anyone to carry it out, even people we least expect. Moses' attempt to extend the same protection he had experienced foreshadows his future role as a deliverer to a people he already claims as his own (Genesis 2:11). God does not excuse the action but honors the motivation, developing that motivation further until Moses is ready to take on the role as God defines it.

THE LESSON APPLIED

There were deep injustices that jeopardized Moses's existence, just as there are injustices that threaten the lives of African-American children today. Because of social injustices and the way in which capitalism creates gross inequities, many children are not able to receive adequate healthcare, well-balanced meals, are being mis-educated in their school systems, and are being criminalized by law enforcement and the criminal justice system. What are some ways that Christians can cleverly and creatively address the structural injustice on their behalf? This may be a great opportunity to create a social justice ministry at your church to have representation at city council meetings, school board meetings, city planning, and budget meetings. A great way to organize in an effort to hold politicians accountable for their campaign promises—consider organizing your church to write letters or emails to your mayor, councilperson, senators, and congressional representatives to express your disapproval of injustice and speak up for the voiceless. It is an opportunity to lobby for those things that you care about.

LET'S TALK ABOUT IT

1. Consider what God might be doing right now in your life, community, church, and city for the good of His people. What miracle is God looking for you to take part in courageously and creatively?

God's plan looked unknown, small, and insignificant, as parenting can sometimes feel, but God was engineering a miracle. God was up to something massive that would be known to the world and to many generations to come.

HOME DAILY DEVOTIONAL READINGS
OCTOBER 3–9, 2022

MONDAY	TUESDAY	WEDNESDAY	THURSDAY	FRIDAY	SATURDAY	SUNDAY
God Calls and Equips	God Brings Victory	God Saves, Provides, and We Follow	God Expects Obedience	God Offers Eternal Rest	God Promises a Homeland	God Is Perfect and Just
Exodus 3:1–15	Exodus 14:21–31	Psalm 105:26–27, 37–45	Hebrews 3:7–19	Hebrews 4:1–11	Deuteronomy 1:1–8	Deuteronomy 32:3–14, 18

SONG OF MOSES

| ADULT TOPIC:
EXPRESSING THANKFULNESS | BACKGROUND SCRIPTURE:
DEUTERONOMY 31:30–32:47 |

DEUTERONOMY 32:3–6, 10–14, 18

King James Version

BECAUSE I will publish the name of the LORD: ascribe ye greatness unto our God.

4 He is the Rock, his work is perfect: for all his ways are judgment: a God of truth and without iniquity, just and right is he.

5 They have corrupted themselves, their spot is not the spot of his children: they are a perverse and crooked generation.

6 Do ye thus requite the LORD, O foolish people and unwise? is not he thy father that hath bought thee? hath he not made thee, and established thee?

• • • • • •

10 He found him in a desert land, and in the waste howling wilderness; he led him about, he instructed him, he kept him as the apple of his eye.

11 As an eagle stirreth up her nest, fluttereth over her young, spreadeth abroad her wings, taketh them, beareth them on her wings:

12 So the LORD alone did lead him, and there was no strange god with him.

13 He made him ride on the high places of the earth, that he might eat the increase of the fields; and he made him to suck honey out of the rock, and oil out of the flinty rock;

14 Butter of kine, and milk of sheep, with fat of lambs, and rams of the breed of Bashan, and goats, with the fat of kidneys of wheat; and thou didst drink the pure blood of the grape.

New Revised Standard Version

FOR I will proclaim the name of the LORD; ascribe greatness to our God!

4 The Rock, his work is perfect, and all his ways are just. A faithful God, without deceit, just and upright is he;

5 yet his degenerate children have dealt falsely with him, a perverse and crooked generation.

6 Do you thus repay the LORD, O foolish and senseless people? Is not he your father, who created you, who made you and established you?

• • • • • •

10 He sustained him in a desert land, in a howling wilderness waste; he shielded him, cared for him, guarded him as the apple of his eye.

11 As an eagle stirs up its nest, and hovers over its young; as it spreads its wings, takes them up, and bears them aloft on its pinions,

12 the LORD alone guided him; no foreign god was with him.

13 He set him atop the heights of the land, and fed him with produce of the field; he nursed him with honey from the crags, with oil from flinty rock;

14 curds from the herd, and milk from the flock, with fat of lambs and rams; Bashan bulls and goats, together with the choicest wheat—you drank fine wine from the blood of grapes.

MAIN THOUGHT: And he said unto them, Set your hearts unto all the words which I testify among you this day, which ye shall command your children to observe to do, all the words of this law. (Deuteronomy 32:46, KJV)

DEUTERONOMY 32:3–6, 10–14, 18

King James Version	*New Revised Standard Version*
• • • • • •	• • • • • •
18 Of the Rock that begat thee thou art unmindful, and hast forgotten God that formed thee.	18 You were unmindful of the Rock that bore you; you forgot the God who gave you birth.

LESSON SETTING
    Time: Unknown
    Place: Sinai Wilderness

LESSON OUTLINE
  I. **Israel's Indictment**
     (Deuteronomy 32:3–6)
  II. **God's Care & Provisions for Israel**
     (Deuteronomy 32:10–14)
  III. **Israel's Rejection of God**
     (Deuteronomy 32:18)

UNIFYING PRINCIPLE

We sometimes fail to remember what others have done for us. How can we maintain an attitude of appreciation and gratitude? Moses instructs Israel to remember God's blessings and to teach their children about the promises God fulfilled on their behalf.

INTRODUCTION

In the lesson, Moses presents his song that indicts Israel. God brings a lawsuit against Israel. God accuses Israel of a breach of contract. When God made a covenant with Israel to be their God and they His people, both parties would be faithful to each other. Moses calls himself as a witness and uses his first-hand knowledge to deliver a testimony against Israel. Moses then testifies how he witnessed first hand God's goodness and faithfulness to Israel and Israel's infidelity to God. Moses caused the Israelites to remember God their own experience with God, God's faithfulness to Israel, and how His faithfulness led to their deliverance from Egypt and other foreign powers. This lesson is a glimpse into the eternal courtroom where Moses is the plaintiff and Israel is the defendant.

EXPOSITION

I. ISRAEL'S INDICTMENT (DEUTERONOMY 32:3–6)

The introduction of the song is made up of two parts. The first is the formal introduction (v. 1–3). It reflects a legal format very common to the ancient Near East. The song begins as a testimony against Israel. Here through Moses, God charges Israel with a lawsuit. God charges Israel with a breach of contract in contrast to God's faithfulness to them. The intent of Moses's song is to evoke praise and adoration to God as well as confession.

The text of the lesson, Moses's song, begins with the declaration of Moses proclaiming the name of the Lord and invites others to credit greatness to God (v. 3). Even though the song's purpose is to express God's dissatisfaction with Israel's commitment, Moses suggests that there is never a time not to praise and adore God. Not only is the proper response to God's actions worship and praise; it is also clear that such a response is the natural, sincere response to seeing God at work. Worship and praise flow out of our God experience.

The first two words of verse 4 indicate the theme, "The Rock." Moses uses the metaphor of a rock to remind Israel that God is strong, stable, and one that can be depended upon. It is a poetic way of saying that God is faithful, God can be counted upon, God can be trusted, and God is steady in which they can anchor themselves upon. The imagery of God as a rock was repeated five times throughout the song in reference to God and twice to idols. Moses then proclaims that God's works are perfect; no blemish is found in God's work because there is no blemish in God. This imagery should give every believer hope and reason to endure because we have a solid, dependable God who is committed to us who will not give way when the waves and winds of life blow. We have a steadfast and stable God.

Though God had been faithful, just, dependable, and faultless in His dealings with Israel. Israel had been quite the opposite of God: unreliable, erratic, temperamental, unstable, and often going back on their commitment to God. Moses seemingly expresses amazement that the Israelites would respond to such a steady and faithful God. Moses says that Israel acted corruptly toward God (v. 5). God has kept up His end of the bargain, but Israel has not. The covenant relationship depends upon each party keeping faith. Moses' song testifies that Israel has not done so. God had been faithful to Israel even when Israel had turned its back on God and created idols, frustrating and angering Moses. Israel refused to be faithful to God. Moses is so astonished and appalled by Israel's behavior he reckons or

likens them to a rebellious, bratty, willful child who's been afforded love, luxury, and forgiveness and forsakes the parents who have provided. Remembering God's actions leads us to ponder God's character as revealed by God's actions. Here God is a parent, demonstrating God's love through both caring for and disciplining God's children (see 32:19). Before we point our pretentious noses at Israel, we must remember that we too have not always been faithful to God. All of our stories are that God has been reliable and we have not been faithful; God has been good when we have not been good. We have built idols out of our careers, significant others, bank accounts, ourselves, and much more. We have allowed other entities to possess more devotion and dedication than God. We, too, have been rebellious and forgot to hold up our end of the covenant with our God. Thankfully God's faithfulness is not predicated upon our ability to be faithful.

To further prove his point, Moses asks Israel two forceful questions. He asks, "Is this the way you repay the Lord all foolish and wise people (v. 6)?" The question causes Israel to look back at their outrageous behavior and their response to God's blessings. Moses is reminding Israel that God is the originator of the nation, the promiser, the liberator, deliverer, and their sustainer. God not only created Israel, but then God also paid the price for their freedom, delivering them from Egyptian slavery. Then Moses says God made and formed Israel, which described the Lord's direct hand in establishing the nation through Moses. Many believers take this same attitude; once we receive the blessing that we've prayed for, we fail to be dedicated to God but instead, rely on ourselves and our abilities and forget that it is only by the grace of God we exist.

II. God's Care & Provisions for Israel
(Deuteronomy 32:10–14)

Moses says God found them in a desert barren and howling waste (v. 10). This description illuminates how God found Israel in a desolate, desperate, and hope-less time. It is a reminder of Israel's time in the wilderness and God's care for them as they journeyed. The Israelites were an unorganized group of people in an inhos-pitable environment at the time. From this humble beginning, God entered into a covenant with them and brought them into affluence. Moses reminds the Israelites of their humble beginnings in Egypt. The Lord made a covenant with Israel not because they were a mighty nation. Moses notes that Israel was in a desperate circum-stance when God found them, unlike how the Israelites romanticized their time in the wilderness. Moses reminds Israel of how hopeless and pitiful of a nation they were when God attaches himself to them and makes them the apple of his eye.

There in the middle of the desert, the Lord shielded and cared for Israel (v. 10). Israel's journey in the wilderness is portrayed as one of a harsh life where survival was possible only by the Lord's provision. It is where the young nation learns how to live and where they were trained in the proper ways by the mother eagle (v. 11). It is in the desert that the Lord shielded and cared for Israel like an eagle caring for its young babies as they are taught to fly. While in the wilderness, God acted as a parent eagle, protecting Israel from becoming prey and providing nourishment for the young nation. The eagle stirs up its nest, pushing the young eagles out into the air to test their wings, but the parent eagle does not leave them all together on their own. The parent eagle remains close within eyesight to catch the fluttering little one on its outspread wings as they begin to descend and then return them to the nest. Likewise, the Lord took Israel out of Egypt into the desert of Sinai but did not leave them without help and without His watchful eye. God caught and supported Israel with His wings like an eagle and supported and at times propped the Israelites up in Sinai. The eagle both challenges and protects its child just like God does.

The Israelites were aware of polytheism because of the Egyptians. Polytheism is the belief or the worship of multiple gods. The Egyptians, Canaanites, and most peoples of the day practiced polytheism. Moses reminds the Israelites that God alone was the leader and sustainer of Israel (v. 12). God is omnipotent, has unlimited power and, is able to do anything. God is unrivaled, and unlike humanity and Israel, God does not need any assistance. This is not just Israel's testimony but every Christian upon reflection. It was God who allowed them to overcome and to jour-ney forward, and it was God alone who has blessed believers, healed sickness, sustained Christians through a global pan-demic. God does not need assistance from other gods to keep His covenant. .

Moses states that God calls Israel to ride high on the high places of the land (v.13). Moses then moves to Israel's anticipated conquest of Canaan, which is said to be a mountainous land. Moses foretells that God will feed them with the finest foods directly from God's natural provisions. The song views Israel as nourished with the fruit of the fields, honey from the rock, and olive oil from the trees. The song states that Israel will be fed plentifully, nourished, full and satisfied by God's delivery and supply system through nature.

Not only has God provided vegetation to feed Israel, but also animals to contribute to this life and feast of plenty. Israel will receive milk from the cattle. From the milk, they would be able to produce curds, cream, and butter to sustain themselves further. They will receive the fat of lambs, meaning fatten and meaty lambs and goats, and in addition, the people would be provided with "the fat of the kidneys of the wheat," which meant the choices and finest wheat. Lastly, Israel would be provided with the foaming blood of the grape, which means they would have fine red wine to drink.

III. ISRAEL'S REJECTION OF GOD (DEUTERONOMY 32:18)

Moses' song now portrays Israel's future faithlessness. After eating all the fine foods and drinking the choice of red wine provided by God, Israel rejects God. Israel will turn to other gods again, neglecting their covenant to God. Israel will forsake their dependable and solid God, their Creator God, and the God of their ancestors too. Israel would turn their backs on their steadfast and faithful God, who provided them with so much, and embrace new gods who have not proven themselves. Modern-day Christians similarly turn away from God after receiving the blessings. Israel suffered from convenient amnesia, forgetting the God of their past triumphs and the God who created and sustained them.

THE LESSON APPLIED

In his song, Moses recalls God's faithfulness to Israel, even as the song indicts Israel for its failure to be who God had them to be. If you were to write a song what would the lyrics be? How would you celebrate God and perhaps even more important what charges would be levied against you?

LET'S TALK ABOUT IT

1. As you think about God as the Rock what are the adjectives that pop into your mind?
2. Do you think this is an appropriate metaphor?
3. What other metaphors can you come up with to describe who God is for His people?

Believers should not question the steadiness of God, who does not waver.

HOME DAILY DEVOTIONAL READINGS
OCTOBER 10–16, 2022

MONDAY	TUESDAY	WEDNESDAY	THURSDAY	FRIDAY	SATURDAY	SUNDAY
God Is My Portion Forever	Israel Struggles to Remain Faithful	Treasure in Clay Jars	Afflicted but Renewed Daily	God's Grace Is Sufficient	Deliverance Comes from God's Hand	God Calls Gideon
Psalm 73:1–5, 16–17, 21–28	Judges 2:7–8, 11–19	2 Corinthians 4:1–7	2 Corinthians 4:8–18	2 Corinthians 12:1–10	Judges 7:1–8, 16–22	Judges 6:1–2, 7–16

THE CALL OF GIDEON

| ADULT TOPIC: | BACKGROUND SCRIPTURE: |
| CONFIDENCE PROVIDES NECESSARY COURAGE | JUDGES 6:1–27 |

JUDGES 6:1–2, 7–16

King James Version

AND the children of Israel did evil in the sight of the LORD: and the LORD delivered them into the hand of Midian seven years.

2 And the hand of Midian prevailed against Israel: and because of the Midianites the children of Israel made them the dens which are in the mountains, and caves, and strong holds.

• • • • • •

7 And it came to pass, when the children of Israel cried unto the LORD because of the Midianites,

8 That the LORD sent a prophet unto the children of Israel, which said unto them, Thus saith the LORD God of Israel, I brought you up from Egypt, and brought you forth out of the house of bondage;

9 And I delivered you out of the hand of the Egyptians, and out of the hand of all that oppressed you, and drave them out from before you, and gave you their land;

10 And I said unto you, I am the LORD your God; fear not the gods of the Amorites, in whose land ye dwell: but ye have not obeyed my voice.

11 And there came an angel of the LORD, and sat under an oak which was in Ophrah, that pertained unto Joash the Abiezrite: and his son Gideon threshed wheat by the winepress, to hide it from the Midianites.

12 And the angel of the LORD appeared unto him, and said unto him, The LORD is with thee, thou mighty man of valour.

New Revised Standard Version

THE Israelites did what was evil in the sight of the LORD, and the LORD gave them into the hand of Midian seven years.

2 The hand of Midian prevailed over Israel; and because of Midian the Israelites provided for themselves hiding places in the mountains, caves and strongholds.

• • • • • •

7 When the Israelites cried to the LORD on account of the Midianites,

8 the LORD sent a prophet to the Israelites; and he said to them, "Thus says the LORD, the God of Israel: I led you up from Egypt, and brought you out of the house of slavery;

9 and I delivered you from the hand of the Egyptians, and from the hand of all who oppressed you, and drove them out before you, and gave you their land;

10 and I said to you, 'I am the LORD your God; you shall not pay reverence to the gods of the Amorites, in whose land you live.' But you have not given heed to my voice."

11 Now the angel of the LORD came and sat under the oak at Ophrah, which belonged to Joash the Abiezrite, as his son Gideon was beating out wheat in the wine press, to hide it from the Midianites.

12 The angel of the LORD appeared to him and said to him, "The LORD is with you, you mighty warrior."

MAIN THOUGHT: And the LORD said unto him, Peace be unto thee; fear not: thou shalt not die. (Judges 6:23, KJV)

King James Version	*New Revised Standard Version*
13 And Gideon said unto him, Oh my LORD, if the LORD be with us, why then is all this befallen us? and where be all his miracles which our fathers told us of, saying, Did not the LORD bring us up from Egypt? but now the LORD hath forsaken us, and delivered us into the hands of the Midianites.	13 Gideon answered him, "But sir, if the LORD is with us, why then has all this happened to us? And where are all his wonderful deeds that our ancestors recounted to us, saying, 'Did not the LORD bring us up from Egypt?' But now the LORD has cast us off, and given us into the hand of Midian."
14 And the LORD looked upon him, and said, Go in this thy might, and thou shalt save Israel from the hand of the Midianites: have not I sent thee?	14 Then the LORD turned to him and said, "Go in this might of yours and deliver Israel from the hand of Midian; I hereby commission you."
15 And he said unto him, Oh my LORD, wherewith shall I save Israel? behold, my family is poor in Manasseh, and I am the least in my father's house.	15 He responded, "But sir, how can I deliver Israel? My clan is the weakest in Manasseh, and I am the least in my family."
16 And the LORD said unto him, Surely I will be with thee, and thou shalt smite the Midianites as one man.	16 The LORD said to him, "But I will be with you, and you shall strike down the Midianites, every one of them."

LESSON SETTING
    Time: Unknown
    Place: Ophrah

LESSON OUTLINE
  I. Israel's Oppression by the
     Midianites
     (Judges 6:1–2)
  II. The Prophet's Rebuke
     (Judges 6:7–10)
  III. Gideon's Calling
     (Judges 6:11–16)

UNIFYING PRINCIPLE

We sometimes feel inadequate to the task to which God calls us. How do we overcome feelings of fear and insecurity? Gideon received divine reassurance of God's continued presence for the task at hand.

INTRODUCTION

After forty years of peace brought by Deborah's victory over the Canaanites, the Amalekites and other enemies, Israel returned to its pattern of turning away from God and backslid again. Gideon would become the fifth judge of Israel.

EXPOSITION

I. ISRAEL'S OPPRESSION BY THE MIDIANITES (JUDGES 6:1–2)

Once again, the Israelites fell into a pattern of sin (v. 1) that had become too familiar. Unfortunately, they are now at the mercy of the invading Midianites. The Midianites are descendants of Abraham and Keturah according to Genesis 25:1–5. They were desert dwellers from northwest Arabia. Israel watched helplessly as their land was stripped, their homes and villages destroyed, and their lives endangered. For seven long years, the Midianites oppressed

Israel. Like locusts, the Midianites invaded the land of the Israelites. At harvest time, they took Israel's crops and destroyed animals. Israel was deprived of any possibility of thriving. This was a time of poverty, persecution, and powerlessness.

This was not Israel's first quarrel with Midian. The Midianites joined with the Moabites in an attempt to impede the Israelites under Moses (Numbers 22:7; 25:6), but later Moses defeated them (Num. 31:8). For seven years, Israel was not at the mercy of Midian. Israel then falls victim to Midian, a people who they have previously defeated, as a consequence of sin. Sin will have you oppressed by an enemy you have already defeated. Israel is now helpless to resist the invading Midianites and escape to the mountains in an effort to save their lives (v. 2). This is another indication of the desperation Israel was facing. Judges 6:6 literally says that Israel "became small," reflecting not only their economic plight but their emotional and psychological state at the depredations of the Midianites. Yet, even this low state is not an indication of repentance but only of their pain in the situation. Though their nation had been overtaken and their lives impoverished, that was not their main problem. Israel's main problem was that they counted God out. Israel had a spiritual relapse and worshiped the gods of the Amorites (v. 10). Israel was a fickle nation. Previously Israel had high praise and devotion for God, but it could not resist the attraction of other gods.

II. THE PROPHET'S REBUKE (JUDGES 6:7–10)

In their distress, Israel cried out to God. Surprisingly, God did not immediately respond to Israel's cries by sending them a deliverer. Instead, God sent Israel a prophet to remind them of His grace and goodness and to call them to repentance. Sometimes believers who cry to God for deliverance are met with a reminder of indictment. God sent a prophet to tell them that they had forfeited the right to deliverance. Disobedience and faithlessness are the cause of Israel's oppression. Once again, God must remind Israel of His past goodness and how that should have resulted in their devotion. Instead, Israel chooses to worship other gods again. In verse 10, the text says that the Israelites worshiped the gods of the Amorites. But Israel refused to listen to God and now find themselves in a pitiful predicament of their own blame. The prophet recalls the exodus from Egypt and God's gift of Canaan. Both of these acts should have led to Israel's loyalty to God. After all, the book of Judges begins promptly after Israel has promised three times to be faithful to God (Joshua 24:18, 21, 24). The people now under distress cry out to God, but in this case, the prophet does not deliver the people as Deborah did; but instead, the prophet chastises the people. The prophet's speech ended in indictment, leaving Israel unclear on God's intentions about their future. God had demonstrated His grace in delivering Israel from their previous enemies and providing them with their own land. He committed Himself to be their God, so it is no surprise that God demanded Israel's exclusive allegiance. He would not tolerate any other gods.

God expresses His disappointment with Israel "you have not listened to me" (v. 10). God has spoken, but Israel has refused to listen once again. Christians can sometimes behave a lot like Israel. God gives instructions and yet believers do not listen to God and turn to other gods. The narrator's purpose in inserting this prophetic scolding at this point sets the stage for Gideon's call.

III. GIDEON'S CALLING (JUDGES 6:11–16)

Not only does God have a message, God also has a messenger. The Lord's vessel of deliverance was a young man from the tribe of Manasseh named Gideon.

Gideon's call is the most extended and most formal call narrative in the book of Judges, revealing the significance of Gideon's call as well as the author's view of Israel (forgetful) and of Gideon (insecure). Gideon's call indicates God's preference, presence, and performance.

In the passage, we meet Gideon, who does not seem to have much to offer when he first appears in the text, but he is ultimately responsible for delivering Israel from Midianite oppression. Gideon is an unlikely leader from humanity's perspective. All throughout the Bible, there are examples of God's preference to call people that defy the human preference. Gideon was a farmer's son, who worked with his hands, and his father was an idol worshiper (Judges 6:15, 25). Still, God calls and uses Gideon for His service and glory. Gideon's calling strongly reflects Moses' calling (Exodus 3–4), suggesting that the author wants the reader to see Gideon as a potential type of Moses.

An angel of the Lord appeared while Gideon is threshing wheat in Ophrah in a pit to hide from the Midianites. Gideon was threshing wheat by hand in a pit to hide the wheat from the Midianites, which indicates his refugee lifestyle.

While Gideon was hiding from the enemy, the Lord knew exactly where Gideon was and sent a messenger with instructions. The Midianites did not know where Gideon was hiding, but the Lord did! God had His eye on Gideon the whole time. Even when Gideon was unaware of it, God was with him, watching him, protecting him, and guiding him for his future. When the angel speaks to Gideon, he comes with hope and assurance "The Lord is with you, mighty warrior" (v. 12). The angel's words seem incongruent with Gideon's character and circumstance. So far, all that is known about Gideon is he's evading the enemy, and he is from a working-class family, a polar opposite from the angel's greeting.

Gideon challenges the validity of the angel's claim and wonders why a present God would allow His people to suffer. Where was God when his nation was being overtaken by the Midianites? If God was present, why did God allow such horrible conditions? The same questions can be asked about present circumstances in the world. Gideon contrasted the miracles he heard of his ancestors to the Lord's current inactivity. God is always present amid suffering and has a plan for deliverance. God has given believers the same promise as Gideon (Hebrews 13:5; Matthew 28:20; John 14:17–18); the Lord has promised to be with believers in every situation. The Lord's presence was not just a reminder but also intended to encourage Gideon, similar to how the Lord did to assure and encourage Moses to deliver Israel out of Egypt (Exodus 3:12–14). Gideon's response to God's calling is reminiscent of what Moses did when the Lord called him at the burning bush. Both men came up with excuses as to why they could not do what the Lord said they could do. Both men felt inadequate but God assures both that God is with them.

Then the Lord says something that is amazing. He looks at Gideon and calls him "a mighty man of valor." Again, this seems to be the opposite of Gideon's reality. Here is Gideon so afraid of the enemy that he is hiding behind a winepress threshing wheat. He is full of fear, but God saw past his present predicament and spoke to Gideon's future. Gideon focused on his frailties, but God saw past that and into his potential. God anticipates Gideon's bravery. God specializes in using those who humans feel are weak to accomplish His will.

The vision is cast, and Gideon knows what is required of him by the Lord. He is sending Gideon to rescue His people who have been mistreated and abused. He is to save Israel out of the hands of the Midianites. In verse 16, the Lord reaffirms His choice and Gideon's call. God reminds Gideon that He would resource him. God promised to be with him.

The Lesson Applied

Gideon is full of doubts excuses as to why he can not fulfill God's calling. Believers often make the same mistake of doubting God's calling on their lives. The excuses may change, but Christians throughout centuries have been afraid to go and do what God was calling them to. Gideon's view of himself was much different than God's view of himself. I Samuel 16:7 says, "The Lord does not look at the things man looks at. Man looks at the outward appearance, but the Lord looks at the heart." God is not interested in societal status, pedigree, appearance, but the Lord looks at hearts. The heart reveals whether one can be trusted and if they are willing vessels. Gideon was about to allow his past to define what his future looked like, but thankfully God had other plans for him. God has plans that outweigh all believers' past and doubts.

Let's Talk About It

Gideon's call was in response to a particular issue. He was to be a deliverer for Israel. Often we are called to particular situations and people. Has there been an instance in which God has called you to serve a particular people or cause?

Is God calling you to serve His people in a way that is significant? God calls us to people, places, and causes that furthers His will.

HOME DAILY DEVOTIONAL READINGS
OCTOBER 17–23, 2022

MONDAY	TUESDAY	WEDNESDAY	THURSDAY	FRIDAY	SATURDAY	SUNDAY
A Prayer for Protection and Boldness	A Desire to Be Like Others	God Is the King of Nations	The Lord Is Robed in Majesty	God Chooses Saul	God's Spirit Will Possess You	Behold Your King!
Acts 4:23–31	1 Samuel 8:1–9	Revelation 11:15–19; 15:2–4	Psalm 93	1 Samuel 9:3–17	1 Samuel 9:27–10:8	1 Samuel 10:17–27

WHO IS KING?

ADULT TOPIC: BACKGROUND SCRIPTURE:
ISRAEL REJECTS GOD IN FAVOR OF A HUMAN KING   1 SAMUEL 8:1–9; 10:17–26

1 SAMUEL 8:4–7; 10:17–24

King James Version

THEN all the elders of Israel gathered themselves together, and came to Samuel unto Ramah,

5 And said unto him, Behold, thou art old, and thy sons walk not in thy ways: now make us a king to judge us like all the nations.

6 But the thing displeased Samuel, when they said, Give us a king to judge us. And Samuel prayed unto the LORD.

7 And the LORD said unto Samuel, Hearken unto the voice of the people in all that they say unto thee: for they have not rejected thee, but they have rejected me, that I should not reign over them.

••• 1 Samuel 10:17–24 •••

AND Samuel called the people together unto the LORD to Mizpeh;

18 And said unto the children of Israel, Thus saith the LORD God of Israel, I brought up Israel out of Egypt, and delivered you out of the hand of the Egyptians, and out of the hand of all kingdoms, and of them that oppressed you:

19 And ye have this day rejected your God, who himself saved you out of all your adversities and your tribulations; and ye have said unto him, Nay, but set a king over us. Now therefore present yourselves before the LORD by your tribes, and by your thousands.

20 And when Samuel had caused all the tribes of Israel to come near, the tribe of Benjamin was taken.

New Revised Standard Version

THEN all the elders of Israel gathered together and came to Samuel at Ramah,

5 and said to him, "You are old and your sons do not follow in your ways; appoint for us, then, a king to govern us, like other nations."

6 But the thing displeased Samuel when they said, "Give us a king to govern us." Samuel prayed to the LORD,

7 and the LORD said to Samuel, "Listen to the voice of the people in all that they say to you; for they have not rejected you, but they have rejected me from being king over them.

••• 1 Samuel 10:17–24 •••

SAMUEL summoned the people to the LORD at Mizpah

18 and said to them, "Thus says the LORD, the God of Israel, 'I brought up Israel out of Egypt, and I rescued you from the hand of the Egyptians and from the hand of all the kingdoms that were oppressing you.'

19 But today you have rejected your God, who saves you from all your calamities and your distresses; and you have said, 'No! but set a king over us.' Now therefore present yourselves before the LORD by your tribes and by your clans."

20 Then Samuel brought all the tribes of Israel near, and the tribe of Benjamin was taken by lot.

MAIN THOUGHT: And ye have this day rejected your God, who himself saved you out of all your adversities and your tribulations; and ye have said unto him, Nay, but set a king over us. Now therefore present yourselves before the LORD by your tribes, and by your thousands. (1 Samuel 10:19, KJV)

1 Samuel 8:4–7; 10:17–24

King James Version	*New Revised Standard Version*
21 When he had caused the tribe of Benjamin to come near by their families, the family of Matri was taken, and Saul the son of Kish was taken: and when they sought him, he could not be found.	21 He brought the tribe of Benjamin near by its families, and the family of the Matrites was taken by lot. Finally he brought the family of the Matrites near man by man, and Saul the son of Kish was taken by lot. But when they sought him, he could not be found.
22 Therefore they enquired of the LORD further, if the man should yet come thither. And the LORD answered, Behold he hath hid himself among the stuff.	22 So they inquired again of the LORD, "Did the man come here?" and the LORD said, "See, he has hidden himself among the baggage."
23 And they ran and fetched him thence: and when he stood among the people, he was higher than any of the people from his shoulders and upward.	23 Then they ran and brought him from there. When he took his stand among the people, he was head and shoulders taller than any of them.
24 And Samuel said to all the people, See ye him whom the LORD hath chosen, that there is none like him among all the people? And all the people shouted, and said, God save the king.	24 Samuel said to all the people, "Do you see the one whom the LORD has chosen? There is no one like him among all the people." And all the people shouted, "Long live the king!"

LESSON SETTING
Time: 960 BC
Place: Mizpah

LESSON OUTLINE
I. **Israel Demands a King and Rejects God**
   (1 Samuel 8:4–7)
II. **Samuel's Message to Israel**
   (1 Samuel 10:17–19)
III. **Saul's Selection**
   (1 Samuel 10:20–24)

UNIFYING PRINCIPLE
We tend to be influenced by the people around us, for good or for ill. How do we discern which voice to listen to? The elders chose to listen to the people rather than following the leadership of God.

INTRODUCTION
Israel was truly God's chosen people. God provided His love and allegiance to them. Israel was a nation born of promises. It was an entire nation that could trace its lineage back to one man, Abraham, a man who had received an outlandish set of promises from God. Along the way to these promises being fulfilled, Israel experienced oppression and abuse at the hands of the pharaoh and the Egyptians. Israel cried, and God heard their cries and delivered Israel from oppression. In the wake of their liberation, God renewed His covenant with Israel, and Israel pledged its allegiance and devotion to God.

Samuel was the first of the prophets after Moses and was the last judge of Israel. Samuel had a high devotion to God. He was the son of Elkanah and Hannah, born in the hill country of Ephraim. He was brought to the tabernacle at Shiloh as a child to serve God in fulfillment of a vow made by his mother, and he succeeded Eli as the high priest and judge of Israel.

As the judge and high priest, Samuel made annual tours through Bethel, Gilgal, and Mizpah to judge the people and ensure unity. At the time of the lesson, Israel was under constant threats from other nations and internal threats within Israel's own tribes. The people were dissatisfied with Samuel's sons, who he appointed to judge the people in his place as his successor. The Israelites rejected Samuel's sons because of their corruption. Samuel was not a warrior, but he was essential to Israel's flourishing. Like Moses, Samuel was a hero who was able to rally his people to keep their hope and faith in God amid oppression.

EXPOSITION

I. ISRAEL DEMANDS A KING AND REJECTS GOD
(1 SAMUEL 8:4–7)

What a difference a chapter makes. In chapter seven, Samuel is effective as a judge, and the people are pleased and content. Samuel is an effective leader and is beyond reproach. Israel had existed as a confederation of tribes for roughly two centuries, dependent upon unity, faith and covenant with God. But now, suddenly, everything has changed in chapter eight. Samuel is old and still in charge, but his sons, who are judges, are failures. Samuel's sons have convoluted the judicial process by taking bribes and being unjust (v. 3). They have deliberately perverted justice, corrupting Israel's judiciary system. Other nations like the Philistines had strong armies equipped with weapons and chariots. Israel was desperate to strengthen its resistance to the Philistine threat, who were encroaching on Israelite territory.

The people are disappointed in the trajectory of Israel's justice system. The elders address Samuel with Israel's concerns. The elders propose a new model of power. If anyone in Israel should have known better, the elders should have.

They were knowledgeable about how God had continually provided for Israel. The elders knew about God defeating Israel's enemies and delivering them from the brutalities of oppression. The elders were fully aware of God's goodness to Israel, yet they chose to listen to the people instead of following God and God's leadership. The elders requested a king. Some scholars suggest that the motivation for the request was to protect the wealthy. Scholars suggest that the wealthy wanted a strong government to protect their wealth. The text does not explicitly inform of the elders' motivation, but whatever the motivation may have been, it is clear that the elders believed Israel's condition to be dire. The elders proposed a comprehensive withdrawal from the current system of social organization.

The elders desire a governance "like the other nations" (v. 5). The request was horrendous and probably jarring to Samuel. This request would completely transform Israel. Israel was God's chosen people, and in return, Israel vowed its loyalty and devotion to God. Since its inception on Mount Sinai, Israel was to pledge its allegiance to God, trusting and relying on God's promise, mercy, and love. There is a danger in desiring to mimic others. Israel wanted to be like other nations and, in doing so, would deny what made them unique, being God's chosen people. Samuel recognized the implications of the elders' request and was displeased. Their request had severe consequences and repercussions and would shift Israel's social order, governance, and void their allegiance to God. Samuel is displeased (v. 6) because he considers their demands sinful. The request to have a king felt like a rejection to Samuel. Rightfully so, after all, he was then appointed by God, judge of Israel, and the people were pleased with him, but now their contentment has transformed to disdain, and the people want a king. Samuel prayed to God. While in this uncomfortable situation, Samuel prays, God is his first resort.

God's response was surprising to Samuel. He tells Samuel to grant Israel's request for a monarchy. Though a monarchy is not God's intended course of action, God gives in to Israel's request. God has reservations about Israel's proposal. First, the monarchy is not a political problem, but a theological problem. The problem is not so much that Israel desires a monarchy, but that Israel's desire is to abandon God. The desire for a monarchy is not a rejection of Samuel, but a rejection of God (v. 7). This rejection was understood to be a turning away from God because as a theocratic confederation, God was to be Israel's king. Secondly, this rejection of God is nothing new but a continued characteristic of Israel's behavior toward God. Israel has a storied history of forsaking and abandoning God for lesser gods. So, while the request for a monarchy surprised Samuel, it was not a surprise to God. While God does not endorse Israel's choice, God does not prevent it either. God is so merciful that He gives people their desires even if they go against His plan. It was undeniably evident that Israel was in need of leadership. Still, the political answer God's people chose could never solve the spiritual problem they faced and would only further strain their relationship with God, yet God granted their request.

II. Samuel's Message to Israel (1 Samuel 10:17–19)

Samuel calls the people to hear an announcement by God at Mizpah. Samuel is a herald for God and is able to speak on God's behalf. He begins the message by rehashing God's benevolence to Israel (v. 18). Samuel reminds Israel that God has been merciful and kind to Israel throughout its history. He reminds Israel that it was God who delivered them from the oppressive plight of Pharaoh in Egypt and all the other nations who beleaguered them. God has been gracious to Israel, and now Israel rejects their kind and delivering God. It is ironic that Samuel delivers this message at Mizpah. Mizpah [MIZ pah] means watchtower. It is no coincidence that at Mizpah, God reminds Israel He alone has been their watchtower, watching and protecting them from dangers seen and unseen.

But Israel is too afraid to keep trusting God. Israel thought God could not take care of them, so they wanted a human king with a military presence to defend and protect them. Monarchies are not inherently evil or wrong, but Israel's lack of trust in God was sinful. God's care for them had been more than sufficient, delivering them from their enemies. In chapters 4–6, it is apparent that Israel viewed the Philistines as a threat to overtake them. Israel was terrified that the Philistines would enslave them, much like the Egyptians did to their ancestors. Israel was too fearful and too heavily reliant on their own abilities to remember that God's intervention was why they could overcome their detractors. Israel completely rejects God, forgetting how God has been their security in the past warning them about dangerous situations, protecting them from predators, and delivering them from evil. Israel imagines a different kind of security, which causes Israel to reject its memory of God's goodness and place its trust in a monarchy.

III. Saul's Selection (1 Samuel 10:20–24)

Despite Samuel's objections, it was time to select a king. God and Samuel had conceded and would allow a king. Samuel called all the tribes of Israel, and the tribe of Benjamin was chosen through the process of casting lots (v. 20). The only other time we see this method of elimination in the Old Testament is when God singles out Achan as the source of rebellion against God (Joshua 7:16–18), suggesting that Saul's appointment should be seen as a judgment on Israel for abandoning God's spiritual leadership by choosing a king.

Casting lots was not uncommon to Israel (Leviticus 16:8–10; Joshua 7:10–26; 18:6). Lot casting would have probably included stones or pieces of wood with marks on them that were thrown like dice in a board game. Depending on which marks appeared, they would select an option between the choices. The casting of lots (v. 20–21) comes after the mention of the rush of spirit (v. 9–13), followed by the selection. The text is similar to the first two chapters in Acts when there is a selection made by lots and the rush of the Spirit. Both texts confirm that God nor God's selection cannot be confined to tradition or conventional methods. The process begins with twelve tribes, narrowed down to the clans of that tribe, then to families, and then to any sons in that family.

There were thousands of people to choose from, but God was still in control and still the cosmic conductor of Israel's fate. The secret anointing of Saul in (v.1) has now become public and confirmed. The lot falls to Saul, and Saul is chosen as Israel's first king. God was actively involved in the process. Saul had already been chosen, and God used the lot to affirm this choice before the people. God orchestrated this event. God does not always initiate or cause events to happen, but God can certainly work through humanity's choice.

Saul is not desirous of the title or responsibility of being king. Saul is afraid of being king. Of course, he was aware that he was the one and thus knew the result was coming, and he hid (v. 21). In fact, Saul is not even present for the "drawing," but he had to be found. It was God who informed the people where Saul was hiding (v. 22). Even though the people had rejected God, He had not rejected them and was always available and at their disposal. Saul's hiding was an indicator of Saul's weaknesses and fear. Instead of stepping up in faith to fulfill God's purpose for him, Saul hides and hopes that Israel will find another king. God informs the people that Saul was hiding among the baggage/supplies. Biblical translations vary in the translation of Saul's place of hiding; it could refer to anything from general utensils to battle equipment; the context suggests the latter, armor.

Saul is found. When he is found, Israel notices his height. Saul is tall (v. 23). In the ancient Near East, a man's height was seen as an indication of his physical ability and power, which were good outward characteristics for royalty. Saul's height acts as confirmation to his being chosen as king. Other than his height, the text does not mention any other distinguishing trait of Saul's. Saul appears ideal on the outside but internally is irresponsible and undisciplined (10:21).

Samuel vouches for Saul as God's selection (v. 24). Samuel strongly affirms Saul as God's chosen. Samuel says, "there is none like him among all the people" is not a reference to his height. Saul is the one who God has selected to be the king of Israel, which makes him unique and within a class of his own. This phrase had been traditionally reserved for Israel elites like Moses (Deuteronomy 34:10–11) and Josiah (2 Kings 23:25). What a strong endorsement for such an unqualified and unproven leader. Saul is really God's choice and, therefore, the best person for the job. The people, in turn, are accepting and responsive and acclaim Saul as their king. Israel enthusiastically pledges their allegiance to their new king by shouting, "Long live the king (v. 24)." The people affirmed Saul's selection without thought of his character, his background, or his capabilities, just his appearance. Saul's kingship begins with innocence and no indicator of his later indiscretions, which were avoidable if the elders listened to God rather than the people.

THE LESSON APPLIED

It is not uncommon for people to experience fear concerning the calling they have been given or have a sense of unworthiness for that calling. However, those feelings should not keep believers from serving as the Lord has appointed them to perform. If God has called you to a task, it is not a sign of humility to let fear keep you from serving where God has called you to. Though everyone called by God has feelings of inadequacy, know that the same God who calls is also faithful to equip.

LET'S TALK ABOUT IT

Israel wanted a king to help them organize their forces so that they could strongly defend their borders. If you were a part of the collective that made the decision, would you have made a different choice to install a human king?

Though Israel made the wrong choice, it is important that most of us would have made a similar choice if given the opportunity. Whereas, most of us do not live in societies where a monarchy is an acceptable form of governance, safety is a top priority for all people. We have also made decisions as a people that dishonored God in the name of our safety and way of life.

HOME DAILY DEVOTIONAL READINGS
OCTOBER 24–30, 2022

MONDAY	TUESDAY	WEDNESDAY	THURSDAY	FRIDAY	SATURDAY	SUNDAY
God Rejects Saul	God's Kindness and Severity	God's Begotten Son	Jesus the Heir of David	The Bright Morning Star	Making Melody to God	A Higher Perspective
1 Samuel 15:1–11	Romans 11:13–24	Psalm 2	Acts 13:21–31	Revelation 22:12–17	Psalm 89:20–29, 34–37	1 Samuel 16:1–13

DAVID ANOINTED AS KING

ADULT TOPIC:	BACKGROUND SCRIPTURE:
THE HEART OF A LEADER	1 SAMUEL 16:1–13

1 SAMUEL 16:1–13

King James Version

AND the LORD said unto Samuel, How long wilt thou mourn for Saul, seeing I have rejected him from reigning over Israel? fill thine horn with oil, and go, I will send thee to Jesse the Bethlehemite: for I have provided me a king among his sons.

2 And Samuel said, How can I go? if Saul hear it, he will kill me. And the LORD said, Take an heifer with thee, and say, I am come to sacrifice to the LORD.

3 And call Jesse to the sacrifice, and I will shew thee what thou shalt do: and thou shalt anoint unto me him whom I name unto thee.

4 And Samuel did that which the LORD spake, and came to Bethlehem. And the elders of the town trembled at his coming, and said, Comest thou peaceably?

5 And he said, Peaceably: I am come to sacrifice unto the LORD: sanctify yourselves, and come with me to the sacrifice. And he sanctified Jesse and his sons, and called them to the sacrifice.

6 And it came to pass, when they were come, that he looked on Eliab, and said, Surely the Lord's anointed is before him.

7 But the LORD said unto Samuel, Look not on his countenance, or on the height of his stature; because I have refused him: for the LORD seeth not as man seeth; for man looketh on the outward appearance, but the LORD looketh on the heart.

New Revised Standard Version

THE LORD said to Samuel, "How long will you grieve over Saul? I have rejected him from being king over Israel. Fill your horn with oil and set out; I will send you to Jesse the Bethlehemite, for I have provided for myself a king among his sons."

2 Samuel said, "How can I go? If Saul hears of it, he will kill me." And the LORD said, "Take a heifer with you, and say, 'I have come to sacrifice to the LORD.'

3 Invite Jesse to the sacrifice, and I will show you what you shall do; and you shall anoint for me the one whom I name to you."

4 Samuel did what the Lord commanded, and came to Bethlehem. The elders of the city came to meet him trembling, and said, "Do you come peaceably?"

5 He said, "Peaceably; I have come to sacrifice to the LORD; sanctify yourselves and come with me to the sacrifice." And he sanctified Jesse and his sons and invited them to the sacrifice.

6 When they came, he looked on Eliab and thought, "Surely the Lord's anointed is now before the Lord."

7 But the Lord said to Samuel, "Do not look on his appearance or on the height of his stature, because I have rejected him; for the Lord does not see as mortals see; they look on the outward appearance, but the LORD looks on the heart."

MAIN THOUGHT: But the LORD said unto Samuel, Look not on his countenance, or on the height of his stature; because I have refused him: for the LORD seeth not as man seeth; for man looketh on the outward appearance, but the LORD looketh on the heart. (1 Samuel 16:7, KJV)

1 Samuel 16:1–13

King James Version	*New Revised Standard Version*
8 Then Jesse called Abinadab, and made him pass before Samuel. And he said, Neither hath the LORD chosen this.	8 Then Jesse called Abinadab, and made him pass before Samuel. He said, "Neither has the LORD chosen this one."
9 Then Jesse made Shammah to pass by. And he said, Neither hath the LORD chosen this.	9 Then Jesse made Shammah pass by. And he said, "Neither has the Lord chosen this one."
10 Again, Jesse made seven of his sons to pass before Samuel. And Samuel said unto Jesse, The LORD hath not chosen these.	10 Jesse made seven of his sons pass before Samuel, and Samuel said to Jesse, "The Lord has not chosen any of these."
11 And Samuel said unto Jesse, Are here all thy children? And he said, There remaineth yet the youngest, and, behold, he keepeth the sheep. And Samuel said unto Jesse, Send and fetch him: for we will not sit down till he come hither.	11 Samuel said to Jesse, "Are all your sons here?" And he said, "There remains yet the youngest, but he is keeping the sheep." And Samuel said to Jesse, "Send and bring him; for we will not sit down until he comes here."
12 And he sent, and brought him in. Now he was ruddy, and withal of a beautiful countenance, and goodly to look to. And the LORD said, Arise, anoint him: for this is he.	12 He sent and brought him in. Now he was ruddy, and had beautiful eyes, and was handsome. The LORD said, "Rise and anoint him; for this is the one."
13 Then Samuel took the horn of oil, and anointed him in the midst of his brethren: and the Spirit of the LORD came upon David from that day forward. So Samuel rose up, and went to Ramah.	13 Then Samuel took the horn of oil, and anointed him in the presence of his brothers; and the spirit of the LORD came mightily upon David from that day forward. Samuel then set out and went to Ramah.

LESSON SETTING
Time: 1000 BC
Place: Bethlehem

LESSON OUTLINE
I. Samuel's Commission
   (1 Samuel 16:1–5)
II. Rejection of Jesse's Sons
   (1 Samuel 16:6–11)
III. David Anointed
   (1 Samuel 16:12–13)

UNIFYING PRINCIPLE

People choose leaders based on human standards. How should those who rule be chosen? According to 1 Samuel, God selects leaders based on a person's heart rather than by human standards.

INTRODUCTION

Can you believe that the scouting report on NBA superstar Steph Curry was once that his explosiveness and athleticism are below standard? Many scouts believed he could not be successful in college basketball because of what they saw in his stature, speed, height, or body build. He had boyish looks, a very thin frame and he was barely 6ft tall. He was not heavily recruited; most colleges overlooked him. A small college named Davidson College took a chance on Curry and offered him the opportunity to walk on the team. Davidson recognized what other colleges, coaches and recruiters could not. The Davidson coach saw and recognized Steph's work ethic, how coachable Steph was, his behavior, leaders, and character, and liked what he saw in Steph. Because his coach looked beyond the surface and saw Curry's character, he went on to become one of the NBA's all-time greatest shooters and helped to change the way basketball is played. Steph went from being an overlooked recruit to an NBA champion, superstar, and MVP. The story of Steph Curry's rise from obscurity to NBA legend is reminiscent of the story of David. King David was once overlooked because he did not have the physical appearance of a king.

David is one of the most notable characters in the Bible. He is known as a man after God's own heart. David is one of the most mentioned characters in the Bible. Besides Jesus, David is perhaps the most popular person in all of Scripture. Out of all the people in Scripture, David is only one of few listed as having a unique pursuit of God. Though David ascends to become the second king of the united kingdom of Israel, ancestor of Jesus Christ, mighty warrior, and writer of many beloved psalms, Scripture does not introduce David as royalty but as a runt. David is the runt of his brothers and is shepherding his father's sheep in the text when his life takes a dramatic shift. God through Samuel chooses David, He picked David from the sheep pasture and anointed him to be king. David was chosen not because of his physical appearance but because of his heart for God.

EXPOSITION

I. SAMUEL'S COMMISSION (1 SAMUEL 16:1–5)

When the text opens, Samuel is grieving for Saul and now the season of grief has passed, and it is time for God to do a new thing. Samuel has been prophet and counsel to Saul and he's been a part of Saul's reign so it is understandable why Samuel would be grieved. Saul has been rejected by God as king (1 Samuel 15). God has decided that he is exhausted by Saul's disrespect and God sends word that He is firing Saul. God says to Samuel, "I have provided for myself a king among [Jesse's] sons" (v. 1). The Hebrew word that is translated here as "provided" literally means "to see" ra'ah); as in English, Hebrew uses "to see"—"I have seen to it"—idiomatically with the sense of "to provide." God has seen Israel's needs even before they know their needs. Only God can keep you in position and place and still fire you. Saul was fired with the crown on his head. Now God and Samuel are preparing for a new king. Samuel has the arduous task of anointing a new king. Samuel is commissioned to go to Jesse in Bethlehem outside the reach of Saul's kingdom and outside Samuel's Ramah-Bethel-Mizpah circuit. The new king would come from a new territory. To this point, the text has not given much background information about Jesse. God says to Samuel, "I have provided a king among his sons." The selection of David was secured before Samuel even begins his journey. Similarly, Saul was selected as king by God, not by accident, coincidence, or political strategy but because God engineered it. God tells Samuel to fill his horn with oil (v.1). The oil Samuel possessed would have been an exquisite olive oil, carried in a ram's horn and been used exclusively for anointing a new king.

Samuel understandably has reservations about his new assignment (v. 2). Anointing a new king while the throne was still occupied could result in death. The throne was not vacant. Saul was not ill nor was he considering abdicating or renouncing his position and power. Anointing another king is considered traitorous and would make Samuel an enemy of the king. Samuel expresses his apprehensions about his assignment. God does not cancel the assignment because of Samuel's apprehension instead God instructs Samuel how to avert being discovered by Saul. The Lord tells Samuel to operate in a covert manner to not raise suspicions and take a young cow with you and say that you are there to offer a sacrifice and invite Jesse and I will show you whom to anoint. Samuel arrives in Bethlehem with his anointing oil and a young cow. The elders are terrified and full of anxiety about his arrival. They are fully aware that whenever high officials of the king's cabinet visit trouble and negative consequences were typically what followed. They were vulnerable to King Saul and his army and the elders were rightfully suspicious and leery of Samuel. He must act covertly. Samuel is only given access when he announces that he is visiting peacefully to make a sacrifice. In order to not raise suspicions in the area, he invites everyone but especially Jesse to consecrate themselves to make themselves in better covenant with God. Sanctification was the process of making oneself holy. In preparation for the sacrifice, one would sanctify themselves by means of ritual washing and avoidance of unclean items, people, and actions such as contact with corpses, unclean animals, or sexual discharge.

II. REJECTION OF JESSE'S SONS (1 SAMUEL 16:6–11)

After a period of consecration, Samuel gets an audience with Jesse and invites Jesse and his sons to the sacrifice. When they arrive Jesse proudly parades his sons one by one before Samuel. His eldest son Eliab who looked kingly and attractive in stature to the point that Samuel presumptuously takes out his oil flask and is ready to anoint him the next king. Fortunately, God's criteria for the next king was not Samuel's criteria. God's responds to Samuel's assumption by saying, "Do not look on his appearance or on the height of his stature, because I have rejected him; for the Lord does not see as mortals see they look on the outward appearance, but the Lord looks on the heart" (v. 7). God speaks to Samuel and precautions him not to look at Eliab's physical appearance. Eliab's height and appearance were reminiscent of Saul, whom God had rejected. Looks can be misleading.

In verse 7, God introduces an essential principle that what matters most for a person is not their outward appearance but the inner qualities, heart, and character. God looks beyond human surfaces and sees what is in a person's heart. Both God and Israel need a king with a heart that desires to please and follow God. Eliab is rejected by God. Jesse then parades Abinadab and Shammah and the remaining four sons, but each time they were rejected as God's chosen one (vv. 8–10).

Samuel had to be confused and wondered that did he not hear God clearly about this assignment. Jesse was flabbergasted. He had brought out what he believed to be the best he had to offer and yet his best was not good enough. Samuel asks, "Are these all the sons you have because God said the next king would come from this house but none of the sons that have been brought forth are chosen. Are there any more sons?" Jesse answers reluctantly that he has an additional son, but he is outside taking care of the sheep. The eighth son was the youngest or the runt of the sons. Thankfully, God did not see his runt status as eliminating him for service. God valued and sought out someone to lead Israel who had a love for Him and would be obedient. For God, it did not matter that David was a runt but more about David's purpose and posture. Samuel halts the whole process and commands Jesse to summon his eighth son. Samuel, Bethlehem's elders, Jesse, Jesse's seven older sons, and the household must all stand and wait for the arrival of David. All of the people who overlooked him now must wait on David (v. 11). While David is out being a good shepherd, God has engineered a moment to take him from the pasture to the palace.

III. DAVID ANOINTED
(1 SAMUEL 16:12–13)

David finally physically appears in the narrative. The first thing that is noted about David is his appearance. He is ruddy which is also the word used to describe Esau (Genesis 25:25), meaning reddish hair and complexion. It is also noted that David has beautiful eyes and is handsome. It is rather interesting that the first information given about David is his physical appearance; especially because this text explicitly states that God is not concerned with physical appearance. While Samuel scanned David's physical appearance God scanned David's heart. He tells Samuel

that David is the one and to anoint him (v. 12). God's approval of David's character is not explained here but can be understood considering David's words in Psalm 40:6–8. David expresses his understanding that God desires whole-hearted loyalty and sincere obedience, not religious observance without love. Jesus was born in Bethlehem and did not have the outward appearance or pedigree that people expected. He was despised and rejected because He came from a poor town and His stepfather was a carpenter, but He went on to become the King of all kings and ultimately gave humanity salvation.

David's anointing (v. 13) takes place in a private ceremony, in the presence of his family, the same ones who had looked over and dismissed him. The oil is poured on David as a symbol of the marriage between God, Israel, and David. David is now Israel's new king chosen by God. His entire life is about to change not just because he will become Israel's next king, but also because the Spirit of the Lord comes upon him powerfully and took control from that day forward. The chief difference between Saul and David's anointing is that the Spirit of God took control of David and not Saul. This transformation was not caused by oil, but by Spirit. David is qualified for anointment by his heart. All of his physical attributes are irrelevant.

Take note that throughout the narrative, David does not speak. Not one word is uttered from David during this entire spectacular and life-altering event. David is silent through all thirteen verses, even though he is being anointed king. When God has made someone His choice you do not have to speak, you allow the anointing to speak for you.

Verse 13 states that the Spirit of the Lord came upon David from that day forward. Throughout David's life, it is evident that God's anointing was present in his life. When God chooses a king (David) verses when the people chose a king (Saul), God leaves a lasting stamp through anointing.

THE LESSON APPLIED

Like David, many believers have been rejected and overlooked. Unfortunately, sometimes our rejection has come from those who are closest to us. David's father overlooked and rejected him. Jesse minimized David and relegated him to be the pasture. Jesse rejected David and the very idea that he could be king by not bothering to bring David in for consideration. Thankfully, God saw in David what his father did not see. It does not matter who rejects you or overlooks you when God accepts and appoints you. We should take time to scan our lives and see whom we have overlooked or rejected because they did not have an acceptable physical appearance. You never know you may be rejecting the person who will be pivotal in your life: your significant other, a mentee or mentor, spiritual leader, or a great friend, all because they do not appear in the ways that ascribe to societal norms. As believers, we should be challenged to see as God does, not at the outward appearance but at the heart.

LET'S TALK ABOUT IT

In what sense does this lesson have application in a our current cultural context?

The text reverberates in a contemporary cultural context. Humanity relies on sight for almost everything but often that sight is myopic therefore untrustworthy. Advertisers exploits this, saturating our televisions, email inboxes, social media with provocative images of luxury and excess. For instance, models usually fit a certain body image to make consumers believe that if they purchase the product somehow their lives will be transformed. Unfortunately, many people select politicians, spouses, employees, and leaders based solely on appearance. The text offers a powerful, countercultural message to look at a person's heart, character, and places that cannot be seen with a human eye. Often outward appearances are not reliable and lead to misjudgments. We often forget that time and gravity have a way of catching up with all of us, so it would behoove us to base decisions on more than appearance like God tells Samuel.

HOME DAILY DEVOTIONAL READINGS
OCTOBER 31–NOVEMBER 6, 2022

MONDAY	TUESDAY	WEDNESDAY	THURSDAY	FRIDAY	SATURDAY	SUNDAY
Receive the Holy Spirit	Renounce Sinful Practices	God Is My Light and Salvation	Chosen in God's Providence	You Are God's Chosen People	The Way, the Truth, the Life	God's Eternal Plan of Salvation
Acts 19:1–12	Acts 19:13–20	Psalm 27	Esther 4:5–17	Deuteronomy 7:1–11	John 14:1–14	Ephesians 1:1–14

GOD PICKED YOU!

ADULT TOPIC:	BACKGROUND SCRIPTURE:
GOD CHOOSES US	REVELATION 2:1–7; ACTS 19; EPHESIANS 1:1–14

EPHESIANS 1:1—14

King James Version

PAUL, an apostle of Jesus Christ by the will of God, to the saints which are at Ephesus, and to the faithful in Christ Jesus:

2 Grace be to you, and peace, from God our Father, and from the LORD Jesus Christ.

3 Blessed be the God and Father of our Lord Jesus Christ, who hath blessed us with all spiritual blessings in heavenly places in Christ:

4 According as he hath chosen us in him before the foundation of the world, that we should be holy and without blame before him in love:

5 Having predestinated us unto the adoption of children by Jesus Christ to himself, according to the good pleasure of his will,

6 To the praise of the glory of his grace, wherein he hath made us accepted in the beloved.

7 In whom we have redemption through his blood, the forgiveness of sins, according to the riches of his grace;

8 Wherein he hath abounded toward us in all wisdom and prudence;

9 Having made known unto us the mystery of his will, according to his good pleasure which he hath purposed in himself:

10 That in the dispensation of the fulness of times he might gather together in one all things in Christ, both which are in heaven, and which are on earth; even in him:

New Revised Standard Version

PAUL, an apostle of Christ Jesus by the will of God, To the saints who are in Ephesus and are faithful in Christ Jesus:

2 Grace to you and peace from God our Father and the Lord Jesus Christ.

3 Blessed be the God and Father of our Lord Jesus Christ, who has blessed us in Christ with every spiritual blessing in the heavenly places,

4 just as he chose us in Christ before the foundation of the world to be holy and blameless before him in love.

5 He destined us for adoption as his children through Jesus Christ, according to the good pleasure of his will,

6 to the praise of his glorious grace that he freely bestowed on us in the Beloved.

7 In him we have redemption through his blood, the forgiveness of our trespasses, according to the riches of his grace

8 that he lavished on us. With all wisdom and insight

9 he has made known to us the mystery of his will, according to his good pleasure that he set forth in Christ,

10 as a plan for the fullness of time, to gather up all things in him, things in heaven and things on earth.

MAIN THOUGHT: Blessed be the God and Father of our Lord Jesus Christ, who hath blessed us with all spiritual blessings in heavenly places in Christ. (Ephesians 1:3, KJV)

EPHESIANS 1:1—14

King James Version	New Revised Standard Version
11 In whom also we have obtained an inheritance, being predestinated according to the purpose of him who worketh all things after the counsel of his own will:	11 In Christ we have also obtained an inheritance, having been destined according to the purpose of him who accomplishes all things according to his counsel and will,
12 That we should be to the praise of his glory, who first trusted in Christ.	12 so that we, who were the first to set our hope on Christ, might live for the praise of his glory.
13 In whom ye also trusted, after that ye heard the word of truth, the gospel of your salvation: in whom also after that ye believed, ye were sealed with that holy Spirit of promise,	13 In him you also, when you had heard the word of truth, the gospel of your salvation, and had believed in him, were marked with the seal of the promised Holy Spirit;
14 Which is the earnest of our inheritance until the redemption of the purchased possession, unto the praise of his glory.	14 this is the pledge of our inheritance toward redemption as God's own people, to the praise of his glory.

LESSON SETTING
Time: AD 60
Place: Ephesus

LESSON OUTLINE
  I. **Greetings**
     (Ephesians 1:1–2)
 II. **God Chooses Us**
     (Ephesians 1:3–6)
III. **Jesus' Work**
     (Ephesians 1:7–10)
 IV. **The Power of God in Human Lives**
     (Ephesians 1:11–14)

UNIFYING PRINCIPLE
In a competitive climate, we strive to be selected and we desire the benefits of being chosen. How do we thrive in a culture where not everyone is chosen? In Christ, God has already chosen and gifted us to be holy, blameless, and forgiven.

INTRODUCTION
Ephesians was written primarily to Gentiles to encourage them on their Christian journey. It was a reminder that salvation was not bound just to the Jewish people. In fact, salvation is not bound by ethnicity, locality, heritage, or any other social system. God's kingdom is open to all who put their trust and belief in God. This first section of the letter to the church of Ephesus sets the stage for how the rest of the letter should be read and interpreted using the themes: the blessing of being chosen, adoption, redemption, and the fullness of restored creation, in the end, all of this in Christ.

EXPOSITION

I. GREETING
(EPHESIANS 1:1–2)
The introduction to the entire book of Ephesians is found in the first two verses. The writer uses it to set the stage for the rest of the letter. The opening of the letter is lacking the more detailed greetings found in Paul's other letters. The author uses Paul's name followed by his apostolic authority to address the church at Ephesus. Apostle means sent one. An apostle is

someone who comes into a situation with credentials from the person in authority. In Paul's case, the person of authority is Jesus. Paul was an ambassador for Christ.

Some believe that this letter was actually a circular letter not written to any particular congregation but meant to be circulated to many congregations in multiple cities. Some ancient manuscripts have a blank space or an omission in place of the word Ephesus which helps to affirm that theory. Ephesus was an important city to Paul's ministry and a place where he spent considerable time laboring and ministering to and with the people. Hence, it is no surprise that the letter was intended for Ephesus. At the same time, it is reasonable to assume that the letter was also designed to be a general letter and circulated among cities and churches because of Paul's role as a missionary and evangelist. The writer greets the readers warmly, referring to them as faithful saints in Ephesus. Nonetheless, the greeting emphasizes essentials to Christian life faithfulness and holiness.

Verse 2 is a typical Pauline salutation of "grace" and 'peace." Grace is favor or kindness shown without regard to the merit of the person who receives it. God offers grace by redeeming and restoring a wayward humanity. God confers the grace to society with no expectation of return. Grace is what sustains believers in the Christian life. Peace refers to the inner rest of the soul knowing that God's will and grace are at work. The writer knew how essential grace and peace from God are necessary for the life of believers and knew that receiving God's grace comes ahead of peace in God.

II. GOD CHOOSES US (EPHESIANS 1:3–6)

Following the greeting, Paul delivers a monumental passage filled with theological truth, profound mystery, and beautiful knowledge of the work of God. The writer begins verse 3 with a celebration of God for His blessings. The writer is celebrating God because He has blessed His people. The letter called for a blessing upon the Father recognizing His glory, honor, and goodness because the Father has already given believers spiritual blessings. God's resources are always available for believers with certainty and assurance. The writer urges the recipients of the letter to bless God because God has blessed them. Believers are obligated to live lives that are reflective of the blessings, love, grace, and mercy that has been received from God. Charles Spurgeon once said, "He has blessed us; and therefore, we will bless him. If you think little of what God has done for you, you will do very little for him; but if you have a great notion of his great mercy to you, you will be greatly grateful to your gracious God." The letter says that God has blessed believers with every spiritual blessing. Reflection upon God's blessings necessitates blessing God because every good and perfect gift comes from God (James 1:17).

The verses that follow will expound on the blessings that are alluded to in verse three. The mention of heavenly places foreshadows the letter's later attentiveness to sacred truths. It also reminds us that God does not hold back when it comes to blessing His children. These blessings are spiritual blessings that far outweigh material blessings. Spiritual blessings are higher and better and more secure than material blessings. These blessings cannot spoil, rust, or be stolen, but the Almighty God secures them. Jesus urges believers in Matthew 6:19–20, "Do not store up for yourselves treasures on earth, where moths and vermin destroy, and where thieves break in and steal. But store up for yourselves treasures in heaven, where moths and vermin do not destroy, and where thieves do not break in and steal." While material blessings have their place and should also solicit gratitude, we should aim for spiritual blessings. Spiritual blessings are often blessings that the human eyes cannot see.

In verse 4, believers are chosen by God before humanity was introduced to the earth and before they could have done anything to warrant God's choice. God's selection should give assurance to the stability of God's plan and love. God did not randomly choose believers by some capricious method. God chose believers because they are His children according to His will. God's choice is not just for blessings or salvation but comes with the responsibility for personal holiness and blamelessness in love.

Verse 5 discusses how the Lord predestined believers to be adopted as children through the redemptive power of Christ's death and resurrection. How remarkable, the author does not say that God looked ahead to figure out who would later become His children or suddenly realized who His children were. The writer says that God chose His children and predestined them for adoption because of divine love and inspiration. In ancient Roman adoption, when the adoption was complete, the adopted would have all the rights of a biological child of their new family and while losing their rights, debts, and obligations to their old family as if they had never existed. The adopted would become a new person. The letter's audience would be familiar with this concept of adoption and appreciate the illustration. The idea of adoption is also similar to 2 Corinthians 5:17, in which Paul declares that anyone in Christ is a new creation. But wait, there is more; not only did the adopted become a part of a new family but they are freed and often elevated by the status of that new family. The father's inheritance would now go to the adopted child. The imagery is that believers are not only adopted by God through Christ, those who can inherit all that has to give. Adoption in its Roman practice was ultimately about inheritance as only men could adopt another man, if he had no legitimate heir. This is why the adopted received the inheritance, it was the intention of this transactional relationship. Verse 6 emphasizes a relational element again by using the descriptive word "accepted." Here accepted means to be highly favored or full of grace as in Luke 1:28. The letter states that every believer is now accepted because of God's grace. God entirely accepts believers.

III. JESUS' WORK (EPHESIANS 1:7–10)

Earlier in the text, "every spiritual blessing" was mentioned (v. 3); now, the writer explains through Christ believers are able to receive these blessings. Because of Jesus' sacrifice of shedding His blood on the cross believers have been forgiven, freed, and redeemed. Forgiveness of sins and the debt of sin have now been paid.

Redemption is typically a price or action being paid to regain possession or cancel a debt. Jesus redeemed believers through love by shedding His blood on Calvary's cross. Christ paid for liberty. Believers are abundantly free, no longer chained and shackled by the shame of misdeeds. Verse 7 refers to the Old Testament imagery of the sacrificial system, drawing the church into the story of God's interactions with His people by placing them into the Passover story (Exodus 12), not as encroachers but as legitimate children of God through grace.

Redemption and forgiveness of sins are just a portion of the work of Christ. In addition, believers are given the knowledge of the mystery of His will (v. 9). The mystery of His will is God's great plan and purpose, which was hidden but revealed through Jesus Christ. It infers that God's great plan is hidden to non-believers but clear to believers. Believers are assured that while they may not know the specifics of God's plan, they find resolve in the knowledge that God is in control and will reveal this plan in the fullness of time. Purpose in Christ is an open secret only hidden so no one can claim superiority or exclusivity. God did not let us know His plan out of His own good will because humanity could not handle the weight of God's plan. It is in the goodness of God that God withholds some mystery and revelation. God hides what humans could not handle so that humanity can come to know the fullness of God through Christ. If God's revelation were divorced from goodwill, society would not be able to handle it. The letter then goes on to sum up, those mysteries in verse ten. The universe will find its meaning through its source, sustainer, and establisher, Christ. God will reconcile heaven and earth together in unity.

IV. THE POWER OF GOD IN HUMAN LIVES (EPHESIANS 1:11–14)

The writer now turns his attention to the process in which God's saving power impacts the human experience. The text now shifts to practical explanations and approaches for his current context. Jesus makes an inheritance possible for believers (v. 11). It is only through Christ that believers are able to find out who they are. Believers are predestined by God, meaning long before believers even knew or thought about Him. There was an eternal purpose, a deliberate plan that was in the works as part of the overall purpose that He is working out in everything and everyone. God crafted this plan carefully before the earth had formed and according to an eternal purpose. God not only planned it but works to fulfill it. Counsel stands for deliberate arranging so that every detail, way, and means are considered, carried out, and provided.

Verse 13, "you also," is inclusive of Gentile believers and readers. The writer is reminding the church that God has a place for both Jew and Gentile; both are now members of the universal Church through the work of Jesus Christ. This addresses what was widely believed and accepted that Jewish people were God's chosen people given an inheritance and having all rights and privileges while the Gentiles had no privileges. The writer states that in Christ, both Jew and Gentile have a place and will be recipients of God's inheritance because Christ has made this possible.

Jewish people no longer own exclusive rights to the inheritance, but it is now available to all believers.

Verse 13 also states that in Jesus when you heard and believed. Even though the Godhead did the work of predestination, one must listen to and believe, and upon that would be sealed with the Holy Spirit. Believers receive the blessings of God, are predestined by God, and secured by Christ, and sealed by the Holy Spirit. Not only did God make a promise, but God sealed the promise by the Holy Spirit. What an amazing reality that those in Christ have a changed life and an eternal future that is sealed, and nothing or no one can break this seal. Believers can be hopeful and confident in the outlook about the future because God is sure to bring completion to the work that Christ started on the cross. The pericope alludes that what believers are experiencing now is a down payment of what will come to a complete redemption through God's plan, Christ's sacrifice, and the Holy Spirit's power working. This is the miracle of God. Believers should grow more profound in the hope that comes from the Holy Spirit, being assured that God has already chosen and gifted them to be holy, blameless, and forgiven through the work of Jesus Christ.

THE LESSON APPLIED

Remember that God chose you! That by itself is a revolutionary revelation if you fall amongst those who are downtrodden, lost, or locked out. Jesus chose you before the foundation of the world to be a part of God's plan. This translates that there is none among us who are mistakes, oops babies, or unplanned pregnancies. As believers we do not think that God leaves anything up to chance and that includes us as well. There is purpose to your life and God has called you to something. It is now your job to figure out the specifics to God's calling on your life. Remember that God chose you!

LET'S TALK ABOUT IT

1. **What does it mean for you to be chosen by God?**
2. **As one who has been adopted into God's family, how is that personally revolutionary for you and contributes to your sense of identity in a world that often attempts to define us differently than the way God does?**

Being chosen for anything is a big deal for many people who feel rejected by the systems of power and favor. Being chosen by God has the ability to bolster one's sense of somebodiness, self-assurance, and confidence. How might you use this information to correct any dim spots in your assessment of self-worth.

HOME DAILY DEVOTIONAL READINGS
NOVEMBER 7–13, 2022

MONDAY	TUESDAY	WEDNESDAY	THURSDAY	FRIDAY	SATURDAY	SUNDAY
The Gospel Threatens Vested Interests	Encouraging Disciples and Saying Farewell	The Gospel Bestows an Inheritance	The Lord Is My Chosen Portion	Be Strong and Courageous	Rejoice in God's Salvation	A Glorious Inheritance
Acts 19:21–31	Acts 19:32–20:1	Acts 20:17–21, 26–35	Psalm 16	Joshua 1:1–9	Isaiah 25	Ephesians 1:15–23

CHRIST IS WISDOM

EPHESIANS 1:15–23

King James Version	New Revised Standard Version
WHEREFORE I also, after I heard of your faith in the Lord Jesus, and love unto all the saints,	I HAVE heard of your faith in the Lord Jesus and your love toward all the saints, and for this reason
16 Cease not to give thanks for you, making mention of you in my prayers;	16 I do not cease to give thanks for you as I remember you in my prayers.
17 That the God of our Lord Jesus Christ, the Father of glory, may give unto you the spirit of wisdom and revelation in the knowledge of him:	17 I pray that the God of our Lord Jesus Christ, the Father of glory, may give you a spirit of wisdom and revelation as you come to know him,
18 The eyes of your understanding being enlightened; that ye may know what is the hope of his calling, and what the riches of the glory of his inheritance in the saints,	18 so that, with the eyes of your heart enlightened, you may know what is the hope to which he has called you, what are the riches of his glorious inheritance among the saints,
19 And what is the exceeding greatness of his power to us-ward who believe, according to the working of his mighty power,	19 and what is the immeasurable greatness of his power for us who believe, according to the working of his great power.
20 Which he wrought in Christ, when he raised him from the dead, and set him at his own right hand in the heavenly places,	20 God put this power to work in Christ when he raised him from the dead and seated him at his right hand in the heavenly places,
21 Far above all principality, and power, and might, and dominion, and every name that is named, not only in this world, but also in that which is to come:	21 far above all rule and authority and power and dominion, and above every name that is named, not only in this age but also in the age to come.
22 And hath put all things under his feet, and gave him to be the head over all things to the church,	22 And he has put all things under his feet and has made him the head over all things for the church,
23 Which is his body, the fulness of him that filleth all in all.	23 which is his body, the fullness of him who fills all in all.

MAIN THOUGHT: The eyes of your understanding being enlightened; that ye may know what is the hope of his calling, and what the riches of the glory of his inheritance in the saints. (Ephesians 1:18, KJV)

LESSON SETTING
Time: AD 60
Place: Ephesus

LESSON OUTLINE
I. Praise
   (Ephesians 1:15–16)
II. The Prayer
   (Ephesians 1:17–19)
III. Power
   (Ephesians 1:20–23)

UNIFYING PRINCIPLE

In our media age, we have access to multiple sources of information. Who or what can we trust as our source for wisdom? The opening prayer of Ephesians proclaims Christ as the ultimate source of hope and wisdom.

INTRODUCTION

Everyone has had to ask someone else for advice at one point or another. Hopefully, we have a proper perspective from which to receive guidance. Most people do not ask their two-year-old family member for career advice because they could not offer wisdom. When seeking counsel, it is essential to give ear to those who have wisdom. There are a multitude of voices attempting to inform, persuade, and compete for our attention. Television shows, social media, friends, family, music, movies, books, Internet websites and etc., all wrestle for our eyes, ears, and minds. Believers have to learn to which voices can provide hope and wisdom. God is the ultimate source of knowledge. God graciously places wise individuals in our lives to help guide us in the decision-making process.

The previous verses in chapter one list the spiritual blessings (Ephesians 1:3–14). Those verses reassured believers about God's commitment to humanity by remembering the cross and that God lavished us with love, forgiveness, and mercy. God has blessed His followers with an eternal inheritance and sealed it with Jesus Christ and the promise of the Holy Spirit.

In the lesson's passage, the author gives his response: God's spiritual blessing is to worship God. He thanks God for the faith and love of the believers, prays their knowledge of God will increase as their understanding of their hope, inheritance, and God's power grows. The prayer concludes with praise to Christ for His authority both now and forever.

EXPOSITION

I. PRAISE
(EPHESIANS 1:15–16)

The text began with the author praising the works, faith, and love that he heard about the Ephesian church (v. 15). The writers thanking of God is reflective of the faith and love of the recipients are part of God's vast blessings toward them. The statement that he "heard" furthers the speculation that the writer was very familiar with the community. By hearing it indicates that the author most likely had a relationship with the church as a whole, but more likely special relationship(s) with members of that community. It helps to demonstrate that the author, presumably Paul, kept tabs on a community of faith that he helped found. Their acts of faith lived out through love were the topic of discussion not as a mere profession of faith but as a reflection of active trust in what God has done and will do. Believers should live out their faith so that people hear of their faith and begin to spread the good news of their works. The news of their faith and its expression of love to others had reached the author. Faith translates to *pistis* and love *agape*. The faith mentioned is not faith directed toward Christ but toward fellow believers. The Church is commended, not because of their love for God, but for their love for all the saints. The evidence of God's work or changed lives is not one's allegiance to God but how we love His people. Can the same be said about the current Church of the living and true God? Has the universal Church's work caused believers and unbelievers to speak highly about it and share about the faith and love it possesses? Now more than ever, the Church has tools at its disposal to share its faith in love far and wide. Instead the news that is heard is divisive or about a particular personality instead of the unifying power of Christ. The Christian community should always have great works of faith and love in action to share with the world. The faith and love mentioned will be elaborated upon later in the letter. The faith and love mentioned is an act towards unity, reconciliation between Jewish believers and Gentile believers to create a universal Church or body of Christ (v. 23). The Ephesians are praised for having an active love not simply in word or attitude; Paul's concept of love frequently carries themes of social justice, compassion and life shared together (see 1 Corinthians 13; 1 Timothy 1:5; compare 2 Thessalonians 1:3 and Acts 2:42).

It is important to note that love must carry along with it justice. Love without justice is simply sentimentality. In others words, it is a bunch of ineffective mushy feelings. Coupled with justice, love enables those who embrace it both to live and move in compassion for others. On the other hand, justice without love typically becomes brutality and cruelty. Truthfully, love and justice need each other for balance.

Thanking God for the readers' faithfulness and love is an affirmation for the believers. The prayer of thanksgiving transforms into intercession on their behalf. The writer specifies that he continually remembers and intercedes for them in prayer based on hearing of their good works and faith (v. 16). The author not only gave thanks for God's work among the Ephesians but also prayed that it would continually grow more robust. Pastors and other Christian leaders should look to the text as an example to not only evangelize the lost but to pray and cover their church and community. This is the duty of pastors and church leaders. It is through prayer that those who are under their charge are most effectively cared for. In all honesty, there are times in which we are able to help those we care for but in most instances they are made the better through prayer, and prayer alone. Intercessory prayer is one of the best things that a church leader can have in his or her back pocket. This is what enables us to not become angry, disillusioned, anxious, or faithless, but it is through prayer that God steps in to fix that which is not in our power to do.

II. THE PRAYER (EPHESIANS 1:17–19)

The writer details what he petitions God on their behalf for. He prays that God would grant them spiritual wisdom and revelation in the knowledge of God so that they may be enlightened and know God better. These prayer requests are not so that the Ephesians can see into the future and predict events or that they would be able to investigate others' lives as judges. The author wanted them to have a growing knowledge of God so that they would know God's will and purpose. The emphasis lies on the hope that God will make known to the community God's wisdom, riches, hope, and power. The knowledge is for the benefit of living in community and relationship with one another through love and purpose. The Christian life should be centered around God's purpose. The author also wanted the Ephesians to have accurate knowledge of God. This was important because they would encounter false prophets who would attempt to sway them with incorrect teachings and false prophecies. The Ephesians would need wisdom and revelation to understand the difference between the false teachings and the actual teachings of God. They would only know the truth. By using wisdom, they would be able to use the spiritual gift of discernment (1 Corinthians 12:10).

False prophets were not just a problem in the ancient world, but even in contemporary times we must tarry in the Spirit for the gift of discernment. False prophets come in many different shapes and sizes and it is up to the believer to determine what she or he is encountering in the moment. This points to the need of each and every believer to study for him or herself. If we are to discern, then we must know sound teaching for ourselves. It is hard to pull the proverbial wool over one's eyes when he or she knows the Word for himself or herself.

He then prays that they would understand everything that God afforded them in Christ (v. 18–19). If the Ephesians knew all that God has given them through Jesus Christ, it would require a supernatural work. It will require that the eyes of their understanding be illuminated. The author uses the expression "eyes of your heart" (v. 18); the heart is synonymous with understanding. God honors heart oversight. Sight is factual, sight does not require faith or courageousness, but heart involves trust and faith.

The author wanted the readers to know the hope of His calling (v. 18). This is the first object of knowledge, the hope of God's calling. The writer suggests that believers should find security and enduring hope in knowing that God called them for His purpose and His service. God's calling should give every believer confidence knowing that believers have a glorious future of eternal life free from sin and the troubles of the world. Verse 18 ends by mentioning knowledge of inheritance. Inheritance is a recurring theme and emphasis in chapter 1. Inheritance refers to what children of God have coming to them. While the text does not explicitly state much about the inheritance, it does reflect amazement believers are to meditate on what God has in store for His children. The requirement for the believer equipped with this knowledge is to live now in light of that future. This inheritance is sure and secured by Christ. This prayer of intercession is essential and needs to be continuous because this kind of knowledge gives confidence for living in the present. Confidence in the future frees believers to live wholly in the present.

Lastly, the writer prays that believers come to understand the immeasurable greatness of His power (v. 19). Immeasurable translates to *huperballon*, which means to throw over or beyond, which means that God's power defies human description and measurement. The author wants the reader to know that God's power for us is excellent and beyond comprehension for those who believe and put their trust in God. Not only is God's power great for the believer, but it is also great in the believer. Not only is the believer a recipient of God's great power but also a trustee and representative of His power. This realization should bring great joy and excitement to the believer to have the power of the Almighty working within. But as the famous quote states, "with great power comes great responsibility." The believer is also responsible for using their power to partner with God on God's mission for the world. The power at work for believers is the same power that has created, sustained, and resurrected Jesus Christ from the dead. How powerful could the Church be if it realized the power that believers possess and then operated accordingly? Believers have the power of creativity like God. This means believers should be innovative in worship experiences, evangelism, and stewardship. Believers have the power to resurrect dead situations, relationships, and churches. Believers need to tap into the unlimited power that is available to them.

III. POWER
(EPHESIANS 1:20–23)

The author begins verse 20, describing what God has done for Jesus; God raised Him from the dead, gave Christ a heavenly throne, and elevated Him above every power and place. The writer is clear Christ is also a recipient of God's power. Doing so indicates the lengths God's power has been extended toward humanity. The author wants the reader to know the journey of Christ. The power of God restored Christ to preeminence. Humanity is also fixed and reconciled through the power of God to its rightful purpose and position. Not only is Christ above all past and current powers, leaders, governments, and names but forever (v. 21). Christ is in charge of it all and has an ultimate say forever. Both political leaders and monarchies have limited reigns; either their time or another power catches up to them but not Christ. There is no limit to Christ's power. He will reign forever and ever, and no one will overthrow him.

Lastly, verse 22 states that through divine power, Christ has been made the head over all things through the Church. This is the first mention of the Church in the letter to the Ephesians. Here the Church is translated to *ekklesia*, which means the called out. The letter is not pointing to the local church in Ephesus but to the universal Church. The universal Church is the beneficiary of God giving Christ as the head of all things. The Church is the body of Christ, benefiting from the power of Christ.

The imagery of the body would have been familiar to the readers, and it refers to the broad scope of believers. Unlike in Corinthians, where the body is used as an image to refer to the relationships between believers. The purpose of the metaphor or reference of the Church to the body is not about hierarchy but reminds believers how interwoven the Church is with Christ. The Church is to be involved and partner with

Christ in His mission and power. Christ has been given power over all things. There is nothing that is capable of stopping Christ and His Church. The power Christians have is not intrinsic power but a power that comes from God. Because there is no rival to God, believers do not have to look anywhere else to find the power they need for life. What they need is in Christ.

The latter section of verse 23 introduces the idea of the fullness of Him. Scholars debate the writer's meaning. This verse raises several questions. Is it Christ who fills the Church? Or is Christ being fulfilled by the Father? Clearly, the Church is the recipient of God, and Christ fills the Church with His blessings and presence. The implication is Christ's body is involved in the filling of all things. The Church is the fullness God is using to reconcile humanity.

THE LESSON APPLIED

In this passage, the author thanks God for the faith and love of the believers in Ephesus and prays that their knowledge and relationship with God will grow. Often believers' knowledge of God is neither deep nor intimate. If Christians are unaware of His eternal purposes, His great love for us, and His incomparable power, we don't know God. Intimacy with God should be every believer's goal. Pray this prayer and think about the steps that can be taken to know God better. How can you grasp the hope that can be found in Christ better and His great power for those who believe?

LET'S TALK ABOUT IT

In this passage the author moves from simple praise for the believers at Ephesus into intercessory. Why is intercessory prayer such an important type of prayer?

Intercessory prayer essentially means to stand in the gap for another. When we practice intercessory prayer we are learning selflessness, humility, and love as we seek answers on behalf of another. In terms of building a congregation, there is no better tool to help create a collective bond between the saints. As we pray for others the lessons that the Gospel teaches that we ought to think more of others than ourselves is reinforced and we get the opportunity to watch God at work, as we look for His solution to the issue at hand. It is in intercession that we learn most how to be like Jesus. It is where we learn to set our needs, wants, desires, problems, and issues to the side and focus on someone else. Indeed, this is what Jesus did by coming to earth and then give His life.

HOME DAILY DEVOTIONAL READINGS
NOVEMBER 14–20, 2022

MONDAY	TUESDAY	WEDNESDAY	THURSDAY	FRIDAY	SATURDAY	SUNDAY
Grace Overflowed for Service	Live in Peace, Godliness, and Dignity	Qualifications for Church Servant Leaders	Do Justice, Love Kindness, Walk Humbly	Trust in God and Do Good	Speak for Your Servant Is Listening	Created for Good Works
1 Timothy 1:1–4, 12–17	1 Timothy 2:1–8	1 Timothy 3:1–13	Micah 6:1–8	Psalm 37:1–9, 37–40	1 Samuel 3:1–10	Ephesians 2:1–10

WE ARE GOD'S HANDIWORK

ADULT TOPIC: GOD MADE US FOR A PURPOSE	BACKGROUND SCRIPTURE: REVELATION 2:1–7; ACTS 19; EPHESIANS 2

EPHESIANS 2:1–10

King James Version	New Revised Standard Version
AND you hath he quickened, who were dead in trespasses and sins;	YOU were dead through the trespasses and sins
2 Wherein in time past ye walked according to the course of this world, according to the prince of the power of the air, the spirit that now worketh in the children of disobedience:	2 in which you once lived, following the course of this world, following the ruler of the power of the air, the spirit that is now at work among those who are disobedient.
3 Among whom also we all had our conversation in times past in the lusts of our flesh, fulfilling the desires of the flesh and of the mind; and were by nature the children of wrath, even as others.	3 All of us once lived among them in the passions of our flesh, following the desires of flesh and senses, and we were by nature children of wrath, like everyone else.
4 But God, who is rich in mercy, for his great love wherewith he loved us,	4 But God, who is rich in mercy, out of the great love with which he loved us
5 Even when we were dead in sins, hath quickened us together with Christ, (by grace ye are saved;)	5 even when we were dead through our trespasses, made us alive together with Christ—by grace you have been saved—
6 And hath raised us up together, and made us sit together in heavenly places in Christ Jesus:	6 and raised us up with him and seated us with him in the heavenly places in Christ Jesus,
7 That in the ages to come he might shew the exceeding riches of his grace in his kindness toward us through Christ Jesus.	7 so that in the ages to come he might show the immeasurable riches of his grace in kindness toward us in Christ Jesus.
8 For by grace are ye saved through faith; and that not of yourselves: it is the gift of God:	8 For by grace you have been saved through faith, and this is not your own doing; it is the gift of God—
9 Not of works, lest any man should boast.	9 not the result of works, so that no one may boast.
10 For we are his workmanship, created in Christ Jesus unto good works, which God hath before ordained that we should walk in them.	10 For we are what he has made us, created in Christ Jesus for good works, which God prepared beforehand to be our way of life.

MAIN THOUGHT: For we are his workmanship, created in Christ Jesus unto good works, which God hath before ordained that we should walk in them. (Ephesians 2:10, KJV)

LESSON OUTLINE

I. **The Walking Dead
   (Ephesians 2:1–3)**

II. **But God
   (Ephesians 2:4–7)**

III. **Saved By God for a Good
   Work (Ephesians 2:8–10)**

UNIFYING PRINCIPLE

People often look for a purpose in life. How do people find meaning and direction for their lives? Ephesians reminds us that God's creative design is embedded in each of us and through Christ we join in the good work God prepares us to do.

INTRODUCTION

Regardless of the discipline, genre, or medium artists possess extraordinary talents and abilities. One of the fantastic abilities artists have is the ability to take blank canvases or something of little to no value and transform it into a masterpiece. Artists can take a surface that is worthless and turn it into something valuable. Similarly, God takes the blank canvases of believers' lives and transforms them into a masterpiece. The text is a celebration of how God graciously transforms and liberates believers who were once the walking dead into new people with a new focus and direction. God does not just transform us, but God gives a new purpose and new work objectives to complete. The writer illustrates for the readers a before and after picture of Christians' lives and the impact God has made. The writer wants the believers in Ephesus to understand God's redemptive and transformative work in their lives and the nature of their salvation.

EXPOSITION

I. THE WALKING DEAD (EPHESIANS 2:1–3)

The second chapter of Ephesians is a continuation of chapter 1. The writer begins by saying you were once dead in sin. Before God, those who would become believers are lifeless and incapacitated. Romans 3:10–18 describes what it means to be dead. The writer takes the time to remind the believers where they started and from where they have come. Life without God is a living death. The imagery used is remarkable. The writer uses death because he is pointing to the hopelessness and finality of the situation. Believers were dead because of disobedience and sin. Before they were believers, they were controlled by sin. Sin means to miss the mark and the writer reminds the readers that no matter where or how they are currently situated in life, they were once guilty of missing the mark.

The author says that believers were dead because they were under the evil influence of the forces at work in their lives. To be dead is to be unconscious, ignorant, or unaware. Death is the natural consequence of the three effects of evil influence. The first of the named forces is the world or cosmos. The world presents a constant pressure to make you assimilate, conform, and be controlled. There was a time when believers were addicted to the world and its ways. The world's ways are the opposite of God's ways. The world tells believers to look out solely for themselves and to trust no one, which is the antithesis of God's way. The writer points to the culturally pervasive attitudes and values that tempt and entice humanity to rebel and reject God. There was a time when believers chase after the values of the world like greed, selfishness, deception, and idolatry.

The second influence was the devil (v. 2), the ruler of the air who once had control of believers (v. 2). The Ephesians were once under the control of Satan, the accuser of the brethren (Revelation 12:10), the father of all lies and deceit. The devil once swayed and influenced their behavior. The writer reminds the Ephesian believers that Satan once ordered their thoughts, actions, and lives.

The last characterization of evil, he said there was an internal enemy, the cravings of the flesh led us astray into behaviors that did not honor God (v. 30). Things like deceitfulness, evil desires, loss of temper, anger, jealousy, pride, lying, and arrogance once had control of the believers. He wanted to remind them of this so that they would remain humble and with the zeal to reach others who were dead just like they were. Indeed, this is still true in a modern context. In every city in the world, there are some dead people who need to be reached with the Gospel of Jesus Christ, and believers should be on a mission to seek out the dead and introduce them to the Christ who is able to resurrect.

II. BUT GOD
(EPHESIANS 2:4–7)

The writer takes the first three verses and unpacks the tragic and pitiful condition that believers were in once. Verse four begins with the conjunction, ""But God.""
A conjunction is a word used to connect clauses. "But God" in the text means that something is about to be modified. A conjunction informs the reader that something is about to happen and change, and those two words change everything "but God" you were dead and stuck in sin, but God got involved, intervened, and did something about your sin situation. Thank God for a "but God" because it will change conditions and your circumstances. Think about how marvelous and gracious God is. Emergency personnel, doctors, and EMTs do not extend life-saving care for patients who have been declared dead. They do not use their life-saving resources on the dead. Believers were once declared dead, and the cause of death was sin. "But God," who is full of mercy and grace, resurrected them. "But God" is arguably the two most important words in the entire letter because it sets up the marvel known as grace. "But God" sums up the good news of the Gospel. The expectation in verse 3 is the consequence of God's anger and punishment because of "but God," the believer experiences God's mercy and love. The author reminds the Ephesians that they were on their way to hell, "but God" rescued them from the penalty of sin with the wealth of God's mercy and love.

Wealth describes God as rich or excessive in mercy. Mercy is forgiveness shown for someone even when you possess the power to punish. Mercy is usually given to those who are desperate. The Bible says that the wages of sin are death (Romans 6:23). The entire of humanity was desperate because there was a sin debt that needed to be paid, but that thankfully God's mercy paid the debt through Jesus Christ. Jesus paid it all. The measurement for God's mercy and love for humanity is inconceivable; it boggles human understanding. The dead toward whom God has sown mercy are drawn from precisely the ranks of the living dead detailed in Ephesians 5:5. God's mercy is rooted in God's great and radical love, a disposition that has guided God's actions since before creation (Ephesians 1:4). Love is the reason God made a covenant with Israel and the reason why God went to such extraordinary measures to fulfill the covenant. God did not wait to love humanity. God intervened in humanity's pitiful condition and intervened on humanity's behalf. God did not wait to love humanity until humanity was lovable. Christ shared in humanity's death so that believers could share in His resurrected life. The old person is crucified and resurrected as new creations in Jesus with old things passed away (2 Corinthians 5:17).

Not only did God give humanity mercy but verse 5 points to God's grace. It is only by the grace of God that one can receive grace. The work of God's grace does not involve human merit. The rescue from spiritual death is God's work done for the undeserving. By God's grace and mercy, those who were dead have been made alive (v. 5). It is because God is so gracious that followers are saved or liberated

God raised believers from the dead along with Christ (v. 6) and seated them together in heavenly places with Jesus Christ. Just as Jesus had a resurrection, so also has the believer. While Jesus's resurrection was a physical one, the believers' is a spiritual one. We are seated in heaven no matter where we find ourselves seated currently. Believers can be assured that their place has been reserved in heaven.

This gives the Ephesians security in who they are and where they stand in Christ Jesus. It is a reminder that they have already been seated in heavenly places having dual citizenship in both earth and heaven. What God did for Christ, God has also done for His followers.

In the future, God will continue to show the exceeding riches of His grace (v. 7). God will continually show grace and kindness. The letter does not have an impending end, as Paul's letters usually contain. The verse (v. 7) implies an indefinite future in which God's grace will be shown. It also highlights the author's belief or expectation that God's grace will be preached for many years to come.

III. SAVED BY GOD FOR A GOOD WORK (EPHESIANS 2:8–10)

It's only because of our connection with Christ that believers can now experience a new reality. Now the author begins a new sentence by repeating verse 5 and broadened it: "you have been saved by grace through faith." This verse points toward salvation. Salvation means that believers are no longer under the control of the devil and now are under the power of the mighty God. Those who were once dead have been saved through faith. Faith that is mentioned in this verse is translated to as trust. Believers must trust that God has secured their salvation. The work of salvation is God's gift (v. 8). Salvation is the liberation of oppressed sinners is not an act that sinners initiated or something that can be gained through human effort. Salvation is God's love in action, taking the initiative to save His children. The work of salvation is God's gift (v. 9).

Ironically grace translates to the Greek word *charis*. Charis means grace and also gift. The writer wanted to ensure that the readers were fully aware that salvation was not something that could be earned or bought, but it was a gift given to each believer. Suppose salvation was the accomplishment of humanity, then humans could brag and boast about it. Since God alone is responsible for salvation, then God alone should receive the glory for it. Believers should boast about the transformational power of God and how only a loving and powerful God is able to save.

In verse 10, the text reminds the reader that God saves believers not merely to save us from the wrath of sin, which is rightly deserved, but God saves believers to make something beautiful, a masterpiece out of their lives. Believers are God's workmanship which is translated from the Greek word *poiema*. Masterpieces are only valuable because of the work of the craftsman. Believers should find their value, not in their own deeds or works, but that they are a product of God's hand. Workmanship is a work of art. It means to be crafted by a skilled worker. Believers are God's handiwork and thus are saved to do good work. God's love is transformational. It finds humanity wherever they are located and transports it to where it should be going. God's expressions of love are capable of saving the soul and also capable of changing lives. Charles Spurgeon once said, "The spiritual life cannot come to us by development from our old nature. I have heard a great deal about evolution and development, but I am afraid that if any one of us were to be developed to our utmost, apart from the grace of God, we should come out worse than before the development began."

God creates believers for the purpose of a new manner of life. They are to walk into good works. The new way of life is reflective of God's likeness as an instigator of justice and holiness. Believers are created in Christ Jesus for good works. God activates believers in good works. These works are also a part of God's predestined plan as much as any other promise of salvation. These good works are evidence of the life of God's chosen. If someone claims to be a believer, but there is no evidence of good works, then they are not indeed God's chosen. Works cannot save the believer, but they are the proof of living a changed life. Changed people do God's work in the world. Every believer has been ordained to do good works, and these works have been prepared in advance even before the believer's birth; the work has already been set assigned to be completed by the believer. God has assigned believers the good work of fighting injustices, correcting systems that have marginalized and othered people for far too long. God has given believers the good work of taking a stand against racism, sexism, capitalism, and classism. God has created believers anew to do good works like serving and shepherd God's people; it's a good work to share the Gospel and to care for sick, lost, widowed, orphaned, and imprisoned. It is good work to correct a criminal justice system that traditionally has oppressed people of color. There should be evidence of good works like loving yourself, loving your family, and loving your neighbor as yourself. Good works are not always easy to carry out, but believers should remember God has prepared them for this. Good works are not payment for salvation, but the product of salvation and every believer should have evidence of good works.

THE LESSON APPLIED

God has prepared for every believer good works even before the foundation of the world. Effectively this means each one of us is called to do something that will be a blessing to someone else. The question in a real sense becomes, what should I do?

One of the ways to answer that question very simply is to quote, "Do to others what you would have them to do to you." Even as the verse above is often quoted, it usually misquoted or misunderstood. It literally means that those things that we want another to do for us, it is that which we should do for another. Many times people believe that they ought to do to or for another what has been done to or for them. That is not the intention of the verse. The point of the verse looks at the self more than it looks to the other. What we then do for or to others is direct reflection of what we feel about ourselves.

Each time we do to or for others as we would want another to do for us we are living out our true calling to good works. With this the "Golden Rule" in place we honestly do not need any more guidance. It is in this space that our good works come from a place of security in God and not as an opportunity to gain favor or earn salvation. It is also in this space that we can begin to think critically, not only about our personal impact on the world and people around us but understand ourselves as part of various larger systems and structures. It is in this space that we are able to see and fight various injustices. The natural concern for self preservation is taken away because the concern for self is removed, rather concern for the other is that which is first. It is in this light that we should walk, so that we understand that even in positions of comfort and relative ease, we must stand with and on behalf of those who are not in the same position as us.

LET'S TALK ABOUT IT

1. Verse 4 uses the phrase "But God". The exposition explains what that phrase means and its effect. What personal experience have you had with, "But God"?

2. Has God ever placed the conjunction in the sentence of your life and changed its trajectory?

Many people have experienced a "But God" moment in their lives. Spend some time talking about how God is able to change our circumstances with a simple phrase.

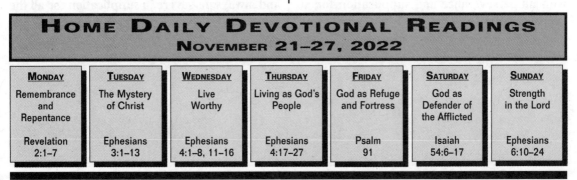

HOME DAILY DEVOTIONAL READINGS
NOVEMBER 21–27, 2022

MONDAY	TUESDAY	WEDNESDAY	THURSDAY	FRIDAY	SATURDAY	SUNDAY
Remembrance and Repentance	The Mystery of Christ	Live Worthy	Living as God's People	God as Refuge and Fortress	God as Defender of the Afflicted	Strength in the Lord
Revelation 2:1–7	Ephesians 3:1–13	Ephesians 4:1–8, 11–16	Ephesians 4:17–27	Psalm 91	Isaiah 54:6–17	Ephesians 6:10–24

GOD GIVES TOOLS FOR OUR PROTECTION

ADULT TOPIC:
TOOLS AVAILABLE TO WITHSTAND INJUSTICE AND EVIL

BACKGROUND SCRIPTURE:
REVELATION 2:1–7; ACTS 19; EPHESIANS 6:10–24

EPHESIANS 6:10—18

King James Version	New Revised Standard Version
FINALLY, my brethren, be strong in the Lord, and in the power of his might.	FINALLY, be strong in the Lord and in the strength of his power.
11 Put on the whole armour of God, that ye may be able to stand against the wiles of the devil.	11 Put on the whole armor of God, so that you may be able to stand against the wiles of the devil.
12 For we wrestle not against flesh and blood, but against principalities, against powers, against the rulers of the darkness of this world, against spiritual wickedness in high places.	12 For our struggle is not against enemies of blood and flesh, but against the rulers, against the authorities, against the cosmic powers of this present darkness, against the spiritual forces of evil in the heavenly places.
13 Wherefore take unto you the whole armour of God, that ye may be able to withstand in the evil day, and having done all, to stand.	13 Therefore take up the whole armor of God, so that you may be able to withstand on that evil day, and having done everything, to stand firm.
14 Stand therefore, having your loins girt about with truth, and having on the breastplate of righteousness;	14 Stand therefore, and fasten the belt of truth around your waist, and put on the breastplate of righteousness.
15 And your feet shod with the preparation of the gospel of peace;	15 As shoes for your feet put on whatever will make you ready to proclaim the gospel of peace.
16 Above all, taking the shield of faith, wherewith ye shall be able to quench all the fiery darts of the wicked.	16 With all of these, take the shield of faith, with which you will be able to quench all the flaming arrows of the evil one.
17 And take the helmet of salvation, and the sword of the Spirit, which is the word of God:	17 Take the helmet of salvation, and the sword of the Spirit, which is the word of God.
18 Praying always with all prayer and supplication in the Spirit, and watching thereunto with all perseverance and supplication for all saints;	18 Pray in the Spirit at all times in every prayer and supplication. To that end keep alert and always persevere in supplication for all the saints.

MAIN THOUGHT: Wherefore take unto you the whole armour of God, that ye may be able to withstand in the evil day, and having done all, to stand. (Ephesians 6:13, KJV)

LESSON SETTING
Time: AD 60
Place: Ephesus

LESSON OUTLINE
I. **Preparation for Battle**
(Ephesians 6:10–13)
II. **Uniform**
(Ephesians 6:14–17)
III. **Prayer**
(Ephesians 6:18)

UNIFYING PRINCIPLE
We live in a violent world. How do we resist the forces that undermine peace and unity? The armor of God strengthens believers to withstand the forces of evil that daily threaten peace on earth.

INTRODUCTION
As the letter to the Ephesians comes to an end, Christ's church has emerged at the center of God's saving power in action. In ancient times letters like Ephesians would have been shared by communal reading in the temple. The writer of Ephesians knew that and used the final chapter as a spiritual pep rally to rouse up believers for battle. The writer calls for believers to be empowered with God's power and prepare for battle by putting on the armor of God. The use of armor would have been an excellent illustration because first-century believers were quite familiar with seeing soldiers.

EXPOSITION

I. PREPARATION FOR BATTLE (EPHESIANS 6:10–13))
As the letter to the assemblies of believers in Ephesus and throughout the great cities of Asia Minor closes, the author offers a final extended metaphor for how a believer in Jesus Christ should be empow-

ered. The author has carefully established the believers' place in Christ, the world, and the church. This is the last section addressing the believers' witness in the earth. The author says "finally" (v. 10) in light of all that God has done for and to you, "be strong in the Lord and in the power of His might." The writer lists these words together to reference power as a way to describe God's power. Previously, the author has described God's power in Ephesians 1:19 as so excessive that it raised Jesus Christ from the dead. The author is commanding believers to strengthen themselves in the Lord. The writer says before you go into combat for the Lord, you need to get some power. It is much like an athlete preparing for athletic competition before one can earn a uniform; they must first be strengthened through conditioning, weight training, and practice. If not, when it's time to put on the team uniform and play the game, the athlete will fail, so the writer says before you grab ammunition get some strength.

It is within the Lord's might and power that believers are strengthened. God has vast inherent might and power. They are a reserve of power put into action. The author urges believers to rely on God's power and might as they enter into battle. They are not permitted to sit and allow God to do all the work. No, the writer is attempting to convey that believers must rely on God's power and might through faith and then put their faith in action by fighting the battle.

Verse 11 urges the believers to put on the complete armor of God. The armor is needed to be victorious against forces of evil. God gives believers a complete set of equipment. God provides everything believers will need to be successful in battle at their disposal. The phrase armor of God is reminiscent of Isaiah 59:17, but the predominantly Gentile readers would have interpreted it in the context of the equipment of a Roman soldier and of Roman military tactics. Roman soldiers were trained to hold their ground and not retreat. The writer is urging believers to mimic soldiers by being strong, putting on the complete armor, and standing their ground against the wiles of the devil. This call to stand is not a passive stance; standing is resistance. In Exodus 14:13, "standing" is the stance for the people who God was defending. The lesson text tells believers to become warriors or soldiers, and the power and armor of God enable them to resist and unravel the strategies of the devil. Standing is not just showing up for the battle, but it is an act of defiance and opposition. Believers express the strength and faith that they have in God by standing against the schemes of the devil. Satan's traps for the people of God cannot prevail when they stand against them in the power of God.

Verse 11 informs the reader that the enemy is the devil. Verse 12 stipulates that the struggle is not against flesh and blood. The struggle is a spiritual battle. The descriptions of supernatural powers (v.12) echo standard Jewish terms for pagan deities or evil spirits, which the Christians in Ephesus would be familiar. The author wants the believers to know who their real enemy was and against whom they are struggling. Sometimes believers confuse who they are struggling against and misdirect their stand.

Believers do not struggle against members of different denominations, religious organizations, or even hateful people. The author says Christians must resist the evil spirits at work. Christians must resist the temptation to see hostile or disagreeable people as the actual enemy. God has not called believers to physically battle others in God's name. In actuality, God has called believers to struggle against the enemy, not against the victims of that enemy. The text uses a variety of terms to refer to spiritual enemies. Regardless of the term, these spiritual enemies are all a part of an army under the leadership of the devil with the mission of knocking Christians off their standing and discrediting the witness of the believers.

The proper response is given in verse 13. When believers find themselves in spiritual warfare, the author reiterates the call to put on the whole armor of God. This time the author details why believers need the armor of God. He states the purpose of the armor is so that believers may be able to "withstand in the evil day, and having done all, to stand (v. 13)." The author alludes that without the whole armor and strength of God, it is impossible to be protected, resist, and withstand the attacks from spiritual enemies. Satan will attempt to stop Christians from fulfilling the mission and purpose God has given. The writer says that when Satan tries to intimidate and prevent believers from doing the Lord's work, believers should stand. In ancient warfare, soldiers standing at the end of a battle was a sign of victory. Standing is a sign of strength in battle. Believers should stand in grace, courage, strength, faith, liberty, and unity.

The verse indicates that there will be a day when all believers will have to face an attack from the enemy, but when that day comes, believers should put on their spiritual armor and stand because they will be victorious.

II. Uniform
(Ephesians 6:14–17)

Christians can only stand victoriously when equipped with the correct armor. The text now elaborates on the armor in which believers should wear. The armor is the virtues and actions associated with the various pieces of armor. These are the only useful tools needed to battle evil powers. Those who wear the armor are doing God's work. The armor of God in the following verses is used to help the believers do as God has commissioned them to do, stand.

The first piece of armor listed is the belt of truth (v. 14). Truth is symbolically represented as a belt that protects and keeps the other garments and armor in place so that the soldier can stand within the struggle. Truth acts in the same manner. It is honesty, integrity and that which is worthy of trust. A believer cannot stand effectively, if they do not exercise truth. Truth is what separates God's people from the world because the world and the evil powers operate under the cloak of lies and dishonesty. Satan is the father of lies (John 8:44), and every lie finds its origin in him. When operating in anything other than the truth, believers are no longer under the guidance of God. Truth means speaking the truth to the powers that be. Truth is having the courage and integrity to speak up when something is wrong. Truth is a liberation tool too. Jesus said in John 8:31–32, "If you hold my teaching, you are really my disciples. Then you will know the truth, and the truth will set you free." Truth is also the only defense against lies and deceit.

The next piece of armor is the breastplate of righteousness. Righteousness is represented by a breastplate that provides protection for essential organs like the lungs and heart. Most people are familiar with the definition of righteousness that means being made right or using appropriate Christian actions. An often-overlooked meaning can be found in the Greek translation of righteousness, *dikaiosunē,* which is the same word for justice. It is this version that the text uses. Righteousness is justice in action. Just as a soldier could not effectively go into a battle without a breastplate so also can not a Christian battle evil without righteousness and justice.

The preparation of the Gospel is represented as shoes. Preparation is readiness. Christians should live in a constant state of readiness and mobility to bring the Gospel of peace. Verse 15 brings to light an unusual component for battle, peace. Peace according to the text makes a Christian soldier ready for battle. The text says that believers should have their feet ready to bring the good news of peace. The gospel of peace provides the footing for everything believers do. Having the right footwear enables a soldier to withstand certain attack.

In addition, the writer urges the Ephesians to take the shield of faith to protect and fend off fiery darts (v. 16). The shield described in the verse is large and oblong that would cover and protect the entire body. In ancient warfare, attacks were launched at all sides of the soldier in large quantities in an attempt to catch the soldier unprotected and cause panic. The evil forces attempt the same strategy. Faith or confidence in God like the shield helps to block the attacks. Satan attacks Christians with doubts, fear, lies, and confusion, but faith shields the believer, not allowing those attacks to overtake or make the believer quit the battle. The shield was an integral part of the soldier's equipment because they were needed it specifically to thwart the launch of arrows. Arrows used in ancient warfare were often dipped in flammable substances and set afire before being launched into the air. In this way, a massive archery attack was terrifying. Fire literally flying through the air. It was the large shield that could protect the soldiers. Further, the large Roman shield would often be covered in leather and then dipped in water. The wet leather retard the flames of the arrows. Our shield of faith does the same thing for us. As we are wet with faith, the evil one's darts that cause doubt, faithlessness, shame and so much else are stopped and cannot set us on fire.

Ephesians now turns to a specific element of God's armor, the helmet of salvation. The helmet is symbolic for salvation. The writer commands the Ephesians to "take up the helmet of salvation (v. 17), which makes it doubtful that the text was intended to be an assurance of salvation. After all, believers' salvation has already been assured since the moment of belief, which was proven in Ephesians 2. I believe the author was urging the Ephesians to take the Good News of salvation with them and offer it and liberation to those who were still in the bondage of sin.

This piece of equipment was massively important for the soldier because it protected the head. It is good to have the other protective equipment, but the head is to be protected at all cost. However, when we consider that Satan attacks through wiles, deceitfulness, and schemes it is easy to understand that Christians must protect their minds. The helmet of salvation does just that. The helmet of salvation is in some ways analogous to the lyrics of an old song, "I woke up this morning with my mind stayed on Jesus." This aligns with Isaiah 26:3, "Thou wilt keep him in perfect peace, whose mind is stayed on thee: because he trusteth in thee." With one's mind focused on God, it is impossible for Satan to gain a foothold. Thus the helmet must be taken up and used.

The last piece of equipment is the sword of the Spirit, the Word of God. The Word of God is not to be used as a book full of quotes to be memorized and recited. There are other instances where Scripture refers to the Word as a sword. In Hebrews 4:12, "For the word of God is alive and active. Sharper than any double-edged sword." To effectively use the sword, believers must practice and train as a soldier would. Soldiers would have practiced before battle to develop instinct and skill to position themselves to be a superior fighter. Therefore, effectively using the sword takes practice. It is important to note that the sword was the only weapon that could be used for close quarter combat, it is that which is used to defend and advance. All other pieces of equipment listed are defensive but the sword can be used offensively and so in this way it is that which is to be used to advance the cause of Christ. It is important to note that we fight Satan with the Word of God. Pay attention to Jesus as He only spoke words of Scripture to the evil one (Matt. 4:1–11). Even for the Son of God, the only way to defeat the devil was to use the Word of God.

III. PRAYER
(EPHESIANS 6:18)

Verse 18 highlights the importance of continual prayer. Continuous prayer means to use every opportunity and moment for prayer, which is why the text says that believers need to be alert. It is only through prayer that the armor of God and strength can work. Prayer is also a sign of unity with other soldiers. Praying for other believers is a way to assist in meeting others' needs. Soldiers are not only intended to be warriors fighting against the oppressive powers of evil but also intercessors for fellow believers who are also fighting the same battle. The armor should not make believers blind to the struggles and cries of others.

The recognition of prayer in this way reemphasizes that the battle is not against flesh and blood. It is important to remember that our fight is not against those whose earthly reality is no different than our own, but belongs to the higher realms where God is.

THE LESSON APPLIED

The armor of God is a metaphor that suggests to Christians that there is a spiritual battle in which each believer must take part. Thankfully, believers are not left without protection from the dangers of evil, and there is protection available to believers. God is always watching and protects His children with ferocity. The full armor of God gives us built in protection. Christians should reflect upon the ways in which they wear God's armor. In what ways has the armor protected you as you go about your daily life? Is there any piece of armor that is worn incorrectly or missing? Are there any actions that need to be taken to ensure full protection?

LET'S TALK ABOUT IT
What is the armor of God?

The armor of God has been given to each child of God as a tool of protection and defense. The armor of God is symbolic of what Christians should be doing daily to fight against evil powers. God is enlisting good soldiers to fight the good fight. Have Christians successfully been defending the faith? What do you think it entails to defend the faith? Do you even believe at this juncture in time with a type of pervasive cultural Christianity present, is a defense of Christianity even necessary?

HOME DAILY DEVOTIONAL READINGS
NOVEMBER 28–DECEMBER 4, 2022

MONDAY	TUESDAY	WEDNESDAY	THURSDAY	FRIDAY	SATURDAY	SUNDAY
My Sheep Hear My Voice	Guided by the Spirit	God Will Rise Up with Mercy	Recounting God's Goodness	God's Everlasting Love	Zechariah's Prayer Is Answered	Hear and Believe
John 10:22–30	John 16:1–15	Isaiah 30:18–26	Psalm 103:1–12	Psalm 103:13–22	Luke 1:5–17	Luke 1:18–25

SECOND QUARTER

December

January

February

ZECHARIAH HEARS FROM GOD

ADULT TOPIC:	BACKGROUND SCRIPTURE:
GOD'S PROMISE	LUKE 1:5–23

LUKE 1:8–20

King James Version

AND it came to pass, that while he executed the priest's office before God in the order of his course,

9 According to the custom of the priest's office, his lot was to burn incense when he went into the temple of the Lord.

10 And the whole multitude of the people were praying without at the time of incense.

11 And there appeared unto him an angel of the Lord standing on the right side of the altar of incense.

12 And when Zacharias saw him, he was troubled, and fear fell upon him.

13 But the angel said unto him, Fear not, Zacharias: for thy prayer is heard; and thy wife Elisabeth shall bear thee a son, and thou shalt call his name John.

14 And thou shalt have joy and gladness; and many shall rejoice at his birth.

15 For he shall be great in the sight of the Lord, and shall drink neither wine nor strong drink; and he shall be filled with the Holy Ghost, even from his mother's womb.

16 And many of the children of Israel shall he turn to the Lord their God.

17 And he shall go before him in the spirit and power of Elias, to turn the hearts of the fathers to the children, and the disobedient to the wisdom of the just; to make ready a people prepared for the Lord.

18 And Zacharias said unto the angel, Whereby shall I know this? for I am an old man, and my wife well stricken in years.

New Revised Standard Version

ONCE when he was serving as priest before God and his section was on duty,

9 he was chosen by lot, according to the custom of the priesthood, to enter the sanctuary of the Lord and offer incense.

10 Now at the time of the incense offering, the whole assembly of the people was praying outside.

11 Then there appeared to him an angel of the Lord, standing at the right side of the altar of incense.

12 When Zechariah saw him, he was terrified; and fear overwhelmed him.

13 But the angel said to him, "Do not be afraid, Zechariah, for your prayer has been heard. Your wife Elizabeth will bear you a son, and you will name him John.

14 You will have joy and gladness, and many will rejoice at his birth,

15 for he will be great in the sight of the Lord. He must never drink wine or strong drink; even before his birth he will be filled with the Holy Spirit.

16 He will turn many of the people of Israel to the Lord their God.

17 With the spirit and power of Elijah he will go before him, to turn the hearts of parents to their children, and the disobedient to the wisdom of the righteous, to make ready a people prepared for the Lord."

18 Zechariah said to the angel, "How will I know that this is so? For I am an old man, and my wife is getting on in years."

MAIN THOUGHT: But the angel said unto him, Fear not, Zacharias: for thy prayer is heard; and thy wife Elisabeth shall bear thee a son, and thou shalt call his name John. (Luke 1:13, KJV)

LUKE 1:8–20

King James Version	*New Revised Standard Version*
19 And the angel answering said unto him, I am Gabriel, that stand in the presence of God; and am sent to speak unto thee, and to shew thee these glad tidings.	19 The angel replied, "I am Gabriel. I stand in the presence of God, and I have been sent to speak to you and to bring you this good news.
20 And, behold, thou shalt be dumb, and not able to speak, until the day that these things shall be performed, because thou believest not my words, which shall be fulfilled in their season.	20 But now, because you did not believe my words, which will be fulfilled in their time, you will become mute, unable to speak, until the day these things occur."

LESSON SETTING
Time: 5 BC
Place: The Temple in Jerusalem

LESSON OUTLINE
I. A Faithful God
(Luke 1:8–19)
II. A Faithful Promise
(Luke 1:20)

UNIFYING PRINCIPLE
People struggle with doubts and fears that limit their ability to hope. What impact do our doubts and fears have on our lives? While there is a consequence to Zechariah's doubt, it does not nullify God's hope-filled promise.

INTRODUCTION
The story of Zechariah and Elizabeth introduces us to the Advent season, the time of expectation and anticipation of what God is about to do among His people. It is worth noting that this season begins with a couple who had limited expectations because of their life situation. They are an older couple and are beyond the time of seeing some of their hopes and dreams come to pass. They live in a land under foreign occupation where being a Jew in public space could lead to harm. The head of the nation is a puppet ruler from their own ranks that carries out his own form of oppression and cruelty among his people. It is this context that the couple lives a committed life of faith to each other and to God. It is not always easy remaining loyal to one's faith and to each other when life has dealt so many disappointments. However, Zechariah and Elizabeth are blameless walking in all the commandments and ordinances of God. Yet, they have no children, no one to carry on the family name nor inherit the responsibility of being a priest as a son of Aaron or a wife for a priest. When Zechariah entered the temple to carry out his priestly duty, he did so knowing, he would be the last in his family line to fulfill this all–important role because they were without a child. There are times when we least expect it that God shows up to change our circumstance for His glory and our good.

EXPOSITION

I. A FAITHFUL GOD
(LUKE 1:8–19)
The story of Zechariah and Elizabeth is introduced in a way that emphasizes their faithfulness. Zechariah and Elizabeth are faithful to each other and faithful to God.

Although life has not worked out the way they planned and hoped, their circumstance does not alter their commitment to each other or their commitment to God. One of the hardest things in life to do is not to bend to the will of circumstances. If we are not thoughtful, determined and have a higher preceptive the things that happen to us can mold us in ways that make us bitter, pessimistic and burnout from fighting a battle we seem to always be losing. Zechariah and Elizabeth hold on to what they know to be right. They refuse to allow disappointment to determine their response to each other and their response to God. Zechariah and Elizabeth did not blame each other for what had gone wrong in their lives but supported each other.

Support is always a sign of faithfulness and what it means to be present for others in ways that affirm their value in our lives. As a faithful family, Zechariah and Elizabeth provide a model for others in the community to follow. One of the ways a family demonstrates faithfulness is in accepting responsibility. When Zechariah's turn came to serve as priest in the temple it fell his lot to burn the incense at that altar. There were multiple functions that priests served in the temple. Some roles appeared to be more important than others and Zechariah is given one of the less important roles, but he accepts his responsibility as a sign of his faithfulness. There is no reluctance on Zechariah's part to perform his assignment. He is willing to accept responsibility and do what is expected of him. Being faithful is not always about doing the larger things in life, being faithful is often about doing the small assignments well that come our way.

Zechariah and Elizabeth provide the model of a faithful family, faithful to each other and faithful to God.

Although it is not mentioned explicitly, it is reasonable to understand that one of the reasons Zechariah and Elizabeth were chosen to be John the Baptist's parents was because of their faithfulness. In this lies a principle. Often it is our faithfulness that sets us apart for service. Given their faithfulness, despite their circumstances, God recognized that they could be trusted with such a awesome task of rearing to one who would be the forerunner of Christ. It is important to note that John would be required to live as a Nazirite from birth. As his parents, this would require them to teach him what that meant and the kind of commitment that it would require. Only parents who were used to modeling faithfulness would be able to properly carry out this task.

While Zechariah is serving in the temple, an angel from the Lord comes to him with a word about how his prayers have been heard. With serendipity, the angel appears, not as Zechariah prayed, but as there was a group praying outside of the temple. Clearly, there is a lesson in the power of corporate prayer. By all means, it was God's plan to answer Zechariah's prayer to have a child, but the assembly gathered in prayer set the appropriate atmosphere for the angelic entrance. It is already noted that Zechariah was working in the temple as this theophany took place pointing to the necessity of prayer during and throughout worship. Whereas, we do not know what the group was praying for, but the fact that Luke mentions it signals that it signified that it was worth paying attention to.

The prayer that Zechariah had prayed most was a prayer for a child. Children were a sign of God's favor and blessing to a family. Children represented a visible expression of God's grace at work in the life of a family. The presence of children ensured that the family line would continue and given that Zechariah was a descendant of Aaron it meant that the child if he was a male would be a priest and if a girl would be the wife of a priest. This is a matter of legacy, bloodline, and yes, property. There was much at stake in Zechariah and Elizabeth having a child, but when the angel appears to Zechariah about God hearing his prayer, he is not prepared to have his prayers answered. Zechariah had moved to the place in life when he no longer expected anything to change. It is possible to be engaged in the work of faith and lose focus on what faith can make possible. Zechariah had no expectation for anything being different when he left the temple and being in the presence of God than when he went into the temple. In a very real sense, this points to the kind of beating the Jews had been subjected to under the Romans. It is possible to miss God's movement when our eyes are focused only on what is in front of us. Herod would still be in charge. The Romans would still occupy his homeland. Jews would still be subject to oppression. The practice of religious rituals alone cannot change us or make us ready for change. We need a divine encounter that exceeds our expectation. The good news is that God's faithfulness is not tied to human expectation. Even when our lives are filled with doubts and questions God can show up with a word of hope and promise. God's faithfulness to humanity is a function of God's love for us. God loves Zechariah and Elizabeth enough to overcome doubts and difficulties to meet them with a word of promise.

Despite Zechariah's faithfulness, he was overwhelmed by fear when meeting the angel. Not only does this signal that he had given up hope on realizing the birth of a child but it points to the reverence that he had for the things of God. On one hand, that may seem to be automatic given his status as a priest, however, there were many examples of unfaithful priests. Zechariah recognized that he was in the presence of a divine figure and as such there was a level of respect that was due the moment. In most instances in which humans come into contact with an angel in the biblical text, the person in question is gripped by fear. Whereas, believers understand that we have not been given a spirit of fear there are times in which fear is the appropriate response. We cannot be controlled by fear but it can be very helpful. Fear allows us to walk with caution when necessary and not fall victim to wanton recklessness. Zechariah was afraid because he recognized that he was in the presence of one who was more powerful than himself.

God's faithfulness is not just expression in what the child to be born will do for Zechariah and Elizabeth, the child will also do something for the nation. Zechariah's son will not follow the tradition of the priesthood, but he will be a prophet that will lead Israel toward repentance. Zechariah's son will help turn a nation back to God. In his role as prophet, John the Baptist will confront, not just individual sin, but the sins of a nation that had become institutionalized in ways that removed the witness of justice. John the Baptist will remind the nation of God's vision for people that will make justice a cornerstone to society. In hearing Zechariah and Elizabeth's prayer for a child, God was also hearing the prayers of people for relief from oppression and a return to justice. Zechariah's son is also the forerunner to the Messiah.

John has the role of preparing a people to rethink the kingdom of God, not as a distance location, but a present reality at work among us because God is working through His people the plan of redemption. God in His faithfulness, had not forgotten Zechariah and Elizabeth nor had God forgotten Israel.

II. A FAITHFUL PROMISE (LUKE 1:20)

Zechariah's response to the angel's message with doubt does not cause the angel to alter God's promise. God does not need Zechariah to believe what the angel has said in order to bring it to pass. Whereas, faith always plays a vital role in religious practice, it is not faith only that causes God to act on our behalf. Because God is sovereign, He can do whatever He chosen to do in whatever way He chooses to fulfill His purposes. God's promise is not changed because of Zechariah's lack of faith, but Zechariah is marked by his encounter with the angel in ways that leaves him speechless. Zechariah is not able to share his doubts; he must continue his service as priest unable to speak. Zechariah is forced to reflect upon what the angel said and to think about the promises of God in ways that we sometimes only do in silence. There is a power to

silence that can still us and return us to a sense of awe and the mystery about God. Zechariah seem to have lost that sense of awe and mystery about God at some point in his life. When he leaves the temple still unable to speak, he cannot tell others the good news that the angel shared with him in the Temple. Zechariah is unable to tell Elizabeth about his encounter in the temple and the promise of God. Zechariah returns home different in many ways, but the way he is most different is in his trust in God's promise. The witness of Zechariah's trust in God's promise is in how he does not let his age prevent him from being husband to his wife, and in God's own time Elizabeth conceived. Immediately Elizabeth recognized her conception is an act of God—God was honoring a promise that Zechariah had been unable to tell Elizabeth. God's promise often comes to those who seem insignificant and limited by the standards of the world. However, it is the humble, the poor and the old that God selects first in the season of Advent to change expectations and to reveal how nothing is impossible with God.

THE LESSON APPLIED

It is possible, even for the faithful, to question whether things will ever change when they continually witness oppression and abuse. Whereas Zechariah is faithful in his religious duty, his environment had dulled him to the possibility of change. Zechariah is completely unprepared to have his prayers answered and incapable of being responsive to the angel with faith to believe in a different reality. The continued tragic events of the loss of black life at the hands of law enforcement as well as that the hands of black–on–black violence makes many wonder if anything will change. Marches, prayer vigils and even a world–wide pandemic had not slowed the lost of life for any reason. The absence of the respond that we seek should not make us lose hope. Our religious expressions should mean more than ritual and we should always be open to the ways that God may respond. What we may discover is that God wants to use us in ways to bring about the change that seeks. Countless prayer had been offered seeking an end to segregation in public spaces. The Jim Crow law held firm until four students sit down at a lunch counter in Greensboro, North Carolina and struck a blow that was the beginning of the end of segregation in the south.

The students had no idea of what their sit in at a lunch counter would accomplish when they started, but God used their efforts to answer prayer. We never know how God will answer prayer or when God will answer prayer therefore, we should live with the expectation that any day is a day we may witness the answer to prayer.

LET'S TALK ABOUT IT

Why do you think the angel made Zechariah speechless until the birth of John?

Doubt can spread like an infection when persons are able to continue to give voice to what they think is not possible. When Israel spied the land that God had promised, the majority of those that spied the land declared the reality of a land flowing with milk and honey, but they also spoke about their doubts as well because the land was occupied by others that appeared stronger than them. The report of the majority caused the heart of the people to melt and led to forty years of wandering in the dessert when the land of promise was within their reach. In Zechariah's initial response to the angel, he spoke of his limitations as well as the limitations of his wife Elizabeth. If Zechariah maintains his ability to speak, he may use it to spread his doubts about God's promise. Zechariah may become like the spies that gave the majority report and cause the hearts of those near him to become doubtful as well. There are times when we are better off not being able to share our doubts. There are moments when we are to lend into our faith and trust that God's power will give us what we need when we need it most. This is part of the reason God shut his mouth. If Booker T. Washington would have listened to the voices of doubt, a school that changed the world would not have built in ritual Alabama–Tuskegee Institute, and we may have never heard of its most famous professor, George Washington Carver. There are times when our doubts should be muted for our faith to thrive.

HOME DAILY DEVOTIONAL READINGS
DECEMBER 5–11, 2022

MONDAY	TUESDAY	WEDNESDAY	THURSDAY	FRIDAY	SATURDAY	SUNDAY
God's Messenger Is Coming	God Calls Israel to Return	The Prophet Elijah Is Coming	Prophets Speak God's Word	God Will Preserve David's House	God Opens Zechariah's Mouth	Blessed Be the God of Israel
Malachi 3:1-6	Malachi 3:7-18	Malachi 4:1-6	2 Peter 1:16-21	Zechariah 12:1-10	Luke 1:57-66	Luke 1:67-80

ZECHARIAH SPEAKS

ADULT TOPIC: ZECHARIAH REDEEMED	BACKGROUND SCRIPTURE: LUKE 1:57–80

LUKE 1:57–66, 76–79

King James Version	*New Revised Standard Version*
NOW Elisabeth's full time came that she should be delivered; and she brought forth a son.	NOW the time came for Elizabeth to give birth, and she bore a son.
58 And her neighbours and her cousins heard how the Lord had shewed great mercy upon her; and they rejoiced with her.	58 Her neighbors and relatives heard that the Lord had shown his great mercy to her, and they rejoiced with her.
59 And it came to pass, that on the eighth day they came to circumcise the child; and they called him Zacharias, after the name of his father.	59 On the eighth day they came to circumcise the child, and they were going to name him Zechariah after his father.
60 And his mother answered and said, Not so; but he shall be called John.	60 But his mother said, "No; he is to be called John."
61 And they said unto her, There is none of thy kindred that is called by this name. And they made signs to his father, how he would have him called.	61 They said to her, "None of your relatives has this name." Then they began motioning to his father to find out what name he wanted to give him.
63 And he asked for a writing table, and wrote, saying, His name is John. And they marvelled all.	63 He asked for a writing tablet and wrote, "His name is John." And all of them were amazed.
64 And his mouth was opened immediately, and his tongue loosed, and he spake, and praised God.	64 Immediately his mouth was opened and his tongue freed, and he began to speak, praising God.
65 And fear came on all that dwelt round about them: and all these sayings were noised abroad throughout all the hill country of Judaea.	65 Fear came over all their neighbors, and all these things were talked about throughout the entire hill country of Judea.
66 And all they that heard them laid them up in their hearts, saying, What manner of child shall this be! And the hand of the Lord was with him.	66 All who heard them pondered them and said, "What then will this child become?" For, indeed, the hand of the Lord was with him.
• • • • • •	• • • • •
76 And thou, child, shalt be called the prophet of the Highest: for thou shalt go before the face of the Lord to prepare his ways;	76 And you, child, will be called the prophet of the Most High; for you will go before the Lord to prepare his ways,

MAIN THOUGHT: And thou, child, shalt be called the prophet of the Highest: for thou shalt go before the face of the Lord to prepare his ways. (Luke 1:76, KJV)

LUKE 1:57–66, 76–79

King James Version	New Revised Standard Version
77 To give knowledge of salvation unto his people by the remission of their sins,	77 to give knowledge of salvation to his people by the forgiveness of their sins.
78 Through the tender mercy of our God; whereby the dayspring from on high hath visited us,	78 By the tender mercy of our God, the dawn from on high will break upon us,
79 To give light to them that sit in darkness and in the shadow of death, to guide our feet into the way of peace.	79 to give light to those who sit in darkness and in the shadow of death, to guide our feet into the way of peace."

LESSON SETTING
Time: 5 BC
Place: Jerusalem the Temple

LESSON OUTLINE
I. **Affirming God's Promise** (Luke 1:57–60)
II. **Supporting God's Actions** (Luke 1:61–66)
III. **Praising God's Work** (Luke 1:76–79)

UNIFYING PRINCIPLE
The birth of a child is a transformative experience. How does the birth of a child bring hope to a community? With John's birth, God fulfills a promise to Zechariah, who proclaims a larger promise to all the world.

INTRODUCTION
The dedication of a child in Jewish culture occurs within the temple as a religious service. The service requires the couple to offer a sacrifice and then proceed to the actual naming of the child which represents the first time the name is spoken within the community. The custom requires the father to give the child his name. However, Zechariah is unable to speak after being made mute by the angel Gabriel for his unbelief in God's promise of giving Zechariah and Elizabeth a child in their mature years. Elizabeth tells the community the child's name is to be John. However, her standing in the community as a woman makes them question the choice and by custom ask Zechariah what the child's name will be. Zechariah confirms what Elizabeth said and at that moment his speech is returned to him. The sudden return in Zechariah's speech and his praise of God makes the community know that there is something unique not just about the birth of John, but something is unique in what John will grow up to do. John is the forerunner to the Messiah, the one who will prepare the way of the Lord.

EXPOSITION

I. AFFIRMING GOD'S PROMISE (LUKE 1:57–60)
After the birth of their child, Zechariah and Elizabeth bring him to the temple to be dedicated to the Lord. The dedication service is an outward expression of religious faith that affirms God's promises to them. God had indeed kept His word and allowed this older couple to conceive and give birth to a healthy child. The entire community and the families of Zechariah and Elizabeth were present for the dedication service as a sign of their support,

but also to bear witness to God's grace to the couple and the gift of a child to both the family and community. Each time a child is born, that child is a gift not just to their families but to the community as well. We rarely know what children will grow up to do and be later in life, but the dedication service provides an opportunity for the community to pledge their support and assistance to help the child be all that they can be. During the dedication service, Elizabeth tells the community the child's name. She declares his name is John.

Although Zechariah is unable to speak, he has found some way to communicate with Elizabeth about his experience in the temple with the angel and how he had been given a name to give to the child upon its birth. The name of the child would be as important as the birth of the child, and Zechariah and Elizabeth were to be obedient to the plan of God by calling their newborn son John. Elizabeth affirms God's promise by calling the child what the angel told Zechariah in the temple; she names him John.

The community resists Elizabeth's choice and thinks that the first-born son should be named after his father or for some other male member of the family. Their protest about his name is interesting given that naming a boy after his father was not a first-century cultural habit among Jewish people. People were not given surnames at this point in history (last names). Instead, male children were known by their relations, such as John, son of Zechariah. To name a son after his father would make it confusing, consider, Zechariah, son of Zechariah. Elizabeth held to her position of the child's name.

Those who pay close attention to the text may question, how does she know the name? Clearly, Zechariah has not spoken to her, and we should not suppose that she was given a separate angelic visitation. It is likely that in the same way Zechariah wrote down the name for the onlookers, he did the same thing for Elizabeth at some point during her pregnancy. He most likely wrote for her the entire episode and the included prophecy. She knows the name and is going to make sure that her son is named in accordance with the prophecy given to her husband. Sometimes the promises of God must be affirmed in moments of resistance from those who are well-intended. Not every effort to move us from what God desires for us comes to us from those who mean us harm. What we need most is discernment and commitment to the way and will of God that allows us to say no to any effort that would keep us from affirming God's promise in our midst. Moreover, it is important to hold to the promises of God. Often, we can become discouraged or even faithless, but it is because of Elizabeth's tenacity to hold to God's promise that in this moment she is able to affirm that which God has promised. Elizabeth demonstrates the strength of a strong woman that will stand up for what she believes is right in the face of opposition. The courage of Elizabeth to say no to family and community in order to affirm God's promise should not be overlooked. Strong women play a vital role in the Advent season, and they help to prepare the way of the Lord. What an important affirmation for the strong women in our midst. Strong women help us all and particularly make sure God's plan comes to fruition.

II. SUPPORTING GOD'S ACTIONS (LUKE 1:61–66)

In the scene of the dedication of John in the temple Zechariah largely plays a supporting role. The main actor is Elizabeth, the determined mother and wife who is committed to following the plan of God. When the community resists Elizabeth's efforts to name the child John, they turn to Zechariah with the expectation he would agree with their assessment and offer a different name than the one given by Elizabeth. However, Zechariah responds by writing on a tablet "his name is John." Zechariah supports Elizabeth in what she has communicated to others about what the child's name will be. There is no disagreement between husband and wife on the actions they are to take in naming their son. The community will not be able to sway Zechariah to go in a direction different than the one his wife has stated. The witness of unity between Zechariah and Elizabeth reveals their commitment to follow God's will. This is an important point for married couples. Agreement and proper support between husband and wife is a two-way street. It is also necessary for a proper and loving relationship. Zechariah does not just play a supporting role to Elizabeth, but Zechariah plays a supporting role to God's actions as well. When Zechariah affirms that the child's name is to be John, he stands in agreement with what God has made possible. When Zechariah supports the actions of God his speech impediment is lifted, and he is able to speak again. The return of Zechariah's speech at the very moment he demonstrates his support of God's action leaves the community feeling awe and mystery over the ways God's power has been manifested among them. Although we recognize God's sovereignty there is a place for our support of God's actions. One of the ways we can show our support of God's action is by affirming God's work. John's birth is a sign of God's action in the world to bring new possibilities and preparation for the way of the Lord. It is an action that Zechariah and Elizabeth support in their dedication of the child in the temple. As well as an action they support by obeying the command of the angel to name him John.

To indicate the child's name, Zechariah motions for and then writes on a tablet. This in itself seems unremarkable; it is the most logical thing to do in a world in which there are no voice boxes to aid speech. However, given that for the most part, the Greco-Roman world is mostly preliterate it is amazing. It is estimated that somewhere between 90-95% of people could not read or write. Zechariah's ability to do both indicates a higher level of class. This is an important designation given that John would be a prophet and need familiarity with the Scriptures of Israel. This speaks to the education that John would be guaranteed as the son of a literate priest. In some ways, even as John would embrace the things of God, he would reject the privilege of his upbringing. As the son of a priest, not only would he have access to a certain kind of education, but he was guaranteed a position as a priest based on his ancestry. John would use his education to interpret the Scriptures in a new light that called the people to repentance and entrance to the Kingdom of God. Even so, John's calling was not to the privilege of the temple complex but the dirty work of preaching in the wilderness. He would reject the vestments of the priesthood in favor of clothing made from camel's hair.

Zechariah in many ways represents the perfect reactionary character at this moment in the narrative. Whereas, he had his moment of doubt when the angel gave him the prophecy, he understands now and will not be deterred from proper alignment with God's plan. So much so that after supporting and agreeing with his wife, his tongue is freed, and he can speak. The first thing he does is praise God. The word used here is *eulogeo* or ευλογεω. There is a good chance that this word looks familiar, as its English cognate is *eulogy*, a literal translation is "good word." In this context, the translation "praise" is one sense in which the word can be used. The other is "bless," as in "Zechariah began to bless God." This points to what happens when we praise God in recognition of His grace and goodness. Zechariah recognized that God had blessed him with a son and once again the ability to speak. For his blessing, Zechariah turned around and blessed God. This is quite literally the proper response to a blessing from God. When we bless God, in a real sense we magnify His initial blessing. It is a blessing on the blessing.

To this, fear came upon the neighbors as they wondered what they had just witnessed. It was at this moment that John would become someone who was somebody. Their fear should be thought of more like amazement than the angst that something bad was getting ready to happen. Rather, it was the exact opposite. They knew they were witnessing something special. Something that only their God, the God of Israel, could bring to pass.

III. Praising God's Work (Luke 1:76–79)

Once Zechariah is able to speak, he offers praise to God for the gift of a son as well as the role that John would play. Zechariah's praise is like the praise offered by Mary. After the announcement by the angel, she would give birth to the Savior of the world. Both Zechariah and Mary's praise show God's remembrance of those who have been oppressed and how God has overcome the powerful, not with force, but with the gift of a child. Zechariah acknowledges that John's role will be different from his own; John will be a prophet to God. It was the tradition that the sons of a priest would become priests as well. Children of priests were introduced to rituals that the priests performed and were instructed in the Torah. The priesthood was an occupational position, and the work of the priesthood would become the life's work of a male child born to a priest. It is not a small matter for Zechariah to let go of any notion that his son would follow him as a priest. The priesthood also carried community respectability as a main stead in the life of the community. However, prophets were viewed differently by the community. Prophets were often called troublemakers. Their message was often rejected, and some were even put to death for challenging community values and choices. Despite the difficulties that prophets often experienced in the community, the community still acknowledged the value of prophets in communicating God's message to the people. John would be a prophet in the tradition of the prophets that communicated God's message to the people to prepare the way of the Lord.

Zechariah accepts that his son will not just have a different name, but he will have a different responsibility than his father. John will be the prophet that will prepare the way of the Lord.

At some point John leaves home and lives in the wilderness. The Essenes were a Jewish religious group that retreated to the wilderness away from the city in order to have no distractions that could keep them from hearing the voice of God. John may have very well been a part of the Essene community. Within the Essene community, John would have been introduced to religious beliefs about coming judgment for sin, the need for sanctification, and preparing for the Lord. The Essene movement predates John's birth and had a religious focus absent of social or political concerns.

Zechariah prophesies over his son with partial knowledge of what was to come. Not only is Zechariah's own spiritual and theological adeptness on display, but his love for his son. If nothing else, Zechariah wanted John to live out God's calling on John's life. There is nothing better than a father can have for his son.

THE LESSON APPLIED

Elizabeth is an example of a strong woman who would not be swayed by others but stood firm upon her faith conviction. It takes strength to hold firm when there are others that would tell you that you are making the wrong decision and they support the claim with appeals to tradition, law, and family values. There will be times when we will have to defend our choices. Elizabeth says no to those who would have her name her child, Zechariah. Conviction informed by faith is what gives believers the courage to stand, from Martin Luther to Joan of Arc. In the same vein, we must also bless God like Zechariah. In the same way that we hold to our convictions, we also must praise Him for what we've seen.

LET'S TALK ABOUT IT

How does Zechariah respond to the community about John's role as a prophet as opposed to a priest? Does Zechariah owe the community an explanation when John does not enter the priesthood?

Parents often want their children to succeed them in a family business or a family tradition that identifies the family to the larger community. The expectation of the community was that John would become a priest like his father. Zechariah's own desire would probably have been for John to become a priest, given the uncertain responses given to prophets. Even still from the record, it is clear that Zechariah gave his son the opportunity to be himself and live into his calling in God.

HOME DAILY DEVOTIONAL READINGS
DECEMBER 12–18, 2021

MONDAY	TUESDAY	WEDNESDAY	THURSDAY	FRIDAY	SATURDAY	SUNDAY
The Word Became Flesh	John's Testimony	Here Is the Lamb of God!	Come and See!	Prepare the Way of the Lord	Wait on the Lord	John's Confession of Faith
John 1:1-14	John 1:15-28	John 1:29-42	John 1:43-51	Isaiah 40:1-11	Isaiah 40:21-31	Luke 3:2-6, 15-18

JOHN THE BAPTIST

ADULT TOPIC:	BACKGROUND SCRIPTURE:
JOHN PREPARES THE WAY	LUKE 3:1–20; JOHN 1

LUKE 3:2–6; 15–18

King James Version

ANNAS and Caiaphas being the high priests, the word of God came unto John the son of Zacharias in the wilderness.

3 And he came into all the country about Jordan, preaching the baptism of repentance for the remission of sins;

4 As it is written in the book of the words of Esaias the prophet, saying, The voice of one crying in the wilderness, Prepare ye the way of the Lord, make his paths straight.

5 Every valley shall be filled, and every mountain and hill shall be brought low; and the crooked shall be made straight, and the rough ways shall be made smooth;

6 And all flesh shall see the salvation of God.

• • • • • •

15 And as the people were in expectation, and all men mused in their hearts of John, whether he were the Christ, or not;

16 John answered, saying unto them all, I indeed baptize you with water; but one mightier than I cometh, the latchet of whose shoes I am not worthy to unloose: he shall baptize you with the Holy Ghost and with fire:

17 Whose fan is in his hand, and he will throughly purge his floor, and will gather the wheat into his garner; but the chaff he will burn with fire unquenchable.

18 And many other things in his exhortation preached he unto the people.

New Revised Standard Version

DURING the high priesthood of Annas and Caiaphas, the word of God came to John son of Zechariah in the wilderness.

3 He went into all the region around the Jordan, proclaiming a baptism of repentance for the forgiveness of sins,

4 as it is written in the book of the words of the prophet Isaiah, "The voice of one crying out in the wilderness: 'Prepare the way of the Lord, make his paths straight.

5 Every valley shall be filled, and every mountain and hill shall be made low, and the crooked shall be made straight, and the rough ways made smooth;

6 and all flesh shall see the salvation of God.'"

• • • • • •

15 As the people were filled with expectation, and all were questioning in their hearts concerning John, whether he might be the Messiah,

16 John answered all of them by saying, "I baptize you with water; but one who is more powerful than I is coming; I am not worthy to untie the thong of his sandals. He will baptize you with the Holy Spirit and fire.

17 His winnowing fork is in his hand, to clear his threshing floor and to gather the wheat into his granary; but the chaff he will burn with unquenchable fire."

18 So, with many other exhortations, he proclaimed the good news to the people.

MAIN THOUGHT: And he came into all the country about Jordan, preaching the baptism of repentance for the remission of sins (Luke 3:3, KJV)

LESSON OUTLINE
   I. **The Preaching of John the Baptist**
      (Luke 3:2–3)
   II. **The Prophetic Work of John the Baptist**
      (Luke 2:4–6)
   III. **The People Who Came to Hear John the Baptist**
      (Luke 2:15–18)

UNIFYING PRINCIPLE

People are looking for someone with power, authority, and compassion to lead them out from under the weight of oppression. Where can such a leader be found? John proclaims the good news of one more powerful than he, who is coming and will baptize with the Holy Spirit and fire.

INTRODUCTION

John the Baptist appears on the scene as a preacher in the tradition of the prophets. His preaching focuses upon a call for national and personal repentance. There is a clear social gospel implication in what John has to say in his call for persons to treat others fairly. Fair treatment is not just dependent upon personnel reformation but also requires a reforming of the systems of oppression that hold persons in bondage and make the powerful believe there are no other options. John's preaching, like many of the prophets before him, occurs away from the religious center of the temple and the rituals of Jewish worship. John goes to a remote place to preach that which requires the people to have to come to him. Working in remote places as a religious witness was a practice followed by the Essenes.

The Essenes were a religious community that operated in isolation and focused on practices consistent with monasticism. The Essenes believed themselves to be the people of the New Covenant. They understood the concept of the New Covenant to be a renewal of strict adherence to Mosaic Law, the separation from a society that was corrupt and sinful. They had a strong belief in national existence for Israel, free from foreign intervention. Given the Essene desire for national independence, they were always of interest to the Romans and seen as a possible threat. This concern about the threat that the Essenes represented meant that both Roman and Jewish government authorities sought to keep them from becoming a force powerful enough to lead a revolution. John the Baptist is the strongest single character to emerge from the tradition of the Essenes, and his preaching carries both religious and political implications. His preaching is welcome news to some and troubling news to others. One of the ways that John the Baptist prepares the way for the Lord is to inform the community that change is necessary, and change is coming, welcomed or not.

EXPOSITION

I. THE PREACHING OF JOHN THE BAPTIST (LUKE 3:2–3)

Before we tackle John's preaching, verse 2 requires some explanation. Biblical, readers are confused that there are two men named high priest at the same time. To be clear, the role of high priest was a religious role and not a political one, however, the Romans made it function as the latter. The role was also supposed to last for a lifetime, not unlike a Supreme Court

Justice. However, the Romans changed that as well. The Romans would replace the high priest as it pleased them, and this led to multiple persons having served as high priest in a lifetime. As Luke writes the names of Annas and Caiaphas, it is likely that because the high priest position was hereditary that these two men were related. It is also most likely that one of them was the high priest and the other a former high priest that exerted power from behind closed doors.

John the Baptist begins his preaching ministry with the introduction of the phrase, "the word of the Lord came to John." This phrase is unique to the call and preaching of Old Testament prophets. John is viewed in the tradition of the Old Testament prophets and often compared to Elijah. The preaching of Old Testament prophets was a particular type of preaching that was informed by what God wanted to be changed in society because of sin and oppression. Prophetic preaching often came with pronouncements of pending judgment if conditions did not change and if people did not change. All prophetic preaching started with "the word of the Lord" coming to the prophet since the prophet is the instrument God uses to communicate. The word is not of the prophets making or ideas about what needs to occur. "The word of the Lord" is that which comes from God to the prophet often when the prophet was not seeking it. It is not until we hear "the word of the Lord came to John the Baptist" that he starts his preaching ministry. Gerhard von Rad in his book *The Message of the Prophets* states "the word of Yahweh is both a necessary precondition of prophetic preaching and also forms its subject matter– through, indeed, it is fundamental basis of the prophets' existence– they only occasionally made it the subject of theological reflection." When the word of the Lord came to the prophets, they saw their only responsibility was to speak the word and leave the result up to God. When the word of the Lord came to John the Baptist, it was a word about the need for repentance. Repentance in this instance is literally a change of mind. A change of mind is reflected in a change of action. Repentance in John's preaching demanded a change in actions as well a change in the heart. It is the combination of the change in actions and heart that provided the authentic witness of repentance. Included in John the Baptist's preaching ministry was the act of baptism. Ritual baptism was not new to Israel. The temple had various pools where persons participated in ritual cleansing before or after leaving worship. The Essene community of which John may have been a part, practiced ritual cleansing traditions as well. However, John gives baptism a new meaning that surpasses ritual cleansing and causes baptism to be viewed as an outward expression of a decision to change how one lived. Baptism was a commitment to lead a life of worship to God but to also honor God with a commitment to justice in how one lived. John's preaching called for a life of transformation that helped to usher in a world consistent with what God desired. Preaching with purpose that leads to transformation is how John's preaching helped to prepare the way of the Lord. John's preaching was ultimately about introducing the idea of the Kingdom of God. In this preaching, he was making a way, or making the way of Jesus smooth and plain.

II. THE PROPHETIC WORK OF JOHN (LUKE 2:4–6)

Luke attributes Isaiah's prophecy to John the Baptist. Luke takes this position for several reasons: First, because of the location of John the Baptist's ministry. John is in the region of the Jordan River, an area away from the busy noise of the city of Jerusalem and the people of the villages. The desolation of the wilderness is the place that God uses to teach His people about the new thing He is doing. Just as the wilderness was used as a training ground to teach Israel as they journeyed from Egypt, the wilderness will again be a training ground for all of those who will come and hear what John the Baptist has to say. Moses was given the Ten Commandments in the wilderness; John the Baptist is given the word of the Lord in the wilderness. Moses had the tablets; John has the voice. There are things that God has for His people that can only be obtained through the prophet in the wilderness. It is in the wilderness that there is enough solitude for one to be able to correctly hear from God. John's ministry in the wilderness enables him to listen intently for God, and it also serves as a place of separation from the hustle and bustle of a system that John will stand in a position of opposition against. John's presence in the wilderness was just as much about protest against that which he would speak out about as it was about spiritual discernment and clarity. John understood that there is a purity found in nature that allows one to hear from God and not get lost in the values of the world.

Second, Luke believes that John the Baptist serves the role of preparing others for what is to come. What becomes abundantly clear early in the ministry of John the Baptist is that he is viewed by some as a possible messianic candidate.

John quickly puts to rest any questions about him being the Messiah and defines his role as one that is preparing the way for the Messiah that will come. John prepares the way in part by making persons sensitive to the interest of God. God has a particular vision of Israel and the world; John wants persons to seek God's interest as opposed to their own. Lastly, Luke views John's role as helping to make access to God possible by the removal of barriers. Mountains, valleys, crooked places, and rough ways can all be barriers to access for some people. For all persons to have access, the barriers have to be removed. In ancient times, whenever the king was going to visit a community, one of the things that happen was a group went to the community ahead of time to ensure that the route of the king had all barriers removed. As a part of that, the army would go before the king and make the way. Often, there would be new roads created and the necessary earth moving that this required. In the same way that new roads require hills to be brought low and valleys filled up for our roads, the same was true in the days of old, even without any heavy machinery. This was done to ensure that the king would be safe as he traveled. The last thing that an empire would want is for its leader to be attacked or killed while in route to a part of the empire. Those who went before were making sure that the king would be safe by removing those barriers. John the Baptist plays the role of helping to eliminate the barriers so that when the King comes His route is clear.

III. THE PEOPLE WHO CAME TO HEAR JOHN THE BAPTIST (LUKE 2:15–18)

The people who came to hear John the Baptist came with messianic hope that John might be the deliverer the people long sought. Messianic hope in Israel had its roots in nationalism and the belief that God would provide a national leader to overthrow the Romans and return Israel to the glory days of King David. The Essene community that John the Baptist may have been part of was long viewed as the logical source from which such a leader would emerge. This was due to at least two reasons, 1) the Essene's strict loyalty to the Law of Moses; 2) their condemnation of appeasement with the Romans that provided a visible sign of resistance. The power of John's proclamation and conviction he spoke attracted a growing audience to the wilderness to hear him speak. The presence of the crowd adds to the hope that John just might be the One, the Messiah that the Jews had longed to see. John quickly dashes the hopes of the crowd and clarifies his role as one of preparing the way for the true Messiah. John makes no messianic claims, nor does he accept the claims of the Messiah that the crowd would thrust upon him. Amidst a growing popularity, John the Baptist remains true to his central role of preparing the way of the Lord. John communicates his secondary role to the coming Messiah by drawing a contrast in their ministry. John's ministry has included baptism as a ritual to provide an outward confession of change. However, the coming Messiah would baptize persons with the Holy Spirit and fire. The Messiah would be able to empower persons in ways that John could not. John does not have the ability to direct the Holy Spirit, but the coming Messiah would pour out the Holy Spirit upon those who followed him. Persons would be empowered to live out their witness of faith in ways that exceed the practice of rituals alone. The coming Messiah would not just empower, but true to prophetic proclamation, the Messiah would also judge those that resisted the claims of God upon them. The burning of chaff is an indication that judgment is real and the call for repentance and preparation has a time limit. The time for change, the time to be ready is now because the Messiah is coming.

The preaching of John the Baptist speaks very clearly to a very prominent apocalyptic point of view that was a part of his understanding. Ultimately, John's message is one of urgency. It wasn't just that the people needed to repent but they needed to repent at once because the Messiah was on His way. John's message was one about God's prerogative to interrupt whatever plans humanity may have devised. God, through the Messiah and His kingdom, was breaking into the normalcy of the day. It was in this way that all would need to be sure of the inauguration of something new. God was doing something new that referenced the old and John was responsible for introducing it. All needed to know what was coming and John simply made sure that all who would listen would receive this good news.

THE LESSON APPLIED

John the Baptist is a leader that will not be swayed away from God's call in his life. John does not fall prey to a crowd that would quickly anoint him as the Messiah and the leader of a revolution. John remains true to his call of preparing the way for the coming Messiah, Jesus Christ of Nazareth. It is not always easy to accept a secondary role given human egos and pride that can lead us toward paths of temptation. However, John the Baptist is able to do so because he is dependent upon the word of the Lord that God sends to him. John is not willing to step outside of what the word of the Lord has told him even if the crowd attempts to get him to do so.

John knows his purpose and his place and is committed to doing the work that God has given him. Saying no to the crowd could have come at a cost. Since John did not meet their expectations of what he should do, so they may have no longer come to hear him preach. They may have sought to get others not to go hear John. Yet John finds the strength to remain true to the prophetic ministry God had given him, even if it meant accepting a secondary position to Jesus. The humility of John the Baptist, along with his conviction as he preached a message of repentance, makes John a unique character in Scripture. This was absolutely part of the reason Jesus said John was greater than the prophets of old even as he did no miracles. John was emblematic of one who understood God's plan and he was fine with doing his part for the kingdom of God.

LET'S TALK ABOUT IT

What role did Messianic hope play in getting people to come to the wilderness to hear John the Baptist preach?

Israel never stopped looking for a Messiah after the fall of Jerusalem and the Babylon exile. The prophets had long spoken of a day when the cloud of judgment upon the nation would be removed, and the Messiah would come to them. Messianic longing gave rise to groups that fought foreign domination. Messianic longing gave rise to deeper religious devotion to discern the times and the person who would be the Messiah. It was messianic hope that initially brought people to the wilderness to hear John the Baptist. In time, other groups than those who had messianic hope would go out to the wilderness to hear John the Baptist, including tax collectors and soldiers. However, it was the hope of the coming Messiah that caused the first group of persons to go to the Jordan to hear John the Baptist. Advent is a season of hope and expectancy. During Advent, Christians have a heightened sense of awareness of the ways that God might break into the routine of life with new possibilities that bring glory to Him and work toward our good.

HOME DAILY DEVOTIONAL READINGS
DECEMBER 19–25, 2022

MONDAY	TUESDAY	WEDNESDAY	THURSDAY	FRIDAY	SATURDAY	SUNDAY
The Birth of Jesus	The Ruler from Bethlehem	A Son Is Given	A Shoot from Jesse's Stump	The Lord Is with You	Blessed among Woman	My Soul Magnifies the Lord
Matthew 1:18-25	Micah 5:1-15	Isaiah 9:1-7	Isaiah 11:1-10	Luke 1:26-38	Luke 1:39-45	Luke 1:46-55

MARY MARVELS AT GOD'S CHOICE

ADULT TOPIC:	BACKGROUND SCRIPTURE:
OPEN TO BEING CHOSEN	LUKE 1:46–55

LUKE 1:46–55

King James Version	New Revised Standard Version
AND Mary said, My soul doth magnify the Lord,	AND Mary said, "My soul magnifies the Lord,
47 And my spirit hath rejoiced in God my Saviour.	47 and my spirit rejoices in God my Savior,
48 For he hath regarded the low estate of his handmaiden: for, behold, from henceforth all generations shall call me blessed.	48 for he has looked with favor on the lowliness of his servant. Surely, from now on all generations will call me blessed;
49 For he that is mighty hath done to me great things; and holy is his name.	49 for the Mighty One has done great things for me, and holy is his name.
50 And his mercy is on them that fear him from generation to generation.	50 His mercy is for those who fear him from generation to generation.
51 He hath shewed strength with his arm; he hath scattered the proud in the imagination of their hearts.	51 He has shown strength with his arm; he has scattered the proud in the thoughts of their hearts.
52 He hath put down the mighty from their seats, and exalted them of low degree.	52 He has brought down the powerful from their thrones, and lifted up the lowly;
53 He hath filled the hungry with good things; and the rich he hath sent empty away.	53 he has filled the hungry with good things, and sent the rich away empty.
54 He hath helped his servant Israel, in remembrance of his mercy;	54 He has helped his servant Israel, in remembrance of his mercy,
55 As he spake to our fathers, to Abraham, and to his seed for ever.	55 according to the promise he made to our ancestors, to Abraham and to his descendants forever."

LESSON SETTING
Time: 3–4 AD
Place Nazareth

LESSON OUTLINE
I. **The Focus of Mary's Praise (Luke 1:46–49)**
II. **The Concern of Mary's Praise (Luke 1:50–53)**
III. **The Belief in Mary's Praise (Luke 1:54–55)**

UNIFYING PRINCIPLE
People may be chosen to serve based on their power, wealth, and authority. How should we view those who are chosen to serve? According to Luke, Mary was chosen to become the mother of Jesus because of her humble servant attitude.

MAIN THOUGHT: And Mary said, My soul doth magnify the Lord, And my spirit hath rejoiced in God my Saviour. (Luke 1:46–47, KJV)

INTRODUCTION

This section of Luke's gospel is commonly referred to as the Magnificat. The Magnificat is a poem of praise by Mary after being chosen by God to give birth to the Savior of the world. The poem follows many of the themes found in Hannah's prayer of thanksgiving after the birth of Samuel. Both women acknowledge the power and the grace of God for His kindness with the gift of a child. Each woman believes that God has something special in store for the children they birthed. Both stories are a part of the barren woman's motif that runs throughout the Bible. In all these stories a woman who is not able to get pregnant does so. In most cases, this is due to difficulty in conception, in Mary's case it is because of her virginal status, nonetheless the effect is the same. A woman who is not supposed to be able to have children miraculously conceives. Mary's praise reveals a particular position about God's concern for the poor. Mary is a young, poor village girl who is viewed as powerless in the eyes of the world, yet she experiences the empowering of God's Spirit in her that causes her to see the liberating power of God in fresh ways. The hungry are filled and the rich are sent away empty. Mary also understands in her praise that what God has done for her was not just for Mary, but an indication of how Mary would be the instrument God would use to fulfill His promise to Israel. Mary's praise has social implications that speak to God's view of a just society where the powerful are not in charge, but God is, and He can use whomever He wills for His purposes, even poor village girls.

EXPOSITION

I. THE FOCUS OF MARY'S PRAISE (LUKE 1:46–49)

The focus of Mary's praise is on the power of God and what has been accomplished that could only be done by God. Our praise of God is always a recognition of the power of God at work in our lives and the world. Praise is one of the ways we acknowledge God's power as well as our own limitations. Mary was helpless to change her condition of poverty and oppression. She lived in a world where the powerful used force to take what they wanted without concern about how their actions impacted others. Mary certainly wanted something better out of life but was powerless to bring the change by herself. Thus, her praise magnifying God and rejoicing in her spirit acknowledges what God has done for her. Mary's praise also incorporates humility that confesses that God did not have to use her but looked upon her low estate and had regard for her still as an unworthy vessel. Part of the strength of Mary's praise comes from the place of all the things that God was willing to overcome to choose Mary as the mother of the Savior of the entire world.

Mary was already engaged and planning a wedding, but God was willing to overcome the prior plans of another. There were countless reasons that could have been used for not choosing Mary. There was only one reason Mary was chosen, because of a sovereign God decided to make Mary His choice. Mary's praise also reveals her understanding of the Jewish longing for the Messiah–all generations will call me blessed. In Judaism what gave motherhood its deepest meaning was the possibility that her son might be the long-hoped-for deliverer of Israel. Mary gives praise to God because she knows that her son is the Messiah. Mary's praise gives voice to all the ways that God had worked on her behalf to use Mary to fulfill His purpose. Any time God is willing to use us to make a difference in the world, that is reason enough to give Him praise.

Mary's praise is partly predicated on the fact that she acknowledges God as her Savior. The language of verse 47 is interesting given that Jesus, her son, is to be the Savior of the world. This pun plays on the fact that even as Mary is a part of the story of salvation, she is not the central character but is also in need of salvation. Interestingly, God is called Savior about 35 times throughout the Old Testament. This reference points backward and portends the future simultaneously. It is a point of connection bridging the work of salvation between God the Father and God the Son, who is coming. Mary happens to be the point of connection between the two.

Mary is clear about her role in all that was getting ready to take place. She refers to herself as a servant of the Lord. Inasmuch as this demonstrates her humility, it also points to her place in the story of salvation. She is not the birth of salvation but a medium through which it would come to the world. Her humility is based on her self-understanding that she is at the nexus of a miraculous world event of which she was simply drafted to be a part.

It is important to note that Mary's spontaneous praise came about as Mary was visiting her cousin, Elizabeth, who was pregnant with John the Baptist. Imagine the level of excitement for both of these women, not just because they were having sons, but because they were getting to be a part of God's plan. It was at this point that Mary was overwhelmed and exploded into praise. Her song of praise was not just about her or what God was doing for her but also Elizabeth and the entirety of Israel.

She declares that Yahweh is the Mighty One. In this, she references God's greatness. She understands that God is even beyond that which He is doing at the moment. To declare God the Mighty One is not only to recognize what He is doing in the moment, but also that His greatness extends beyond her immediate concern. For God to be the Mighty One, He must have completed mighty acts in the past, and she trusts that He will also complete mighty acts in the future. His might is seen continually, and for this Mary gives Him praise.

II. The Concern of Mary's Praise
(Luke 1:50–53)

The concern of Mary's praise speaks to what God has done for His people. It is a praise filled with components of liberation and social justice. Mary declares that God has turned the tables on the powerful by putting down the mighty from their thrones and bringing to nothing the plans of the proud. The meek and lowly are vindicated by God's actions.

Their trust in Him has not gone without reward and Mary's praise affirms what God has done for those who put their trust in Him. The only way for the humble to be lifted above their situation is for God to do the lifting. In the gift of the Savior, through a babe born of a woman, God exalts the humble in ways that exceed their imagination. The birth of Jesus does not just have theological implications, but in Jesus, Christ God is righting the social and economic order. Jesus is the sign that God is filling the hungry with good things. Yet, at the same time, He is sending the rich away empty. Those who depend upon their ability and resources miss what God is doing. Blinded by status and privilege they continue to lean on their own power as opposed to humbling themselves before the power of God. Only the humble can truly see what God is up to, and when they see it, they cannot help but praise God. Mary's praise is a prayer of praise that all the humble can participate in because it connected the entire community to what God is doing in Jesus Christ. Our praise may begin with a focus on the power of God, but after seeing God's power at work we should be able to see how that power impacts others as well.

God's mercy runs from generation to generation. This alone is good news for those that will hear of it. This takes the long view of history and considers what God does for each and every generation of people that walk on the face of the earth. Even as God is showing Mary mercy, she could trust that His mercy would be available to those who came after her. She was sure that those who came before her had experienced God's mercy as she would have known of God's mighty acts of the past. This in itself is important to note because in Jesus God's mercy went to a new level. If mercy is not receiving that which is deserved, Jesus' birth is a celebration of mercy. It is through Him that all punishment and judgment that is deserved by humankind will not be experienced. As Mary exclaims God's mercy, she realizes that His mercy is not just for her at this moment but for all of humankind. Mercy is the compassion that is aroused when viewing the affliction of another. In this sense, God looks upon the miserable circumstance of humankind and decides to act. Though not explicitly referenced, it is easy to make the connection to God's action in the Exodus story. Yahweh tells Moses, "I have indeed seen the misery of my people in Egypt. I have heard them crying out because of their slave drivers, and I am concerned about their suffering." (Exodus 3:7) In this instance, it is easy enough to understand what mercy is and how God displays it. As it relates to our Lucan text, God acts precisely because He understands that unless He does something, humanity will remain lost. His mercy in choosing Mary is but only a portion of His total mercy. His mercy towards Mary is a microcosm of the mercy that He is dispensing to the whole of the world. This is why Mary rejoices with great excitement.

III. THE BELIEF IN MARY'S PRAISE (LUKE 1:54–55)

Mary's praise reveals a belief in God's promises to Abraham. Mary sees what God has done for her as a sign that God was keeping His promise to a nation because of the father of the nation Abraham. It is because God remembers that Mary is the benefactor of God's memory. God makes a covenant with Abraham and promises to give him and his descendants all of the land of Canaan for an everlasting possession and that he would be their God. (Genesis 17:7–8). Mary's pregnancy with the gift of the Savior is proof of God's faithfulness. Israel long believed in God's covenant-keeping promise often referred to in the Hebrew as *hesed* translated as loving-kindness. *Hesed* was long believed to be an attribute of God and often one act of *hesed* was to be responded to in kind. In other words, lovingkindness is to be shown in reciprocation. In essence, as God demonstrates lovingkindness to His people, in this instance Mary, lovingkindness should be shown back to God. Lovingkindness is not supposed to be a one-way street but rather bi-directional. God's lovingkindness, therefore, is relational in that He displays hesed to His people, and He does so from His covenantal choice. His lovingkindness, therefore, is about His covenantal faithfulness.

Mary makes the connection of God's goodness toward her with God's promise to Abraham and declared that God has helped Israel. The Messiah would be the fulfillment of all that God promised to ensure the deliverance of Israel from the domination of sin. It is another example of His lovingkindness to His people. The belief in Mary's praise comes from a heart of conviction that understood the promises of God.

Although Mary is a young girl she has been exposed enough to the Torah and heard the Word of God enough to know the promises of God and claimed them as her own. Mary's praise is undergirded by a working knowledge of the Torah and understanding of the stories, rituals, and traditions that accompanied her faith. Thus, Mary's praise provides an insightful theology that involves far more than just joy for being chosen but shows a woman of mature faith and a vessel ready to be used by God. In this, we might surmise that Mary's usefulness is at least partly determined by her understanding of the things of God before her interaction with the angel. One's usability by God is determined by one's ability to comprehend God's past with humanity and the ways in which God moves in and out of history. For Mary, this meant that she had a command of some of Israel's basic history and God's actions within it. As she understood Abraham's story, she was able then to see God's movement and thus properly avail herself to be used by God. The maturity of her faith was at least in part determined by her knowledge of the things of the past. There is a good word implanted for those who work with or are responsible for rearing young people. Often young persons are not concerned with history and yet it is in the past that we can learn of God and develop faith and hope for the future. It is impossible to learn faith solely on the now, there is too much uncertainty, rather faith is learned from the past and those who were a part of it. Mary knew she could trust God in part because of

Abraham's story and Israel's history with Yahweh. She did not doubt because all that was happening had already been promised, and she understood that God's word cannot return to Him void.

THE LESSON APPLIED

Mary's praise in the Magnificat provides us informed praise with a sound theological understanding of the ways that God operates as well as what God had said in His Word. Informed praise keeps persons and the church on a path that is consistent with how God works in the world. Whereas praise involves an emotional component and surely Mary was emotional when she declared "my soul magnifies the Lord." Mary's praise ties her emotions to a learned theology that was a part of the tradition in which she was reared. There is a value in being socialized into the life of the Church that allows us to learn its stories, rituals, and traditions until we discover ways to apply them to our lives. Praise should never be separated from the theology of the One we praise. God expects those who praise Him to know something about Him, and the praise we offer is also our offering what we say we know about Him. Mary's praise helps us to see the connection between praise and theology.

LET'S TALK ABOUT IT

Does God's delay mean that He will not honor His promises of the past?

An important part of Mary's praise is that God remembered His covenant with Abraham. Although Israel has fallen prey to multiple national powers that have looted and oppressed the nation, God has not forgotten His promise to Abraham. The delay in the Messiah's coming was no indication that God would not fulfill His promise. There are times when we may feel that God has forgotten us. An extended illness, and economic hardship, a family crisis can all make us wonder if God has forgotten us. Mary's praise affirms that we serve a God who remembers. In God's own time, He will remember, and when He remembers He will act on our behalf because He is faithful. We should always take courage that we serve a God who is faithful. In the words of the saints in days gone by, "He may not come when you want but when He comes, He is always on time." God is above time and thus is not constrained to the timing that we think is best. Rather because of His unique position God is able to complete His promises as He sees fit.

HOME DAILY DEVOTIONAL READINGS
DECEMBER 26–JANUARY 1, 2022

MONDAY	TUESDAY	WEDNESDAY	THURSDAY	FRIDAY	SATURDAY	SUNDAY
God Will Bless the Faithful	Choose Life	God Forgives the Penitent	Christ the Atoning Sacrifice	We Are God's Children	Solomon Dedicates the Temple	A Call to Walk Faithfully
Deuteronomy 30:1-10	Deuteronomy 30:11-20	1 John 1:1-10	1 John 2:1-11	1 John 3:1-10	2 Chronicles 7:1-11	2 Chronicles 7:12-22

GOD PROMISES TO HEAR AND FORGIVE

ADULT TOPIC: BACKGROUND SCRIPTURE:
PROMISES AND CONSEQUENCES   2 CHRONICLES 7:1–22

2 CHRONICLES 7:12–22

King James Version	*New Revised Standard Version*
AND the LORD appeared to Solomon by night, and said unto him, I have heard thy prayer, and have chosen this place to myself for an house of sacrifice.	THEN the LORD appeared to Solomon in the night and said to him: "I have heard your prayer, and have chosen this place for myself as a house of sacrifice.
13 If I shut up heaven that there be no rain, or if I command the locusts to devour the land, or if I send pestilence among my people;	13 When I shut up the heavens so that there is no rain, or command the locust to devour the land, or send pestilence among my people,
14 If my people, which are called by my name, shall humble themselves, and pray, and seek my face, and turn from their wicked ways; then will I hear from heaven, and will forgive their sin, and will heal their land.	14 if my people who are called by my name humble themselves, pray, seek my face, and turn from their wicked ways, then I will hear from heaven, and will forgive their sin and heal their land.
15 Now mine eyes shall be open, and mine ears attent unto the prayer that is made in this place.	15 Now my eyes will be open and my ears attentive to the prayer that is made in this place.
16 For now have I chosen and sanctified this house, that my name may be there for ever: and mine eyes and mine heart shall be there perpetually.	16 For now I have chosen and consecrated this house so that my name may be there forever; my eyes and my heart will be there for all time.
17 And as for thee, if thou wilt walk before me, as David thy father walked, and do according to all that I have commanded thee, and shalt observe my statutes and my judgments;	17 As for you, if you walk before me, as your father David walked, doing according to all that I have commanded you and keeping my statutes and my ordinances,
18 Then will I stablish the throne of thy kingdom, according as I have covenanted with David thy father, saying, There shall not fail thee a man to be ruler in Israel.	18 then I will establish your royal throne, as I made covenant with your father David saying, 'You shall never lack a successor to rule over Israel.'
19 But if ye turn away, and forsake my statutes and my commandments, which I have set before you, and shall go and serve other gods, and worship them;	19 "But if you turn aside and forsake my statutes and my commandments that I have set before you, and go and serve other gods and worship them,

MAIN THOUGHT: If my people, which are called by my name, shall humble themselves, and pray, and seek my face, and turn from their wicked ways; then will I hear from heaven, and will forgive their sin, and will heal their land. (2 Chronicles 7:14, KJV)

2 Chronicles 7:1–22

King James Version

20 Then will I pluck them up by the roots out of my land which I have given them; and this house, which I have sanctified for my name, will I cast out of my sight, and will make it to be a proverb and a byword among all nations.

21 And this house, which is high, shall be an astonishment to every one that passeth by it; so that he shall say, Why hath the LORD done thus unto this land, and unto this house?

22 And it shall be answered, Because they forsook the LORD God of their fathers, which brought them forth out of the land of Egypt, and laid hold on other gods, and worshipped them, and served them: therefore hath he brought all this evil upon them.

New Revised Standard Version

20 then I will pluck you up from the land that I have given you; and this house, which I have consecrated for my name, I will cast out of my sight, and will make it a proverb and a byword among all peoples.

21 And regarding this house, now exalted, everyone passing by will be astonished, and say, 'Why has the LORD done such a thing to this land and to this house?'

22 Then they will say, 'Because they abandoned the LORD the God of their ancestors who brought them out of the land of Egypt, and they adopted other gods, and worshiped them and served them; therefore he has brought all this calamity upon them.'"

LESSON SETTING

Time: 970–960 BC
Place: The Temple in Jerusalem

LESSON OUTLINE

I. A Chosen Place
(2 Chronicles 7:12–16)
II. A Promised Position
(2 Chronicles 7:17–18)
III. An Unnecessary Penalty
(2 Chronicles 7:19–22)

UNIFYING PRINCIPLE

Relationships involve blessings, expectations, and consequences. How do we honor and maintain good relationships with other people? When God declared Solomon's temple as home, the honor came with obligations and promises.

INTRODUCTION

Solomon completes the building of the temple that David longed to build. The temple provides a central location for religious rituals and worship. The centralization of worship was a powerful unifying force for the nation and brought all the tribes together to worship in one place. National unity would be possible because of the God the entire nation worshiped and served. In the first worship service held in the new temple, Solomon leads the people in worship through his sacrifice on the altar and his prayer before God. The people witness in Solomon a leader who takes seriously his responsibility to God and the people. Solomon is a leader who leads by example. Solomon's prayer during the dedication of the temple is for God to use the temple as a place that the nation may come to hear His word, to make sacrifice to Him as a sign of their dedication, but Solomon also prays that the temple might be a place that the people can come to when they have sinned and find forgiveness. Solomon prays that the temple might always be a place where the people may be able to turn to God.

Solomon's prayer demonstrates that God would use sacred space differently from all spaces as the means that the people might find forgiveness and restoration. Turning to God and God turning to the people is made possible because there is a place set aside where both parties can meet and turn to each other. When Solomon finished his prayer, God answered with. Now the nation knows that the temple is a place where God's power is at work. Later, God appears to Solomon and informs him He has heard his prayer and tells Solomon what He expects of the nation that would worship and serve Him as His own.

EXPOSITION

I. A CHOSEN PLACE
(2 CHRONICLES 7:12–16)

Whereas Solomon builds the temple, it is God that chooses the temple as a place His Spirit will reside among the people. Just as God chooses persons, God also chooses places that He will use to bear witness to His presence at work in the world. The places God chooses can create within us a deeper sense of God's presence and we approach such places with mystery and awe. God tells Solomon He has chosen the temple and tells Solomon what it means for God to have chosen the temple. The selection of the temple by God carries responsibility and blessing.

The people will not be able to come to worship in the temple and expect the blessings of God if they are not following the will of God. God is always concerned about how power may be used by others in ways that takes advantage of the weak, the needy, and the poor. Israel will have to display the witness of a just society where all people are treated fairly if they expect the temple to be a place of blessing. Religious rituals in the temple will not excuse abuse of people or acts of idolatry. The presence of the temple will not remove the possibility of judgment if the people do not worship God with whole hearts and treat others the way God expects. Idolatry and abuse will cause God to act. The actions of God are described as shutting up the heavens where there is no rain (see 1 Kings 17:1–2), commanding the locust to devour the land, and sending pestilence. The environment will turn against an agricultural economy in ways that will make it impossible to succeed. The blessings of God relate to the obligations of the people of God. Disobedience to God will have consequences. Through repentance, humility, and prayer God promises restoration and healing of the land. When the people turn back to God, the environment that once worked against them will again work for them. God's restoration includes both people and things when the people turn back to him. The temple is the place that God has chosen in the community where the people may come to turn to him, and he will turn to them.

The theology of verses 14 and 15 are representative of the theology of those books considered to be of deuteronomic origin. Deuteronomic theology is simple in that it attributes the welfare of the people to their faithfulness or lack thereof to their attendance to their covenant with Yahweh. If Israel carried out His wishes all would go well, however, if not then they would be punished. Many scholars have pointed out that the words here are very likely the partial work of later redactors who are explaining Israel's exile and the destruction of Jerusalem and the temple by the Babylonians. In this sense, God's answer to Solomon acts as a prophecy for that which would take place several centuries later. The temple would be fine based on their own faithfulness to God.

It is at this juncture that it is important to note several things about the placement and building of the temple. The temple functioned more like a royal chapel. The temple was a part of the larger palace complex, as it sat adjacent to the royal palace. This is important to note as it points to one of the larger themes that is present in this passage and the entire narrative of the Chronicles. As a part of the royal structure, its building reflected a royal theology that imbued the royal family with covenantal status as the chosen rulers (v. 17, 18).

The building of the temple demonstrated the kind of social and economic stability of a society that had sound borders and national security. Long ago were the days when Israel was concerned with the constant raiding of their neighbors (Judges 6:3–6). The excitement of the people was not just because there was a place for worship and national festivals, but that it was representative of national strength that had been built through the reigns of David, and Solomon was ruled over a unified kingdom. This was their moment to celebrate that they had arrived. Israel was not just a band of people grouped together by tribal affiliation, but a true nation-state.

II. A Promised Position (2 Chronicles 7:17–18)

The Davidic covenant was God's promise to David that someone from his family would always sit on the throne of Israel. This is affirmed again by God to Solomon. The Davidic covenant comes with certain conditions and those conditions are that Solomon would follow David's example of trusting God and keeping the laws of God. The king does not have absolute power to do as he wills if he desires to remain on the throne. The king has a responsibility to God, to follow God and to lead the people in ways that allow them to follow God as well. If Solomon will follow the commands and ordinance of God, the blessing of the Davidic covenant will flow to him and his descendants. The Chronicler is causing the reader to hear that it was God who established Solomon's rule because of his faithfulness to God. Solomon's faithfulness can serve as a model for the nation. Given Solomon's wealth, extensive building programs, as well as his international trade, there may have been competing voices in his time on what made Solomon a great king. The Chronicler weighs in to connect Solomon's successful reign with a promised position that God gave Israel's most celebrated king–David. The witness that Solomon remained on the throne to his death was an indication that he fulfilled God's expectation of him. The birth of the Messiah was the continued fulfillment of God's promise to David that someone from his line would sit on the throne of Israel forever–Jesus was born in Bethlehem because Joseph was from the line and house of David.

The Davidic covenant is an everlasting covenant, but one with conditions. It is important to point out the conditional statements of verses 17 and 18. Though this is a covenant, its execution does not rest wholly on divine shoulders. Rather its conditions are attached to that of the king and the people. God's promise was given to Solomon as it was given to his father before him, yet the promise could be broken by the humans who were a part of it. We should all take pause and notice that we have a role in ensuring that God's promises come to pass. Even as God makes promises to His people, we can invalidate those promises by not fulfilling the duties that He has outlined for us. Whereas the promise was to David and his family it was affective of all of Israel as it rested upon their ability to do that which would cause them to flourish. What kind of king they would have would determine the fate of the nation? In this way, the covenant was not just about the royal family's right to rule, but about whether they would dwell in the land God was giving them. This covenant was then tied back into the Mosaic covenant before it. The main difference is that the future of the people was now linked with the fortunes of the royal line as well.

Whereas, the promise was to David and his family it was affective of all of Israel as it rested upon their ability to do that which would cause them to flourish. What kind of king they would have would determine the fate of the nation. In this way, the covenant was not just about the royal family's right to rule, but about whether or not they would dwell in the land God was giving them. This covenant was then tied back into the Mosaic covenant before it. The main difference is that the future of the people was now linked with the fortunes of the royal line as well.

III. An Unnecessary Penalty (2 Chronicles 7:19–22)

God provides a warning to Solomon about what could happen to a nation that turned away from Him. The focus of the warning is not on individual sin but the sins of a nation. When a nation allows greed to take advantage of the poor and creates systems that keep people in poverty, that nation is responsible for wrong. Much of what harms persons are acceptable forms of institutionalized sin, like racism and poverty. God's warning to Solomon as the king is to prevent the institutionalization of sin in ways that the nation turns away from God. Continue to remind the people of their responsibility to God and each other as the people of God. Israel is to be a light to the nations about what it means to place God at the center of national life and make worship and service to Him the nation's aim.

Israel is to be a nation guided by its theology. The question always for the nation is not what is in their interest but what is in the interest of God and how God wants to use the nation to accomplish His will. If the nation will put God's interest over their own interest, they can avoid the penalty of turning away from God. The penalty begins with the promise of exile, God will remove the people from the land. The land meant everything to Israel and the blessings of God were often seen in connection with the land. To lose the land for a people that had known bondage could cause them to lose hope in the future. In addition to losing the land, God's presence would leave the temple and the place once of reverence would be viewed with discontent. The symbol of national unity would be gone, and the people would not know how to find God or where to find God. The last part of the penalty was a public shame as a result of others asking why God treated these people so badly.

The response would be because they worshiped other gods of their own making as opposed to the God that made the nation. All of this could be avoided if the nation will not turn away from God.

THE LESSON APPLIED

No nation can hide behind religious language while mistreating others. We are not always privy to knowing the ways that God will respond to the sins of a nation. Whereas it is true that God is patient, in His own time He will respond to sin.

The greed of some has led to the stripping of natural resources in ways that the environment and certain wildlife are at risk. Global warming has long since been accepted by most persons as scientific fact, but the nations of the world cannot find common ground on reducing greenhouse gases and our planet is in peril. Each passing year we witness more violent storms and more damaging wildfires. Sensible gun laws could reduce the violence we see in our communities and our schools, but powerful lobbying groups continue to stand in the way of practical solutions to make our communities safe. State and local officials have banned teaching the nation's history on race and made voting more difficult for persons that have been historically disenfranchised. The global pandemic has exposed glaring disparities that are making some question if democracy can survive. There are many reasons we need a national movement of repentance and a turning to God. Just saying God bless America will not be enough. Israel ultimately failed the test of repentance and spent 70 years in exile. The temple was destroyed and once they returned to the land under foreign domination. A penalty that could have been avoided was made a reality because of a nation that did not heed the message given to Solomon.

LET'S TALK ABOUT IT

Why was the temple so important as a place of prayer for Israel?

The temple was a special place for Israel because it represented the place that God's Spirit resided. For many, local churches serve that same purpose; they represent the place that believers feel they can find God. Although God can be found anywhere, there are places that are unique and give us historical connection with family and others. Often, these are places where we know that God heard our cries. The very first thing that people who had been slaves built as their own within their communities were churches. The churches they built were an indication of their faith and their desire to have a place where all might go to hear the voice of God.

HOME DAILY DEVOTIONAL READINGS						
JANUARY 2–8, 2023						
MONDAY	**TUESDAY**	**WEDNESDAY**	**THURSDAY**	**FRIDAY**	**SATURDAY**	**SUNDAY**
God Will Make a Way	Dry Bones Shall Live	Israel Will Be God's People	God's Restoring Love	Stand Firm in the Spirit	The Lord Is a Faithful Protector	God Restores God's People
Isaiah 43:14–28	Ezekiel 37:1–14	Ezekiel 37:15–28	Hosea 11	2 Thessalonians 2:3–15	2 Thessalonians 3:1–5, 13–17	Isaiah 43:1–13

GOD PROMISES RESTORATION AND PROTECTION

ISAIAH 43:1–4, 10–12

King James Version

BUT now thus saith the LORD that created thee, O Jacob, and he that formed thee, O Israel, Fear not: for I have redeemed thee, I have called thee by thy name; thou art mine.

2 When thou passest through the waters, I will be with thee; and through the rivers, they shall not overflow thee: when thou walkest through the fire, thou shalt not be burned; neither shall the flame kindle upon thee.

3 For I am the LORD thy God, the Holy One of Israel, thy Saviour: I gave Egypt for thy ransom, Ethiopia and Seba for thee.

4 Since thou wast precious in my sight, thou hast been honourable, and I have loved thee: therefore will I give men for thee, and people for thy life.

• • • • • •

10 Ye are my witnesses, saith the LORD, and my servant whom I have chosen: that ye may know and believe me, and understand that I am he: before me there was no God formed, neither shall there be after me.

11 I, even I, am the LORD; and beside me there is no saviour.

12 I have declared, and have saved, and I have shewed, when there was no strange god among you: therefore ye are my witnesses, saith the LORD, that I am God.

New Revised Standard Version

BUT now thus says the LORD, he who created you, O Jacob, he who formed you, O Israel: Do not fear, for I have redeemed you; I have called you by name, you are mine.

2 When you pass through the waters, I will be with you; and through the rivers, they shall not overwhelm you; when you walk through fire you shall not be burned, and the flame shall not consume you.

3 For I am the LORD your God, the Holy One of Israel, your Savior. I give Egypt as your ransom, Ethiopia and Seba in exchange for you.

4 Because you are precious in my sight, and honored, and I love you, I give people in return for you, nations in exchange for your life.

• • • • • •

10 You are my witnesses, says the LORD, and my servant whom I have chosen, so that you may know and believe me and understand that I am he. Before me no god was formed, nor shall there be any after me.

11 I, I am the LORD, and besides me there is no savior.

12 I declared and saved and proclaimed, when there was no strange god among you; and you are my witnesses, says the LORD.

MAIN THOUGHT: But now thus saith the LORD that created thee, O Jacob, and he that formed thee, O Israel, Fear not: for I have redeemed thee, I have called thee by thy name; thou art mine. (Isaiah 43:1, KJV)

LESSON SETTING
Time: 550 BC
Place: Babylon

LESSON OUTLINE

I. **A New Day and A Different Time**
(Isaiah 43:1–2)
II. **Redemption's Work**
(Isaiah 43:3–4)
III. **God's Presence Among God's People**
(Isaiah 43:10–12)

UNIFYING PRINCIPLE

People struggle through challenges and trouble. How do we have hope in spite of life's difficulties? Isaiah reminds us that even when circumstances seem hopeless, God offers help and hope.

INTRODUCTION

Most biblical scholars believe that the Book of Isaiah was written by three distinctively different authors. Isaiah 1–39 was written by the prophet Isaiah who once served as a priest during the reign of Uzziah. Isaiah 40–55 was written by the Deutero–Isaiah who writes during the Babylon exile period. A third prophet writes Isaiah 56–66 and very little is known about him. Today's lesson is attributed to Deutero–Isaiah whose speech is informed by several critical facts. First, he comes to light at a time of exile when the people living in exile could make no sacrifices as a part of their worship ritual, thus worship was highly dependent upon an oral element of worship. Second, he was one with the people in believing that the downfall of the nation was the result of divine judgment and all that remained for the survivors was to acknowledge the justice of the sentence

(Westermann, 1969 p. 7). Third, he is probably a product of the synagogue movement that began in exile to keep people connected to their faith traditions while in captivity. Deutero–Isaiah pivots from a word of judgment to a word of hope. It is the hope that Yahweh offers even while persons are in bondage and the community is called to focus upon the hope. The elements of hope include the presence of God in life's difficult moments, the peace of God to grant security in uncertainty, and the promise of God for coming deliverance. Isaiah 43 encompasses all of the dimensions of hope God offers to people living in exile. The presence of hope eliminates fear and moves the community to a newfound trust in the power of God. Deutero–Isaiah's message is a message of salvation that causes the community to interpret their present moment as one filled with possibilities because God is in their midst.

EXPOSITION

I. A NEW DAY AND A DIFFERENT TIME
(ISAIAH 43:1–2)

The prophet begins his oracle with the declaration of a new day and a different time. The community is to no longer focus solely on the condition of exile but see the ways that God's presence and power can make a difference. They are now invited to apply discernment to their condition that can see the hand of God at work among them. The phase is both personal and communal. The words of the prophet are meant for the entire nation living in exile, but they are heard with the power of personal appeal. The prophet was obliged to address individuals and they had to be won to accept his message (Westermann, 1967 p. 116). The prophet connects the new day that God is creating during exile to God's past acts on Israel's behalf. The implied witness that the prophet has in mind is the nation. They are to reference their deliverance from Egyptian bondage. When God delivered Israel from Egypt he did so at a time when Israel was in crisis and had no expectation of change in their condition. However, God raised up a deliverer and leader in Moses that not only led them out of bondage but helped to give birth to a nation formed upon the laws of God and the witness of God's faithfulness to them. God chose Israel as the nation He would claim as His own. The new day that God brings into bearing does not come without struggle. There were moments such as the Red Sea crossing, wilderness wandering, and even a time of exile, but God has promised to be with the nation and sustain them and keep them no matter what comes their way. The redemption of the nation is never in question because God is its redeemer. Thus, there is no reason to fear because God has committed Himself to be with the nation He has chosen. The prophet's words of national salvation are spoken in ways that individuals in the community may be able to see how they may benefit from what God is doing because they are a part of the community. The sustaining power of God is not found in isolation but through connection to a larger community that bears witness to God's work within the community. Whenever we can turn our focus away from our condition alone and look to discern the witness of God among us, we are in position to experience a new day and different time.

Verse 1 points to God's creating work when He formed Israel. He took them from a group of disconnected tribes to a full nation with an identity. As a part of His work of creation, He gave them a name, His own name. In this sense, they belonged to Him as a possession but much more than a possession of utility but one of precious value. As God's chosen people there was a work prepared for them. God's work in forming Israel references His work in the creation of the world. God as the only God should not have been in question from Israel's perspective. They had a first-row seat to witness all that He had done. Who God was to Israel was without question as the One who formed and called them into being. It was His calling, liberation, and provision that enabled their existence.

As His redeemed, they had been bought by God's own ransom. Their redemption is not as much a reference to deliverance from the yoke of sin but the price that God paid to bring them out of the bondage of Egyptian slavery and possibly the exile of Babylon. In God's redemption is the formation of the nation. In this way, redemption is about identity, as it demonstrates that they belong to God. Redemption in the ancient world was a familiar concept as debt slavery was not uncommon. After a person was enslaved due to a debt, the only way for them to be released was for the debt to be paid or for them to be redeemed. Essentially to be redeemed therefore is to have someone pay a debt on behalf of another and for that person, then to be released from the bondage and obligation of that debt. God paid the debt for Israel to be set free from every form of bondage that it had ever encountered.

Israel had passed through many waters and fires through the years. Most biblical interpreters believe that the waters and fire that are referred to in verse 2 is the hard time of exile and return to the homeland. God promises Israel that even as they would face some difficult moments, they would survive. It is in this that we might not reference God's protection, but rather His ability to grant them enough strength to endure hardship. Not only would God grant them passage through the worst they would encounter, but they would emerge as those who had a better understanding of God and His might. It is easy to shout and sing about God's ability to redeem if you've never been tossed aside and needed actual redemption. They would pass through the waters but would not drown, they would learn how to swim. They would be singed by the fire but not burned to a crisp, they would learn to wet some rags to protect their skin. It would not be easy, but God would see them through, and they would emerge better. Therefore James 1:2 tells us, "My brothers and sisters, whenever you face trials of any kind, consider it nothing but joy..." They and we can be joyful because God has guaranteed that we'd make it through and come out better equipped than before.

II. REDEMPTION'S WORK
(ISAIAH 43:3–4)

Redemption's work in Israel begins with God's selection of Israel to be the nation He chose as His own. The prophet's point is that there is nothing that can happen to the nation that will change God's selection of Israel as His own. God in His sovereignty decided that He would favor poor and marginalized people without resources or military. God's selection means the nation has continued access to the power of God. Thus, God may use His power at any moment to change the condition of exile to liberation. God uses His power to bring liberation by working through the political and military conditions of the times. Foreign nations may be called into service by God to assist in Israel's liberation from bondage. Cyrus becomes one of the foreign kings that God will use to help rebuild Israel after exile. God's work of redemption may take on many forms: sometimes using foreign nations to assist and sometimes using people that call the community to repentance and hope. The central theme that the prophet wants to get across to the community is how special they are in God's eyes. They are not to allow their condition of exile to shape their view of their worth and dignity.

God loves them and has chosen them as His own people. They are precious to Him. What comes across in the prophet's words is what gives rise to understanding covenant faithfulness. God will not forget His promise to Abraham, nor will He forget His promise to David. Because Israel is His chosen, He will redeem them. God will pay the price to ensure that the nation is restored to its proper glory.

III. GOD'S PRESENCE AMONG GOD'S PEOPLE
(ISAIAH 43:10–12

God affirms His presence among His people by informing the people they are witnesses to His power and presence. This is a call to remember and reflect upon the ways that God has demonstrated His presence and power in the past. The primary point of reference for this national remembrance is deliverance from Egyptian bondage. The most critical component in the deliverance from Egypt was the Red Sea crossing. There was no other power or any other god that was able to do what God did for Israel when their enemies were behind them, and the Red Sea was in front of them. Israel had nowhere to turn and no army to fight for them, but God delivered them and destroyed their enemies. All of God's past actions on behalf of the Israelites help to create a national memory that could be called upon to see the ways that God has always been present among His people.

In as much as they had the memory of Egyptian deliverance, there were many events that they could reference. As God's witnesses, they were called upon to testify only to that which they knew to be true. As His witnesses, they were being called forth to a metaphorical trial in which they would help to do as Jeremiah says, "boast in the Lord." (9:24) They were to look over their personal and collective history and reflect on the various mighty acts that He had performed. Beyond their deliverance from Egyptian bondage, as a people, there are various instances for which they had seen God act in mighty power. The act of witnessing is also an act of service. They are to witness because they are servants of the Most High God.

Interestingly, their status as witnesses is intertwined with the call to service. This highlights the fact that witnessing is not done to the benefit of the one who testifies, rather it is helpful only to the ones who receive the testimony. It is in giving that testimony that service is rendered as those who receive the truth are elucidated. Both those who receive the testimony and the one who is positively testified about are served in and through the act of witnessing. One is shown in a positive light and the other receives truthful information that can be helpful in being whom they are supposed to be in God. The witness that they are called to participate in is no different from that which the apostle says when he writes, "You yourselves are our letter, written on our hearts, to be known and read by all; and you show that you are a letter of Christ, prepared by us, written not with ink but with the Spirit of the living God, not on tablets of stone but on tablets of human hearts" (2 Corinthians 3:2).

The prophet also affirms there are no rival gods that compare to what Yahweh has done for Israel. Living in exile, Israel was exposed to the idol gods of their captors, but the prophet wants them to know that these gods are powerless. The God of Israel who chose the nation as the object of His favor and delivered them out of bondage has no rival gods. There is no god like Israel's God. The human-made gods and idols that surrounded Israel were worshiped by those that believed the gods had to be pleased to keep punishment away. The God that Israel worshiped and served was a God that chose the nation, not because they pleased Him, but because He loved them. Out of God's love for Israel, He promised to be present among the people and would use the people to be a light to the nations of the world. Even in exile, Israel is not to forget what God has done for them. Furthermore, Israel is to continue to be witnesses to who God is and the ways He is present among the people in exile.

It is the presence of God that provides the hope for a future that will be brighter than the current moment.

THE LESSON APPLIED

Personal and national memory about God's actions on behalf of an individual or a nation can serve as a means of hope and inspiration in times of difficulty. Memory provides a historical reference point that recalls when the change in condition or circumstances occurred and the ways God made the change possible. The prophet's use of language that evoked memory changes the community narrative from desperation to hope. Exile may be a part of the story, but it is not the whole story. God is able to work on behalf of the community to bring deliverance even in the midst of exile. Memory also plays the key role in maintaining religious practices when rituals are not possible. At a time when the community is dependent upon an oral tradition used by the prophets to communicate faith, the memory of God's past acts and memory of the prophet's word keep the flame of hope alive. Whenever we remember the faithfulness of God, we are empowered to face whatever is before us with courage and conviction that the Lord will make a way somehow.

LET'S TALK ABOUT IT

Why did God choose Israel and no other nation?

A bedrock belief in the Christian tradition is the sovereignty of God and God's ability to choose whom He wills for His purposes. The lesson today makes clear that Israel is God's choice of the nation that He would claim as His own and grant His favor upon. Because Israel is a nation that is precious in the eyes of God, He has used the events of history to demonstrate His faithfulness to Israel. Whereas Israel may experience setbacks and difficulties over the years, God would continue to show Himself faithful to the nation He had chosen as His own. Much of what informs American foreign policy in the middle east is connected to the belief that Israel holds a special place with God. However, holding a special place with God does not mean that Israel should be able to restrict the property rights of others and limit the opportunities of those within its borders that are different. Being a light to the nations of the world means in part living out God's vision of shalom peace built upon a just society. It is understanding that the land on which Israel sits has been and will always be contested. Those who are not Israeli have always be there too.

GOD PROMISES TO GUIDE OUR WAY

ADULT TOPIC:	BACKGROUND SCRIPTURE:
NOT BY OUR OWN DEVICES	ISAIAH 48:1–22

ISAIAH 48:3–8, 17

King James Version

I HAVE declared the former things from the beginning; and they went forth out of my mouth, and I shewed them; I did them suddenly, and they came to pass.

4 Because I knew that thou art obstinate, and thy neck is an iron sinew, and thy brow brass;

5 I have even from the beginning declared it to thee; before it came to pass I shewed it thee: lest thou shouldest say, Mine idol hath done them, and my graven image, and my molten image, hath commanded them.

6 Thou hast heard, see all this; and will not ye declare it? I have shewed thee new things from this time, even hidden things, and thou didst not know them.

7 They are created now, and not from the beginning; even before the day when thou heardest them not; lest thou shouldest say, Behold, I knew them.

8 Yea, thou heardest not; yea, thou knewest not; yea, from that time that thine ear was not opened: for I knew that thou wouldest deal very treacherously, and wast called a transgressor from the womb.

• • • • • •

17 Thus saith the LORD, thy Redeemer, the Holy One of Israel; I am the LORD thy God which teacheth thee to profit, which leadeth thee by the way that thou shouldest go.

New Revised Standard Version

THE former things I declared long ago, they went out from my mouth and I made them known; then suddenly I did them and they came to pass.

4 Because I know that you are obstinate, and your neck is an iron sinew and your forehead brass,

5 I declared them to you from long ago, before they came to pass I announced them to you, so that you would not say, "My idol did them, my carved image and my cast image commanded them."

6 You have heard; now see all this; and will you not declare it? From this time forward I make you hear new things, hidden things that you have not known.

7 They are created now, not long ago; before today you have never heard of them, so that you could not say, "I already knew them."

8 You have never heard, you have never known, from of old your ear has not been opened. For I knew that you would deal very treacherously, and that from birth you were called a rebel.

• • • • • •

17 Thus says the LORD, your Redeemer, the Holy One of Israel: I am the LORD your God, who teaches you for your own good, who leads you in the way you should go.

MAIN THOUGHT: Thus saith the LORD, thy Redeemer, the Holy One of Israel; I am the LORD thy God which teacheth thee to profit, which leadeth thee by the way that thou shouldest go. (Isaiah 48:17, KJV)

UNIFYING PRINCIPLE

People want to know what the future holds. Can they figure it out on their own? Isaiah tells us that God alone knows the future and revealed it to the Israelites despite their obstinance and stubbornness.

INTRODUCTION

Isaiah 48:1–ff summarizes the section of the book that concludes with chapter 48. The chapter emphasizes God's actions in the affairs of human history and prepares the stage for Cyrus, the king God will use to overthrow Babylon. Whereas Israel may be guilty of idolatry and oppression that led to God's judgment, God will also judge the nation that carried His chosen away in exile. The prophet makes clear in his pronouncement that deliverance comes to the nation, not because of some foreign source like idols or kingdoms, deliverance will come because God has moved on behalf of Israel. God's commitment to Israel is such that not even their continued rebellion will stand in the way of God bringing redemption to His own. For the sake of His own name, God will keep His promises. God will bring deliverance to a nation prone to rebellion. God's willingness to continue to show kindness to Israel gives us a window into the grace of God and how grace is never dependent upon our actions but on God's compassion toward us. In this way, grace is always God-directed and based on His bottomless pit of love.

EXPOSITION

I. GIVING PROPER CREDIT (ISAIAH 48:3–5)

In this section, the prophet of comfort becomes a prophet of confirmation. These words are probably spoken in a synagogue setting and layout the basic problem with Israel, its willingness to discard the grace that God has poured out. Israel is prone to rebellion and sin no matter how gracious God has been. To make matters worse when deliverance comes there are those that would give credit for their deliverance to some other source than God. The willingness to attribute the work of God to idols further highlights the problem of sin. Given all that God had done for Israel in its history, it should have been enough for them to recognize the hand of God moving in their lives. Time and time again God had used events and history to work for the nation's good. The failure to discern leads to the acceptance of false realities that would give credit to the wrong thing or the wrong person. Instead of God becoming frustrated with the nation's response, He continues to make new expressions of grace possible. The prophet's words thus become a celebration of grace more than a call to repentance.

One might expect repentance to be the focus when a nation has turned from God, but the prophet points to how God's grace is still at work among His people. In showing the people the grace of God in the light of their sin, He provides an effective way to produce godly sorrow.

The grace of God can show us the heart of God, and when we see that God's heart is for us it can lead us to repentance. It is God who receives the credit for the nation's deliverance, and it is God who receives the credit for a nation's repentance.

God's new work is an erasure of all those things of the past. Inasmuch as Israel has been punished for her sins against Yahweh, they are now in the process of being renewed. The call to forget the things of the past in many ways is related to the words of the Psalmist who writes, "as far as the east is from the west, so far he removes our transgressions from us." (Psalm 103:12) Israel has sinned but God's recompense has been satisfied and thus a new era is about to begin. At this juncture they are to forget the pain and heartache of Babylon, exile is no longer but they will once again inhabit the land that the Lord promised their ancestors.

Verse 3 is an invocation of the start of the canon, as Genesis opens by saying, "In the beginning." The kind of invoking of a biblical precedent is to be a reminder of God's creative power and His ability to do away with those things that have previously existed. Not unlike God's work in the beginning where the "Spirit of God hovered over the face of the deep" taming the chaos of the waters and other materials from which He formed the world, He now is using the chaos of Israel's exile to re-form His people and re-create His nation. This moment is a kind of "ground zero" for the Israelites, particularly given the fact that many of those who were going to be returning to the Holy Land had never been there before. For those who had been born in Babylon and elsewhere, indeed God was doing a new thing that they had never seen before. They were going to go to a place that they had never seen before. In this way, this generation of Israelites was like the generation that marched into the Promised Land under Joshua's direction. In both instances, God was doing a new work and bringing His people to a new place in purpose.

II. NEW THINGS (ISAIAH 48:6–8)

The prophet makes a bold declaration in the new thing that God is about to do, God will overthrow Babylon and use a foreign king to do so. The prophecy of Babylon's overthrow comes before the actual events. However, knowledge of the coming of events was to inspire those living in exile to a life of faithfulness to God. Moreover, the prophecy was given so that Israel could bear witness. Witness bearing to God's activity in the life of community was critical to maintaining commitment to the distinct practices of Judaism. God does not always tell the nation what He will do in the affairs of the world but on the occasions when He does tell the nation through the prophets, they are to bear witness. The fact that God at times reveals His plans for humanity means that Israel is to live in trust and her dependence upon the events that God has orchestrated for her good. These events could not be known in advance except for God's intervention to share with them. Bearing witness in exile is seen as new responsibility. Israel is called to reorder their thinking about deliverance to where it is not restricted to immediate relief but how God might use them and the moment to bring glory to Himself and work for the good of the nation. Bearing witness in exile creates what Walter Brueggemann calls fresh, imaginative theological work, recovering the old theological traditions and recasting them in terms appropriate to the new situation of faith in an alien culture (Brueggemann, 1997 p. 116). This is the kind of theology Joseph used with his brothers when they were reunited in Egypt after Joseph had become prime minister. Joseph tells his brothers that they may have meant what they did to him for evil, but God meant it for good. Through their actions, God was sending him ahead of them so in the right moment Joseph might be the source for deliverance for a family caught in the grips of a famine. Bearing witness in exile seeks to discover the ways that God is present and how His presence is a sign of His continued faithfulness.

It is in these verses that God's creative ability is invoked. These verses demonstrate God's ability to create from nothing and on the spot. In this, God's awesome power is invoked as that which has no equal. Verses 6 and 7 are very clear that the action that is about to take place has not been previously done or even conceived. It is in this way that it is clear that the happenings that are about to take place in human affairs are not human derived. Whereas, the Persians will invade the Babylonians and set the Israelites free, the idea did not begin in Cyrus' mind. God is omnipotent and uses the events of history to make His purposes come to pass.

Some scholars believe this to be a revolutionary idea in that it represents a radical monotheism that found its genesis in this Israelite era. The thought is that during the period of exile there was a shift in their understanding of Yahweh. He was previously understood to be a national deity, but He is now known to be much more. This is a shift because prior to this period foreign gods were not necessarily thought of as idols but simply as foreign gods. Now that they have witnessed Yahweh's ability and strength beyond their own borders, they should know He is God and all others are idols. At this juncture all of their questions of Yahweh's character and ability should have been answered.

Nonetheless, Israel is rebuked as those who from the very beginning had been rebellious against God and their covenant with Him. For Israel to be called a rebel is an acknowledgment of their own participation in their estrangement. Verse 8 points to the fact that there has not been a time in which Israel has been completely loyal to their God. Their rebellious nature can be recalled at the beginning of the nation as the people complained against Moses and God in the wilderness. (Exodus 16:3) As rebels, they would not incline their ears to the word of the Lord that was coming by way of the prophet.

III. THE GOD THAT GUIDES (ISAIAH 48:17)

The prophet proclaims in this passage the historical relationship of God with Israel. He begins his description of the relationship as the God who redeems. At the forefront of Israel's understanding of God is that God is a redeemer. The conception of God as a redeemer has its roots in the nation's formation and deliverance from Egyptian bondage. Repeatedly God refers to Himself and the nation refers to Him as the One that delivered from Egypt. The idea of God as a redeemer played a large role in keeping the hopes of those living in exile alive of a day of return to their homeland.

Beyond God being a redeemer, the prophet declares the holiness of God. God is the nation's deity, not just the deity of individuals, He is the God of Israel. God has chosen a nation on the earth and its people to be those whom He would allow His favor to reside. Israel has not earned God's favor; God's favor had been granted to them out of His own holiness. God decided to be the Holy One of Israel.

Inasmuch as God is with Israel as the Holy One, this title indicates His otherness. The word "holy" communicates the separation and sacredness of something over and against that which is common. Isaiah has a very high theology in that this concept of God is of One who is "high and lifted up, whose train of glory filled the temple" (6:1). Above all else, God is separate from that which He created, other passages in Isaiah also point to Yahweh's transcendence. For instance, consider, "It is he who sits above the circle of the earth, and its inhabitants are like grasshoppers; who stretches out the heavens like a curtain, and spreads them like a tent to live in" (40:22). As the Holy One of Israel, Yahweh is to be respected as transcendent and sacred even above Israel, His chosen people. The title is a reminder that the people and their God are not the same, they are separate, even in relationship.

As the Holy One of Israel and the Lord their God, the prophet is placing emphasis on the relational aspect of God to the people. Because of the relationship that the people have with God, God leads them. The ways that prove God's guidance is seen as He teaches for their profit/good. Israel's God is not the type of deity that teaches to punish only, but He teaches to aid and help and to move the people forward toward His goal for them. In exile, God has not stopped guiding the nation. The words of Deutero–Isaiah assures a community living in exile that God is still with them, and God is still guiding them. Trust in God is the central claim of this passage, even in moments when we do not fully understand how God is leading and where God is leading. In time, we will discover the ways the hand of God has been with us because we serve a God that leads His children.

God's teaching is not always that which makes His children feel the best, nonetheless, His teaching does benefit us. His teaching undoubtedly has its root in the Torah, which is most often thought of as the law, but its translation is closer to that of "teaching". By considering this verse in light of the Torah, we might be able to gain a closer understanding of that which Yahweh actually teaches His people. As Isaiah writes this passage, this teaching is not necessarily novel but that which finds its basis in the Scriptures of Israel. This is why Yahweh can rightly call the people obstinate in verse 4. They are an obstinate people because that which He teaches in the present moment has already been taught so that even as He prepares them for a new thing, His new thing is to be trusted because of the old things that have already been done and taught.

THE LESSON APPLIED

There may be nothing more difficult than finding the strength to bear witness to God in times of difficulty. It is easy to feel overwhelmed and moved to a position of complaint or compliance. The prophet stirs the community to rise above their condition and see the way God might use exile to draw the community closer in their religious commitment. To bear witness in moments of difficulty requires a faith rooted in the belief of the goodness of God even when times are not good. The lesson also reveals that such a trust in God does not go without reward. When we are willing to stand up and do what God expects of us as His witnesses God sometimes responds with unexpected blessings. The prophet is given a view to the future where deliverance will surely come. Babylon will fall to a foreign king that will provide the resources and the people for Israel to return to their homeland and rebuild it. Bearing witness to God is every believer's responsibility, no matter the times we live.

LET'S TALK ABOUT IT

Do we think of the ways that God may be using current events today to move the world in the direction that is consistent with His will? How are believers to interpret these events?

The prophet invites the community to see the ways the hand of God is at work in human affairs moving things in the direction that God desires for the good of His people. The Scripture tells us "all things work together for good for them that love the Lord and have been called according to his purpose" (Romans 8:28). Believers need discernment and wisdom to respond in ways that reflect our commitment to bear witness to God. God is always at work in the world but we do not always see the work as His. When we look at the events of the world through a theological lens, it will lead us to ask a different set of questions than those raised by journalists. A global pandemic has taught us as a nation that there are national limits. The wealth and power of the nation could not hold back the spread of a virus that has claimed more than one million lives in the United States of America alone. Whereas we applaud the work of researchers in their ability to develop a vaccine in record time, the national political divide continues to contribute to the unnecessary loss of life. We may want to take the position of Abraham Lincoln who was reported to have said that he did not know what side God was on in the great war; he only hoped to be on God's side.

HOME DAILY DEVOTIONAL READINGS
JANUARY 16–22, 2023

MONDAY	TUESDAY	WEDNESDAY	THURSDAY	FRIDAY	SATURDAY	SUNDAY
Passing from Death to Life	You Are Light in the Lord	Christ Will Shine upon You	God's Word Lights My Path	Your Light Has Come	Jesus the Light of the World	Joy in Obeying God
1 John 3:14–24	Ephesians 5:1–10	Ephesians 5:11–20	Psalm 119:97–112	Isaiah 60:1–8	John 8:12–20	Isaiah 58:1–14

God Promises Light in the Darkness

ADULT TOPIC: LIVING RIGHT OVER EMPTY RITUALS	BACKGROUND SCRIPTURE: ISAIAH 58:1–14

Isaiah 58:6—10

King James Version

IS not this the fast that I have chosen? to loose the bands of wickedness, to undo the heavy burdens, and to let the oppressed go free, and that ye break every yoke?

7 Is it not to deal thy bread to the hungry, and that thou bring the poor that are cast out to thy house? when thou seest the naked, that thou cover him; and that thou hide not thyself from thine own flesh?

8 Then shall thy light break forth as the morning, and thine health shall spring forth speedily: and thy righteousness shall go before thee; the glory of the LORD shall be thy reward.

9 Then shalt thou call, and the LORD shall answer; thou shalt cry, and he shall say, Here I am. If thou take away from the midst of thee the yoke, the putting forth of the finger, and speaking vanity;

10 And if thou draw out thy soul to the hungry, and satisfy the afflicted soul; then shall thy light rise in obscurity, and thy darkness be as the noon day.

New Revised Standard Version

IS not this the fast that I choose: to loose the bonds of injustice, to undo the thongs of the yoke, to let the oppressed go free, and to break every yoke?

7 Is it not to share your bread with the hungry, and bring the homeless poor into your house; when you see the naked, to cover them, and not to hide yourself from your own kin?

8 Then your light shall break forth like the dawn, and your healing shall spring up quickly; your vindicator shall go before you, the glory of the LORD shall be your rear guard.

9 Then you shall call, and the LORD will answer; you shall cry for help, and he will say, Here I am. If you remove the yoke from among you, the pointing of the finger, the speaking of evil,

10 if you offer your food to the hungry and satisfy the needs of the afflicted, then your light shall rise in the darkness and your gloom be like the noonday.

LESSON SETTING

Time: 530 BC

Place: Jerusalem

LESSON OUTLINE

I. **The Social Responsibility of Faith**
(Isaiah 58:6–7)

II. **The Meaning of Peace**
(Isaiah 58:8–9)

III. **The Approval of God**
(Isaiah 58:10)

UNIFYING PRINCIPLE

People want to manipulate tradition or customs for their own selfish ends. How can we avoid empty ritual and tradition? Isaiah tells us that God cares more about a person's sincere prayer than performing empty rites.

MAIN THOUGHT: And if thou draw out thy soul to the hungry, and satisfy the afflicted soul; then shall thy light rise in obscurity, and thy darkness be as the noon day (Isaiah 58:10, KJV)

INTRODUCTION

This passage is attributed to the third writer of Isaiah commonly referred to as Trito–Isaiah. The prophet writes during the time of the reign of Cyrus after the fall of Babylon in 6th century BC. In the first year of his reign, Cyrus allows some of the Jews living in exile to return to Jerusalem. Along with their return to their homeland, Cyrus returns the religious vessel and symbols that had been taken from the temple during the war with Babylon. The exiles provided the resources and people necessary to begin the rebuilding of Jerusalem, and the first building project is to rebuild the temple. The construction of the temple allows Israel to return to a centralized form of worship as well to institute the old rituals that were not possible in exile, such as sacrifice. The first part of the temple that was repaired was the altar. The establishment of ritual worship at the temple did not prevent those who had returned from exile from taking advantages of the less fortunate. It appears not everyone living in exile returned under the same economic condition. There were probably those who had gained Cyrus' favor as they prepared for the return home and may have been able to personally profit from the resources Cyrus made available to rebuild the city and the temple. From their advantaged position these individuals begin to take further advantage of those who had less. The prophet informs the community that God is not interested in rituals without righteousness. Trito–Isaiah challenges the people to live up to God's expectation of a community built upon justice and righteousness. To trust in ritual without doing what was right in the eyes of God could lead to another judgment. Trito–Isaiah agrees with the prophet Micah that the Lord does not desire fasting but kindness, justice, and mercy.

EXPOSITION

I. THE SOCIAL RESPONSIBILITY OF FAITH (ISAIAH 58:6–7)

David Pleins in his work, the *The Social Vision of the Hebrew Bible*, states that God has a vision for the community built upon justice and peace most often referred to as Shalom. Where there is no justice there can be no peace. Trito–Isaiah demonstrates a keen awareness of economic and political oppression and its impact of the welfare of the community.

Israel is to be different from the nations of the world and show the world how it is possible to live together in ways where the powerful do not take advantage of the powerless. In God's vision for Israel the powerful are to use their power to protect the weak and to ensure that the weak and those in need benefit from the grace of God manifested in the community of his people. The prophet informs the people that the powerful cannot curry the favor of God through religious ritual if they neglect the duty of their religion to care for the needs of others. Faith has a social responsibility not just a personal responsibility. We live within communities among others, and faith is a lived-out practice that requires the faithful to live out the meaning of faith in their lives in ways that makes the community better. The social responsibility of faith involves ethics. Ethics provides boundaries that the community is to live within to ensure a set of community values that are consistent with God's desires. The

Ten Commandments and the law codes were examples of ethics. The ethical consideration that the prophet raises is the treatment of the poor. Israel is to share its resources (food, clothing and shelter). Israel is not to ignore the needs of the poor they are aware of by hiding themselves from them. The prophet presses the point of responsibility even more by calling those in need their own flesh. The poor are not to be viewed as outsiders or less than, but they too are the people of God, whom God has provided a nation, a faith, and rituals to worship and serve Him. When the nation honors the tradition of the faith with its demand of social responsibility then the nation can experience the blessings of God that are not limited to a select few but are provided for all.

As stated earlier, the poor are not just to be considered the kin of the powerful but through actual lineage are a part of Israel. They are not just to be considered but are the actual kinsfolk of the elite. Israel as a nation was built upon the notion of kinship ties, as the nation was subdivided into various groups of relationalities. There were varying numbers of tribes, who took there names from eponymous ancestors. Furthermore, tribes were broken down into clans, and clans into families, and families into households. The basic premise of the nation was not the individual, or subject, like it is for our modern nations. From that standpoint, each one is a brother or a sister and thus to deny anyone is to deny the benefit of family. It is important to note that for the ancients this was their form of a security net. In a world in which there was no social security the best that a society could do was to depend on familial relations to provide for those who otherwise would be destitute. Consider Deuteronomy 15:4–5 which states the following, "There will, however, be no one in need among you, because the Lord is sure to bless you in the land that the Lord your God is giving you as a possession to occupy, if only you will obey the Lord your God by diligently observing this entire commandment that I command you today." Clearly in this instance, the command to care for the poor is tied to a greater sense of social responsibility. God's community is better when all of His people have what they need to sustain and flourish in life. To remain in proper covenant with God, there were certain ethical demands that the law placed upon the Israelites that had to be followed.

II. THE MEANING OF PEACE (ISAIAH 58:8–9)

Shalom, the peace that God gives a community, is always conditional and the condition is based upon acts of justice. If Israel will do its part in treating the poor fairly and providing for their needs as opposed to oppressing them, then God will respond with a blessing for the nation that will give it peace. The way that Israel will experience the blessings of God begins with the vividness of God's presence among the nation. If Israel wants to be able to see God's presence among the people, it will have to include a commitment to justice in its treatment of the poor. God's presence is defined as the light that will then break forward. Light in the Hebrew understanding in reference to God had multiple meanings. Light could provide direction. In this case, it would be the direction that the nation needed to complete the work of rebuilding both the city of Jerusalem and the temple. Israel would experience multiple rebuilding efforts with mixed results. The most common problem hindering the rebuilding effort was the lack of direction. Light was also associated with righteousness or the ability to follow the will of God. If Israel would treat the poor in the ways God expected a nation to do that carried His name, He would provide the light of righteousness for the nation to walk. Light also represented a new beginning. The return home of the exiles was a new beginning. However, to make the new beginning successful, Israel would need the light of God. God's light would remind the nation who they are and what God expected of them. Those returning from exile were not to bring the oppression from exile with them to their homeland. Israel was to be different, but to be different they would need the light. The healing that the prophet mentions involves the restoration of the city and the temple through the rebuilding project that the community was engaged. The completion of the rebuilding was dependent upon the treatment of the poor and those without.

God is not interested in seeing a temple or a city rebuilt that denies justice and oppresses the poor. The city and temple that bears God's name are to reflect the values and vision of its Maker. The glory of the Lord is a reference to the temple's dedication in the days of Solomon when the glory of the Lord filled the temple. If Israel will give attention to the social responsibility of the faith, then the glory of the Lord will not just fill the temple, the glory of the Lord will be their protector. Peace is witnessed in the presence and power of God in a city and a temple that honors God and allows grace to be experienced by all.

Verse 9 points to covenantal language as it is conditional. Its language revisits the conditions of the Mosaic covenant as spelled out in the Torah. Consider Deuteronomy 15:7–11, "If there is among you anyone in need, a member of your community in any of your towns within the land that the Lord your God is giving you, do not be hard-hearted or tight-fisted toward your needy neighbor. You should rather open your hand, willingly lending enough to meet the need, whatever it may be. Be careful that you do not entertain a mean thought, thinking, 'The seventh year, the year of remission, is near,' and therefore view your needy neighbor with hostility and give nothing; your neighbor might cry to the Lord against you, and you would incur guilt. Give liberally and be ungrudging when you do so, for on this account the Lord your God will bless you in all your work and in all that you undertake. Since there will never cease to be some in need on the earth, I therefore command you, 'Open your hand to the poor and needy neighbor in your land.'"

As a part of the second law, this excerpt is but one example of the covenantal relationship that the Israelites were to have with one another that in turn placed them in proper relationship with God. Their blessing was directly tied to righteous relationships within the larger community.

This should serve as an example of that which the Lord requires of His people in all times and ages. Whereas, there are those among us who are favored in regards to their personal material resources, those resources are not for the exclusive blessings of the recipients. Rather, those blessings are to be for the benefit of all. In a very real sense a rising tide lifts all boats. As God causes the tide to rise for some, it was their/our job to make sure all boats are lifted just a little higher.

III. THE APPROVAL OF GOD (ISAIAH 58:10)

The prophet informs the community how God's approval is found. Ritual worship alone will not gain God's approval. There must be a commitment to addressing the needs of the poor. God places His interest in the poor to show that the poor are not without someone who will champion their cause. The poor may not have access to the powerful, but God does, and God uses the prophet to call those in power into account. Those in power are called to pour themselves out for the hungry. The resources of the powerful are not to be viewed as their private position but they are to be used to help meet the needs of others. The powerful are told to pour out themselves for the hungry. Those who have returned from exile are expected to remember a time during exile when they were in need and God poured out to them. Whereas the rise of Cyrus as king may have improved their economic condition, had left them better than others, they should not forget what it means to be hungry for they too were once hungry. Whenever we remember what God has done for us it should inspire us to show the grace we have received to others. Beyond pouring out to the hungry, the powerful of God's kingdom are to satisfy the desires of the afflicted. There is no greater desire among the afflicted than the desire for justice. The afflicted are those most often taken advantage of because of their lack of status or standing in the community. The afflicted are marginalized and treated as less than. The community must implore a system of justice where the afflicted can receive their due. As long as injustice reigns within the community, no amount of ritual worship will win God's approval. The prophet again makes a reference to the light that will come when the nation turns away from acts of darkness.

If Israel follows God's way of living then their light will shine brightly. Simply by caring for the most destitute in their midst, the nation that has experienced a lot of darkness by way of exile and oppression will help to demonstrate a different way of being. This in part is what it means for them to be a holy people, that is, those who are set apart for God's own purposes. The theme of light in the 58th chapter figures prominently over the next two chapters. Consider Isaiah 60:1–3, "Arise, shine; for your light has come, and the glory of the Lord has risen upon you. For darkness shall cover the earth, and thick darkness the peoples; but the Lord will arise upon you, and his glory will appear over you. Nations shall come to your light, and kings to the brightness of your dawn." The light that Israel would experience was twofold. One, as they returned from the darkness of oppression their light would return as those who experienced freedom and the ability to worship without encumbrances in the land of their ancestors. Two, their light would burn as they lived to demonstrate the ways of the Lord to the world. The brightness of their light was contingent upon covenant faithfulness as they cared for the poor. They were to be a light to the nations.

THE LESSON APPLIED

The prophet takes on a nation that would so easily take advantage of the poor. The exiles return home with a significant amount of wealth as well as their religious symbols. They have been provided what they needed to start to rebuild their community. However, as they started to rebuild the community, they institutionalized the mistreatment of the poor through the lack of access to food as well as uneven justice system that benefited the powerful at the expense of the poor. The prophet informs the nation that God would not approve the worship of those who took advantage of the poor. America often refers to itself as a godly nation. Historians speak of the founding fathers as persons of faith. Prayer is a part of the opening of Congress each day and religion is constantly referred to in some form or another as the basic for some American policy position, both domestically and around the world. However, American treatment of the poor leaves something to be desired. There are more homeless, those without health insurance and in prison than any industrialized nation in the world. Poverty continues to be the leading cause of crime, lack of education and limited opportunity than any other factor.

More and more of the national wealth is concentrated among handful of persons. Yet persons fill churches every week and offer the ritual worship they believe will gain God's approval. The words of the prophet have as much meaning today as it did then. God does not desire ritual worship; God desires compassion and justice.

LET'S TALK ABOUT IT

Sharing what one has with the poor is seen by some as socialism. A member of Congress resisted an effort to provide financial assistance for families through a child tax credit but, the same member voted for the 2017 tax cuts that increase the wealth of the top one percent. Even during a global pandemic, CEO-pay at major corporations continued to grow as benefits and wages were cut for employees through layoffs and automation. There needs to be a recognition that Christian faith has a social responsibility element where God expects us to care for those in need to the best of our ability. We are not to hoard the resources that God makes available, but use them to show God's grace at work in the world through God's people. It is time to call the nation and the Church to live up to the confession of their faith by using resources, influence and everything God has provided to help the poor and to ensure justice for the oppressed. Pure religion calls for us to care for the underprivileged and underserved.

HOME DAILY DEVOTIONAL READINGS
JANUARY 23–29, 2023

MONDAY	TUESDAY	WEDNESDAY	THURSDAY	FRIDAY	SATURDAY	SUNDAY
Christ Has Come in the Flesh	God's Love Revealed among Us	The Testimony in Our Hearts	God Will Go with You	The Lord, Merciful and Gracious	God Is Near Despite Adversity	God Will Pour Out the Spirit
1 John 4:1–8	1 John 4:9–21	1 John 5:10–21	Exodus 33:12–23	Exodus 34:5–17	Joel 1:1–4, 14–20	Joel 2:18–31

GOD PROMISES TO BE PRESENT

ADULT TOPIC: BACKGROUND SCRIPTURE:
PROMISES OF RESTORATION AND GLADNESS   JOEL 1:1–4; 2:18–31

JOEL 2:21–27

King James Version

FEAR not, O land; be glad and rejoice: for the LORD will do great things.

22 Be not afraid, ye beasts of the field: for the pastures of the wilderness do spring, for the tree beareth her fruit, the fig tree and the vine do yield their strength.

23 Be glad then, ye children of Zion, and rejoice in the LORD your God: for he hath given you the former rain moderately, and he will cause to come down for you the rain, the former rain, and the latter rain in the first month.

24 And the floors shall be full of wheat, and the vats shall overflow with wine and oil.

25 And I will restore to you the years that the locust hath eaten, the cankerworm, and the caterpiller, and the palmerworm, my great army which I sent among you.

26 And ye shall eat in plenty, and be satisfied, and praise the name of the LORD your God, that hath dealt wondrously with you: and my people shall never be ashamed.

27 And ye shall know that I am in the midst of Israel, and that I am the LORD your God, and none else: and my people shall never be ashamed.

New Revised Standard Version

DO not fear, O soil; be glad and rejoice, for the LORD has done great things!

22 Do not fear, you animals of the field, for the pastures of the wilderness are green; the tree bears its fruit, the fig tree and vine give their full yield.

23 O children of Zion, be glad and rejoice in the LORD your God; for he has given the early rain for your vindication, he has poured down for you abundant rain, the early and the later rain, as before.

24 The threshing floors shall be full of grain, the vats shall overflow with wine and oil.

25 I will repay you for the years that the swarming locust has eaten, the hopper, the destroyer, and the cutter, my great army, which I sent against you.

26 You shall eat in plenty and be satisfied, and praise the name of the LORD your God, who has dealt wondrously with you. And my people shall never again be put to shame.

27 You shall know that I am in the midst of Israel, and that I, the LORD, am your God and there is no other. And my people shall never again be put to shame.

MAIN THOUGHT: And ye shall know that I am in the midst of Israel, and that I am the LORD your God, and none else: and my people shall never be ashamed. (Joel 2:27, KJV)

LESSON SETTING
>   Time: 5th century BC
>   Place: Judah

LESSON OUTLINE
   I. **Restoration of the Land
      (Joel 2:21–22)**
   II. **Restoration of the People
      (Joel 2:23–25)**
   III. **Restoration of Israel's Faith
      as God's People
      (Joel 2:26–27)**

UNIFYING PRINCIPLE

People have a tendency to mess up the world and their lives. Will the world and human life ever be better than they are? God promises to restore what has been ruined due to human actions and inactions.

INTRODUCTION

Joel is one of the minor prophets and is different from most prophets in that he is considered a cultic prophet. In most cases, the prophets concentrate on social injustices and the link to faith and religion. Joel is a prophet whose ministry takes place within the temple and uses liturgical forms to convey a message that is transmitted through priestly circles. Some scholars refer to Joel's prophecy as classical prophecy that borrows from past prophets because much of the past prophecy has yet to be fulfilled. Joel views some of the past prophecies as those things that are coming to pass in his time but views other parts of past prophecy as those things that are still waiting fulfillment in some future time. At the time of the passage in today's lesson, Judah had recently experienced a locust plague that had taken a toll on the nation's food supply. An agricultural economy dependent upon a fruitful harvest was devastated. The prophet believes the locusts that devoured

the food supply were a result of God's judgment upon a nation that did not live out the social responsibility of their faith in the treatment of the poor and those in need. If Israel will repent and turn to God surely God will answer and restore all that was lost and provide even more. Chapter 2 begins with an announcement statement that points to a cataclysmic moment but concludes with the expressed belief that God would hear their prayer and restore the land and the people. Joel affirms that the God of Israel is a keeper of promises and a restorer of all that have been lost.

EXPOSITION

I. RESTORATION OF THE LAND (JOEL 2:21–22)

The restoration process that Joel envisions God making possible starts with the land. The land had suffered because of Israel's sin and the choices they made as a community. The locust that devoured the land came as a result of God's punishment for the nation's sin to live up to God's vision for the community that would bear His name. The destruction of the land by locusts was widespread and took away not just Israel's primary food supply but the food supply of livestock as well. The loss of pastures meant that much of the livestock would not survive.

In addition to the damage created by the locust, the land also suffered drought from the lack of rain. In every way, the land was paying the price for the nation's sin.

Thus, when God begins His work of restoration, He begins with the land. The land is vital to Israel and the land was one of the primary ways that testify to the blessing of God. Land as the Bible uses it is the symbol that represents the wholeness of joy and well-being characterized by social coherence and personal ease in prosperity, security, and freedom. Land is central if not the central theme of biblical faith (Brueggemann, 1977 pp. 2–3). The announcement of coming restoration for the land is given in typical prophetic announcement fashion, "fear not." Joel is not the first prophet to use the phrase "fear not" to announce God's coming activity. The announcement of "fear not" is to inform the community of an alternative response to the current condition. The community is called to respond in faith before the events of restoration fully take place. A sign of the community's change and turn toward God can be displayed if they are able to let go of fear and trust that God will do as He promised. The longing for things to return to what the community has known as normal may provide the necessary inspiration to believe. The land and the people can rejoice because restoration is on the way. The promise of restoration is stated as the thing that God has made possible. God has made it possible for the pastures to return to their past state, for trees to bear fruit and for vines to yield their harvest. The damage caused by locusts and drought was not irreversible. God can and will restore.

It is important to note that Israel's covenant with God was centered around land. God's promise to Abraham and his descendants focused on their dwelling of the land. Land was a central theme for Israel's ancestors, a place of home and a place of prosperity. "Then the Lord appeared to Abram, and said, "To your offspring, I will give this land" (Genesis 12:7). It is based on this promise that Israel is founded and finds its identity. God's announcement of restoration is ultimately then about covenant faithfulness. God's plan of restoration is about Him keeping His word not only to the current generation but those who proceeded them.

It should not be missed that Joel and the Chronicler are both products of the post-exilic period. Joel is a little bit earlier than Chronicles, but both have a similar set of concerns given their closeness in date. As texts written during the Persian period, they are concerned with Israel's reestablishment in the land that the Lord gave them. As such when reading Chronicles, much of the theology present is anachronistic and offers an explanation for the people's exile, punishment, and return to Palestine. As such, it makes sense that Joel and Chronicles would share in their attention of the practice and establishment of cultic rituals in relation to Israel's land covenant with Yahweh. Second Chronicles 7:14 states, "if my people, who are called by my name, will humble themselves and pray and seek my face and turn from their wicked ways, then I will hear from heaven, and I will forgive their sin and will heal their land." This quote coming from God's appearance to Solomon after the dedication of the first Jerusalem temple indicates the importance of the land in regards to Yahweh's covenant faithfulness. It is through the promise and establishment of the people in the land that they are to know that they are favored by God.

In like manner, Joel's attention to the restoration of the land and its inhabitation relates to Israel's most central story. Israel was formed and created through its deliverance from Egyptian bondage and God's promise to bring them into a new land. "So I have come down to rescue them from the hand of the Egyptians and to bring them up out of that land into a good and spacious land, a land flowing with milk and honey—the home of the Canaanites, Hittites, Amorites, Perizzites, Hivites and Jebusites" (Exodus 3:8). At a time when they were returning to the land after being delivered from the Babylonian captivity, the resonance of their initial story was tantamount to their understanding of what God was doing at the moment. As Ecclesiastes reminds us, "there is nothing new under the sun" and God often works in ways that are familiar to His people, even in new moments. As they were delivered from the exile, they needed a reminder that God has promised the land to them and that He would restore all that had been lost.

Lastly, the reframing of the promise of land was important, given that many of the people who were "returning" to the land were not returning but a generation or two removed from having ever lived in Palestine. As such, being reminded of the covenant through Joel's prophecy was appropriate as they had not experienced God's favor in the form of liberty and land. The promise of the restoration of the land therefore was a reestablishment of the covenant with an entirely new generation of God's people.

II. RESTORATION OF THE PEOPLE (JOEL 2:23–25)

The prophet's announcement of the restoration of the people does not begin with the phrase "fear not" but with "be glad" in verse 23. The people are called upon to rejoice in what God is about to do in their midst. "Be glad" is an invitation to praise and give glory to God. Joel proceeds to give the community the reasons they have for being glad in what God will do. He speaks as if God has already done the things that He shares with the community. Some of what Joel mentions may have already begun, particularly the rain. In this region of the world, there are distinct rainy seasons. The early rain would occur in October and November. The latter rain would happen in March and April. The rains would make planting and harvesting of food possible as well as provide water for pastureland that livestock would need. The rain was a sign of God honoring his covenant relationship with the people. The rain told the people that they would be provided for. Joel indicates that the rain would come in abundance and the rain would be a witness of the community's vindication. There are several things that the rain would make possible that would work for the good of the people. The rain would make the grain harvest plentiful until the threshing floor would be full. Vats that held wine and oil would also overflow. The excess food crop could be stored, used for trade or turned into other items of use that would be of benefit to the people. The surplus that God would make possible would be the proof that God had restored all that had been lost by the locust and the other insects that had harmed the land and created a food crisis for the community. Joel describes God's restoration as the things that God provides in abundance. There is more than what the community needs to meet their need. Restoration is an act of grace that exceeds what sin has marred because grace is always greater in its impact than sin. Grace is what places us in right relationship with God. The restoration of the people is not just a restoration of things but a return of the people to right relationship with God. The work of -restoration removes the shame of loss.

Both the community and the surrounding nations will be able to see the results of restoration in ways where the nation will feel honor and give glory to God for all that He has made possible.

These verses point to the theological understanding that all can be attributed to God's hand. Even the weather is understood to be controlled by God. This contrasts with our understanding that the weather is controlled by invisible natural forces. Even something like the rain is to bring rejoicing and praise of God because it is His doing. The rains make clear God's own plan to prosper His people and make provision for all their needs in excess. Their shame is removed because they are no longer the scorn of their God rather, they are His favored. The rains are a metaphor for their drenching in His love such that He would honor every promise made to them and their ancestors. In this way, it becomes abundantly clear that God's restoration of His people was very explicitly tied to the restoration of their land. Without the land, the people could not be restored because it was the land that was the resource by which God would provide for them.

III. RESTORATION OF ISRAEL'S FAITH AS GOD'S PEOPLE (JOEL 2:26–27)

The work of restoration by God of the land and the people will demonstrate that God has not abandoned Israel. Whereas the sins of the nation may lead to God's displeasure in ways that brings punishment, God has not abandoned the nation that He has chosen as His own. There may have been those within the community that wondered if the locust and the drought and all that was lost was a sign that the nation had completely lost the favor of God. The influence of foreign deities may have made some question whether they should seek help from another source. Joel informs the people that when God does the work of restoration, then the people would know that God is still in their midst and there is no other god that can restore what had been lost. God is still working on behalf of the nation. The witness of God working to restore should rekindle the nation's faith in God. Restoration of Israel's faith in God will move the nation to worship God in ways that fulfill God's intent for them when they return from exile. Israel will now become a nation more committed not just by performing the rituals of temple worship, but more committed to their social responsibility to others because they now know the meaning of being restored. The shame of the past has been taken away by the power of God and Israel looks to the future with hope because their faith in God has been restored.

As God's people, they could expect to be recipients of His faithful favor. Their previous shame was related to their rejection as they underwent judgment. Their faith needed a revival, particularly given that many of them had not witnessed the mighty acts of God in the nation's history. They would now witness the magnanimity and grand power of God as they were brought back to their rightful place.

As it is prophesied that Israel would once again become that which God had purposed, it should serve as an impetus for faith for all who have seen God's ability to restore that of the past. This text is a reminder that despite the struggles and difficulties of a community, God is faithful to His promises of the past, if we will avail ourselves to His will. Israel's faith would grow because they were no longer listening to the stories of the past, but God had made the determination to be in their midst and include them in salvation history at that particular moment. This is a cause for great rejoicing. This is the reason for exceeding gladness. Any time that one is included in God's work in the world, this is reason enough to give Him praise.

THE LESSON APPLIED

There are times when the decisions we make have a negative impact on those around us and the things we are dependent upon. Israel had strayed away from God and as result experienced the judgment of God in the form of locusts and drought. The environment suffered along with the people because of decisions some of the people made. We should never see our actions as those things that only affect us because every action carries consequences or blessings dependent upon what we do. The good news is that when our actions are bad, and we turn to God in repentance God is willing to restore us. God's work of restoration does not just include us. God can restore all the harm we may have created. We serve a God that heals and restores people, nations, and land.

LET'S TALK ABOUT IT

How are we to understand Joel and what happened to his land in the light of our current planet's condition? Is there a role the church should play in the discussion and debate about global warming? What work of restoration can we be engaged that is consistent with our Christian faith?

God's judgment in the lesson was seen by its impact on the environment. The locust and drought led to a famine that eliminated food supply and put people at risk. Environmentalists tell us that global warming is putting our entire planet at risk. The primary contributor to global warming is greenhouse gases from human-made products. The decision by many companies to deny the science of global warming as well the desire to maximize corporate profits at all costs has allowed global warming to continue at a dangerous rate. Our world is now experiencing more violent storms than ever before with increased frequency. Wildfires and drought are more common with lives and homes lost on a regular basis. God's judgment is seen in every which way imaginable as we continue to see the erosion and destruction of that which He has given us as His stewards.

HOME DAILY DEVOTIONAL READINGS
JANUARY 30–FEBRUARY 5, 2023

MONDAY	TUESDAY	WEDNESDAY	THURSDAY	FRIDAY	SATURDAY	SUNDAY
The Last Will Be First	God, Teach and Guide Me	How Majestic Is God's Name!	God Will Build You a House	Who Am I Before God?	God Confounds the Wise	God Chooses the Lowly and Despised
Matthew 20:1, 6–16	Psalm 25:1–15	Psalm 8	2 Samuel 7:1, 4–17	2 Samuel 7:18–29	1 Corinthians 1:18–24	1 Corinthians 1:25–31

NOT MANY ELITE CALLED

ADULT TOPIC:	BACKGROUND SCRIPTURE:
WISDOM AND FOOLISHNESS	1 CORINTHIANS 1:18–31

1 CORINTHIANS 1:18–31

King James Version

FOR the preaching of the cross is to them that perish foolishness; but unto us which are saved it is the power of God.

19 For it is written, I will destroy the wisdom of the wise, and will bring to nothing the understanding of the prudent.

20 Where is the wise? where is the scribe? where is the disputer of this world? hath not God made foolish the wisdom of this world?

21 For after that in the wisdom of God the world by wisdom knew not God, it pleased God by the foolishness of preaching to save them that believe.

22 For the Jews require a sign, and the Greeks seek after wisdom:

23 But we preach Christ crucified, unto the Jews a stumblingblock, and unto the Greeks foolishness;

24 But unto them which are called, both Jews and Greeks, Christ the power of God, and the wisdom of God.

25 Because the foolishness of God is wiser than men; and the weakness of God is stronger than men.

26 For ye see your calling, brethren, how that not many wise men after the flesh, not many mighty, not many noble, are called:

27 But God hath chosen the foolish things of the world to confound the wise; and God hath chosen the weak things of the world to confound the things which are mighty;

New Revised Standard Version

FOR the message about the cross is foolishness to those who are perishing, but to us who are being saved it is the power of God.

19 For it is written, "I will destroy the wisdom of the wise, and the discernment of the discerning I will thwart."

20 Where is the one who is wise? Where is the scribe? Where is the debater of this age? Has not God made foolish the wisdom of the world?

21 For since, in the wisdom of God, the world did not know God through wisdom, God decided, through the foolishness of our proclamation, to save those who believe.

22 For Jews demand signs and Greeks desire wisdom,

23 but we proclaim Christ crucified, a stumbling block to Jews and foolishness to Gentiles,

24 but to those who are the called, both Jews and Greeks, Christ the power of God and the wisdom of God.

25 For God's foolishness is wiser than human wisdom, and God's weakness is stronger than human strength.

26 Consider your own call, brothers and sisters: not many of you were wise by human standards, not many were powerful, not many were of noble birth.

27 But God chose what is foolish in the world to shame the wise; God chose what is weak in the world to shame the strong;

MAIN THOUGHT: And base things of the world, and things which are despised, hath God chosen, yea, and things which are not, to bring to nought things that are: That no flesh should glory in his presence. (1 Corinthians 1:28–29, KJV)

1 Corinthians 1:18–31

King James Version	New Revised Standard Version
28 And base things of the world, and things which are despised, hath God chosen, yea, and things which are not, to bring to nought things that are:	28 God chose what is low and despised in the world, things that are not, to reduce to nothing things that are,
29 That no flesh should glory in his presence.	29 so that no one might boast in the presence of God.
30 But of him are ye in Christ Jesus, who of God is made unto us wisdom, and righteousness, and sanctification, and redemption:	30 He is the source of your life in Christ Jesus, who became for us wisdom from God, and righteousness and sanctification and redemption,
31 That, according as it is written, He that glorieth, let him glory in the Lord.	31 in order that, as it is written, "Let the one who boasts, boast in the Lord."

LESSON SETTING
Time: 56 AD
Place: Corinth

LESSON OUTLINE
I. **The Folly of the Cross**
   (1 Corinthians 1:18–21)
II. **The Power of God**
   (1 Corinthians 1:22–25)
III. **The Chosen of God**
   (1 Corinthians 1:26–31)

UNIFYING PRINCIPLE

Humans can be strengthened through maintaining daily relationships with those who provide good counsel. Where do we find true wisdom when facing life's challenges? God calls us into relationship with Jesus who is the source of wisdom, understanding, and guidance.

INTRODUCTION

Paul writes to the church at Corinth from Ephesus in response to questions the church had raised to him, as well as because of rumors of division within the church. The Corinthian church had been established by Paul on one of his missionary journeys sponsored by the church at Antioch. Paul remained in Corinth for 18 months before leaving because of persecution and to continue his missionary work of establishing churches in Asia Minor. Corinth was a major city at the center of the Roman province of Achaia. The city was an important trade route with a seaport and brought a diverse group of travelers to its shores. As a former Greek city, the influence of Greek culture, philosophy, and education continued to play a vital role in the communities of understanding. Discussions concerning philosophy and religion were commonplace. Thus, Corinth was an ideal city for Paul to share the gospel and plant a church in order to spread the message of the cross. In Paul's letter to the Corinthians, he provides his theological position about the cross and how the cross is central to the message of salvation. The cross is a symbol of shame to the larger community because it is an instrument used to execute criminals. However, Paul views the cross as a symbol of divine wisdom that was employed by God for the work of redemption and salvation.

I. THE FOLLY OF THE CROSS
(1 CORINTHIANS 1:18–21)

Wisdom and power were the primary things that grabbed the attention of the masses in Corinth. Wisdom and power were the steps on the ladder to an elevated social standing in the eyes of the world. Paul deconstructs the Corinthians' ideas about wisdom and power and replaces them with the word of the cross. Paul begins with what the Corinthians believe has power and demonstrates something they did not know; the cross had more power. Paul is seeking to build a Christian community and to do so, he knows he must change the community's thinking about what has value. He challenges the church to see the world through God's eyes which will require a different understanding of power and wisdom.

Corinthians were familiar with the cross as a tool of execution used by the Romans, but the idea of God using the cross to bring salvation was completely new to them. To accept Paul's position on the cross as an instrument of redemption, the Corinthians would have overcome the shame often associated with the cross. Death on a cross was reserved for the worst criminals or those that the Romans wanted to make an example of who may have threatened Roman power. Crucifixion as means of deterrence and state execution existed before the Romans. However, some of the most gruesome examples of this form of state-sanctioned death are from Roman history. For example, in the 1st-century B.C. there was a great revolt of enslaved people on the Italian peninsula. It was known as the Third Servile War and was led by the gladiator, Spartacus. The rebellion lasted for about two years and began with a small band but eventually amassed some 120,000 people. The Romans were able to defeat Spartacus after two years. To discourage any more revolts they set up crucifixions along a road entering the city of Rome. There were some 6,000 people hung on 120 miles of road as a visual reminder that this is what happened to slaves who stepped out of place.

Although this is one of the more gruesome examples of mass crucifixion, it should be noted that it was normal that crucifixion often took place at the entrance or along the entering road of a city. In most cases, the bases for the crucifixes would remain in place as permanent fixtures as reminders of the power of the state over life and death. In this manner, Jesus' death on the cross was very much like other Roman crucifixions. He was led to Calvary, right outside of the city gates, there He hung between two other men, and a sign was placed over His head as a warning, "King of the Jews." This was a political message, "this is what happens to supposed kings without Roman sanction."

Paul tells his community that Jesus' death on the cross was an indication of how God in His wisdom uses the weak things in the world to bring the change that God desires for God alone to receive the glory. The preaching of the cross would always appear foolish to those absent of faith. However, for those that trust God the preaching of the cross has power. In the cross, we see the love of God at work on the behalf of humanity in order to cancel the debt of sin. The cross represents the sacrifice that Jesus made as an obedient son of God to carry out God's plan. Several times Paul tells the Corinthians he knows that what he is saying about the cross will be folly to those who continue to follow the world's understanding of wisdom and power. Paul knows he is making a case for a different way of thinking and further builds on his position with a set of contrast later in the text. If the Corinthians cannot shift in their thinking about power and wisdom and see what God has done through the cross, it will be difficult for the Corinthian church to survive. Some of the very struggles the church was undergoing during the time of Paul's letter were founded in the old ways of thinking about wisdom and power that built division. The cross becomes the thing that the entire church can rally around as a symbol of faith and God's power at work paying the cost of redemption.

II. THE POWER OF GOD (1 CORINTHIANS 1:22–25)

Paul continues to make his case about a shift in thinking by providing an example of how others think. The Jews demand a sign. Much of the Jewish faith centered around some form of revelation that God was moving in a specific manner. The demand for a sign was asked by Moses when God selected him to lead the people out of bondage. During Israel's wandering years, they were guided by signs: a cloud by day and fire by night. The Jews looked for a Messiah that would vanquish all foreign oppressors and restore the throne of David. The proof for the Jews that the Messiah was whom He claimed would be determined if He could fulfill their political, social, and religious hopes. For many, Jesus could not have been the Messiah precisely because He died in shame like other political prisoners. They wanted a sign to be sure; however, Jesus as the Christ required faith. Faith and signs are not completely antithetical to one another however, signs are not to be the impetus for faith. Signs are to be a confirmation of faith not to be the birth of faith. John's gospel says as much when Jesus states, "'Have you believed because you have seen me? Blessed are those who have not seen and yet have come to believe'" (20:29).

Whereas some Jews demanded a sign, the Greeks sought wisdom. The influence of Greek philosophy ran deep in Corinth and the market centers were occupied constantly by those who were debating some position on philosophy and religion. The use of argument and persuasion was an art form employed to gain followers of a particular position. Paul would not promise a sign, nor would he participate in philosophical discussions to demonstrate his wisdom. Paul had only one message and that message was Jesus Christ crucified for the sins of the world. The story of God's faithfulness and humanity's salvation is summed up in what God has done through the cross. Greek scholar Michael Gorman states that the term Paul used most to describe himself was the apostle of the crucified. Paul was convinced that God's power was made known at the cross and that the cross is where the church can continue to discover God's power at work, using suffering and weakness for redemptive purposes. The demonstration of God's power through suffering and weakness will always be a stumbling block for both Jews and Greeks as well as all those that view power through the traditional ways of the world as they knew it.

It is not until one's thinking has been reordered that he/she will be able to see what God has done. Paul believes this is a function of the church to reorder thinking to where persons can see the power of God at work among them. In so many ways this is the transformation for the renewing of the mind. In order for one to accept that God's power was made manifest in the death of a man hung as a criminal requires that one's mind be made over that is not driven by those things that are considered to be powerful. This means that God's power looks different than what we are accustomed to; God's power is indeed otherworldly. It is not otherworldly in the sense that there is no impact on the world in which we live but that God chooses to manifest His omnipotence in ways that defies our preconceptions of power.

III. THE CHOSEN OF GOD (1 CORINTHIANS 1:26–31)

Paul invites the Corinthians to reflect upon their own calling by God. What made them respond to the gospel message when it was preached? What background did they come from that caused God to choose them to receive His message and share that message with others? Paul asks the Corinthian church to do theology, to reflect upon God and their relationship to Him. The reflections would make something obvious. Firstly, God is not impressed by the status quo of wisdom and power because God has chosen so few of their number that falls within that category. God has chosen to build the Corinthian church primarily from those on the low end of the social ladder. His Kingdom receives the have-nots and shares with them the life-changing power of the Gospel. God works with the weak and desperate to shame the world and its ideas of strength. Secondly, God works with the weak and desperate not because

they are better, but God does so to prove His strength so no one may steal the glory that belongs to Him alone. Paul says no one should understand what he has said better than those who know their limitations and their weaknesses but have seen how God has used them for His own glory. God's chosen are not to become divided over issues of leadership. God's chosen are not to use the standards of the world as the model for success. God's chosen are to acknowledge that the source of their strength lies in Jesus Christ. Thus, Paul's final appeal is to keep Jesus the primary focus and trust Him. The Gospel is not a philosophy to be followed but a message about the cross and Jesus that is to be received and shared with others to the glory of God. When the Church keeps its focus upon Jesus and receives the message of Christ and the cross, the Church can boast in the way Paul suggests where boasting is celebrating the wisdom of God and how God uses weakness and folly in the world's eyes to accomplish His purposes in the world.

God does not use the normal conventions of the world to bring about that which He has chosen. He uses that which is considered foolish, rubbish, and even poppycock. This points to God's ability and even desire to produce unlikely outcomes and reversals. These point to His extraordinary power and that He has a soft spot for the downtrodden and unlikely of the world. As one even considers Israel as God's chosen, it is important to remember that Israel was a small nation of disconnected tribes when it began. It was from that that God was able to form a full-fledged nation-state.

As one considers from whence Jesus came, He fits a similar model. Jesus hails from a small town that was not known or distinguished for anything in particular. He came from an uneducated family and was born as the result/during controversy. As He grew in strength and power, at His height Jesus had just 12 disciples that followed Him exclusively. However, it was through this man of a lowly birth that God chose to bring salvation.

THE LESSON APPLIED

One of the greatest temptations that faces the church every generation is to lose focus and reflect the culture as opposed to maintaining the church's witness in the culture. Paul makes clear that the central concern of the Church should be the preaching of the cross. The preaching of the cross is a Gospel of redemptive suffering and how God uses the things we would be tempted to draw back from to show the ways His power is at work among us. In a culture given to ideas of success, the preaching of the cross could appear outdated. The Christian faith is not built upon ideas of success but upon faithfulness. God has shown His faithfulness toward us in that while we were sinners Christ died on the cross in our stead. We are now heirs of salvation and recipients of grace. May we always glory in the cross of Christ, because it is in the cross that our salvation is found.

LET'S TALK ABOUT IT

A secondary concern Paul makes in today's lesson is the need for Christian discernment. How do we balance the practical wisdom of our time against the ways God may be moving among us or wanting to use us?

Christian discernment seeks to apply the witness of the Holy Spirit, Scripture, experience, and sacred traditions in ways that bring us to a decision about God's leading. For the Corinthian church to be able to change from concern about power and wisdom in ways that created division, they would need to apply discernment to Paul's message in order to institute change. Discernment would allow them to hear the message of Paul, not just as the words of their founding leader, but the words God had for them to hear to become what God desired the church at Corinth to be a multicultural church of Jews and Gentiles, rich and poor, men and women, young and old, living out the meaning of following Christ in a world of Roman domination. Our process of discernment must include that which is usable. Even as this passage seemingly downplays the wisdom of the world, Paul does use familiar conventions in his work as an apostle. There are those conventions that can be used to advance the Kingdom, and we must figure out what those are and use them accordingly.

HOME DAILY DEVOTIONAL READINGS
FEBRUARY 6–12, 2023

MONDAY	TUESDAY	WEDNESDAY	THURSDAY	FRIDAY	SATURDAY	SUNDAY
God's Children and Heirs	A Holy Nation	Abide in Christ	Chosen by Christ	Be Holy	Keep God's Statutes in Holiness	Kindle God's Gift within You
Galatians 4:1–7	Exodus 19:1–8	John 15:1–14	John 15:15–27	Leviticus 19:2–4, 9–18	Leviticus 20:22–26	2 Timothy 1:3–14

CALLED WITH A HOLY CALLING

2 TIMOTHY 1:3–14

King James Version

I THANK God, whom I serve from my forefathers with pure conscience, that without ceasing I have remembrance of thee in my prayers night and day;

4 Greatly desiring to see thee, being mindful of thy tears, that I may be filled with joy;

5 When I call to remembrance the unfeigned faith that is in thee, which dwelt first in thy grandmother Lois, and thy mother Eunice; and I am persuaded that in thee also.

6 Wherefore I put thee in remembrance that thou stir up the gift of God, which is in thee by the putting on of my hands.

7 For God hath not given us the spirit of fear; but of power, and of love, and of a sound mind.

8 Be not thou therefore ashamed of the testimony of our Lord, nor of me his prisoner: but be thou partaker of the afflictions of the gospel according to the power of God;

9 Who hath saved us, and called us with an holy calling, not according to our works, but according to his own purpose and grace, which was given us in Christ Jesus before the world began,

10 But is now made manifest by the appearing of our Saviour Jesus Christ, who hath abolished death, and hath brought life and immortality to light through the gospel:

11 Whereunto I am appointed a preacher, and an apostle, and a teacher of the Gentiles.

12 For the which cause I also suffer these things: nevertheless I am not ashamed: for I know whom I have believed, and am persuaded

New Revised Standard Version

I AM grateful to God—whom I worship with a clear conscience, as my ancestors did—when I remember you constantly in my prayers night and day.

4 Recalling your tears, I long to see you so that I may be filled with joy.

5 I am reminded of your sincere faith, a faith that lived first in your grandmother Lois and your mother Eunice and now, I am sure, lives in you.

6 For this reason I remind you to rekindle the gift of God that is within you through the laying on of my hands;

7 for God did not give us a spirit of cowardice, but rather a spirit of power and of love and of self-discipline.

8 Do not be ashamed, then, of the testimony about our Lord or of me his prisoner, but join with me in suffering for the gospel, relying on the power of God,

9 who saved us and called us with a holy calling, not according to our works but according to his own purpose and grace. This grace was given to us in Christ Jesus before the ages began,

10 but it has now been revealed through the appearing of our Savior Christ Jesus, who abolished death and brought life and immortality to light through the gospel.

11 For this gospel I was appointed a herald and an apostle and a teacher,

12 and for this reason I suffer as I do. But I am not ashamed, for I know the one in whom I have put my trust, and I am sure that he is able

MAIN THOUGHT: Hold fast the form of sound words, which thou hast heard of me, in faith and love which is in Christ Jesus. (2 Timothy 1:13, KJV)

King James Version	*New Revised Standard Version*
that he is able to keep that which I have committed unto him against that day. 13 Hold fast the form of sound words, which thou hast heard of me, in faith and love which is in Christ Jesus. 14 That good thing which was committed unto thee keep by the Holy Ghost which dwelleth in us.	to guard until that day what I have entrusted to him. 13 Hold to the standard of sound teaching that you have heard from me, in the faith and love that are in Christ Jesus. 14 Guard the good treasure entrusted to you, with the help of the Holy Spirit living in us.

LESSON SETTING

Time: 64 AD
Place: Ephesus

LESSON OUTLINE

I. **Recalling What Matters (2 Timothy 1:3–7)**

II. **Reclaiming the Work of Ministry (2 Timothy 1:8–10)**

III. **Remembering What is Required for Faithful Ministry (2 Timothy 1:11–14)**

UNIFYING PRINCIPLE

We struggle with trusting our own abilities. How do we know we have what is required to succeed in life? When we put our trust in Jesus, we have assurance that we can accomplish what He has called us to do.

INTRODUCTION

Second Timothy is one of three epistles that make up the pastoral epistles. The primary concern of the pastoral epistles is church order and proper conduct in the church. The pastoral epistles are written to local pastors as opposed to letters written to entire Christian communities. The pastoral epistles provide the pastors with a play book to guide their actions and demonstrate their responsibility in the life of the church. Many of the themes and concerns of 2 Timothy are present in 1 Timothy. Central among the themes and concerns is holding fast to the truth. As the Church moves away from the time of Jesus' physical presence and the death of many eyewitnesses, it feels the pressure of the culture to comfort. The Church also faces serious questions about the meaning of being Christian at this time. In a world of pagan influences, the Church was viewed as just another group and no different from the countless other religious groups in a pagan society. Once persons came into the church with such a background, there would be attempts to change the church and make it more acceptable to the views of those who make up the church.

There may have been no danger more pressing for the church than the possibility of being remade in ways that were not consistent with what it meant to be in Christ. The response of church leaders is for the church to reflect upon its origins and traditions and to reestablish them in the forms of doctrine that could be communicated and followed. Second Timothy informs the reader that the Church has a history and tradition that extends beyond the temporary moment. There are established doctrines and values that the Church holds that are to be passed down to succeeding generations. In moments of difficulty and crisis these doctrines and traditions can provide the ground upon which one can take their stand for the truth. To stand for the truth of the Gospel may lead to suffering but failure to stand would bring shame upon the leader and the Church that Christ died to birth.

Paul's own ministry had been marked by suffering and hardship for the cause of the Gospel, and he expects that experience to continue in some form for all those who stand for the truth. There is a spiritual war being waged in local church leaders, therefore Timothy must be prepared to do their part in the battle.

I. RECALLING WHAT MATTERS (2 TIMOTHY 1:3–7)

Paul begins by appealing to his close personal relationship with Timothy as a basis for all that will follow in the rest of the letter. Paul is not providing instructions as a distant leader acting in his authority. Paul's instruction to Timothy comes from a heart that is concerned about Timothy and his well–being. Timothy has benefited from a family that shared the faith with him at young age and nurtured him in his understanding of the Way. Timothy has benefited from a start that not many persons had at the beginning of the Church age. There were mature believers that taught him and modeled for him what it meant to be in Christ. Beyond the investment of his family, Timothy had received the investment and support of Paul. Paul had trusted Timothy with important work in establishing churches throughout the Roman Empire. Timothy served as envoy for Paul on multiple occasions to communicate the message to churches that were struggling with various issues, none more famous than the church at Corinth. Timothy has served as Paul's traveling companion and had the privilege of being mentored by Paul in how the ministry was to operate. Timothy is reminded of the special gifts for ministry he had received by the laying of hands. Early in the Church's history, the laying on of hands by church leaders represented a symbolic empowerment given to another to serve the Church in some special capacity. Paul himself had received the laying of hands by leaders of the church at Antioch, and it empowered him for outreach mission abroad. To recall the laying of hands would encourage Timothy to remember that he had been called to participate in the same Spirit-empowered ministry that Paul has exercised. The point that Paul seeks to make is that ministry will not be easy, even when doing the right thing for the right reason. Paul's own ministry record reflects that truth. Timothy is to be encouraged that the same Spirit that motivated and empowered Paul to keep going in moments of hardship is at work within him, if he would heed the moving of the Spirit within him. In order to move forward in the desired way, Timothy will need to rekindle or to stir up the gift. The stirring up of the gift is a call to reflect upon what God has done for Timothy and from that reflection Paul expects the Spirit to empower Timothy to endure suffering, to love both the work of the church and the people of the church, and to create courage and discipline to be able to face whatever dangers may manifest themselves. These are the things that matter and if Timothy will remember them, he may be encouraged to continue in the work of the ministry.

II. RECLAIMING THE WORK OF MINISTRY (2 TIMOTHY 1:8–10)

Most scholars agree that Timothy was serving the church at Ephesus and that at some point became distressed over the ministry and may have been on the verge of leaving Ephesus. The issues that contributed to Timothy's emotional and spiritual injury are not clear. However, what is clear is that Timothy was not taking a hard enough stance to protect the truth and keep the church on a sure foundation. Therefore, Timothy is encouraged by Paul to reclaim the ministry. In order to reclaim the ministry, Timothy would have to act and it would have to start with a change in thinking. He could not be ashamed of the Gospel or what is required to protect the truth of the Gospel.

Paul believes the presence and power of the Spirit empowers one to be able to endure suffering for the cause of Christ. Thus, Paul invites Timothy to be a participant in the suffering that ministry can sometimes bring. Suffering must replace shame because shame leads to inaction, but suffering provides a witness. Shame often leads to inaction because as a feeling it erodes the mental, emotional, and spiritual strength needed to publicly bear witness. Shame causes one to look inward and question his/her value in light of whatever is the perceived undesired trait. The witness of Christ suffering to birth the church through his shed blood and the witness of Paul's own suffering should inform Timothy that there will be times when church leaders are required to stances that can lead to suffering in order to protect the truth of the gospel. Reclaiming the work of ministry

also means knowing that God has a purpose for what occurs in the life of the church and the life of the church leader. Paul reminds Timothy that the call to ministry has not come because of the works of individual church leaders, but the call has come in accordance with God's purposes. If God's purpose can lead to the call and empowerment for ministry, then God's purpose should be the over arching concern for those engaged in ministry.

The author chides Timothy not to be ashamed of the Gospel with the understanding that for the Church to grow it would take dedicated servants who stood tall, even in the face of opposition. To not be ashamed in this instance is to hold to the doctrine of faith that was passed on to him by his mother, grandmother, and others who stood on a strong faith foundation. In a very real sense, Timothy was told to be bold in his proclamation about Jesus, even if that meant suffering. Boldness without the possibility of suffering or difficulty is not really boldness, it is simply saying what one wants in a safe environment. The author tells Timothy, even when it is not safe, testify and tell it all.

His use of salvation language concerning the work of Jesus Christ who has abolished death and brought immorality to light through the Gospel is a further appeal to the power of God to uphold one in suffering and even deliver from suffering. Trust in God can provide the courage necessary to reclaim the ministry and protect the truth of the Gospel. It also points to a great fact for this herald of the Gospel that we are all saved to a calling. This asks and answers the following question: For what purpose are we saved? In God's grand plan we are not saved just for the sake of being saved but to play a part in His great cosmic play. Whereas our salvation is contingent only upon Jesus, our salvation is attached to a calling. Even as God called Timothy, each one who is saved by His grace is also called into the work of boldness of testimony to who He is and what He has done.

III. Remembering What is Required for Faithful Ministry (2 Timothy 1:11–14)

For Paul a faithful ministry begins with accepting responsibility. Whereas Paul acknowledges the call of God in his life to ministry. Paul must be willing to accept the responsibility that goes along with the call. Paul defines his responsibility to Timothy in terms of the duties he has fulfilled as a preacher, apostle and teacher. The three roles in Paul's mind are all different but are related to the work of ministry. His primary role he sees as a preacher of the good news of Jesus Christ. As one proclaiming the Gospel Paul developed a method of preaching that focused upon the life, death, resurrection and return of Jesus Christ. At the heart of the Gospel was the need for persons to hear the news about Jesus as the Savior of all of humanity, both Jew and Gentile. As an apostle, Paul acts with spiritual authority to direct the work of ministry primarily among the Gentiles. He is commonly referred to as the apostle to the Gentiles. As a teacher, Paul views his task to determine what are the critical things about ministry that need to be passed on to succeeding generations. As a teacher Paul becomes the church's theologian. Whereas Timothy may not be required to do all that Paul has done, there is a responsibility that comes with ministry that Timothy is expected to fulfill. Paul shares two levels of trust that are necessary for a faithful ministry. The first level of trust is the things we trust to God's keeping. The sustaining force for Paul in his lowest moments was confidence that God would keep what he had committed to His care. The keeping power of God eliminates any reason for shame. God will guard, protect, keep safe what we entrust to Him. Indeed, part of the reason why suffering is to be endured is because even our very lives are to be entrusted to God. For Paul, " to live is Christ and to die is gain" and thus he able to trust God with everything, even the very breath the he drew because even in death he would be take of by God (Philippians 1:21). The second level of trust is what God has entrusted to ministry leaders. God has entrusted to ministry leaders the truth of the Gospel. Therefore, the ministry leaders have a responsibility to guard, to protect and keep safe the truth. The Gospel will encounter those that will resist sound teaching but the ministry leader must hold the line and guard what has been entrusted to their care. To guard the truth of the Gospel is to guard it with a type of purity and hold to the ancient way, even as the Gospel has a way of speaking new and afresh in new circumstances. As much as we are to guard the Gospel we are to do so with imagination and creativity. It is in this way that the Gospel shall always live and provide salvation to all who will hear it. Paul's life has provided a pattern, others can follow, and Timothy is encouraged to follow his pattern for in doing so he will have a faithful ministry.

THE LESSON APPLIED

The work of ministry is always difficult and can lead to ministry burnout. In recent years the church has experienced large numbers of clergy that are leaving church ministry to pursue ministry in other areas such as non-profits that work with the poor, and justice causes that work toward criminal justice reform.

Although work of leading a church may be difficult, it is still important work that requires clergy with courage and conviction to teach and preach sound doctrine in a world so focused on inclusion that the message of the cross could be offensive, even to those within the church. Paul's words to Timothy were to serve as a motivation to summon the courage and commitment necessary to honor his call to ministry and the investment that others had made in him. Ministry leaders should take courage in knowing they are not alone. God always has partners ready to assist and serve alongside of those willing to stand for what is right, even if we do not always know who they are or where they can be found. At the right time, God will reveal them for our good and His glory.

It is important to remember that inasmuch as it is difficult work, it is work to which you are called. The conviction of one's calling is able to sustain us in the darkest of hours. It is in this that we are to be confident that the same God who called us is able to complete the good work that He has entrusted to us. Ministry is very much a walk of faith in which one must put one foot in front of the other in darkness, often alone. Timothy is blessed in that he has Paul who writes to encourage him, it is important to lean on brothers and sisters who know the difficulty of the walk and can offer words of comfort and encouragement.

LET'S TALK ABOUT IT

What are ways that laity can assist in addressing clergy burn out?

There are far too many clergy that feel they are solely responsible for the ministry of the church and do not believe they have enough effective partners in ministry. The church can help to combat this problem by being more intentional in the way it supports clergy. The support could come in multiple ways that range from providing a date night outing for clergy and their families to the church to having more volunteers or staff that take on more of the day-to-day responsibility of operating the church. Another critical means of support of clergy and the work they do is a church committed to biblical literacy where a deeper understanding of issues of faith make the work of ministry a joy and not a burden. Be creative in your effort to support clergy.

HOME DAILY DEVOTIONAL READINGS
FEBRUARY 13–19, 2023

MONDAY	TUESDAY	WEDNESDAY	THURSDAY	FRIDAY	SATURDAY	SUNDAY
Pure and Undefiled Religion	Defender of the Oppressed	Father of Orphans, Protector of Widows	Defend the Poor and Needy	Good News for the Poor	Coming Miseries upon the Rich	God Has Chosen the Poor
James 1:19–27	Amos 5:7–15	Psalm 68:1–13	Proverbs 31:1–9	Luke 4:16–30	James 5:1–11	James 2:1–12

GOD CHOOSES THE POOR

ADULT TOPIC: THE RICH AND THE POOR	BACKGROUND SCRIPTURE: JAMES 2:1–12

JAMES 2:1–12

King James Version

My brethren, have not the faith of our Lord Jesus Christ, the Lord of glory, with respect of persons.

2 For if there come unto your assembly a man with a gold ring, in goodly apparel, and there come in also a poor man in vile raiment;

3 And ye have respect to him that weareth the gay clothing, and say unto him, Sit thou here in a good place; and say to the poor, Stand thou there, or sit here under my footstool:

4 Are ye not then partial in yourselves, and are become judges of evil thoughts?

5 Hearken, my beloved brethren, Hath not God chosen the poor of this world rich in faith, and heirs of the kingdom which he hath promised to them that love him?

6 But ye have despised the poor. Do not rich men oppress you, and draw you before the judgment seats?

7 Do not they blaspheme that worthy name by the which ye are called?

8 If ye fulfil the royal law according to the scripture, Thou shalt love thy neighbour as thyself, ye do well:

9 But if ye have respect to persons, ye commit sin, and are convinced of the law as transgressors.

10 For whosoever shall keep the whole law, and yet offend in one point, he is guilty of all.

New Revised Standard Version

My brothers and sisters, do you with your acts of favoritism really believe in our glorious Lord Jesus Christ?

2 For if a person with gold rings and in fine clothes comes into your assembly, and if a poor person in dirty clothes also comes in,

3 and if you take notice of the one wearing the fine clothes and say, "Have a seat here, please," while to the one who is poor you say, "Stand there," or, "Sit at my feet,"

4 have you not made distinctions among yourselves, and become judges with evil thoughts?

5 Listen, my beloved brothers and sisters. Has not God chosen the poor in the world to be rich in faith and to be heirs of the kingdom that he has promised to those who love him?

6 But you have dishonored the poor. Is it not the rich who oppress you? Is it not they who drag you into court?

7 Is it not they who blaspheme the excellent name that was invoked over you?

8 You do well if you really fulfill the royal law according to the scripture, "You shall love your neighbor as yourself."

9 But if you show partiality, you commit sin and are convicted by the law as transgressors.

10 For whoever keeps the whole law but fails in one point has become accountable for all of it.

MAIN THOUGHT: Hearken, my beloved brethren, Hath not God chosen the poor of this world rich in faith, and heirs of the kingdom which he hath promised to them that love him? (James 2:5, KJV)

JAMES 2:1–12

King James Version	*New Revised Standard Version*
11 For he that said, Do not commit adultery, said also, Do not kill. Now if thou commit no adultery, yet if thou kill, thou art become a transgressor of the law.	11 For the one who said, "You shall not commit adultery," also said, "You shall not murder." Now if you do not commit adultery but if you murder, you have become a transgressor of the law.
12 So speak ye, and so do, as they that shall be judged by the law of liberty.	12 So speak and so act as those who are to be judged by the law of liberty.

LESSON SETTING
Time: 47 AD
Place: Jerusalem

LESSON OUTLINE
   I. **The Correct Attitude (James 2:1–4)**
   II. **Discerning God's Choice (James 2:5–7)**
   III. **Love and the Law (James 2:8–12)**

UNIFYING PRINCIPLE

People make judgments about one another. What is our standard for valuing some people more than others? God directs us to value people based on their God-given value and not on our own standards.

INTRODUCTION

The book of James is one of the general epistles of the Bible and carries that label because it is written to a Jewish audience that is spread over Palestine. It is to those within the twelve tribes of Israel that have become Christian that James writes. James writes under the influence of his Jewish faith, so the letter has considerable ethical instruction about the fair treatment of all persons, regardless of social status. James's instructions could be called community rules for the church to live by. Just as the Law of Moses provided ethical rules for the Israel live by, as a sign of covenant commitment the church needed community rules to order its social relationships as well. James is particularly concerned about the fair treatment of the poor. Although he is a leader in the church in Jerusalem, James is fully aware of the impact of poverty on individuals as well as the community. James' own experiences with poverty after the loss of his father may have been a contributing factor as well. James desires a church that is free of the favoritism that marks the broader society in both religion and politics. The practical aspect of Christianity also demonstrates how Christianity is different from many of the other religions in the Roman Empire. The practical aspect of faith can become an effective evangelism tool, although James does not address evangelism as a consideration in his letter. For James, the practical aspects of Christianity become the way that faith and works come together to build an authentic Christian witness. Faith without works has no value and what better way to put faith to work than through the social aspects of Christianity in the needs of others and treating all persons fairly.

EXPOSITION

I. THE CORRECT ATTITUDE (JAMES 2:1–4)

The issues of partiality/favoritism based upon economic status is a major concern for James and one that he believes threatens the very witness of the church. If the church is to be different from the culture it cannot refrain from using the culture's values as means of determining worth in the body of Christ.

Partiality based upon economic status is a form of discrimination and as such is a sin. If the church allows such a witness of sin to go unaddressed, the entire witness of the church will be in jeopardy. James uses an illustration to prove his point by giving an example of what could happen in a local church. James is careful to build the description of the rich and the poor in stark contrasts. The rich person is presented as a person of influence and power by the gold rings he wears as well as his/her fine clothing. The very physical presence of the person would immediately communicate that the individual was a person of means. The problem is with how persons in the church would interpret those persons as individuals they can garner favor or provide access to power. It is the very thinking of those in the church that persons of influence and power could be used to help those within the church in some form that creates the divide and leads to favoritism to gain favor. This is a problem for James on multiple fronts: 1– It could lead to person becoming more dependent upon those with power than faith in Christ. 2– it could lead to abuses within the church where groups that were seen as powerless were marginalized. 3– it could threaten the peace and welfare of the church as a unified body of believers among a diverse social make-up. After providing an example of a wealthy person who is given preferential treatment, James gives the image of a poor person. The poor man is simply described as wearing shabby clothing. There is no other description that determines his lack of wealth but his dress, he wears the garment of the poor. The poor man is not only denied preferential treatment or even equal treatment, but he is shown a place of lesser value to occupy. "Sit at my feet" is not just a location the poor man sits, but is also an indication that he is below others in the fellowship. A fellowship that was to be defined by its service to Christ and one another is now a place of status and social ranking. If the church participates in this conduct, it demonstrates the wrong attitude. The correct attitude is never judge persons based upon appearance but to treat all persons fairly. The Gospel is in the business of pulling down barriers of separation and the church should never build artificial barriers that divide because we are to be one body in Christ.

Interestingly as James wrote this, it would most likely be hard for him to imagine how many churches in today's world are absolutely separated by social status. For quite a long time in the American church there have been "first", "blue blood", and "silk stocking" churches. Inasmuch as the church is not called to discriminate amongst those who come through the doors, it seems that in many cases we have bifurcated ourselves into haves and have-nots. Instead of discriminating in many cases we simply do not worship next to persons who are of different social statuses than ourselves. Instead of discriminating we simply separate.

II. DISCERNING GOD'S CHOICE (JAMES 2:5–7)

Whereas there may be persons impressed by the presence of the wealthy in the life of the church, James makes it clear that God is not impressed by the wealthy. James goes as far to suggest that God leans in the direction of the poor. God in His sovereignty has often chosen the poor to be His helpers to accomplish His will. The poor who were without material wealth had often showed the ability to exercise great faith. James may have been thinking of the experience of his own mother Mary, a poor village girl used by God to give birth to the Savior of the world and James's brother Jesus. Scholar, Douglass Moo states, "Christians however poor in material possessions they may be both possess spiritual wealthy presently and anticipated greater blessing in the future." James is not making the case for poverty and spirituality being the same. Not all poor are open to the ways of God and not all the rich are closed to the ways of God. However, James does expect his community to be aware of how often God uses those that others would least expect and many times they are the poor. James expects his community to apply discernment that reflects the values the church was built upon. James also informs the community to consider how the rich, those with power, treat them. Writing to those who have been scattered across Palestine from the twelve tribes means his community is aware of the ways power often works against them and not for them.

The church is still a young organization slowly finding acceptance, but also still aware of how persecution never seem to be far away. When the church does experience persecution, it is often at the hands of the powerful. The combination of economic oppression and persecution meant that James's community was always exposed to judicial actions that seized property or political and religious actions that led to possible imprisonment because of their faith in Christ. The actions of the rich are often counter to what the church stands and its Christ.

As pointed out earlier, not all poor are open to the ways of God however, James understands that it is often the poor who must exercise great faith. Paul writes, "Who hopes for what is seen?" (Romans 8:24). Another way to interpret that is "who has hope for what he/she already has?" In other words, those without often must possess faith because without it they would have nothing. It is reminiscent of a quote from Bishop Carlton Pearson who once said, "None of us had very much money... and we didn't have anything in the promise of our future but Jesus." It is hard to believe when one has everything, those who have much often do not hope because there is no need for hope, they have what they need and want. The poor, on the other hand, do not have their temporal needs and desires met and thus must rely on the provision that God grants. It is in these times of need that faith is often forged. One must believe in order to get what they need.

Even as faith is lifted up as that which all who are a part should have, it does not always smooth out the differences within the church nor does it often keep persons from behaving as if it is not real. Even as faith is the model and the church is called to be distinctive from the world, often church is a reflection of the larger society of which it is a part. This should not be. The church should reflect a different set of values not only in word but in practice. This is in part why he questions the high value that is placed on the rich. Not only so, but James also understands that it does not make sense for one to act in ways that are antithetical to one's own flourishing and betterment. He asks, "Why would you lift up those who put you down?" Many times we lift up those who put us down because we want to join their club. The answer is obvious, we often emulate the dominant because we ourselves want to become dominant. However, dominance is not what we are to seek, rather it is love.

III. Love and the Law (James 2:8–12)

The royal law that James refers to is the law of love of neighbor. For the Jews this law is foundational and the one of which all other laws depend. It is interesting that this is one of the few places where James connects to the teachings of his brother. Jesus teaches in Matthew 22:37–40, "'You shall love the Lord your God with all your heart, and with all your soul, and with all your mind.' This is the greatest and first commandment. And a second is like it: 'You shall love your neighbor as yourself.' On these two commandments hang all the law and the prophets." This is basic in terms of the kind of ethics that are to be displayed in the Jesus community. However, if the church showed partiality based upon economic status the law of love has been violated. Because James's community is Jewish there is still a connection to the role of the law in the Jewish church. Although Paul has made the case among the Gentiles for a salvation of grace alone, proper interpretation of Paul's theology understands its proper relationship to the Mosaic Law, especially that which governed social relationships. If a member of the church failed to act upon the law of love by treating rich and poor equally, he/she failed all of the law. The failure to follow the law is a strong argument by James to prevent the church from showing partiality. It was commonly held in the Jewish tradition to violate any part of the law was to be guilty of breaking the entire law. Violators of the law could expect to be judged for their failure to maintain God's standard. It is at this point that James pivots from the law of Moses to the law of grace. James reminds his community, although they may follow aspects of the law of Moses, they are no longer under the law of Moses but under the law of liberty. Liberty is the word that James uses to address the grace of God at work in the life of the believer. The law of liberty is not a written set of rules to be followed. The law of liberty is a law written on the hearts of men and women who have committed themselves to following Jesus. When the community follows Jesus there is no distinction in the treatment of person based upon economic status or by any other form for discrimination. This is the meaning of to speak and act as those judged under the law of liberty. The law of liberty also means that believers have been set free to live into God's law of love more fully. Believers have been set free to love without condition based upon anything except that everyone we encounter has God's image stamped upon his/her essence.

The Lesson Applied

There might not be a problem that threatens the unity of the church more than the claim of partiality. It was claimed by the Hellenist widows over the Hebrew widows about the distribution of food in the church's infancy in Acts 6. The dispute caused such a disturbance in the life of the church it led to the creation of what we now know as deacon's ministry. The same claim was made by Paul against Peter in his treatment of Gentile believers, and it led the church council meeting in Jerusalem in attempt to settle the matter (Acts 15:1–35). Though in both of these instances the questions on the table were related to ethnicity and not social or economic status, the point is made that partiality has no place in God's church. The temptation to recruit and attract persons to the church with financial ability while disregarding those of lesser means is still at work today. Given the western notion of success in economic terms the church can miss the value those have to offer of lesser means. James' words are as meaningful today as they were when he first spoke them. The church is to resist any action that discriminates. Such actions reduce the church's light in a dark world and limits the reach of love.

Let's Talk About It

Why does it seem that God is willing and able to use the poor so often?

Many times, those without material wealth are open to the possibilities of spirituality in ways that wealth can sometimes block. The poor can have a view that is more directed to the eschatological future and do not experience the pull of things that can make one fall in love with things as more than God. Jesus used the parable of the rich man and the poor man as example of how one person trusted his things and the other trusted in what God would provide, even if it was only dogs to lick sores on his body to heal them. Another reason God may so often use the poor is because of God's concern for justice. The persons who have been impacted by injustice are sometimes used by God to oppose oppression and bring to bear the light of God. Such as the case with Amos the prophet or Mary the peasant girl who became the mother of Jesus. It is Mary that declares that God has filled the hungry and sent rich away empty. Poverty does not provide certainty that one will be used by God nor have faith in Him. However, the church should never forget that God so often uses the poor for His glory and the church's good. We cannot forget that our Savior was also born among the poor, rejected, and dejected of the world. If His Father was able and chose to use Him, why not others who are of similar circumstances.

HOME DAILY DEVOTIONAL READINGS
FEBRUARY 20–26, 2023

MONDAY	TUESDAY	WEDNESDAY	THURSDAY	FRIDAY	SATURDAY	SUNDAY
Rescued from Darkness	Paul's Charge to Timothy	God Turns Darkness into Light	God's Word Gives Light	You Are Children of Light	You Belong to God	Live Free in the Light
Colossians 1:9–22	1 Timothy 6:11–16	Isaiah 42:8–17	Psalm 119:121–136	1 Thessalonians 5:1–10	1 Peter 2:1–12	1 Peter 2:13–25

GOD CALLS YOU INTO LIGHT

ADULT TOPIC:	BACKGROUND SCRIPTURE:
AN IMPORTANT ROLE	1 PETER 2:1–25

1 PETER 2:1–10

King James Version

WHEREFORE laying aside all malice, and all guile, and hypocrisies, and envies, and all evil speakings,

2 As newborn babes, desire the sincere milk of the word, that ye may grow thereby:

3 If so be ye have tasted that the Lord is gracious.

4 To whom coming, as unto a living stone, disallowed indeed of men, but chosen of God, and precious,

5 Ye also, as lively stones, are built up a spiritual house, an holy priesthood, to offer up spiritual sacrifices, acceptable to God by Jesus Christ.

6 Wherefore also it is contained in the scripture, Behold, I lay in Sion a chief corner stone, elect, precious: and he that believeth on him shall not be confounded.

7 Unto you therefore which believe he is precious: but unto them which be disobedient, the stone which the builders disallowed, the same is made the head of the corner,

8 And a stone of stumbling, and a rock of offence, even to them which stumble at the word, being disobedient: whereunto also they were appointed.

9 But ye are a chosen generation, a royal priesthood, an holy nation, a peculiar people; that ye should shew forth the praises of him who hath called you out of darkness into his marvellous light;

New Revised Standard Version

RID yourselves, therefore, of all malice, and all guile, insincerity, envy, and all slander.

2 Like newborn infants, long for the pure, spiritual milk, so that by it you may grow into salvation—

3 if indeed you have tasted that the Lord is good.

4 Come to him, a living stone, though rejected by mortals yet chosen and precious in God's sight, and

5 like living stones, let yourselves be built into a spiritual house, to be a holy priesthood, to offer spiritual sacrifices acceptable to God through Jesus Christ.

6 For it stands in scripture: "See, I am laying in Zion a stone, a cornerstone chosen and precious; and whoever believes in him will not be put to shame."

7 To you then who believe, he is precious; but for those who do not believe, "The stone that the builders rejected has become the very head of the corner,"

8 And "A stone that makes them stumble, and a rock that makes them fall." They stumble because they disobey the word, as they were destined to do.

9 But you are a chosen race, a royal priesthood, a holy nation, God's own people, in order that you may proclaim the mighty acts of him who called you out of darkness into his marvelous light.

MAIN THOUGHT: But ye are a chosen generation, a royal priesthood, an holy nation, a peculiar people; that ye should shew forth the praises of him who hath called you out of darkness into his marvellous light. (1 Peter 2:9, KJV)

1 Peter 2:1–10

King James Version	New Revised Standard Version
10 Which in time past were not a people, but are now the people of God: which had not obtained mercy, but now have obtained mercy.	10 Once you were not a people, but now you are God's people; once you had not received mercy, but now you have received mercy.

LESSON SETTING
Time: 65 AD
Place: Roman

LESSON OUTLINE
I. A Change in Direction
(1 Peter 2:1–3)
II. A Work to Be Done
(1 Peter 2:4–8)
III. A Special People
(1 Peter 2:9–10)

UNIFYING PRINCIPLE

People want to know that their lives are going somewhere. Is it possible to feel one's life holds significance? Peter tells us that with Jesus as our foundation, we can be significant partners in building God's Kingdom.

INTRODUCTION

First Peter is a general epistle written to Gentile Christians scattered throughout Asia Minor. Most scholars believe the letter was written by someone that uses Peter's name or uses partial manuscripts by Peter that had not been previously combined and sent out. The Greek language in the letter reflects a person with a broad knowledge of the Greek vocabulary. The style of letter also reveals a classical education, something that a fisherman would not possess. The letter is written as a source of encouragement to Christians that are suffering persecution throughout the Roman Empire. Prior to the reign of Nero, Christians had been viewed as a sect of Judaism and Judaism was a protected religion within the Roman Empire. However, after the city of Rome burned down in 64 AD, Nero used the Christians as scapegoats for the destruction of the city. Christians were easily marginalized because they had many practices that isolated them from the larger society from their views on morality to their closed rituals reserved only for believers. Nero's persecution that started in the city of Rome soon spread throughout the Roman Empire. Christians had property seized, were imprisoned and murdered. First Peter views suffering as a necessary outgrowth of faith because faith in Christ is counter to the culture of the world. Although 1 Peter sees suffering as counter cultural, it does not address the larger counter cultural issues of social relationships. The writer argues for obedience by slaves as opposed to questioning the morality of slavery. First Peter focuses upon an appeal to holiness and from it honors God with a life that looks toward redemption in the future.

EXPOSITION

I. A CHANGE IN DIRECTION (1 PETER 2:1–3)

First Peter is concerned about the persecution taking place to Christians and how that persecution is putting stress on Christian communities. When a community is under pressure there is a tendency to begin bickering and fostering division which only makes the community more vulnerable to outside pressure. Peter calls the community to disassociate themselves with things that can cause division such as malice, deceit, envy, and slander. These particular issues are addressed because of their ability to create division as well as being an indicator of the things that should not be a part of the life of a believer in Jesus Christ. Take off/get rid of provides the image of dirty clothes being removed. The dirty clothes represent the old life prior to conversion. Christians should not be returning to habits that were a part of their old life, but they are to live a life of faith in Christ which demonstrates an alternative way to handle pressure. The alternative that Peter provides is a reliance on the basics that Christ provides. The reference to newborn babies reveals both dependence and a need for what is essential. Milk is a symbol of what it means to desire what God has to offer to sustain life in Him. The church is not to look for other sources to sustain it during persecution. Nor is the church expected to create its own methods of survival in the moment. Just as God provided what was essential for conversion, God will provide what is essential in the present moment, if the churches would seek him. The goal of the church should not be survival, but the goal should be to grow up in salvation. This creates a shift in focus that can eliminate many of the things that contribute to the divisions and the pressure persecution had caused. Peter also offers the kindness of God which the churches have already experienced against the reality of persecution. It is possible for both the kindness of God and persecution to be experienced at the same time. The biggest expression of God's kindness is in what He has done for the churches through Jesus Christ. Salvation and grace have come through Jesus and made the birth of the Church possible. God's kindness can also meet the current need to sustain the churches during persecution when they demonstrate their dependence upon him.

Verse 3 is a redacted version of Psalm 34:8 which says, "O taste and see that the Lord is good." The difference in the two verses is noticeable, while the former is a command or an invitation to taste, the latter indicates that the tasting has already taken place. From this perspective it relates back to verse 2 as the author calls his readers to spiritual maturity. He chides believers to remember and see the goodness of the Lord. This in itself is a type of maturity in understanding the ways in which God has indeed been good. His goodness should press believers forward into drinking milk that will make us strong in the Lord. His goodness should be the impetus that pushes believers forward past malice, guile, insincerity, envy, and slander. Pushing past these is the essence of the milk that believers are to consume. Even as it would seem apparent laying aside the aforementioned character flaws is not a simple matter but requires a deep level of seeking God's face. In this sense, the easy part is acknowledging God's goodness, the difficult part is the action that is required as a result of His goodness and grace.

Lastly, these verses connect with similar ideas that are a part of the canon and remind us that the Spirit was working in and among early Christians such that they were thinking and writing similar thoughts without having access to each others writings, in most cases. Hebrews 5:12–14 states the following, "You need milk, not solid food; for everyone who lives on milk, being still an infant, is unskilled in the word of righteousness. But solid food is for the mature, for those whose faculties have been trained by practice to distinguish good from evil." In the same way Paul writes to the church at Corinth, "I fed you with milk, not solid food, for you were not ready for solid food. Even now you are still not ready, for you are still of the flesh. For as long as there is jealousy and quarreling among you, are you not of the flesh, and behaving according to human inclinations?" (1 Corinthians 3:2, 3). In both of these passages food is used as a metaphor for the nourishment needed to grow in God. Likewise in the Pauline verses, similar character flaws and issues are listed as that which are to be banished from the Christian's life. Maturity in Christ is only facilitated by the nourishment that comes through His Word.

II. A WORK TO BE DONE (1 PETER 2:4–8)

Peter shifts metaphors from that of nourishment to that of security and honor. The metaphor of a stone is used to describe Christ as well as believers. Jesus had used the term stone or rock to describe how he would build a Church that would be able to withstand the assaults of evil forces. Peter sees the Church's security to be able to endure persecution through the image of a stone which can remain firm regardless of the circumstances. The early emphasis on security is given to lessen the tension in the churches and create confidence in what God had already done for them. Once the issue of security is addressed, Peter turned to the role of believers in the present

moment. First, they are to come together as one building in a spiritual house. There should be no freelance Christians doing their own thing. The Church is to be united in message, mission, and purpose. The Church is a living edifice that can only effectively do its work when all parts of the community are engaged. Whereas Paul used the metaphor of the body to describe the Church and the many parts working in unity, Peter uses the image of a building where all the stones/blocks in the building must work together to hold the building in place. Unity within the body is not optional for Paul or Peter, both see it as necessary requirement for an effective witness. The witness of unity will enable the Church to bear witness and show the world what it means to be faithful to Christ and endure hardship for the sake of the Gospel.

Peter's reference to royal priesthood and holy nation seems out of place given he is writing to a Gentile audience, but he seeks to unite his community with what God did for Israel in choosing them. The chosen have the protection of God but the chosen also have responsibility as well. The Church has the responsibility of doing what pleases God. The glory of God is to be the Church's motive. Peter acknowledges that God's glory is not everyone's motive because there are those who have rejected God's offer of salvation. The church is never to make the mistake of others by rejecting what God offers in His gift of salvation. The work to be done is to embrace what God has done and bear witness to His grace, even in persecution.

Verses 6–8 are all quoted from various Old Testament passages. Verse 6 comes from Isaiah 28:16, verse 7 from Psalm

118:22, and verse 8 from Isaiah 8:14. These verses point to the early Christian interpretation of the meaning and developing understanding of who Jesus was and is. The author is looking back over the Scriptures of Israel and sees the connection with the Jesus event and His purpose in the world.

As evidenced by the presence of these three instances, the image of the stone is a popular biblical picture of strength. The stone is to be built upon or in the case of Isaiah 8:14 it is a source of judgment. The stone imagery is ready made in any instance where a new work is being undertaken. First Peter in this sense is right in line with biblical precedent as this is a nascent community of Christians. The Church, in a very real sense, was still being birthed and so it should not come as a surprise that stone building language would show up. Similarly, Paul in Romans 9:33 combines both of the aforementioned Isaian passages, although his conclusions are different than that of the Petrine text. Clearly Romans is similar to Peter in that it was written as the Church was in its formative stages. Jesus is the stone upon which the Church is built and He is also that which causes unbelievers to stumble.

III. A SPECIAL PEOPLE (1 PETER 2:9–10)

The churches are told of their special status with God and Peter makes four declarations to make the special status known. Each declaration is a reference to a Jewish idea of faith in God. Peter is making the case that the Church is now the new Israel. It should be noted that such an interpretation has led to acts of anti–Semitism in the history of the Christian Church and these actions cannot be condoned. Peter calls his community a chosen race. The idea of a chosen race is held in connection with the idea of a covenant God. God has determined to enter covenant relationships with the people He chooses. The choice is God's alone and those that are chosen are recipients of the grace of God. William Barclay states that Christians as a chosen people are chosen for privilege of intimate fellowship with God, to show obedience to God and service for God. A chosen race is one with responsibilities and duties.

In the same vein that this language has led to anti-Semitism, the notion of a chosen race is very inflammatory language. As such it has been used throughout history as a way to justify violence in the name of God. It is important to note that as stated earlier a chosen race is one with responsibility and that responsibility is not to pillage any other group of people, rather calls His people to be a light to the nations. God uses His chosen people to reflect His glory in the world.

Next, a royal priesthood speaks to religious responsibility of the church to the faith it confesses. The priest performed two critical functions: 1– they conduct the rituals of the faith to make access to God possible. 2– they interceded to God on behalf of the people. As royal priesthood each believer has access to God and every believer can intercede with God. The term a holy nation describes how the Church is different. The word holy in Greek is *hagios* meaning separate or sacred. This is why the KJV uses the term peculiar. The difference in God's people is to be seen in a lived experience informed by the Spirit. Peter's final description of the Church's special status is God's own people. The Church represents those who belong to God because they carry God's stamp or impression. A stamp with a seal often represented ownership and authority. The Church not only belongs to God but carries the authority of God to operate in the world on God's behalf as His representative. All of this has been made possible because of the mercy and grace of God. God's grace and mercy has changed their lives and empowered them to serve. These words are written to motivate and inspire for the Church's light to shine through the darkness of the moment.

THE LESSON APPLIED

The Church will always face challenges from time to time that may lead to difficulty and persecution. The tenets of Christian faith can be at odds with the values of mainstream society. In those moments, the Church is expected not to compromise or turn inward but to bear witness to its faith. Perhaps the greatest example in from the mid 20th century and into the early 21st century of what it means to bear witness in the face of persecution is Bishop Desmond Tutu. Bishop Tutu's commitment to Christian faith during the brutal reign of apartheid stirred the conscience of the entire world and help to lead to the removal of apartheid as a governing policy for a nation. Bishop Tutu then led the truth and reconciliation commission that used Christian principles to heal a nation divided by race. Through the commission, persons were able to confess their crimes against humanity and receive forgiveness.

LET'S TALK ABOUT IT

Are their contemporary witnesses of persecution that the Church needs to lend its voice to in our times? Persecution can create a defining moment for the Church. Whereas the Church does not seek persecution, it often finds the Church because the Church challenges the values and choices of the culture. The Church believes it has a responsibility to live out its faith in ways that honors God and helps to build the world God intended centered in peace. Throughout the Church's history, it has made some of its greatest contributions during moments of persecution from the reformation movement with Martin Luther and John Calvin to the civil rights movement with Martin Luther King and Diane Nash. Persecution, in many ways, is broadly defined in that there always are those who are in need of the Church that will stand up and advocate on their behalf. Their persecution is seen through any number of oppressions that we witness on a daily basis. The Church is called to be peculiar in that we do not allow them to be alone in it.

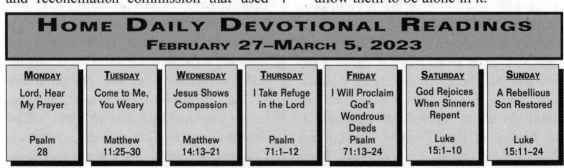

HOME DAILY DEVOTIONAL READINGS
FEBRUARY 27–MARCH 5, 2023

MONDAY	TUESDAY	WEDNESDAY	THURSDAY	FRIDAY	SATURDAY	SUNDAY
Lord, Hear My Prayer	Come to Me, You Weary	Jesus Shows Compassion	I Take Refuge in the Lord	I Will Proclaim God's Wondrous Deeds	God Rejoices When Sinners Repent	A Rebellious Son Restored
Psalm 28	Matthew 11:25–30	Matthew 14:13–21	Psalm 71:1–12	Psalm 71:13–24	Luke 15:1–10	Luke 15:11–24

THIRD QUARTER

March

April

May

THE PRODIGAL SON

ADULT TOPIC:	BACKGROUND SCRIPTURE:
LOVE IN DIFFICULT TIMES	LUKE 15:11–32

LUKE 15:11–24

King James Version	*New Revised Standard Version*
AND he said, A certain man had two sons:	THEN Jesus said, "There was a man who had two sons.
12 And the younger of them said to his father, Father, give me the portion of goods that falleth to me. And he divided unto them his living.	12 The younger of them said to his father, 'Father, give me the share of the property that will belong to me.' So he divided his property between them.
13 And not many days after the younger son gathered all together, and took his journey into a far country, and there wasted his substance with riotous living.	13 A few days later the younger son gathered all he had and traveled to a distant country, and there he squandered his property in dissolute living.
14 And when he had spent all, there arose a mighty famine in that land; and he began to be in want.	14 When he had spent everything, a severe famine took place throughout that country, and he began to be in need.
15 And he went and joined himself to a citizen of that country; and he sent him into his fields to feed swine.	15 So he went and hired himself out to one of the citizens of that country, who sent him to his fields to feed the pigs.
16 And he would fain have filled his belly with the husks that the swine did eat: and no man gave unto him.	16 He would gladly have filled himself with the pods that the pigs were eating; and no one gave him anything.
17 And when he came to himself, he said, How many hired servants of my father's have bread enough and to spare, and I perish with hunger!	17 But when he came to himself he said, 'How many of my father's hired hands have bread enough and to spare, but here I am dying of hunger!
18 I will arise and go to my father, and will say unto him, Father, I have sinned against heaven, and before thee,	18 I will get up and go to my father, and I will say to him, "Father, I have sinned against heaven and before you;
19 And am no more worthy to be called thy son: make me as one of thy hired servants.	19 I am no longer worthy to be called your son; treat me like one of your hired hands."'
20 And he arose, and came to his father. But when he was yet a great way off, his father saw him, and had compassion, and ran, and fell on his neck, and kissed him.	20 So he set off and went to his father. But while he was still far off, his father saw him and was filled with compassion; he ran and put his arms around him and kissed him.
21 And the son said unto him, Father, I have sinned against heaven, and in thy sight, and am	21 Then the son said to him, 'Father, I have sinned against heaven and before you; I am no

MAIN THOUGHT: And the son said unto him, Father, I have sinned against heaven, and in thy sight, and am no more worthy to be called thy son. Luke 15:21, KJV

LUKE 15:11—24

LESSON 1 – LOVE IN DIFFICULT TIMES – MARCH 5, 2023

King James Version	*New Revised Standard Version*
no more worthy to be called thy son.	longer worthy to be called your son.'
22 But the father said to his servants, Bring forth the best robe, and put it on him; and put a ring on his hand, and shoes on his feet:	22 But the father said to his slaves, 'Quickly, bring out a robe—the best one—and put it on him; put a ring on his finger and sandals on his feet.
23 And bring hither the fatted calf, and kill it; and let us eat, and be merry:	23 And get the fatted calf and kill it, and let us eat and celebrate;
24 For this my son was dead, and is alive again; he was lost, and is found. And they began to be merry.	24 for this son of mine was dead and is alive again; he was lost and is found!' And they began to celebrate.

LESSON SETTING
Time: AD 29
Place: On the Way to Jerusalem

LESSON OUTLINE
I. The Younger Son's Request and Reckless Behavior (Luke 15:11–14)
II. The Younger Son's Despair (Luke 15–19)
III. The Father's Forgiveness (Luke 15:20–24)

UNIFYING PRINCIPLE

We all desire to explore the world on our own terms. What do we do when what we find falls short of our expectations? In the parable of the prodigal son, the father demonstrates how only God meets and exceeds the expectations of those who return to God.

INTRODUCTION

Luke 15:11–24 is part of a larger unit that includes Luke 15 in its entirety. This pericope of Scripture consists of three related parables that disclose and display the love of God. Taken together, these three parables are often described by scholars as the "Gospel within the Gospel." The theme of this chapter or of these parables relate to the joy of recovery and return of the lost. In each of the parables something or someone is lost: a sheep, a coin, and a son. The sheep is lost due to its inability to see no further than six feet away, the coin is lost due to carelessness, and the son is lost due to his desire to go his own way. Each one of these parables presents a unique state of *lostness* that fully describes the various situations one can get oneself into. Although the theme of being lost is important, being lost serves the purpose of celebration. Ultimate joy is experienced when each of these is found. Therefore, these parables taken together express the ultimate joy experienced (in heaven), when humanity has been saved. Celebration at the return of what was lost is one of the major themes of this chapter and of the book itself. There is a running thread that weaves from the opening chapter of Luke's Gospel to this text that expresses God's concern for those who are lost, those who are marginalized, and those who are members of an outcast society.

These three parables come in the middle of Jesus' travel across the Judean country-

LESSON 1 – LOVE IN DIFFICULT TIMES – MARCH 5, 2023   **169**

side, in what scholars call the travel narratives (see Luke 9:51-19:27, The Journey to Jerusalem). In terms of form, the first two parables begin with a question, "What man…?" "What woman…?" While the latter parable tells the story of an unnamed old man and his two sons (Luke 15:4, 8, 11). John A. T. Robertson suggests, "Jesus champions the lost and accepts the challenges and justifies His conduct by these three superb stories. The three episodes form a climax: The Pasture—the House—the Home; the Herdsman—the Housewife—the Father; the Sheep—the Treasure—the Beloved Son" (*Word Pictures in the New Testament* by Archibald Thomas Robertson. Volume II. *The Gospel According to Luke*. Nashville: Broadman Press, p. 205). According to Alan Culpepper, defining this pericope of Scripture exclusively as the episodes or deeds of the younger son, works however, to weaken the story. It is three stories in one, with the prodigal son being the first. There is also the story of the waiting father, and the angry son, with the sons' contrasting images and the father caught in the middle seeking to hold his family together. These individual portraits illustrate the significance"of each character and calls attention to the shifting points of view in the parable" (see Alan Culpepper, in *The New Interpreter's Bible: A Commentary in Twelve Volume. Luke/John*. Abingdon Press; Nashville, p. 300). All three viewpoints are vital for the parable to work to achieve its intended purpose.

The three parables are directed to the Pharisees and the scribes, who murmured against Jesus because He gave an audience to publicans and sinners (Luke 15:1–3). The indication here is that they were quite vocal concerning their complaints and that they used them as a weapon to ridicule and demoralize Jesus. Essentially however, the Pharisees revealed they possessed a great character flaw. They did not value the lost and valued themselves superior to the marginalized and the outcast of their society. Their disinclination of others, especially publicans and sinners, moved Jesus to teach them a lesson in love with the hope that they would change their perception and understanding. His presentation of these three stories emphasized heaven's joy of their possible return and of the need of the Pharisees to share this godly concern.

EXPOSITION

I. THE YOUNGER SON'S REQUEST AND RECKLESS BEHAVIOR (LUKE 15:11–16)

The Parable of the Prodigal Son is easily one of the best known and most famous of the illustrations Jesus used to illuminate His message of divine love. It is unique to Luke's Gospel account. Jesus used the allegory form of speech to express beautifully God's *agape* (love). Without hesitation, after completing the first and second parable, Jesus moved quickly to bring the parables to their ultimate climax. He moves into it by pointing to an unnamed man who had two sons. The name of the man and his sons is unimportant probably because Jesus does not want anyone to mistake who the characters represent, God and humanity. The writer's note and emphasis on them as sons also sets us up for the rocky relationship between them that in many ways mirrors the relationship of sons in the Israelitish tradition, Cain and Abel, Ishmael and Isaac, Jacob, and Esau, and parenthetically, Joseph and his brothers. Historically, the relationship has been depicted as one of great animosity between the two. The relationship, though not a part of the textual emphasis for this lesson (vv. 11–24), fairs no differently. The younger son approaches the father with a demand to receive the portion of property that automatically fell to him. The father immediately reciprocated by granting the younger son's wishes. According to Jewish law, the father was not obligated to give into the younger son's demands. He was to allot or bequeath a portion of his estate to his sons that would be transactional after his death. Therefore, for the younger son to demand it while the father was alive was viewed as highly disrespectful and insulting.

According to Israelitish custom a double portion of the father's estate was to be bequeathed to the first–born or elder son. The eldest son, not the younger one, was to receive preferential treatment and was often seen as the strength of the father and the next head of the family or clan (see Genesis 10:15; 22:21; 37:22; 43:33; 44: 12; Exodus 6:14; Numbers 3:2; Deuteronomy 21:17; I Samuel 17:28; *First–Born* by V. H. Kooy, in *The Interpreter's Dictionary of the Bible E–J, Vol. 2*. Abingdon Press: Nashville, pp. 270–272). Looking at the passage from this perspective demonstrates the flagrant cruelty and disrespectable position the younger son took to achieve his inappropriate objective. His request was reckless and mirrors his pending behavior. Although not mentioned until the latter portion of the story, it is quite clear that the imperious desires and demands of the younger son, set into motion a series of difficulties that ate at the elder son who continued to work faithfully for the good of the father's estate. One can sense the drama in the eldest son's expression, "this your son." He sensed that his rights as the oldest son have been violated in at least three ways, first by the imperious demand, second by the younger son flaunting the father's hard–earned resources, and third by usurping his position as the eldest and what should have been the preferred son (see Luke 15:30). The younger son was in effect breaking family ties and treating the father as if he were already dead *(Ibid)*.

The text then explains quite succinctly that the younger son left his father's home and in a relatively short period of time squandered his property in dissolute living. His travel to a distant land (country) is a reference to the abode of the Gentiles, a land separate from God and godly living. He left his home and community to live a despised life, one of living fast and loose (see Proverbs 29:3). The Greek word used here to define dissolute living is used three times in the New Testament. In Ephesians 5:18 it means drunkenness. In Titus 1:6 it is related to rebelliousness. In I Peter 4:3 it describes a variety of vices practiced by Gentiles: passions, carousing, licentiousness, and reveling. The oncoming of a severe panic only serves to hasten his situation, and to paint it as one of desperation. He had made a bad choice to fall away from his father's home and community and here serves as a reflection of humanity's fall in the Garden of Eden, but it was only the beginning of his avalanche. Having detached himself from his family, coupled with living the fast life, he easily and soon depleted his inheritance. The Greek adverb used here denotes a spendthrift, a profligate, a prodigal. The adverb describes the limit of his sinful excesses. Having no real skills to jump start his career, he reduced himself to working a job reserved for the lowest class of Gentiles. This job involved him debasing himself by feeding swine, which was deplorable work for a Jew. It highlighted the great extent of his immense decline because swine were the ultimate symbol of uncleanliness, and represented the disgraceful state of his great demise. To feed them one has to immerse oneself into their filth. Therefore, via his association with swine he was deemed to be as swine himself. Yet no one gave him any of the food (pods from the carob tree) used specially to feed the swine. It is clear from the text that he would have taken the lowest step to accommodate his hunger, yet was deprived of it because no one gave him any. The emphasis is to show that he was in a sinful state, a deplorable state. He was in the deepest depths of despair.

II. THE YOUNGER SON'S DESPAIR (LUKE 15:17–19)

The depths of his despair served however to allow him to see himself as he really was. He came to himself. It is safe to say he saw his image in the cesspool of degradation and did not like what he had become. Robertson said, "He had been as far from himself as he was from home" (Robertson, *Word Pictures in the New Testament* p. 209). Now as he came to himself, he began to acknowledge how good he had it, while at home. The contrast between the two dispositions is startling to say the least. At one time his demands are over the top, now he speaks quietly to himself to confess the error of his ways by acknowledging using the word *many* in verse 17, which indicates

wealth and luxury that, "I have nothing." The mention of hired servants adds to the clearness of his sight. The prodigal clearly sees what he has left behind and understands now the gravity of his mistake. Yet the prodigal is not confused about what he needs to do. Redemption is only possible if he acts. In fact, action is the only recourse to him saving himself, otherwise according to his own words "I perish" (v. 17). He has come full circle to where he had first begun, to reap the full bitter fruit of his foolish behavior and outrageous demands. Seeing himself, considering his present situation, jostled his memory of who he was (the son of a wealthy loving family), while making it perfectly clear he also understood the breadth of what he had done (destroyed any concept of what it meant to be a good Jewish family). He had sinned.

Now the time was ripe for him to redeem himself and reclaim the identity he had so carelessly and foolishly cast to the side. He decides to leave the far country and make his journey home, even if he had to subrogate himself to a life of *servantry*. In comparison, it was better than any of the other alternative before him. He had exhausted any of his rights to claim *sonship* or an inheritance. The now thinking prodigal speaks to himself and convinces himself to accomplish for actions. First, he will appropriately redress his father ("Father," v. 18.). Second, he will confess ("I have sinned against heaven and against you"). Third, he will express contrition ("I am no longer worthy to be called your son"). Fourth, he will petition the father to understand and to forgive him, "make me like one of your hired hands" (see Culpepper, Luke, *The New Interpreter's Bible.* p. 302).

Having rehearsed his plea for forgiveness the young former prodigal takes off for the journey homeward. He deliberately acted on his self–perceived notion to come contrite before his father. His action in this way reveals how important it is for us to acknowledge within ourselves the tragic effect of our sin and to confess it. His return is the equivalent of what it means to repent. Repent means to turn around, to do an about face. That he follows the requisites for repentance are duly noted in the text. First, he comes to himself. It appears "he had been far away from himself as he was from home. He had been away, out of his head, and now began to see things as they really were," according to Robertson (see Robertson, *Word Pictures in the New Testament,* p. 208). Second, he dusts off his sinful boots and arises. Third, He fulfills his self–confessed word and goes home. He does not know what to expect of his father, but at this point it is immaterial. It will not thwart his actions of repentance. His determination to turn back the clock to a happier time is revealed here. He conclusively reveals his intention, "I will arise and go to my father in humility because I did sin." Robertson suggests the prodigal shot his bolt and missed his aim. It is a precursory confession that he will seek to repeat in the father's presence.

III. A FATHER'S FORGIVENESS (LUKE 15:20–24)

As the son goes home, the story shifts to embrace, highlight, and underscore the father's action. The focus is no longer on the son, but on how the father receives the son's return. While he was on the way home, the figure of the father emerges, and his action dominates the scene from this time forth. Evidently, the father had been looking for his son to return. The verb used here expresses the totality of the father's great love and great anticipation for his son's homecoming. The Greek *dragon* (dragon) is used here and means to run. In eager anticipation of the son's returns the father takes the risk of running toward him. Running for an elderly man in the Jewish context meant a loss of dignity. But the father was more than willing to lose any amount of perceived dignity in order to reclaim his long–lost son. The accompanying action of the father is of no less importance than the father's running. He comes to the son and greets him with repeated kisses. The kiss represents full acceptance of the son. He is restored back to his status as a son. The giving of the best robe, a ring, sandals, and the preparation of the fatted calf all come together to emphasize the son's full and complete restoration. The father's action sets the tone for total forgiveness, which means to restore the relation back to what it was before the infraction took place. His action is indicative of what God does. Notice verses 22–24. They complete a series of contrasting images in relationship to the prodigal's wanton experience. His father clothed him with a robe of significant rank and privilege removing the pictures of him ill–clad in shabby clothing of his self–imposed sentence of destruction, via financial and spiritual ruin. The placing of the ring on his finger and shoes upon his feet further show or illustrate he was more than a hired-hand or a slave. The son was a freedman in every sense of the word. To top off the elevation of the younger son, a feast was held in his honor. It contrasts with him being hungry and destitute and longing for the food of swine. The father's action has reversed his downward course. The son has returned to live again. The Greek *kai anezesen*, (kai anezesen) is used here in the emphatic sense and means is alive again. It has connotations of the resurrection. He, who was once in a lost state, has been found. His finding is the cause for merriment. Just as the man rejoiced after finding the lost sheep, the woman rejoiced after finding the lost coin, so the lost but now found son deserves a celebration of sorts.

THE LESSON APPLIED

The story of the prodigal son is a story revealing the love of God for the lost and the outcast. In delivering this parable, Jesus was reaching out to the Pharisee and other respectable religious people to alert them of the fallacy of their ways. Where they would be content to leaving the lost lost, Jesus emphasizes the joy of heaven for them being found. It is a story full of contrasts with the main contrast being the difference between God's concern for the despised human and the human dejection and rejection of others like them. The story is intended to provoke the Pharisee to embrace a new attitudinal disposition for others, and to adopt new ones for themselves. Also, confession plays a major role in this parable. The prodigal acted outside of his normal behavior. Yet, all was not lost because he could rationalize the effect sin had upon him. It had cost him dearly, but when he came to himself and confessed, he discovered and experienced full redemption from the father. Although he had dispensed of the family's resources without regard to what it cost his father or anyone else, he received the ultimate gift of forgiveness and restoration to the family. His reacceptance was nothing short of salvation. Although he missed the mark with his sin, his confession and return more than made up for his error of judgment. The father's love paved the way. It is a microcosm of the human predicament. We erred in judgment and missed the mark God demanded of us. However, His mercy, grace, and love worked together to provide us another opportunity to get it right.

LET'S TALK ABOUT IT

Was the elder son right to exhibit anger for his younger brother?

Anger is a natural emotion but, we cannot allow it to distort our sense of spirituality and forgiveness. In this case, the elder brother's anger led to sin. Rather than be happy that his brother had returned home safely, he held a grudge against him. It also blinded him from being able to comprehend the vastness of his father's love, and prohibited him from proving the forgiveness his brother needed.

HOME DAILY DEVOTIONAL READINGS
MARCH 6–12, 2023

MONDAY	TUESDAY	WEDNESDAY	THURSDAY	FRIDAY	SATURDAY	SUNDAY
Jesus Heals a Gentile Girl	Let the Little Children Come	Learn Wisdom, My Child	Teach Your Children God's Laws	Consecrated from the Womb	The Praises of Children	The Greatest in the Kingdom
Matthew 15:21–28	Matthew 19:13–22	Proverbs 1:7–16	Deuteronomy 4:7–14	Jeremiah 1:1–10	Matthew 21:12–17	Matthew 18:1–9; Mark 10:15

A CHILD IS GREATEST IN THE KINGDOM

ADULT TOPIC:	BACKGROUND SCRIPTURE:
THE WONDER OF CHILDLIKE QUALITIES	MATTHEW 18:1–9; MARK 10:15

MATTHEW 18:1–9

King James Version

AT the same time came the disciples unto Jesus, saying, Who is the greatest in the kingdom of heaven?

2 And Jesus called a little child unto him, and set him in the midst of them,

3 And said, Verily I say unto you, Except ye be converted, and become as little children, ye shall not enter into the kingdom of heaven.

4 Whosoever therefore shall humble himself as this little child, the same is greatest in the kingdom of heaven.

5 And whoso shall receive one such little child in my name receiveth me.

6 But whoso shall offend one of these little ones which believe in me, it were better for him that a millstone were hanged about his neck, and that he were drowned in the depth of the sea.

7 Woe unto the world because of offences! for it must needs be that offences come; but woe to that man by whom the offence cometh!

8 Wherefore if thy hand or thy foot offend thee, cut them off, and cast them from thee: it is better for thee to enter into life halt or maimed, rather than having two hands or two feet to be cast into everlasting fire.

9 And if thine eye offend thee, pluck it out, and cast it from thee: it is better for thee to enter into life with one eye, rather than having two eyes to be cast into hell fire.

New Revised Standard Version

AT that time the disciples came to Jesus and asked, "Who is the greatest in the kingdom of heaven?"

2 He called a child, whom he put among them,

3 and said, "Truly I tell you, unless you change and become like children, you will never enter the kingdom of heaven.

4 Whoever becomes humble like this child is the greatest in the kingdom of heaven.

5 Whoever welcomes one such child in my name welcomes me.

6 "If any of you put a stumbling block before one of these little ones who believe in me, it would be better for you if a great millstone were fastened around your neck and you were drowned in the depth of the sea.

7 Woe to the world because of stumbling blocks! Occasions for stumbling are bound to come, but woe to the one by whom the stumbling block comes!

8 "If your hand or your foot causes you to stumble, cut it off and throw it away; it is better for you to enter life maimed or lame than to have two hands or two feet and to be thrown into the eternal fire.

9 And if your eye causes you to stumble, tear it out and throw it away; it is better for you to enter life with one eye than to have two eyes and to be thrown into the hell of fire.

MAIN THOUGHT: Whosoever therefore shall humble himself as this little child, the same is greatest in the kingdom of heaven. Matthew 18:4, KJV

LESSON SETTING
    Time: AD 28
    Place: Jerusalem

LESSON OUTLINE
  I. **Who is the Greatest?**
    (Matthew 18:1–5)
  II. **Be Service-Minded!**
    (Matthew 18:6–9)

UNIFYING PRINCIPLE

Children are cherished resources with innate qualities and values that often go unappreciated by the larger society. What impedes our ability to be more childlike? Jesus recognized qualities in children that most resemble God's definition of greatness and challenged disciples to relinquish their claims to power or greatness.

INTRODUCTION

Many people conceive of greatness as achieving things that only a few, if others, have achieved. This understanding of greatness carries with it a competitive edge, a feeling of arrogance and superiority over others. It was this type of greatness or definition of greatness that stood out in the minds of the disciples and that they inquired about to Jesus.

Just having confessed that Jesus was the Messiah and being given the keys to the Kingdom of God, the scenario that this passage of Scripture presents is one of personal gain (Matthew 16:13–20). The disciples vied against each other to gain superiority over one another as a benefit or perk for their service. However, Jesus was not having any of that. It was not the type of *followership* that Jesus desired for them to learn in order to carry out His ministry. Jesus had a better way in mind for them to travel and their question provided to Him a teaching moment concerning true greatness. Two things are important in His analysis. First, in answer to their question, Jesus acknowledged the significance of their inquest by calling a little child as a case in point (Matthews 18:1–6). Second, He warns the disciples to stay away from things that may cause them or others to stumble (Matthew 18:7–9). Jesus' point of emphasis is that entrance into the Kingdom of God demands the adoption of a set of divinely–inspired principles that govern human life and the living of which sets humanity on a course of righteousness.

EXPOSITION

I. WHO IS THE GREATEST? (MATTHEW 18:1–5)

This section of Scripture is part of a larger narrative that begin with Matthew 12:22 and continues to the end of the book (Matthew 28:20). The entire pericope deals with the issue of conflict between the Messianic Kingdom and the perception of it as understood by its Jewish proponents (see Eugene Boring. *The Gospel of Matthew, Introduction, in The New Interpreter's Bible*. Vol. VIII. Abingdon Press: Nashville: pp. 122–124). Although conflict is the apparent issue that defines this passage, it points to the establishment of a new community where it is resolved. Precisely, given in the disciples' question is the issue of greatness. Peter's confession of Jesus as the Messiah (Matthew 16:13), His seemingly, yet apparent appointment of Peter as the official second in command (Matthew 16:17–19), and Peter's dominate role in the Transfiguration and in the paying of temple tax (Matthew 17:1–27), probably contributed to the other disciples' belief that Peter had gained a level of authority over them. Jesus addressed the question that ultimately followed in Matthew 18:1.

However, His initial approach is to have them understand that entrance into the Kingdom of God requires the living out of a certain set of principles that contrasted with many of the precepts of Jewish life. This pericope is the one of the first to illustrate Jesus' rejection of automatic entrance into the Kingdom based upon their birth as Hebrews. It is similar to His denial of Jewish relationship to Abraham as a precursor to entrance into heaven as noted in John 8:31–59. The disciples asked Jesus pointedly, "Who is the greatest in the kingdom of Heaven?" Jesus called a little child unto him and set him in the midst of them. What was the point of the Lord's demonstrative act of calling the child before them? According to Eugene Boring, "The disciples had supposed that they were 'in' the Kingdom, and only asked Jesus about their relative rank. Jesus' radical prophetic reply challenges their assumptions: To get 'in' one must be converted, which means to become like a little child" (Boring, *The New Interpreter's Bible*, p. 374). The narrator slaps away any hint of self–serving righteousness as the basis for entrance into the Kingdom. Neither does Jewish heritage, through birth or proselytism, grant automatic entrance into it, either. Both the KJV and the NRSV (Matthew 18:3) argue that it involves the process of an inward change. Definitive change, "to become like a child" is at the center of one gaining access into God's Kingdom. Jesus is direct and focused, and has one goal in mind. In the Jewish world, children were to be seen and not heard. Moreover, they worked as

laborers to advance the family's wealth and prosperity. Rarely did their actions or words have significant meaning. Girls were treated worse than boys, but both found it difficult to gain any parody with parents and the adult world.

Therefore, for Jesus to summon a child and pointedly tell adults they need to assimilate into their own being and life the characteristics of a child was radical, indeed. These characteristics would include but not limited to humility, innocence, openness, accepting, trust, dependency, and being vulnerable. Boring continues, "To become like a little child is to humble oneself, giving up all pretensions of self–importance, independence, and self–reliance and turning to trust in the heavenly Father" *(Ibid, p. 374)*. Emphasis is placed on the word "become," because the call is not one of merely imitating childlike behavior but, it is total transformation by adopting a new concept or idea about one's self. It involves a reassessment of self and indicates the need of a new birth, the need to start over (see John 3:3). Verse five succinctly confirms that whoever successfully obtains and fully embraces childlike humility is the greatest in the Kingdom of heaven.

To become great then is to undergo the process of humility. It is a restatement of Matthew 5:5, "Blessed are the meek: for they shall inherit the earth" (KJV). Life in Jesus' new community of believers requires us to put first things first. That is to say, we must seek after the Kingdom of God and His righteousness. This seeking for God requires us to put on a new mindset that works to control one's desires and ambitions of greatness. It makes one sober–minded. Human greatness and/or superiority over others is not seen as something to strive for as Paul noted in Philippians 2–3. In these chapters, the Apostle Paul called upon the Christians at Philippi to adopt the mind of Christ by opting for a life of humility and service to God. He implies that they are not to be in conflict and competition for greatness and strife for power in the church.

Furthermore, in Philippians 3:3–8, Paul used himself as an example of appropriate Christian conduct and behavior. Although he has attained to achieving great things at several levels, (being a Pharisee, of the tribe of Benjamin, recognized as a conscientious prosecutor), he considered these achievements as dung in light of experiencing Christ's resurrection and the power of the Kingdom of God. Like Jesus' direct comment to the disciples defining greatness as childlike humility, Paul tells the church at Philippi, to govern itself accordingly.

Verse 5 declares that a vital linkage exists between those who receive the humble in Jesus' name. They also receive and accept Jesus. Boring notes here, "'… verse 5 is a concrete illustration of the meaning of humility called for in v. 4. To receive a child is to genuinely humble oneself, for the vulnerable, dependent child can do nothing to further one's selfish ambitions, and receiving the child can have no ulterior motives, no hidden agendas. One who receives a child has been converted to the ethos of the kingdom represented by Jesus, and is no longer concerned about being 'the greatest'" (Boring, *Ibid.* p. 374). It is notable that Jesus identifies and aligns Himself with childlike humility.

II. BE SERVICE-MINDED! (MATTHEW 18:6–9)

In this pericope of Scripture, the scene shifts to encompass what Paul in Romans 15:1 called the "infirmities of the weak." Here the humble defenseless child presented in Matthew 18:1–5 becomes a symbol for the weak, the neglected, exploited and/or immature Christian who must be looked after at all costs. The KJV and the NSV call them, little ones, to emphasis their vulnerability to power and other types of abuses. Like the children noted in the preceding verses, their humility and relative immaturity provide no way for them to grant favors to the powerful. Just the converse is true, the ambitious and the powerful of the church and of the world are implored by Jesus to be the mouthpieces and supporters of the weak and the faint in heart. The use of the Greek word *prosballow* (prosballow) translated offend in the KJV means to harm, to hurt, to attack, or to debase. The point is Jesus warns the strong not to debase the weak or immature ones. Those who are found guilty of such abuse will fair far better if a large millstone were attached to their necks and they were dropped into the sea (v. 6). A millstone was a hand–mill used for grinding grain with a stationary, lower stone, ground against an upper stone that was turned. The device was propelled by a donkey. The weight of the runner stone is significant (up to 3,300 lbs.), and it is this weight combined with the cutting action from the porous stone and the patterning that causes the milling process. The sheer weight of the stone around one's neck assured one's drowning. Thus, there was little hope for one to be rescued if the stone was tied to the body and dropped into the sea. Jesus' words of judgment, noted here in v. 7, reveal His concern for the weak.

Furthermore, His words of caution here in relationship to the little people advised the powerful or mature leaders to avoid condescension. They must govern their behavior or actions toward the little people and exercise their authority appropriately, without placing stumbling blocks in the way of immature or weak members of the new community. The Greek word *woe* as used here is emphatic. It is more than an expression of emotional concern but also carries with it a sense of total disaster as alluded to earlier concerning Christ's judgment. Although Jesus points to those who demonstrate innocence, humility, trust, openness, as children or little ones, He also indirectly acknowledges how those in the world might conceive of those who possess and practice these characteristics as vulnerable and take advantage of them. His terse warning in verses 7–8 is directed to those mature Christians, and to others, who might not be otherwise concerned about the little ones. His identification with them not only signifies His care for them, but also emphasizes that they take care to do so as well. This includes resisting the temptation to overlook or neglect them in any way. Rather than focus on power and achieving greatness, vv. 8–9

contend that the disciples would be better off to focus their efforts on caring for the less fortunate of society.

THE LESSON APPLIED

The greatest in the Kingdom of God are persons who willingly seek to start over by adopting the childlike qualities of humility, innocence, without lust, open and trusting in God, dependent upon Him, and vulnerable to the abuse by the world and others. These believers possess a higher calling to become like Christ who sought not after greatness, but to please God the Father. The lesson posits humility as the key to entrance into the new community of faith established by Jesus for His disciples. It also beguiles leaders to be service–minded and caring for those who are most vulnerable in society.

LET'S TALK ABOUT IT

Why did Jesus point to a child as being the greatest in the Kingdom of God?

The Lord used a child to demonstrate the importance of humility and other virtuous characteristics as a pre–requisite to enter the Kingdom of God. Humility required a sense of soberness about oneself and ones' ability. Humility holds pride and arrogance in check. It also reveals total dependence on the sufficiency of God.

HOME DAILY DEVOTIONAL READINGS
MARCH 13–19, 2023

MONDAY	TUESDAY	WEDNESDAY	THURSDAY	FRIDAY	SATURDAY	SUNDAY
Rivers of Living Water	Worship God Alone	Handling Opposition to God's Plans	Water on a Thirsty Land	Offers Living Water	Worship in Spirit and Truth	Jesus the Savior of the World
John 7:37–43	2 Kings 17:24–34	Ezra 4:1–8, 11–16	Isaiah 44:1–8 Jesus	John 4:1–15	John 4:16–26	John 4:27–29, 31–42

JESUS TALKS WITH A SAMARITAN WOMAN

ADULT TOPIC:	BACKGROUND SCRIPTURE:
DIFFERENT, BUT THE SAME	JOHN 4:1–42

JOHN 4:7–15, 28–30, 39–41

King James Version	*New Revised Standard Version*
THERE cometh a woman of Samaria to draw water: Jesus saith unto her, Give me to drink.	A SAMARITAN woman came to draw water, and Jesus said to her, "Give me a drink."
8 (For his disciples were gone away unto the city to buy meat.)	8 (His disciples had gone to the city to buy food.)
9 Then saith the woman of Samaria unto him, How is it that thou, being a Jew, askest drink of me, which am a woman of Samaria? for the Jews have no dealings with the Samaritans.	9 The Samaritan woman said to him, "How is it that you, a Jew, ask a drink of me, a woman of Samaria?" (Jews do not share things in common with Samaritans.)
10 Jesus answered and said unto her, If thou knewest the gift of God, and who it is that saith to thee, Give me to drink; thou wouldest have asked of him, and he would have given thee living water.	10 Jesus answered her, "If you knew the gift of God, and who it is that is saying to you, 'Give me a drink,' you would have asked him, and he would have given you living water."
11 The woman saith unto him, Sir, thou hast nothing to draw with, and the well is deep: from whence then hast thou that living water?	11 The woman said to him, "Sir, you have no bucket, and the well is deep. Where do you get that living water?
12 Art thou greater than our father Jacob, which gave us the well, and drank thereof himself, and his children, and his cattle?	12 Are you greater than our ancestor Jacob, who gave us the well, and with his sons and his flocks drank from it?"
13 Jesus answered and said unto her, Whosoever drinketh of this water shall thirst again:	13 Jesus said to her, "Everyone who drinks of this water will be thirsty again,
14 But whosoever drinketh of the water that I shall give him shall never thirst; but the water that I shall give him shall be in him a well of water springing up into everlasting life.	14 but those who drink of the water that I will give them will never be thirsty. The water that I will give will become in them a spring of water gushing up to eternal life."

MAIN THOUGHT: And many of the Samaritans of that city believed on him for the saying of the woman, which testified, He told me all that ever I did. John 4:39, KJV

JOHN 4:7–15, 28–30, 39–41

King James Version	*New Revised Standard Version*
15 The woman saith unto him, Sir, give me this water, that I thirst not, neither come hither to draw.	15 The woman said to him, "Sir, give me this water, so that I may never be thirsty or have to keep coming here to draw water."
••••••	••••••
28 The woman then left her waterpot, and went her way into the city, and saith to the men, 29 Come, see a man, which told me all things that ever I did: is not this the Christ?	28 Then the woman left her water jar and went back to the city. She said to the people, 29 "Come and see a man who told me everything I have ever done! He cannot be the Messiah, can he?"
30 Then they went out of the city, and came unto him.	30 They left the city and were on their way to him.
••••••	••••••
39 And many of the Samaritans of that city believed on him for the saying of the woman, which testified, He told me all that ever I did.	39 Many Samaritans from that city believed in him because of the woman's testimony, "He told me everything I have ever done."
40 So when the Samaritans were come unto him, they besought him that he would tarry with them: and he abode there two days.	40 So when the Samaritans came to him, they asked him to stay with them; and he stayed there two days.
41 And many more believed because of his own word;	41 And many more believed because of his word.

LESSON SETTING
Time: AD 26
Place: Samaria

LESSON OUTLINE
I. **The Question That Provoked a Double Question (John 4:7–11)**
II. **The Question That Provoked A Splendid Request (John 4:12–15)**
III. **The Question Answered (John 4:28–30, 39–41)**

UNIFYING PRINCIPLE
People create barriers that can hinder relationships. What can be done to eliminate these barriers? Jesus was able to break the relationship barriers with the Samaritan woman, offering her living water leading to eternal life.

INTRODUCTION
The Bible often deals with subject matter and issues that are not always pleasant to hear. In the Old Testament for example several scandals prevail. Two of the most notable ones are Judah's affair with his daughter-in-law, Tamar, (Genesis 38:1-30) and the rape of Tamar by Amnon her half-brother (2 Samuel 15). Equally, the New Testament deals with real human issues, such as racism, prejudice, and adultery. The presence of scandals or serious human issues show that the biblical record presents a truthful word in relationship to humanity's fallenness, and it does not seek to put forth a utopian view or story of a perfect people.

In the Johannine account before us, the

disciples return from a shopping spree and are amazed that Jesus is talking openly with a woman. Jesus' intentional diversion of His ministry route to include Samaria was a deliberate revelation to Him by the Holy Spirit. The text informs us in John 4:4, "And he must needs go through Samaria" (KJV). His encounter with a Samaritan woman in John 4 is a presentation of multiple issues Jesus confronted: sexism, racism, gender inequality, and adultery, to say the least. These are tough issues to address in the 21st Century, much less at a time when they were readily seen as the norm by more than a few people. John 4:9 is clear "... the Jews have no dealings with the Samaritans." The Samaritan woman words here reveal a firm reality about race relations between these two groups of people. However, little is said about the relationship between the sexes. Not only was she confused and bewildered that a Jew had opened conversation with a Samaritan, but equally bewildering was that Jesus was speaking to a woman, and a scandalous woman at that. This remarkable encounter says a lot about how our Lord dealt with the social issues of His day and how He offers to contemporary people opportunities to challenge socially institutionalized mores. Jesus opened up the dialogue with a question. His question challenged the accepted and conventional norm of the day that Jews and Samaritans had no dealings with each other. In presenting the question that defined the woman's attitudinal disposition, Jesus engages the woman's in conversation. The conversation led to a second inquest and a request for Jesus to supply a real and felt need possessed by the woman. Lastly, by gaining some level of credibility with the woman, Jesus answers her deeper question by revealing to her His identity as the Messiah. In doing so, He also addressed the issues of racism, sexism, and adultery, the very same issues that weigh people down in guilt and sin today.

EXPOSITION

I. THE QUESTION THAT PROVOKED A DOUBLE QUESTION (JOHN 4:7-11)

Jesus' encounter with the woman of Samaria is the focal point of John 4:1-42. John 4:1-6 serves as an introduction to the story. These verses provide the rational and set the stage for His diversion to Samaria. Jesus' popularity had greatly increased and He was already being eyed by the Pharisees, who are suspicious of Him. The Pharisee had already turned violent against John (see Matthew 3:1-10 and Luke 3:19) and may have been the ones' behind John being thrown into prison. With John out of the way, they turned to Jesus with their venom. Knowing His hour had not yet come, Jesus avoided conflict by taking the back roads and the shorter more convenient to the small city (Greek: *polis*). It is a plausible explanation for His route through Samaria (v. 1). He came to Sychar whose location was near the well that Jacob developed and gave to Joseph (see Genesis 33:19; 48:22). However, the purpose of the trip appears to be both geographical and theological. The words *edel edei* in the Greek, meaning *had to* are usually associated with God's plan when used by the Fourth Evangelist (see Gail R. O'Day, *The Gospel of John* in *The New Interpreter's Bible*. Volume 9. Abingdon Press: Nashville, p. 565; John 3:14, 30;

9:4). That Jesus subjected Himself to divine necessity is a staple in this Gospel account. One must not miss the detailed description of the location (Jacob's well), because it is important to understand the divine initiative that Jesus was emphasizing. Overall there are several exchanges between the two parties that end with Jesus making a request or a command.

Verse seven begins with an Old Testament parallel of the story found in I Kings 17:10-11. There Elijah the Prophet requested from the woman of Zarephath water, and a morsel of bread. It is a request of hospitality to a woman who is pursing her duties as a homemaker. The prophetic overtones here will serve as a precursor to the inevitable comparison between Jesus and other Old Testament personalities latter in John's Gospel (see John 6-9). It also points to the woman's gradual, but honorable, elevation of His status once their conversation begins.

Also, O'Day is careful to point out that it is likewise an exchange between a woman and a man similar to the betrothal ones experienced by Isaac Jacob, and Moses (see Genesis 24:10-61; 29;1-20; Exodus 2:15-21). The difference between these encounters and the one between Jesus and the Samaritan woman is Jesus calls her to become a witness, and a herald of the faith to Israel's despised enemies (see *The Interpreters Bible*, p. 565).

Breaking the social norms of the day, Jesus requests of her a drink of water. Her reaction is one of total amazement. With His request, Jesus put a wrench in the social gears of Jewish and Samaritan societies, and all other societies through them that operate and gain strength from racism and sexism. Notice, He did something similar when He offered up the widow of Sidon (Zarephath), Naaman the Syrian, and the Good Samaritan as examples of salvation and good works (see Luke 4: 1-30; 10:25-37).

The woman responded with a question of her own, with the real problem coming out in the aftermath of her inquest. She asked Jesus, '"How is it that thou, being a Jew, askest drink of me, which am a woman of Samaria? for the Jews have no dealings with the Samaritans."' The racial problem between the two groups of people was not a private matter, it was publicly known, and even embraced. Ever the Master Strategist, Jesus ignored the conventional social norms of Judaism and redirected her response to His question in such a way that He gained her complete attention and respect. He used the conditional *if* to denote the vast possibilities of life before her. '"If thou knewest the gift of God, and who it is that saith to thee, Give me to drink; thou wouldest have asked of him, and he would have given thee living water"' (John 4:10, KJV). Abundant life would be the end result of her potential request. His statement provokes her interest denoting she is looking and needing something better than what she currently possesses. This will be brought out a bit later (see vv. 16-18) as He demonstrates the essential qualities that come to bear in the Greek understanding of the word *know*. As noted earlier, she is a by-product of her racial and cultural heritage, and she readily accepted the societal norms of her day and was concerned that Jesus had violated them, hence her amazement. Jewish men did initiate conversation with an unknown woman. Moreover, a Jewish teacher did not engage in public conversation with a woman. Second, Jews did not invite contact with Samaritans. Notice her question and statement, concerning the race problem between the two, did not gain any traction with Jesus. He undoubtably had more pressing matters to attend to, namely the woman's salvation and the salvation of her community. His inaction concerning racial matters illustrates that it was not a barrier that should stand in the way of her salvation. Racial problems should not stand in the way of our salvation, nor should anything else. Jesus treated her with respect and as one entitled to God's umbrella of love, grace, and mercy, regardless of her heritage.

II. The Question That Provoked A Splendid Request (John 4:12-15)

What she hears Him say to her however, deals with her inability to grasp the spiritual significance and truth of His presence. She understands His reference to *Living Water* as fresh running water, especially since He has just offered to her something that He does not appear to possess. She notices, Jesus has nothing within which to carry water in. His seemingly empty-handedness causes her to wonder what Jesus is seeking to accomplish. Jesus had just spoken of her knowing the gift of the Father and who it was that she was speaking to that she would be asking Him for a drink with positive results. Noticing Jesus was empty-handed provoked her to ask Jesus how He expected to draw water from the well and to inquire whether or not Jesus was greater than Jacob. Jesus will answer her indirectly in His comments about the Living Water. One of the keys to better comprehend Jesus' response is to examine the biblical meaning of the word *know*. As meant here in verse 10, *hedeis* (Greek) to know means an intimate knowledge of something or of someone, much like a husband knows his wife or vice versa. If she had an intimate and personal relationship with God she would be aware of the Gift of Life, who was standing before her and speaking to her. She would recognize Him as the Gift that came from above (see John 3:1-6. See Jesus' dialogue with Nicodemus.). This intimate knowledge would be the spark of her later request for living water that quenches thirst forever (v. 12-15). It was this relationship that she was missing, yet one that she desperately needed. Gradually, she would come to make this discovery during the duration of their conversation. At this point, however, Jesus explains the significant difference between the literal water she is inquiring about, the water that comes from Jacob's well, and the Living Water He gives, which is Himself, the Gift from the Father which has come down from above. Her thirst will be forever quenched. He implies by His response to her inquest that He is indeed superior to Jacob, something she will declare herself by her witness to her community.

Although, the woman did not know Jesus, she soon surmised that she was known by Him. After Jesus revealed details of her most intimate history to her, the Samaritan woman found herself leaping over the issue of credibility to embrace Jesus as more than a prophet (John 4:15-18). In this she answered her own question, concerning Jesus' superiority to Jacob.

One greater than Jacob was here and there was no ridicule in His voice, nor was there any indication that He looked down on her. She was being spiritually enlightened. She requested that He give to her the water that would quench her thirst and need to come to the well to draw water.

III. The Question Answered (John 4:28-30, 39-41)

The latter part of this pericope of Scripture finds the woman's response to Jesus' bold declaration of Himself as the Messiah (v. 28). Upon hearing His self-confession as the Messiah, she immediately rushes into action. His confession has generated a need for her to share her new discovery with others in her community. She has even forgotten what she came to the well for. Her action is a throw back to Jesus' earlier comments that those who drink from Jacob's well will thirst again, "but the Water He gives will be in that person as a well of Water springing up into eternal life." Her question, "Is this not the Christ?" even though it begins with a negative particle (Greek: *meti*) anticipates a new discovery, even though she appeals to them from the standpoint of it being a possibility. She had found the Living Water and her need for the running water had been superceded. What she does in return is significant. First, she invites the people of her community to come and see for themselves. Second, she enjoins them to relive her experience. Third, she asks if Jesus could be the Messiah. It appears to be a conclusion she has already come to for herself, but one that she prefers the community to reach for itself. In doing so, she becomes the perfect example of evangelism. She does what a good disciple should be doing. Correspondingly, when they heard His precious words they believed in Him, and He stayed with them two whole days. They came to know Him intimately as the Messiah, the Saviour of the world.

The Lesson Applied

Jesus is the Messiah of God. The salvation that He offers crosses over racial and sexual boundaries. His ministry to the Samaritan woman shows that Jesus is not deterred by our cultural and/or social differences. We are all God's children and in need of His grace and love.

Let's Talk About It

Can we overcome the race problem?

Yes! By imitating Jesus' love for all people. When we come to see others as people like ourselves in need of grace and mercy, we will be less judgmental and less likely to erect barriers to their salvation. Through His power we can come to accept others as made in His image like we are.

Home Daily Devotional Readings
March 20–26, 2023

Monday	Tuesday	Wednesday	Thursday	Friday	Saturday	Sunday
Resist the Devil	The Weapons of Our Warfare	Lord, Remember Your People Psalm 106:1–	Take Refuge in God	Let God's Enemies Be Scattered	Jesus Sets a Demoniac Free	Sent to Bear Witness
James 4:1–10	2 Corinthians 10:1–6	7, 36–41, 47–48	Psalm 34:1–15	Numbers 10:29–36	Mark 5:1–13	Mark 5:14–20

JESUS OVERPOWERS LEGION

ADULT TOPIC:	BACKGROUND SCRIPTURE:
JESUS OVERPOWERS LEGION	MARK 5:1–20

MARK 5:1–13, 18–20

King James Version

AND they came over unto the other side of the sea, into the country of the Gadarenes.

2 And when he was come out of the ship, immediately there met him out of the tombs a man with an unclean spirit,

3 Who had his dwelling among the tombs; and no man could bind him, no, not with chains:

4 Because that he had been often bound with fetters and chains, and the chains had been plucked asunder by him, and the fetters broken in pieces: neither could any man tame him.

5 And always, night and day, he was in the mountains, and in the tombs, crying, and cutting himself with stones.

6 But when he saw Jesus afar off, he ran and worshipped him,

7 And cried with a loud voice, and said, What have I to do with thee, Jesus, thou Son of the most high God? I adjure thee by God, that thou torment me not.

8 For he said unto him, Come out of the man, thou unclean spirit.

9 And he asked him, What is thy name? And he answered, saying, My name is Legion: for we are many.

10 And he besought him much that he would not send them away out of the country.

New Revised Standard Version

THEY came to the other side of the sea, to the country of the Gerasenes.

2 And when he had stepped out of the boat, immediately a man out of the tombs with an unclean spirit met him.

3 He lived among the tombs; and no one could restrain him any more, even with a chain;

4 for he had often been restrained with shackles and chains, but the chains he wrenched apart, and the shackles he broke in pieces; and no one had the strength to subdue him.

5 Night and day among the tombs and on the mountains he was always howling and bruising himself with stones.

6 When he saw Jesus from a distance, he ran and bowed down before him;

7 and he shouted at the top of his voice, "What have you to do with me, Jesus, Son of the Most High God? I adjure you by God, do not torment me."

8 For he had said to him, "Come out of the man, you unclean spirit!"

9 Then Jesus asked him, "What is your name?" He replied, "My name is Legion; for we are many."

10 He begged him earnestly not to send them out of the country.

MAIN THOUGHT: And he departed, and began to publish in Decapolis how great things Jesus had done for him: and all men did marvel. Mark 5:20, KJV

MARK 5:1–13, 18–20

King James Version	*New Revised Standard Version*
11 Now there was there nigh unto the mountains a great herd of swine feeding.	11 Now there on the hillside a great herd of swine was feeding;
12 And all the devils besought him, saying, Send us into the swine, that we may enter into them.	12 and the unclean spirits begged him, "Send us into the swine; let us enter them."
13 And forthwith Jesus gave them leave. And the unclean spirits went out, and entered into the swine: and the herd ran violently down a steep place into the sea, (they were about two thousand;) and were choked in the sea.	13 So he gave them permission. And the unclean spirits came out and entered the swine; and the herd, numbering about two thousand, rushed down the steep bank into the sea, and were drowned in the sea.
• • • • • •	• • • • • •
18 And when he was come into the ship, he that had been possessed with the devil prayed him that he might be with him.	18 As he was getting into the boat, the man who had been possessed by demons begged him that he might be with him.
19 Howbeit Jesus suffered him not, but saith unto him, Go home to thy friends, and tell them how great things the Lord hath done for thee, and hath had compassion on thee.	19 But Jesus refused, and said to him, "Go home to your friends, and tell them how much the Lord has done for you, and what mercy he has shown you."
20 And he departed, and began to publish in Decapolis how great things Jesus had done for him: and all men did marvel.	20 And he went away and began to proclaim in the Decapolis how much Jesus had done for him; and everyone was amazed.

LESSON SETTING

Time: AD 27
Place: Gerasenes

LESSON OUTLINE

I. **Jesus Encounters a Demon-possessed Man (Mark 5:1-5)**

II. **The Demon-possessed Man's Plea (Mark 5:6-13)**

III. **Something to Proclaim (Mark 5:18-20)**

UNIFYING PRINCIPLE

People shun those who are on the margins of society. What can be done for those who are marginalized? After Jesus heals a man marginalized by an extreme disabling condition, He directs him to give witness of his transformation to his community.

INTRODUCTION

Mark 4:36–5:1-20 focuses on Jesus as the great deliverer from powerful storms that threaten human life. Our text for study today shows that Jesus is not only the conqueror of external forces (Mark 4:36-51) that negatively affect humanity, but that He is the deliverer and conqueror of internal storms that adversely affect people as well. This study is part of a larger unit (Mark 1:1-8:26) that emphasizes Jesus' healing and teaching with power (see Mark by Pheme Perkins in *The New Interpreter's Bible: A Commentary in Twelve Volumes. Matthew and Mark. Volume VIII.* Abingdon Press: Nashville, pp. 521-522.). Mark 4:35-6:6A is a smaller unit of the larger section that addresses Jesus' extraordinary power over nature and demons.

In this Scripture passage, Jesus and His disciples left to cross the sea to minister to people who resided in the Decapolis, the 10 Greek Cities. It is an area composed of Gentiles. As they traveled, a big windstorm arose and tossed the boat from side to side. Jesus was asleep at the stern, and the disciples had to awaken Him out of His slumber, asking "Teacher, do you not care that we are perishing?" Jesus woke up and rebuked the wind and sea, commanding them to be still. The disciples were filled with great awe and asked, "What manner of man is this?" "Despite their privileged positions the disciples are unable to grasp the significance of Jesus words and deeds and do not understand who Jesus really is" (Perkins, *Mark, The New Interpreters Bible.* p. 580). Yet at the same time, how does one describe One who commands nature? According to Perkins other miracle workers, exorcists, and magicians were able to perform miracles, but only Jesus could still the raging storm (Perkins, *Ibid.*). This is also evident as revealed in the disciples' self-imposed question, "What manner of man is this." Their question suggests Jesus had remarkable abilities that they had not witnessed before. Yet where the disciples were intrigued and could not believe what they saw, the demon possessed character in our study text promptly identified Jesus as the Son of God, and had no problems acknowledging His power over them (see Mark 5:6-7). The disciples feared the sea storm, but the demons in the possessed man identified themselves as Legion, feared Jesus' rule over them. The contrast between the two miracle stories in which Jesus serves as the central character is amazing, but is a necessary one to illustrate the full range of Jesus' power. He is God over all storms, whether external or internal.

This lesson investigates three things. First it examines, Jesus' encounter with the demon-possessed man. He crosses over the sea to the other side and immediately is confronted by the demoniac, who approaches Him. Was the encounter merely coincidental or was it a part of Jesus' purpose? Second, the man approaches Jesus with a plea. It is evident that he recognized Jesus, but his knowledge of the Lord leaves the demon in fear of judgment. Why? Third, the text shows the man being healed by Jesus. It is a testimony to Jesus' power not only to heal, but also to deliver and transform one from demon-possession to one who proclaims the Good News. How might we apply the meaning of this narrative in our lives as contemporary people is the question that remains?

EXPOSITION

I. JESUS ENCOUNTERS A DEMON-POSSESSED MAN
(MARK 5:1-5)

Many scholars dispute the location where Jesus met the demoniac. Mark and Luke list the area as Gerasenes (see parallel stories in Luke 8:26-39 and in Matthew 8;28-34. Also, see related texts in Mark 8:26; Luke 3:1). Matthew lists it as Gadarenes. In other manuscripts of the Greek text, it contains a variant dealing with the location. Other names for this area includes *Girgash* and *Gadara*. However James Brooks argued that ... "Mark wrote Gerasenes intending to allude to a village on the eastern shore with the Arabic name *Kersa*. *Kersa* is possibly related to the Greek name *Gerasa*, and there are steep hills and cave-tombs about a mile to the south. However uncertainty remains about the exact location of their encounter, except that Mark placed the encounter somewhere on the eastern shore in predominantly Gentile territory" (see James Brooks, Mark in the *New American Commentary: An Exegetical and Theological Exposition of the Holy Scripture NIV Text*. Broadman Press: Nashville, p. 89; see also *The Broadman Commentary. Vol. 8: General Articles Matthew, Mark*. Broadman Press: Nashville, p. 307; see also, Archibald Thomas Robertson, *Word Pictures in the New Testament, Vol. 1. The Gospel According to Mark*. Broadman Press: Nashville, p. 294). These verses (vv. 1–2) indicate a sense of urgency in Mark's Gospel account. Jesus is always in a hurry or the writer is hurling one event on top of another. His approach is to show the urgency of the mission of salvation. The mission is of such great significance that Jesus has no time to lose in fulfilling His divine purpose. Marks notes that Jesus is *immediately* approached by a demoniac.

He provides a vivid description of the demoniac. The man came from amongst the tombs to meet Jesus. Mark identifies the man as having an unclean spirit. He could neither be bound by others or even with chains. Three strong Greek negatives (see v. 3, No man, No, Not with) are used to point out as strong an expression as imaginable (Greek: οὐδεὶς, oudeis, meaning, no one). He could not be bound (*Ibid*, p. 308). He possessed some type of super human strength that allowed him to break

any of the shackles used to bound him. What Mark describes here is more like a wild animal than a person. This is conveyed appropriately by his use of the word tame (KJV). The Greek word used here δαμάσαι, (damasai). It means to subdue, to conquer, to tame. It carries the idea of taming wild animals. This man lived among the tombs. It was a popular belief that cemeteries were haunted by demons. Henry Turlington suggests that the demoniac lived as "an alien from his people and all society, because he was so utterly violent and unmanageable. People tried to control him, but he was unusually strong and did not spare his own body in order to break whatever bonds which they used to restrain him." The Greek *katakopton* (katakopton) means to gush, hack into pieces. He committed the act of self-mutilation (*Ibid.*). This point is of the utmost importance because the emphasis on the inability of the man to be bound by anyone, nor to be able to help himself, coupled with the previous question asked by the disciples, in Mark 4:41, "What manner of man is this?" led to the major confessional in Mark 8:26 that only Jesus Christ, the Son of God, can accomplish these things.

This man lived in a miserable state. His internal storm was a reflection of his being overcome by a series of circumstances that, at the very least, led him to believe that he was tormented by forces he was ill-equipped to deal with. Yet, even for the unruly, Mark presents a Gospel of hope of something better. Jesus has arrived to deal with the most serious and severe of human issues from the inside to the outside. He has come to deal with humanity's external and internal storms.

II. THE DEMON-POSSESSED MAN'S PLEA
(MARK 5:6-13)

Mark points out that when the man saw Jesus from a distance, he approached Him and worshiped Him. The use of the Greek word *proskuneo, (proskuneo)*, for worship is misleading here. One might think the demon is participating in true worship and accepting of Jesus as Lord and Savior. However, the demoniac's intent here is not to submit to Jesus' teachings as a disciple, but to deceive Him, to avoid being cast out of the man (Robertson, *Word Pictures*, p. 295). Pheme Perkins suggests the demoniac is seeking to "reflect a desire to drive Jesus away" to preserve his control and possession of the man's body (*The New Interpreter's, Mark,* pp. 583-584). However, unlike the Jewish religious leaders the demoniac readily acknowledged the divinity of Jesus. Two things are important here: even the ungodly recognize who Jesus is and confess His power. In the earlier story on the ship, the disciples inquired "What manner of man is this?" Here the demoniac answered the question, "He is Jesus the Son of the most high God." Second, Jesus' power and presence troubled the disciples and the demoniac, alike.

Jesus' movement to the other side of the sea is a scene shift. This shift suggests that Satan has lain his claim on this area and implies Jesus' encounter with the evil spirit will not be easy or pleasant. Satan will not easily let go of those areas he has long held in his evil scheme. As it stands, this man is subjected to inner storms of satanic forces just as the disciples at sea were ravaged by torrential winds and walloping waves.

Both were propelled by chaotic forces beyond their control. Both come to Jesus and both receive relief beyond measure. The man with the evil spirit lives among the dead and has living inside of him the one whose objective is his death and the total destruction of humanity. Thus, Jesus' experienced those things that seek to rob humanity of its life and vitality.

Both he and the society that have isolated him are powerless to overcome the chaos his situation represents. The man recognizes Jesus and extends a plea. In ordering the evil spirit out of the man, one is presented with the pervasiveness of evil. Evil desires to live, and to live in such a way that it may thrive and prosper. However, the prosperity is built upon a platform of utter selfishness. Evil wants to live. Yet, its life is always destructive and parasitic. Notice how the evil spirits pleaded with Jesus for mercy to let them live. Yet, they had no mercy on the man whose body they inhabited, selfishly. The previous description of self-mutilation bears this out (v. 5).

Moreover, the evil spirits within the man used a delay tactic to stall its apparent exorcism. Jesus had already repeatedly ordered the demon to come out of the man. In protest, they pleaded with Jesus to allow them to find a new residence (in the swine), not wanting to go back to reside in the abyss, their real home (Robertson, *Word Pictures,* p. 296).

Jesus demanded to know the name of the spirits within the man. They responded, "Legion," meaning many. A legion of Roman soldiers was close to 6,000 men. However, Perkins records that a battalion of 2000 men was often referred to as a legion. Coincidentally, this smaller number almost equaled the number of swine in the story, that the evil spirits desired to enter into (see Matthew 12:43-45, Also, *The Interpreters Bible,* p. 584). If so, it illustrated the cunningness of evil moving to protect and enliven itself. Jesus granted their request. By recognizing Him in the public arena, they make it more difficult for the religious leaders and others to accept Jesus for whom He is. These leaders have already wrongly concluded that Jesus' power comes from Satan. Being identified by the evil spirits probably affirms this misconception in the minds of skeptics. But in their evasiveness they were the ones destroyed. The legion of evil spirits entered the swine and the swine's violent reaction of running into the sea destroyed both the swine and the legion of evil spirits. This passage points to the self-destructiveness of evil. Its attempt to live by evading exorcism leads to its own demise. Jesus set the man free and allowed the spirits of evil to fall into its own pit of destruction.

III. SOMETHING TO PROCLAIM (MARK 5:18-20)

Jesus was leaving to get back into the boat when the man approached Him again. This time the man had regained his humanity and expressed to Jesus a desire to become His disciple. Although the man's intentions were good, Jesus directed Him to a greater mission, to take the message home and evangelize there. He became a forerunner of the Pauline mission to share good news with the people of the 10 Greek cities, the Decapolis.

THE LESSON APPLIED

We are called to trust and to have faith. To do so we must know and confess who Jesus is; He is none other than the "Holy One of God. Thus, all forces of life are under His sovereignty. Mark 4:35-5:1-20 reinforces this truth. The disciples did not fully understand Him or His power, but the demon named Legion fully recognized Him and knew that they were subjected to His holy power. In Jesus, evil will not be able to continuously unleash its fury on human beings. The community may isolate, and incarcerate its social misfits, but Jesus gets to the root of the problem, He restores them as full persons.

LET'S TALK ABOUT IT

How should we react to storms in our lives?

We must allow Jesus to bring healing and restoration into our lives by professing faith and trust in Him as Lord and Savior. When storms arise we must give them over to Him. He will speak to our storms and order them to cease.

HOME DAILY DEVOTIONAL READINGS
MARCH 27–APRIL 2, 2023

MONDAY	TUESDAY	WEDNESDAY	THURSDAY	FRIDAY	SATURDAY	SUNDAY
The Stones Would Shout	Jesus Weeps over Jerusalem	If Mortals Die, Will They Live?	This Is My Body	Why Have You Forsaken Me?	Deliver My Soul, O Lord	The Angels Call the Women
Luke 19:28–40	Luke 19:41–48	Job 14:1–15	1 Corinthians 11:23–34	Psalm 22:1–2, 7-19	Psalm 22:20–31	Luke 24:1–12

THE EMPTY TOMB

ADULT TOPIC: AMAZING ENCOUNTERS	BACKGROUND SCRIPTURE: LUKE 24:1-12

LUKE 24:1-12

King James Version	*New Revised Standard Version*
NOW upon the first day of the week, very early in the morning, they came unto the sepulchre, bringing the spices which they had prepared, and certain others with them.	BUT on the first day of the week, at early dawn, they came to the tomb, taking the spices that they had prepared.
2 And they found the stone rolled away from the sepulchre.	2 They found the stone rolled away from the tomb,
3 And they entered in, and found not the body of the Lord Jesus.	3 but when they went in, they did not find the body.
4 And it came to pass, as they were much perplexed thereabout, behold, two men stood by them in shining garments:	4 While they were perplexed about this, suddenly two men in dazzling clothes stood beside them.
5 And as they were afraid, and bowed down their faces to the earth, they said unto them, Why seek ye the living among the dead?	5 The women were terrified and bowed their faces to the ground, but the men said to them, "Why do you look for the living among the dead? He is not here, but has risen.
6 He is not here, but is risen: remember how he spake unto you when he was yet in Galilee,	6 Remember how he told you, while he was still in Galilee,
7 Saying, The Son of man must be delivered into the hands of sinful men, and be crucified, and the third day rise again.	7 that the Son of Man must be handed over to sinners, and be crucified, and on the third day rise again."
8 And they remembered his words,	8 Then they remembered his words,
9 And returned from the sepulchre, and told all these things unto the eleven, and to all the rest.	9 and returning from the tomb, they told all this to the eleven and to all the rest.
10 It was Mary Magdalene and Joanna, and Mary the mother of James, and other women that were with them, which told these things unto the apostles.	10 Now it was Mary Magdalene, Joanna, Mary the mother of James, and the other women with them who told this to the apostles.
11 And their words seemed to them as idle tales, and they believed them not.	11 But these words seemed to them an idle tale, and they did not believe them.
12 Then arose Peter, and ran unto the sepulchre; and stooping down, he beheld the	12 But Peter got up and ran to the tomb; stooping and looking in, he saw the linen cloths

MAIN THOUGHT: And as they were afraid, and bowed down their faces to the earth, they said unto them, Why seek ye the living among the dead? (Luke 24:5, KJV)

King James Version	New Revised Standard Version
linen clothes laid by themselves, and departed, wondering in himself at that which was come to pass.	by themselves; then he went home, amazed at what had happened.

LESSON SETTING
  Time: AD 29
  Place: Jerusalem

LESSON OUTLINE
  I. **They Went to the Tomb**
     (Luke 24:1–4)
  II. **A Burning Question**
      (Luke 24:5-12)

UNIFYING PRINCIPLE

When we encounter amazing circumstances in life, it's impossible to keep them to ourselves. How do we convey our excitement about amazing experiences? The women visiting the tomb faced the astonishing reality of Jesus' resurrection and shared their excitement with the disciples.

INTRODUCTION

It is remarkable that the Gospel of Jesus provided opportunities for ministry to disenfranchised groups and people who were considered marginal by society's standards. In this quarter's study alone, we have seen Jesus reach out to those who were considered to be unclean (in the Parable of the Prodigal Son). When the issue of greatness came up, Jesus pulled a child to Him and used the child as a model for those who desired to gain entrance into the Kingdom of God. He also broke cultural and social barriers by conversing with a woman of ill-repute, one who has had five husbands and was currently living with a man that was

not her own (John 4). Add to this group the lowly regarded women of this discipleship team who discovered the empty-tomb and you have a ministry punctuated by those categorized as the least likely to succeed. Now, it appears that His whole ministry hinged on a group of women, whose compassion and concern for Jesus to have a proper burial sparks new life into what seems to be a watershed moment for the spudding ministry.

The appearances of Jesus following the resurrection were key to uplifting and restoring the faith of the disciples. During the Passion Week, His followers were emotionally and spiritually as high as they had ever been. The events of the night prior to the Sabbath, however, were devastating. Where did it all go wrong? Fearful of Rome and weak in their own insecurities, the disciples ran at Jesus' arrest and hid. Judas, who handed Jesus over to the authorities, committed suicide. However, the faith and determination of the female disciples would play a pivotal role in sustaining faith in the words and mission of Jesus. We have already seen it was not easy for the male disciples to believe a woman who brought an incredible account of an empty tomb. Afterward, the men mustered the courage to go to the tomb, avoiding both Roman and Jewish authorities, to see for themselves. Although this was only the beginning and there remained much work to be done, this was an occasion for celebration. For through the persistence of these women and the overall courage of the disciples to act upon their word, hope in Jesus' sacrifice sprang anew. In the end they concluded that Jesus was who He claimed to be and the Empty Tomb witnessed to that fact.

EXPOSITION

I. THEY WENT TO THE TOMB (LUKE 24:1–4)

"On the first day of the week, at early dawn" (v. 1, NRSV), the women went to the tomb. They were prepared to anoint Jesus' body with the spices they had already prepared. At the end of Luke 23, we are told that the women accompanied Nicodemus when he placed Jesus' body in the tomb. This was done, Luke tells us, on "the day of Preparation" (v. 54, NRSV). On this occasion, the women themselves "saw the tomb and how his body was laid" (v. 55, NRSV). The day of preparation, according to I. Howard Marshall, "refers to the day of the Jewish week immediately preceding the Sabbath (i.e., Thursday evening to Friday evening)" (*The Gospel of Luke: A Commentary on the Greek Text [Carlisle:* Paternoster Press, 1978], 881). On this day, observant Jews prepared all food to be eaten the following day, so that the sabbath need not be violated by the work involved in preparing it. Joseph of Arimathea had asked for the body of Jesus following the crucifixion (on Friday). This was on the day of Preparation. On that same day, the women prepared spices to bring to the tomb. Since the Sabbath had occurred from sunset to sunrise (the next morning) and Jesus was laid in the tomb

before that Sabbath began, they prepared the spices on Friday and made the trip to the tomb early Sunday morning.

Luke's report that the women came to the tomb with spices is supported by Mark 16:1, but it has a deeper meaning in John's account. There, the spices are connected not to the women but to Nicodemus, who brought "a mixture of myrrh and aloes, weighing about a hundred pounds" (John 19:39, NRSV). Recall that Matthew reports that at the birth of Jesus, the Magi brought gifts, including myrrh. Luke notes that the women brought "spices and ointments" (Gk. *aromata kai myra*). Aroma can speak of any fragrant substance—spices, salve, oil, or perfume—used in embalming the dead.

When they arrived at the tomb, they found that the stone had been rolled away from the entrance. The women must have been frightened even as they were also perplexed. It does not seem in Luke's account that the women had thought about how they would anoint Jesus' body, because the stone would have been too heavy for them to move. This circular stone was set in a trough and was rolled in front of the entrance to the tomb or cave to protect the body from wild animals and grave robbers. Additionally, Matthew reports that a seal was set on the stone by the Roman authorities to denote that the tomb was officially sealed or closed (see Matt. 27:66). This was likely done by connecting the stone to the tomb with a cord and wax so that any tampering could be easily detected. Perhaps the women believed that the soldiers guarding the tomb would assist in rolling away the stone. Knowing Roman customs and the circumstances of the crucifixion, it is highly doubtful that the women would have expected any assistance from the guards. Why then go to the tomb? According to Mark's account, the women asked, "'Who will roll away the stone for us from the entrance of the tomb?'" (Mark 16:3, NRSV). This account suggests that they possibly expected assistance from men nearby, or from the guards. Again, because of the circumstances, it is highly unlikely that any would have become involved. Both Matthew and John concur with Luke in noting that when the women arrived, the stone had already been removed (see Matt. 28:2; John 20:1).

When the women entered the tomb, they discovered that the body of Jesus was missing. Luke reports that they found two men arrayed "in dazzling clothes" (Luke 24:4, NRSV; Gk: *estheti astraptouse*). The same Greek idiom is used of the Transfiguration (see Luke 17:24, using the same root as *astrape*. It means lightning. That is to say, the men had garments of angels (see John A. T. Robertson. *Word Pictures in the New Testament. Volume II, The Gospel According to Luke.* Broadman Press: Nashville, p. 291). In Matthew's account, a single angel appears: "His appearance was like lightning, and his clothing white as snow" (Matt. 28:3, NRSV). Mark likewise reports just one angel (see Mark 16:5–6), while John reports two (see John 20:11–13). The women, already frightened, were now terrified and fell down to the ground.

As previously mentioned, Luke reports that only women came to the tomb, initially. There is some disagreement among the Evangelists as to precisely which women were present at the tomb on this occasion. For our purposes, though, it is not important to pursue this line of inquiry. Luke identifies the women at the tomb as "Mary Magdalene, Joanna, Mary the mother of James, and the other women with them" (Luke 24:10, NRSV). The point of the matter is that none of the other disciple accompanied them to the tomb, but later came to it at the suggestion of the women.

II. A Burning Question (Luke 24:5-12)

The burning question is now posed to the women, "'Why do you look for the living among the dead? He is not here, but has risen'" (v. 5, NRSV). These compelling words reminded them all of the lessons that Jesus had taught. These words were a vindication of the Son of Man in the face of all that was predicted. Joyfully, they remembered the words of Jesus and returned from the tomb to meet with "the eleven and…all the rest" (v. 9, NRSV). As the women reported what they saw and heard, the male disciples who were present initially did not believe them: "But these words seemed to them an idle tale, and they did not believe them" (v. 11, NRSV). But remember that Jesus said that on the third day He would rise again. Peter instinctively regained his faith and ran to the tomb. Upon his arrival, he looked inside the tomb and noticed that the linen wrappings were not disheveled or strewn around the tomb but ordered, as if someone had neatly removed the wrappings.

Remember, when Caiaphas and Annas, the ruling high priest and the former high priest, found out that Jesus' body was missing, they perpetrated the falsehood that the disciples must have stolen His body to give the impression that Jesus had risen. However, if the body had been stolen, the thieves would not have taken time to unwrap it; but even if they had, the wrappings would have been strewn around the tomb, not lying–in perfect order as they were. Moreover, there was the presence of the guards, whose account would eventually be compromised. The disciples could not have secretly removed the body without placing their lives in jeopardy and keeping their deeds among themselves. Remember, they were in fear of their lives and in hiding; they simply did not have the fortitude for this type of covert operation.

The Empty Tomb is to be observed here not as a place where thievery took place, nor is it to be conceived as a place where the disciples gathered to hold a funeral. Rather, the Empty Tomb is to be posited as a witness to the truth Jesus spoke in light of His resurrection. It verifies Jesus' prediction of His life continuing after death, on the third day. It is not coincidental that His prophecy rang true. In Mark 8:31, 9:31, and 10:33-34, Jesus used three passion statement that emphasized He would be raised from the dead to new life. Thus, the Empty Tomb is the voice that bore witness to the greatness of Jesus' claim. Combined with the angelic message that Jesus was not there, it inaugurated hope in the disciples. The women actualized its emptiness and hope sprang up anew, creating a triple witness to the Lord Jesus' resurrection.

THE LESSON APPLIED

We must never forget the centrality of the cross to our faith. We cannot deny the resurrection. Without it, our entire religion would collapse. All four Gospel writers and the Apostle Paul affirms the reality of the Empty Tomb, the resurrection of Jesus Christ from the dead (see Matthew 28:18-20; Mark 16; Luke 24; John 20: and I Corinthians 15). Effectively, the Empty Tomb declared boldly the approval of God of the ministry and life of Jesus. Human beings killed Jesus. More precisely Jesus died at the hands of the Jews and the Romans. But His death is bigger than that. It was essentially the will of God for Him to be the atonement and the propitiation for human sin.

The Apostle Paul so forcefully wrote: "If there is no resurrection of the dead, then Christ has not been raised; and if Christ has not been raised, then our proclamation has been in vain, and your faith has been in vain. We are even found to be misrepresenting God, because we testified of God that He raised Christ whom he did not raise if it is true that the dead are not raised. For if the dead are not raised, then Christ has not been raised. If Christ has not been raised, your faith is futile, and you are still in your sins. Then those also who have died in Christ have perished. If for this life only we have hoped in Christ, we are of all people most to be pitied" (1 Cor. 15:13–19, NRSV).

Without a doubt, the fact of the resurrection is central to our faith. Just as important, though, is the life we live based on the resurrection. Paul has a good deal to say about this as well. He speaks, for example, of desiring to know "the power of [Christ's] resurrection" (Phil. 3:10, NRSV). What is that power? Among other things, it is the power to live a holy life before God characterized by the attitudes and qualities described in Colossians 3:1–11. There, Paul exhorts: "If you have been raised with Christ, seek the things that are above, where Christ is, seated at the right hand of God. Set your minds on thing that are above, not on things that are on earth" (vv. 1–2, NRSV). It is easy to believe something that is in front of our faces, something that we can see and feel. However, Jesus blessed those who believe without seeing (see John 20:29). As believers, we have many means of encountering Jesus. It may be in a moment of solitude that occurs while we are driving our cars. It may be praying while at our jobs. It may be in the worship assembly. These encounters ground us in faith that the tomb is empty.

LET'S TALK ABOUT IT

What is the theological significance of the fact that the tomb was sealed?

Have you ever considered the sealing of the tomb? The Roman soldiers had affixed their seal on the tomb to indicate that Jesus was inside and no one could enter the tomb without their permission. In our society, there are seals on medicine, food containers, and the cargo transported in trucks and vans. As with the Romans, our seals are quite visible. They instill confidence in the consumer and guarantee the purity of the product. Only God could remove the seal on the tomb in such a fashion that would terrify the bravest of men. The seal at the tomb was broken in order to demonstrate the purity of God's Son.

Furthermore, the seal was an indication of the human effort to contain His body. However, it was to no avail because it involved the power of Him who called life into being, originally. Creation began upon the divine initiative that God spoke life into existence. However, when it came to human life God scooped and created people from the dust of the earth and stooped to breath into them the breath of life. What could prevent God then from doing it again? The answer is absolutely nothing. The truth is God did do it again. First, He allowed the Spirit of God to overshadow a virgin to conceive a son, without the aid of a man. Second, when that precious life gave up the ghost, He invigorated it again with His Spirit, calling it back from beyond the grave to new life.

The Empty Tomb testifies that God impregnated death and it gave new life to the crucified Jesus, the One we hail as Lord and Savior. The Empty Tomb continues to witness to the truth of God's salvation for all of humankind. It validates Jesus' ministry and life and provides hope to all who believe and put their hope, faith, and trust in Him. The Empty Tomb is evidence of God's great and majestic eternal victory over death.

HOME DAILY DEVOTIONAL READINGS
APRIL 3–9, 2021

MONDAY	TUESDAY	WEDNESDAY	THURSDAY	FRIDAY	SATURDAY	SUNDAY
I Have Seen the Lord!	Blessed Are Those Who Believe	The Lord Is My Strength	I Shall Not Die, But Live	Jesus Meets Two Disciples	Jesus Opens the Disciples' Eyes	You Are Witnesses of These Things
John 20:11–18	John 20:19–31	Psalm 118:1–14	Psalm 118:15–29	Luke 24:13–24	Luke 24:25–35	Luke 24:36–49

Disciples Come to Believe the Resurrection

Luke 24:13–27, 30–31

King James Version	New Revised Standard Version
And, behold, two of them went that same day to a village called Emmaus, which was from Jerusalem about threescore furlongs.	Now on that same day two of them were going to a village called Emmaus, about seven miles from Jerusalem,
14 And they talked together of all these things which had happened.	14 and talking with each other about all these things that had happened.
15 And it came to pass, that, while they communed together and reasoned, Jesus himself drew near, and went with them.	15 While they were talking and discussing, Jesus himself came near and went with them,
16 But their eyes were holden that they should not know him.	16 but their eyes were kept from recognizing him.
17 And he said unto them, What manner of communications are these that ye have one to another, as ye walk, and are sad?	17 And he said to them, "What are you discussing with each other while you walk along?" They stood still, looking sad.
18 And the one of them, whose name was Cleopas, answering said unto him, Art thou only a stranger in Jerusalem, and hast not known the things which are come to pass there in these days?	18 Then one of them, whose name was Cleopas, answered him, "Are you the only stranger in Jerusalem who does not know the things that have taken place there in these days?"
19 And he said unto them, What things? And they said unto him, Concerning Jesus of Nazareth, which was a prophet mighty in deed and word before God and all the people:	19 He asked them, "What things?" They replied, "The things about Jesus of Nazareth, who was a prophet mighty in deed and word before God and all the people,
20 And how the chief priests and our rulers delivered him to be condemned to death, and have crucified him.	20 and how our chief priests and leaders handed him over to be condemned to death and crucified him.
21 But we trusted that it had been he which should have redeemed Israel: and beside all this, to day is the third day since these things were done.	21 But we had hoped that he was the one to redeem Israel. Yes, and besides all this, it is now the third day since these things took place.
22 Yea, and certain women also of our company made us astonished, which were early at the sepulchre;	22 Moreover, some women of our group astounded us. They were at the tomb early this morning,
23 And when they found not his body, they came, saying, that they had also seen a vision of	23 and when they did not find his body there, they came back and told us that they had

MAIN THOUGHT: Then their eyes were opened, and they recognized him; and he vanished from their sight. Luke 24:31

King James Version

angels, which said that he was alive.

24 And certain of them which were with us went to the sepulchre, and found it even so as the women had said: but him they saw not.
25 Then he said unto them, O fools, and slow of heart to believe all that the prophets have spoken:
26 Ought not Christ to have suffered these things, and to enter into his glory?

27 And beginning at Moses and all the prophets, he expounded unto them in all the scriptures the things concerning himself.

30 And it came to pass, as he sat at meat with them, he took bread, and blessed it, and brake, and gave to them.
31 And their eyes were opened, and they knew him; and he vanished out of their sight.

New Revised Standard Version

indeed seen a vision of angels who said that he was alive.
24 Some of those who were with us went to the tomb and found it just as the women had said; but they did not see him."
25 Then he said to them, "Oh, how foolish you are, and how slow of heart to believe all that the prophets have declared!
26 Was it not necessary that the Messiah[e] should suffer these things and then enter into his glory?"
27 Then beginning with Moses and all the prophets, he interpreted to them the things about himself in all the scriptures.

30 When he was at the table with them, he took bread, blessed and broke it, and gave it to them.
31 Then their eyes were opened, and they recognized him; and he vanished from their sight.

LESSON SETTING
Time: AD 29
Place: The Emmaus Road

LESSON OUTLINE
I. Jesus Appeared
   (Luke 24:13-16)
II. Our Hope is Gone
   (Luke 24:17-24)
III. Blind, But Now They See
   (Luke 24:25-27, 30-31)

UNIFYING PRINCIPLE

We need someone or something to convince us in our struggle to accept the truth of what we cannot explain. What can enable us to believe and trust that which we cannot explain? Jesus appears to the disciples on the road to Emmaus reassuring them of the significance of his crucifixion and reveals the truth of His resurrection as prophesied in Scripture.

INTRODUCTION

It is tough to face our disappointments. When we have invested trust in someone or something and to see it crash places an undue burden on our hearts. This is the way the disciples felt after Jesus was crucified. They had penned their hopes on Him and upon His deliverance of Israel from Roman oppression. But now with His death their hopes had vanished. However, unbeknownst to them, Jesus was alive and appeared among them as they walked on the road to Emmaus. They did not notice it was Him until He began to teach them how the prophecy had to be fulfilled.

Although Luke, the writer of this book, was not an eyewitness to the account, he is held in great esteem as a historian and as a theologian. He wrote to an official addressed as Theophilus and assured him of the factuality of his composition. The book of Acts is a continuation of the Luke-Acts sequence.

Three things are important in their conversation with Him. First, Jesus made the initial move toward them. Divine revelation has to come first before humanity can recognize His presence. God always makes the first move toward humanity to enlighten it and to provide for its salvation. Second, their hopes in Jesus had fallen with His death on the cross of Calvary. All of the information they received steadily decreased their fragile hopes, even the information of apparent sightings of Him after the crucifixion seemed preposterous. Finally, the shekels fell from their eyes and found that the information had not been that far-fetched after all. They had been blinded by their own lack of faith, but at the right moment Jesus revealed Himself and they began to see more clearly.

EXPOSITION

I. Jesus Appeared
   (LUKE 24:13–16)

Luke 24:13–27 is a travel narrative and follows the conversation that took place between the post-resurrected Christ and two of his disciple, although unknowingly to them. It is a part of the larger unit, which includes all of Luke 24. Luke 24 can be divided into several pericopes: the Empty Tomb (vv. 1–12); the Road to Emmaus Conversation (vv. 13–27); Meal (vv. 28–32); and Return to Jerusalem (vv. 33–35); the Appearance to the Disciples, their Commissioning, and Jesus' Ascension (vv. 36–53).

The current focus is on Jesus' appearance to two of the disciples as they travel to Emmaus. It was a small suburb located about seven miles from Jerusalem. Its current location cannot be exactly identified, however (see E. W. Clark in the *The Interpreter's Dictionary of the Bible: An Illustrated Encyclopedia. Emmaus.* Abingdon Press: Nashville p. 98; see also, R. Alan Culpepper. *The New Interpreter's Bible: A Commentary in Twelve Volumes. Volume IX Luke-John,* p. 475).

This travel narrative served to provide the post-resurrected Christ the opportunity to show the disciples how the resurrection was paramount to God's plan for the salvation of Israel and the world, and as the fulfillment of Scripture. They serve similar purposes throughout the biblical record.

For example in the Old Testament, Abraham entertained heavenly travelers in Genesis 18. They were on a mission to enlighten the aged-couple that God would fulfill His promises to provide them with a child. Sarah overheard the prophesy and laughed, but denied it when the men challenged her with the question, "Is anything too hard for God?" (Genesis 18:14). Their prophesy revealed that God, indeed, has power sufficient to meet the needs of His people, and to fulfill His holy purpose.

In the New Testament, Jesus healed the woman with the issue of blood, while He was on the way to heal Jairius' daughter, who was dying (Mark 5;21—43). The narrative's purpose shows that faith activates the healing power of God and brings about the recognition and awareness of the presence of the divine. Furthermore, in the book of Acts, Philip travels directed by the Holy Spirit leads to the baptism of the Ethiopian Eunuch, who did not originally understand the prophetic Word he was reading (see Acts 8:26–40). Yet, because of the prevalence of the Spirit of God his need was met.

Luke 24:1–12 ends with Peter returning home after witnessing the empty tomb. Later that day, two of Jesus' disciples were traveling to the village of Emmaus. The reference probably points out that the appearance of Jesus took place in the vicinity of Jerusalem. They were discussing the events of the past several days when they were joined by a Stranger. The use of the Greek word *omiloun* suggests the conversation may have been lively or heated. The meaning here is that one of the persons discussing the story might be a bit skeptical, while the other person appears to be more inclined to believe it. At any rate, they were unaware that the Stranger was Jesus, the risen Lord, who walked with them. Verse 16 says that their "eyes were holden that they should not know him" (Gk: *ekratounto tou me epignonai auton*). The meaning here is that they were continued being held "from recognizing him" or "from knowing him fully" (John A. T. Robertson. *Word Pictures in the New Testament. Volume II. Luke*. Broadman Press: Nashville, p. 292). The implication is that God withheld them from realizing the that the Stranger was Jesus. Withholding their recognition of Him points to the need for the Stranger to elaborate upon the fulfillment of the prophesy, which He will share with them.

II. Our Hope is Gone (LUKE 24:17–24)

The Stranger asked them what they had been talking about. Again, the Greek here is useful to understand the temperament of their discussion. Luke uses the Greek word "*anti-ballo,* which means to throw in turn, back and forth, like a ball, from one to another, a beautiful picture of conversation as a game of words (Robertson, *Ibid)*. The disciples were going back and forth with each other concerning the events surrounding Jesus' crucifixion and resurrection. Jesus' question arrested them and they looked sad, gloomy, and downcast. Finally, Luke names one of them. He was Cleopas. His name provides a sense of credibility to the story, although nothing else about him is mentioned. With a bit of irony Cleopas reflects Jesus' question back onto Him, as if to say, "Have You been living under a stone. You mean to tell us that You are unaware of the events of the day." "What things?" the unrecognized Jesus asked. This word play illustrates one of O'Day's major points of emphases. "The question assumes Jesus is the only one who does not know of these earth-shattering events, he is the only one who does know the meaning of all that has happened. In classic irony the ignorance of the know it all character (Gk: *alazon*) is exposed by the character who feigns ignorance (Gk: *eiron*) The two disciples assume they know much more about what has happened than does the stranger who has joined them." Jesus plays the "*eiron:*" "What things?" (*pola;* See O 'Day. *The New Interpreter's Bible. Luke*. p. 477).

The next five verses make up their response to Jesus' question. It is a christological confession of Jesus as a mighty prophet of God. However, it reveals their lack of understanding of who Jesus really is and what He came to achieve.

In verse 19, the disciples, primarily Cleopus, relate the events of the day to

Jesus of Nazareth. Identifying not only where He came from, but also His occupation as a mighty prophet by His deeds and by His proclamations. The phrase, Jesus of Nazareth, is typical of Luke to identify Jesus this way. In Luke's birth narrative, the writer shows the family returning to that small village after being honored at the temple by Simeon and Anna (see Luke 1: 26–27; 2:39–40, 51; 4:16–30).

This verse also sums up Jesus' passion and what actually happened to Him. The disciples do not mince words here. They clearly lay the fault at the hands of the Jewish leaders. The people are also exonerated of any responsibility for Jesus' death. Cleophus tied into a long line of offenses committed by the chief priest and others against Jesus (see Luke 9:22; 19:47; 20:1; 19; 22:2, 4; 50, 52, 54, 66; 23:4, 10, 13; 23:13, 35). Even though there was mounting pressure against Jesus to succumb to silence and to abdicate His role as the Messiah of God to appease the Jewish leaders, Jesus refused. His refusal is the reason He was murdered. His murder of course was the destruction of their hopes in Him as the Deliver and Redeemer of Israel. Here, Luke recalls the prophesy of Isaiah concerning Jesus (see Isaiah 41:14; 43:14). With Jesus' death the hopes of the disciples, according to Cleophus, went crashing to the ground. The Greek phrase *hemeis de elpizomen* means, "we were hoping" or "we had hoped" (see v. 21). It is expressed in the imperfect active, which indicates their hopes had vanished. The nail in the coffin of their hope is apparently sealed when Cleophus continued. "Besides all this it's the third day since these things happened. The reference here

either points to ... the Jewish belief that by the fourth day the soul had left the body (Jn 11:39) or possibly to the disciples' slight memory of Jesus' prediction of His resurrection. Cleophus is actually saying "Here it is the third day and to date nothing has happened" (see I. Howard Marshall, *The Gospel of Luke: A Commentary on the Greek Text*. William B. Eerdmans Publishing: Grand Rapids. p. 895).

Verses 22–24 conceptualized their account of the women's testimony that Jesus had indeed appeared to some of the disciples, but as of yet their account lacked sufficient evidence. Jesus had not yet been seen even though the disciples had verified the tomb was empty and their acknowledgement here repeats the sentiments expressed in verses 1-3. Their experience contrasted with that of the other disciples, who had not seen the Lord. They now had seen the risen Lord, but did not know it was Him. Their eyes were holden according to Luke. However, they would gradually come to see Him as their Lord.

III. BLIND, BUT NOW THEY SEE (LUKE 24:25–27, 30–31)

Cleophus and the other disciples were apparently not convinced that the rumors being spread by the women that Jesus was alive and had been seen were solid enough for them to be believed. At this point it appears the risen Lord had had enough. Jesus begins the process of removing His cover. He addresses them as unwise. Luke used the Greek word *anoetoi* to describe them as "unintelligent, foolish ones," or as "foolish men" (v. 25). They were slow of heart or slow to comprehend or to act (Robertson. *Word Pictures in the New Testament. Volume II. Luke*. p. 293). They should have believed the reports of the women at the tomb. Since they did not, the Stranger now lays out the prophetic pattern as if to say, they should have known (Mark 8:31–32; 9:32–32; 10:31–34). In other words, they should have paid greater attention to Jesus' passion statements and to His identification of the coming Messiah to Himself. (see John 4:1–42; Luke 9:26; 21:27). As the Messiah, Jesus had to fulfill the prophesies and Scriptures concerning Himself. Starting with the Law and the prophets, and preceding through the Writings, He related those passages with messianic overtones to demonstrate the path and suffering required of the Anointed One of God, and applied them to Himself. Robertson said, "Jesus found himself in the Old Testament, a thing that some modern scholars do not seem able to do" (*Word Pictures.* p. 294).

When the journey to Emmaus ended, the scene shifts. The Stranger provides the two disciples an opportunity to invite Him into their homes, which He did accept. There was yet unfinished business between them. At the table of fellowship, the unknown Stranger becomes the host. He took the bread, blessed it, and broke it, and gave it to them. These action verbs serve as the stamp of identification and recognition of the Lord. The disciples had seen them before in the feeding of the five thousand and the Last Supper (Luke 9:16, 22:19). They instantly recognized Jesus in this setting and He disappeared from their sight.

THE LESSON APPLIED

This pericope of Scripture is important because it projects that contemporary believers can have a present and current experience with the gloried and risen Lord. As He walked on the Emmaus Road with them, they failed to recognize Him. However, they did get to experience the blessing and joy of table fellowship with Him as they dined together. We too can know Him through the preaching of the Scriptures and when we share bread with Him at His table of fellowship.

LET'S TALK ABOUT IT
Was Jesus a ghost?

No! Our Lord was not an apparition, but He actually rose from the dead to new life. He rose to an incorruptible and an indestructible body. The fact that He ate with His disciples and had the various scars in His hands, feet, and side to prove it, establishes Him as having a unique new body that allowed Him to exercise metaphysical/supernatural powers. The final act of the Eschaton will be to raise us up in bodies similar in nature to His own resurrected body. Hallelujah!

HOME DAILY DEVOTIONAL READINGS
APRIL 10–16, 20231

MONDAY	TUESDAY	WEDNESDAY	THURSDAY	FRIDAY	SATURDAY	SUNDAY
Hospitality and Redemption	Raised with Christ in Glory	Death Is Swallowed Up in Victory	God, Hear My Morning Prayer	Great Is God's Faithfulness	Joy Comes with the Morning	Jesus Appears by the Sea
Luke 7:36–50	1 Corinthians 15:27–31, 35–44	1 Corinthians 15:45–58	Psalm 5	Lamentations 3:21–36	Psalm 30	John 21:1–14

JESUS COOKS BREAKFAST

JOHN 21:1–14

King James Version	New Revised Standard Version
AFTER these things Jesus shewed himself again to the disciples at the sea of Tiberias; and on this wise shewed he himself.	AFTER these things Jesus showed himself again to the disciples by the Sea of Tiberias; and he showed himself in this way.
2 There were together Simon Peter, and Thomas called Didymus, and Nathanael of Cana in Galilee, and the sons of Zebedee, and two other of his disciples.	2 Gathered there together were Simon Peter, Thomas called the Twin, Nathanael of Cana in Galilee, the sons of Zebedee, and two others of his disciples.
3 Simon Peter saith unto them, I go a fishing. They say unto him, We also go with thee. They went forth, and entered into a ship immediately; and that night they caught nothing.	3 Simon Peter said to them, "I am going fishing." They said to him, "We will go with you." They went out and got into the boat, but that night they caught nothing.
4 But when the morning was now come, Jesus stood on the shore: but the disciples knew not that it was Jesus.	4 Just after daybreak, Jesus stood on the beach; but the disciples did not know that it was Jesus.
5 Then Jesus saith unto them, Children, have ye any meat? They answered him, No.	5 Jesus said to them, "Children, you have no fish, have you?" They answered him, "No."
6 And he said unto them, Cast the net on the right side of the ship, and ye shall find. They cast therefore, and now they were not able to draw it for the multitude of fishes.	6 He said to them, "Cast the net to the right side of the boat, and you will find some." So they cast it, and now they were not able to haul it in because there were so many fish.
7 Therefore that disciple whom Jesus loved saith unto Peter, It is the Lord. Now when Simon Peter heard that it was the Lord, he girt his fisher's coat unto him, (for he was naked,) and did cast himself into the sea.	7 That disciple whom Jesus loved said to Peter, "It is the Lord!" When Simon Peter heard that it was the Lord, he put on some clothes, for he was naked, and jumped into the sea.
8 And the other disciples came in a little ship; (for they were not far from land, but as it were two hundred cubits,) dragging the net with fishes.	8 But the other disciples came in the boat, dragging the net full of fish, for they were not far from the land, only about a hundred yards off.
9 As soon then as they were come to land, they saw a fire of coals there, and fish laid thereon, and bread.	9 When they had gone ashore, they saw a charcoal fire there, with fish on it, and bread.

MAIN THOUGHT: Jesus said to them, "Come and have breakfast." Now none of the disciples dared to ask him, "Who are you?" because they knew it was the Lord. John 21:12

JOHN 21:1–14

King James Version	*New Revised Standard Version*
10 Jesus saith unto them, Bring of the fish which ye have now caught.	10 Jesus said to them, "Bring some of the fish that you have just caught."
11 Simon Peter went up, and drew the net to land full of great fishes, an hundred and fifty and three: and for all there were so many, yet was not the net broken.	11 So Simon Peter went aboard and hauled the net ashore, full of large fish, a hundred fifty-three of them; and though there were so many, the net was not torn.
12 Jesus saith unto them, Come and dine. And none of the disciples durst ask him, Who art thou? knowing that it was the Lord.	12 Jesus said to them, "Come and have breakfast." Now none of the disciples dared to ask him, "Who are you?" because they knew it was the Lord.
13 Jesus then cometh, and taketh bread, and giveth them, and fish likewise.	13 Jesus came and took the bread and gave it to them, and did the same with the fish.
14 This is now the third time that Jesus shewed himself to his disciples, after that he was risen from the dead.	14 This was now the third time that Jesus appeared to the disciples after he was raised from the dead.

LESSON SETTING
Time: AD 29
Place: Sea of Tiberias

LESSON OUTLINE
I. **A Restless Crew**
(John 12:1–3)
II. **Jesus Showed Up**
(John 21:4–8)
III. **Jesus Cooked and Fed Them**
(John 21:9–14)

UNIFYING PRINCIPLE
Traumatic losses can lead us to become disconnected from our purpose in life. What helps us recover a sense of wholeness and purpose? Jesus' appearance and fellowship with His disciples at the Sea of Galilee reunified the disciples and restored their sense of purpose.

INTRODUCTION
Without Jesus the disciples were a bundling group of misfits that failed to realize their holy purpose. The crucifixion of our Lord left them even more bewildered than ever before. However, that began to change with Jesus' resurrection from the dead. His resurrection gave them new hope, and inspired them to fulfill the purpose for which He had called them.

This text is the beginning of new opportunities for the disciples to become the evangelists and apostles of the Word that Jesus had called them to be. Having appeared to Mary at the Empty Tomb, Jesus had directed her to go and tell the disciples that He has arisen and would soon ascend to be with the Father. Her word to them was found to be true when the disciples were gathered together and Jesus appeared mysteriously among them later that same day. Eight days later Jesus reappeared to the disciples. This time one of them named Thomas was also present. Thomas had exclaimed previously that He would never believe that it was Jesus, except if he touched the nail prints in His hand and the piercing mark in His side (John 20:24–25). Mysteriously, Jesus appeared unto them again, even though the doors were locked. At this time He commissioned them to the ministry by breathing on them. This commissioning lay in stark contrast to the public commission the disciples received at the Mount of Olive as disclosed in the Synoptic Gospel accounts (see Matthew 28:18–20; Mark 16:15–16; Luke 24:45–49). It is evident that they received several commissions, at least a private one and a public one.

John 21 states explicitly that our text contains the third account of Jesus' appearance to the disciples. It can be aptly described as a miracle story and a recognition story. The miracle of the great catch of fish, like the miracle at Cana of Galilee, (John 2:1–11) is a story of incredible abundance. Simultaneously, it is also a recognition story. The beloved disciple, once again unnamed in the account, reveals his ability to grasp hold of the most significant moments in the narrative. "It is the Lord!" He observed (see Gail O'Day, *John. The Interpreters' Bible. Volume IX. Luke-John.* Abingdon Press: Nashville., p. 856) .

This account shows us three things we must take into consideration. First, we witness firsthand the frustration of the disciples as they tag along with Peter on a fishing expedition. Second, the text reveals that when they had reached their depths of deepest despair that Jesus showed up. His words to them gave them a glimmer of hope that, thirdly, led into a time of fellowship and renewal of their relationship. Although, the passage does not reflect the total impact of Jesus' presence with them on the sea, one can readily observe the positive affect He had on them when they realized who He was. When we come to

acknowledge His presence in our lives, it enlivens our hopes and aspirations for the future. His presence among them also illustrates in a vivid manner the great bond between and the excitement they shared as they anticipated the renewal and continuation of their fellowship.

EXPOSITION

I. A Restless Crew (John 12:1–3)

Clearly the disciples were quite frustrated with the way things were going. Jesus had reappeared to them on two other occasions, but they had no idea of when He would reappear and what His post-resurrection appearances meant for them as a group. The Lord's plan had not been specifically shared with them so they anxiously awaited the next step. Seven of the disciples were together in a place undisclosed by the text. There is no mention of the whereabouts of the other four. Peter, Thomas, and the sons of Zebedee were present and they figure prominently in this post-resurrection appearance of Jesus. Also, Nathaniel appears for the first time since his calling in John 1:45–50. Peter, evidently still to some extent perceived to be the leader of the group, impulsively decided to go fishing. Fishing for people was the reason Jesus had called the disciples to follow Him (see Mark 1:17). Fishing is an unpredictable occupation. It requires patience and skill to do it effectively. There is no guarantee of reward. It requires patience and risk. In faith, the fishermen would throw their nets into the deep water, letting it sink into the lake out of sight, and hoping that the reward for their efforts would be a great catch. Peter and many of the disciples were professional fisherman, and it appeared some of them enjoyed it as a past-time as well.

Fish will not jump into the boat. Fishers must search for them and take a risk by throwing their nets into the water. Could they possibly go through a bunch of work and never get a single fish? Absolutely. That happened multiple times in Scripture. It happened on the occasion before us. After a long night of fishing they, as it had happened many times before, came up empty-handed.

II. Jesus Showed Up
(John 12:4–8)

At daybreak a familiar sight appeared. It was Jesus. He had a knack for showing up at the right time during His post-resurrection appearance. In John's Gospel account, Jesus demonstrated His omniscience as the God who knows all things. He saw Nathaniel near the fig tree. He also saw that in him there was no guile (see John 1:45–50). In several other of His post-resurrection appearances, the Lord mysteriously appeared as if he had been attentively listening to the conversation of the disciples. Thomas complained that he would nor believe the Good News until he had seen Jesus for himself and was allowed to touch the actual prints in His hands and side (see John 20:24–29). Mary, on the other hand was encouraged by the Lord to not touch Jesus as a means to letting Him go physically and to strengthen her faith as a means of continuing her relationship with Him (see John 20:15–18).

Initially, the disciple did not know it was the Lord who appeared to them on the sea, but the Lord spoke out to them and inquired if they had caught anything.

Jesus uses the tender and endearing term (Gk: *paidia,* meaning children*)* to address them. This term is used several times in the Johannine Epistles (see I John 2:1, 18, 28; 3:7, 18; 4:7). The way the question is phrased in the Greek anticipates a negative response (Gk: *mn ti me ti; see* O'Day, *The New Interpreters' Bible Ibid,* p. 857). After they replied, "No!" He instructs them to recast their nets to the other side of the boat. This reveals the two perspectives from which we choose the course upon which we will thread, our's or the Lord's. The disciples' way was found to be a dead-end street as they operating under their own limited insight, came up with nothing, but empty nets. However, at Jesus' direction they recasted their nets on the other side and came up with their largest catch ever. The large catch of fish came at Jesus' direction and firmly identifies Him as the Giver of abundant gifts and as the One who should be glorified as God. The text here shows that it pays great dividends to obey Jesus after He has analyzed the situation and recommended a fix to our emptiness. However, once again Jesus' recommendation must be followed for the payoff to become real for us. Otherwise, it remains only a potentiality.

The revelation of the exact number of the caught fish, 153 of them to be exact have raised quite a number of questions. One question being, what does the number represent, if anything? Some scholars argue that the 153 number represents the various varieties of fish (see O'Day, *John, The Interpreters' Bible* p. 858 for the various arguments on the large catch of fish. Also see, George Beasley-Murray, *The Word Biblical Commentary Volume 36.*

John. Word Book, Publisher: Waco. p. 402).

The emphasis on the 153 fish symbolizes and refers to the miraculous and abundant gift of the gloried Jesus, which is a staple in John's Gospel account. For example, in John 2:1-12 at the wedding of Cana, Jesus is a Guest at the wedding, but He is the One who gives the Gift of the best wine. He does what the host was supposed to do. Additionally, in John 4:1-42 concerning the Samaritan woman at the well, Jesus asked her for a drink, but in the end He is the One who gave her the Gift of Living Water. Jesus is the Life Giver who provides blessings in great abundance. Furthermore, John 11 shows that Jesus is the Giver of abundant life as revealed in the Lazarus' narrative (John 11:1–44). This miracle from death to life is the nail in the coffin that solidified Jesus's apparent death at the influential hands of the Pharisees, and other Jewish leaders, because it sets Him apart as the sole Grantor of Life (John 11:45–50). In essence, Jesus does what God does (John 10:10; John 11:41–44).

The information that it is the Lord comes from the Beloved Disciple. John's Gospel does not tell us who the beloved disciple is. He could be one of the sons of Zebedee or one of the two unnamed disciples. However, tradition records the Beloved Disciple as being John the Apostle. His association and elaborate collaboration with Peter merits some weight here (see Acts 3:1–10; 4:5–21). Murray writes, "The Beloved Disciple recognizes by the miracle that the Man on the shore is the risen Lord. Characteristically, He tells Peter of His intuition, and equally characteristically

Peter throws himself into the sea--not to bring the fish to shore, but to reach the Lord as quickly as he can. The scene is curiously akin to the episode of the empty tomb (2:4–8); if this chapter comes from another Evangelist, we are clearly with a Johannine tradition at one with the former narrative and with a writer whose mind is at one with the Evangelist's" (Murray, *The Word Biblical Ibid.* p. 400).

Revealing his great excitement, Peter quickly dresses and jumps into the sea to go meet Jesus. However, his excitement will be challenged in the succeeding pericope of Scripture (vv. 15–17), when Jesus examined Peter's heart three times asking Him, "If you love Me?" (John 21:15–17).The hard questions to Peter appears to embarrass him and to question his commitment to follow the Lord and to lead the flock. Leading and feeding Jesus' flock will require from Peter a greater sense of courage and faith than what he displayed, while lurking in the shadows near the high priest's office during the Lord's trial (John 18;15–18).

III. Jesus Cooked Breakfast and Fed Them (John 21:9–14)

This text points out that Jesus is the Source of life for the disciples, and for all believers. The connotation here represented in the great catch of fish is that the ministry of salvation is extend from the Father and Son to the disciples. The reference of Peter hauling in the net suggests bringing others to Jesus which is exactly what Peter does in his first sermon in Acts 2. Over 3,000 people were saved. When they had gone ashore they saw a fire with fish and bread. Jesus requested them to bring some of the fish and proceeded to cook them some breakfast. Again He acts as Servant to all and becomes the great Host who feeds them (see John 15). This fellowship meal confirms the intimacy they shared and reminds us of the giving of the Eucharist, where Jesus gave Himself. It also reminds us of the feeding of the 5,000 in John 6. Notice there are also parallels to Luke 24:12–24, the narrative of Jesus encounter with His disciples, while on the Road to Emmaus. Jesus is readily recognized by the disciples within the manner of His giving to them blessings of abundance.

THE LESSON APPLIED

In this pericope of Scripture, the glorified and risen Lord appears to the disciples after His resurrection, and has a fellowship meal with them. This appearance to the disciples is important for several reasons. First It shows that Jesus is their Source of life and the Giver of abundant gifts. The miraculous catch of fish is a clear demonstration of His power. The fact that He prepares for them a meal shows the extensiveness of His provisions.

Second, the text shows Jesus will come to see about us at the time we need Him most. Having fished all night and caught nothing, Jesus came when they least expected it and fulfilled their hopes. Peter was so excited to see the Lord that he jumped into the sea to swim ashore to meet the Lord. The Lord Jesus comes to us and makes Himself known to us through His tender and caring touch, by His concern for our dilemma, and because He desires to strengthen us for the task at hand.

Third, He comes to us to renew our fellowship with Him and with one another. Togetherness and unity are the pillars upon which the disciples are fed with His holy presence and they use it to spread the Gospel throughout the world. May we be so blessed by His presence that we run to meet Him, expect nothing but the best from Him, and to be reconciled to His fellowship.

LET'S TALK ABOUT IT
Does Jesus appear to us today?

The simple answer to this question is yes. Jesus does come to us today. He comes to us in a variety of ways, but we must be open to receive Him and be focused on Him to recognize Him when He comes. He meets us every week through the preached Word and Bible study. He reveals Himself to us through TV shows, movies, other people, and events that take place in our lives. He speaks to us through dreams, visions, and the like. He tenderly works through our conscience to alert us of right and wrong. He speaks to our mind and hearts with His Spirit.

HOME DAILY DEVOTIONAL READINGS
APRIL 17–23, 2023

MONDAY	TUESDAY	WEDNESDAY	THURSDAY	FRIDAY	SATURDAY	SUNDAY
Jesus Brings Danger and Conflict	Peter Denies Jesus	Repent, Turn, and Live	Godly Grief Produces Repentance	O God, Blot Out My Transgressions	Create in Me a Clean Heart	If You Love Me, Follow Me
Matthew 10:28–42	John 18:13–27	Ezekiel 18:13–27	2 Corinthians 7:1–11	Psalm 51:1–9	Psalm 51:10–19	John 21:15–25

JESUS REINSTATES PETER

ADULT TOPIC:	BACKGROUND SCRIPTURE:
RESTORED FRIENDSHIP	JOHN 21:15–25

JOHN 21:15–19

King James Version

SO when they had dined, Jesus saith to Simon Peter, Simon, son of Jonas, lovest thou me more than these? He saith unto him, Yea, Lord; thou knowest that I love thee. He saith unto him, Feed my lambs.

16 He saith to him again the second time, Simon, son of Jonas, lovest thou me? He saith unto him, Yea, Lord; thou knowest that I love thee. He saith unto him, Feed my sheep.

17 He saith unto him the third time, Simon, son of Jonas, lovest thou me? Peter was grieved because he said unto him the third time, Lovest thou me? And he said unto him, Lord, thou knowest all things; thou knowest that I love thee. Jesus saith unto him, Feed my sheep.

18 Verily, verily, I say unto thee, When thou wast young, thou girdest thyself, and walkedst whither thou wouldest: but when thou shalt be old, thou shalt stretch forth thy hands, and another shall gird thee, and carry thee whither thou wouldest not.

19 This spake he, signifying by what death he should glorify God. And when he had spoken this, he saith unto him, Follow me.

New Revised Standard Version

WHEN they had finished breakfast, Jesus said to Simon Peter, "Simon son of John, do you love me more than these?" He said to him, "Yes, Lord; you know that I love you." Jesus said to him, "Feed my lambs."

16 A second time he said to him, "Simon son of John, do you love me?" He said to him, "Yes, Lord; you know that I love you." Jesus said to him, "Tend my sheep."

17 He said to him the third time, "Simon son of John, do you love me?" Peter felt hurt because he said to him the third time, "Do you love me?" And he said to him, "Lord, you know everything; you know that I love you." Jesus said to him, "Feed my sheep.

18 Very truly, I tell you, when you were younger, you used to fasten your own belt and to go wherever you wished. But when you grow old, you will stretch out your hands, and someone else will fasten a belt around you and take you where you do not wish to go."

19 (He said this to indicate the kind of death by which he would glorify God.) After this he said to him, "Follow me."

LESSON SETTING

Time: AD 29
Place: Sea of Tiberias

LESSON OUTLINE

I. The Million Dollar Question
(John 21:15–17)

II. Follow Me!
(John 21:18–19)

MAIN THOUGHT: When they had finished breakfast, Jesus said to Simon Peter, "Simon son of John, do you love me more than these?" He said to him, "Yes, Lord; you know that I love you." Jesus said to him, "Feed my lambs." John 21:15, KJV

UNIFYING PRINCIPLE

Broken friendships often leave us with a sense of guilt and shame that makes it difficult to reconcile with those we love. How do we overcome such feelings and rebuild broken relationships? Jesus transformed Peter's brokenness to wholeness by restoring Peter to a loving relationship with Him, challenging Peter to fulfill his missional purpose.

INTRODUCTION

This passage of Scripture is actually an epilogue to the book of John. It comes at the end of the Gospel account and some scholars believe it was added as an addendum after the original manuscript was completed. However, when it was written does not take away from its importance because it ties together some loose ends that are particular to the Gospel narrative and answers one big question, that of Peter's restoration to the group as the head disciple or apostle. One can rightly frame this pericope of Scripture as one of forgiveness and restoration as far as Peter's purpose and mission are concerned. It shows that Jesus did not want any ambiguity concerning Peter's leadership role. Sure, Peter fell off the bus during Jesus' trial, but it was not the end of the story, nor was it to be the end of Peter's ministry. Thus, this pericope is important in the lives of disciples, then and now because it demonstrates the depth of compassion Jesus has for those who fall short of the glory of God (Romans 3:23).

Both the betrayal of Jesus and the denial of Him were important events in His life and ministry. They reveal deep heartbreak and pain erupting from within the corpus of the disciples. Judas' frantic and desperate effort to move Jesus to adopt the negative and violent action that the Zealots wanted Him to embrace and Peter's cowardice as displayed in His denial of Jesus are stains that punctuate Jesus' ministry, although Peter's objective was meant to protect the ill-tempered disciple from those who accused him of being with Jesus, albeit a poor one. The outcome of these two occurrences are more than accidental mishaps, but they were the direct result of frustration and disappointment in the way Jesus' ministry turned out. Judas had determined that Jesus should share His prospective on the liberation of Israel from Roman authority and would use His mighty powers, the ones expected of the warrior like Messiah, to defend His nation's honor. He was wrong (see Matthew 26:17-25; 47-51; 27:3-10; Mark 14:17-21, 43-47; Luke 23:20-23, 47-53; John 13:21-30; 18:1-11), because Jesus had a better plan to deal with Israel's captivity. Her main problem was sin and idolatry. She must learn the tough road of servantry in order to redeem her former majesty. Judas committed suicide because he could not live with himself and face his life as a traitor.

Likewise, Peter also miscalculated the Lord's ability to read the human mind and heart when he denied the Lord. He dismissed the Lord's omniscience and was hurt and surprised when directly after his blunder he had to face the disappointed Savior. Though he was deeply sorry that he hurt the Lord, Peter continued to minister probably in a wounded fashion. He had lost his way and any claim to the leadership role Jesus had reserved for him (see Matthew 26:32-35, 69-75; Mark 14:27-31, 66-72; Luke 23:31-34, 54-62; John 13:36-38; 17:15-18).

This passage of Scripture sets the record straight and allows for Peter to redeem himself and be forgiven and restored to his role as leader of the disciples. He had denied the Lord three times before the cock crowed, Jesus would have him to rededicate himself to the Lord three times with a penetrating question of love followed by a directive to feed His lambs and to shepherd His sheep. Peter could not ignore Jesus' probing of his heart with His repeated questioning. Nor could he ignore Jesus providing him with another chance to do the work of ministry. It was a touching example of love that was extended to a temperamental person, whose feelings of hurt and embarrassment were enclosed with his acceptance of the restoration offer.

EXPOSITION

I. THE MILLION DOLLAR QUESTION (JOHN 21:15-17)

This is the third of Jesus' post-resurrection appearances. The disciples had just caught a large number of fish (153 large fish), and Jesus invited them to bring some of the fish to the charcoal fire so He could prepare them for breakfast (see Gail O'Day, *John. New Interpreters' Bible: A Commentary in Twelve Volumes*, Abingdon Press: Nashville, p. 856.).

After breakfast, Jesus took Peter aside and interrogated him about the condition of his heart. He was seeking to bring some resolution to Peter's denial of Jesus during His Kangaroo trial before the Sanhedrin Court. Although, Peter had previously boasted that he would never forsake Jesus (see Mark 14:29), the text reveals he did otherwise. He denied Jesus thrice. Peter is identified in these verses as Simon, son

of John, the same name Jesus used when He first met Peter (see John 1:42). It is an acknowledgement that Jesus as the Good Shepherd knows the name of His sheep (see John 10). He asked Peter a point blank question "'Do you love me more than these'" *(Gk: agapas me pleon touton),* meaning, the other disciples. It is a fitting question to one who declared earlier that he would remain by Jesus' side, even if all others ran away (see John 20:6). The intent of Jesus in these verses is to reestablish the relationship they had before He was denied.

Peter's response would govern the relationship from that point forward. Jesus told the disciples earlier "If you love me keep my commandment" (see John 14:15, 21, 23-24;15:9-10). Here His question to Peter fits uniquely within that formula. He asked Peter, "Do you love me," An affirmative response then followed with a directive or a command, "Feed my Lambs/Sheep." Here in verse 15, Jesus used the Greek word for love, *agape.* It denotes the superior love of God. Peter responds in the affirmative. "Yes, Lord," he said to Jesus. "You know that I love you." Peter, however, used a different word for love. He uses the Greek word *phileo* whereas Jesus used *agape.* Gail O'Day argued that the use of two different words here for love suggest that the two words are used interchangeably throughout this Gospel account and does not necessarily invite or ascribe to gradations of meaning (O'Day, *New Interpreters' John.* p. 860). However, this writer begs to differ with that assessment and agrees with the translators of the New International Version (NIV) that their use here implies gradations of meanings into which the apostle must grow. George Beasley Murray noted, "When one contemplates how Jesus had prepared Peter for responsible leadership among the people of the Kingdom and for the mission to Israel and the nations, this was a profound serious failure, which called for a process of re-establishment commensurable with the seriousness of the defection" (see John Beasley Murray. *Word Biblical Commentary. Volume 36. John.* Word Books, Publisher: Waco, p. 405).

Jesus intentionally used *agape* here to help Peter to understand the magnitude of love that would be required of him as the quintessential leader of the disciples. He was not merely to express love for his brethren or fellow persons which is one of the basic requirements for ministry, but he was to keep Jesus' commandments as the primary act of loving God. He was taking on an advanced role in ministry as the apparent heir of the leadership position currently held by Jesus. Therefore, even if he was yet on the way to understanding and practicing that type of love, he would be moving in the right direction. It was certainly not the final destination of love that Jesus intended for him or for any of his disciples, then and now, to possess, but it was a good start. At any rate, Peter affirmed his love for Jesus using the Greek word meaning, "brotherly love." "He does not make any claim here to superior love and even passes by the "more than these" and does not even use Christ's word *agapao* for high and superior love, but the humbler word *phileo* for love as a friend" (John A. T. Robertson, *Word Pictures in the New Testament. Volume 5. John.* Broadman Press, 1932, p. 321). Notice also that Peter

referred the matter to the Lord's complete knowledge and understanding, "'Lord, you know that I love you.'" Jesus replied imperialistically with the commandment, "Feed my lambs." This statement is Jesus' reinstatement of Peter. "Peter's love for Jesus is to be revealed in his care for the Lord's flock" (*Ibid*).

The second time Jesus asked Peter if you love me he dropped "the more than these" (Gk: *pleon touton*) and challenged Peter's own statement of love. The repetition used here was a probing of Peter's heart. By the time the question was asked for the third time, one can clearly see that it aggravated Peter for the Lord to not take his word for it the first time, and certainly by the second time it was asked. He is actually asking Peter can He count on him. Aware that Jesus already knew the deep contours of his heart, Peter explicitly referred the answer to Jesus' omniscience. Peter uses the word know (Gk: *ginosko*) to respond to Jesus' second inquest. This time Jesus commands Peter to, "Shepherd My sheep." The use of the word shepherd (Gk: *boske*) carries the tone of leading and guiding. As the One who gave His life for the Church, Jesus is the Shepherd and Bishop of the Church. Here His words to Peter are instructive. Peter is to watch over the church as both Peter and Paul instructs others to do so in 1 Peter 5:1-3 and Acts 20: 28. Murray adds, 'Both passages speak in the same manner as the risen Lord spoke to Peter on restoring him to the fellowship and to the service of the pastor. The verbs are the same—"my lambs, my sheep... the flock of God, the church of the Lord'" (*Ibid*). "There is no formal difference of meaning in the language by which the risen Lord confirmed in his calling to be shepherd of his sheep from that by which Peter and Paul exhorted the pastor-elders to fulfill their callings as shepherds of the flock of God in 1 Peter 5:1-3 and Acts 20:28" (*Ibid*). Jesus delegated His authority to Peter and Paul, and they subsequently delegated that authority to others who were under-shepherds and in other leadership positions. John 21:15-17 has its fulfillment in Luke 21:32. Here, Peter is advised once he has recovered to strengthen the brethren. Therefore, John 21:15-17 is Peter's restoration to his role as leader of the Church. The third and final exhortation for Peter comes in John 21:17. Here Jesus accepts Peter's humbler statement of love by using the identical word Peter uses (Gk: *phileis me*), meaning I love you as a friend. Peter was cut to the heart with this third question. It undoubtedly reminded him of the three denials he made while in the courtyard of the high priest. Again, Peter's reply to the Lord refers to Jesus' complete knowledge of him. The word "You know" indicates intimate knowledge of Peter's innermost secrets. It is the same type of knowledge revealed to Peter when Jesus prophesied Peter's denial of him. Jesus' final instruction to the lead disciple was to "Feed My sheep."

II. FOLLOW ME!
(JOHN 21:18-19)

Jesus ends His conversation with Peter by pointing out the type of death that Peter would experience. The Lord Jesus reassured Peter he was the apparent leader, but just as he would emulate Christ as being Shepherd, he would also emulate Him in the type of death he would experience. The outstretched hands referred to in v. 18 is a reference to crucifixion. The narrator plainly said it signified the type of death Peter would experience. Jesus' last word to Peter to "Follow Me" is an affirmation to Peter to keep His commandments through the tough road ahead.

THE LESSON APPLIED

Jesus restored Peter to fellowship with Him by asking three times if he loved Him. These three questions equaled the number of times Peter denied the Lord. Jesus took the divine initiative to restore Peter. Christ also offers to us His forgiveness and complete restoration when we confirm our love for Him by keeping His commandments.

LET'S TALK ABOUT IT
Did Peter's denial disqualify him from further service?

No! Jesus forgave and restored Peter. Neither does our failure disqualify us. The Lord can use our failure as a teaching moment and as an opportunity to return us to His love and service. Jesus would restore Peter to His service and He will restore us as well.

HOME DAILY DEVOTIONAL READINGS
APRIL 24–30, 2023

MONDAY	TUESDAY	WEDNESDAY	THURSDAY	FRIDAY	SATURDAY	SUNDAY
Go and Make Disciples	The Day of the Lord Approaches	Jesus Seated at God's Right Hand	Jesus Our Great High Priest	Jesus Has Entered the Holy Place	Lift Up Your Heads, O Gates!	You Shall Receive Power
Matthew 28:1–10, 16–20	Joel 2:1–15	Hebrews 1:1–14	Hebrews 8:1–13	Hebrews 9:8–22	Psalm 24	Acts 1:1–11

A PROMISE IS MADE TO JESUS' DISCIPLES

| ADULT TOPIC:
HOPE AND POWER | BACKGROUND SCRIPTURE:
ACTS 1:1–11 |

ACTS 1:1–11

King James Version

THE former treatise have I made, O Theophilus, of all that Jesus began both to do and teach,

2 Until the day in which he was taken up, after that he through the Holy Ghost had given commandments unto the apostles whom he had chosen:

3 To whom also he shewed himself alive after his passion by many infallible proofs, being seen of them forty days, and speaking of the things pertaining to the kingdom of God:

4 And, being assembled together with them, commanded them that they should not depart from Jerusalem, but wait for the promise of the Father, which, saith he, ye have heard of me.

5 For John truly baptized with water; but ye shall be baptized with the Holy Ghost not many days hence.

6 When they therefore were come together, they asked of him, saying, Lord, wilt thou at this time restore again the kingdom to Israel?

7 And he said unto them, It is not for you to know the times or the seasons, which the Father hath put in his own power.

8 But ye shall receive power, after that the Holy Ghost is come upon you: and ye shall be witnesses unto me both in Jerusalem, and in all Judaea, and in Samaria, and unto the uttermost part of the earth.

9 And when he had spoken these things, while they beheld, he was taken up; and a cloud received him out of their sight.

10 And while they looked stedfastly toward heaven as he went up, behold, two men stood by them in white apparel;

New Revised Standard Version

IN the first book, Theophilus, I wrote about all that Jesus did and taught from the beginning

2 until the day when he was taken up to heaven, after giving instructions through the Holy Spirit to the apostles whom he had chosen.

3 After his suffering he presented himself alive to them by many convincing proofs, appearing to them during forty days and speaking about the kingdom of God.

4 While staying with them, he ordered them not to leave Jerusalem, but to wait there for the promise of the Father. "This," he said, "is what you have heard from me;

5 for John baptized with water, but you will be baptized with the Holy Spirit not many days from now."

6 So when they had come together, they asked him, "Lord, is this the time when you will restore the kingdom to Israel?"

7 He replied, "It is not for you to know the times or periods that the Father has set by his own authority.

8 But you will receive power when the Holy Spirit has come upon you; and you will be my witnesses in Jerusalem, in all Judea and Samaria, and to the ends of the earth."

9 When he had said this, as they were watching, he was lifted up, and a cloud took him out of their sight.

10 While he was going and they were gazing up toward heaven, suddenly two men in white robes stood by them.

MAIN THOUGHT: "You will receive power when the Holy Spirit has come upon you." Acts 1:8, KJV

ACTS 1:1–11

King James Version	*New Revised Standard Version*
11 Which also said, Ye men of Galilee, why stand ye gazing up into heaven? this same Jesus, which is taken up from you into heaven, shall so come in like manner as ye have seen him go into heaven.	11 They said, "Men of Galilee, why do you stand looking up toward heaven? This Jesus, who has been taken up from you into heaven, will come in the same way as you saw him go into heaven."

LESSON SETTING
Time: AD 29
Place: Jerusalem

LESSON OUTLINE
I. Brief summation of the Gospel
(Acts 1:1–5)
II. Emphasis on Jesus departure to heaven and Luke's allusion to the work He left for the Apostles
(Acts 1:6–11)

UNIFYING PRINCIPLE

People want to know how to move forward when they feel powerless. How do we overcome feelings of powerlessness? Jesus tells the disciples to wait for the power that will come to them through the Holy Spirit.

INTRODUCTION

In 2022, some of the key words to understanding American and world society were safe, informed, and connected. Television news stations and a variety of social media outlets underscored the importance of people staying safe, informed, and connected about the events surrounding them throughout the world. As the COVID–19 pandemic continued to spread through our nation and world–wide, there was a great need for people to be alerted of its progress so they could stay safe and protect themselves and their families from serious sickness, and death. Media outlets made making these reports a priority, along with reporting other potential for disasters that adversely-affected people. They encouraged their listeners to stay informed of the events of the day, so they could make the appropriate decisions to maintain healthy and virile families. Acting on the information, provided people with the opportunity to connect the dots, to assimilate the given information into their lives, and to experience the benefits from doing so.

Being safe, informed and connected were also important for the writing of the book of Acts. At the beginning of the book, the disciples were encouraged to remain in Jerusalem to be used by God for the greatest salvific event of all times, the coming of the Holy Spirit in its fullness. This point is of utmost importance because of the emphasis on the man's inability to be bound by anyone or to even help himself, coupled with the disciples' question (Mark 4:41), "What manner of man is this?" Both factors led to the major confessional (Mark 8:26) that only Jesus Christ, the Son of God, can accomplish these things. Without this composition, the Acts of the Apostles, it would be quite difficult to connect the dots between the death of Jesus and the growth and development of the church that He called into being (Matthew 16:33). In other words, the book of Acts provides relevant information for the reader to understand the church's movement away from Judaism and to establish itself as a religious body.

The writer, a physician named Luke, continues his treatise to Theophilus (see Luke 1:1–5 and Acts 1:1–5). His desire is to present an eyewitness account of the happenings pertaining to the salvific ministry of Jesus Christ. He begins Acts with a basic review of Christ's ministry, while interjecting some new instructional details not offered earlier in Luke's Gospel (see the Ascension; Acts 1:1–12). For example, one might think from reading Luke's Gospel that after the disciples assembled that Jesus ascended immediately into heaven. Acts, however informs us that there was a forty–day interval between His resurrection and ascension (Acts 1:3). The forty–day sequence is prominent in biblical literature. Moses was on Mount Sinai forty days when he received the law. Elijah was sustained for forty days when he fled from Jezebel, Jesus meditated and fasted forty days after His Baptism (see *Acts, Broadman Commentary*, Nashville. p. 17).

The Acts account also reveals an inquisitive group, who questioned Jesus about the establishment of His Kingdom (Acts 1:1–8). Jesus' response to them is instructive and reveals the purpose of the book of Acts. The purpose of the book is to show the disciples moving deliberately to share the Gospel of Jesus Christ, while allowing the Holy Spirit to go before them to remove a variety of obstacles to their assigned tasks. The Acts account explores the development of the church, from a small band of disciples hiding in the Upper Room to its vying for power in the palace of Caesar in Rome. Our study today focuses on Jesus' last words to the disciples as He instructed them to tend to the business of evangelism. Two things are important in this study. First, it is imperative that we exam the context out of which Jesus directs the disciples to prepare for the coming of the Holy Spirit to empower them to minister effectively, beginning in Jerusalem. Second, we will exam Jesus' directive for the disciples to be centrally focused to carry on His work of salvation.

I. Brief Summation of the Gospel (Acts 1:1–5)

It is important to point out that Luke was not an eyewitness to all of the events he records in the Luke–Acts sequence. He does pledge to offer, however, an eyewitness account of the activities of Jesus and His disciples. This means His focus is on establishing truth. Originally, the book had no title or name, following the course of traditional Greek literature. Verse one is a reference to the first volume or account of Jesus' ministry to one named Theophilus. This verse ties together Luke's Gospel to the Acts of the Apostles, which is the second volume of writings pertaining to the life and ministry of Christ. However, in this volume we see a change of roles and emphases for the Lord. In volume 1, the historical Jesus is the dominant character. In this volume, Jesus' other self, the Holy Spirit, is the major focus. This point is amply noted by the author in this the second volume and is born out in verse 2, as Luke notes "Until the day in which he was taken up, after that he through the Holy Ghost had given commandments unto the apostles whom he had chosen" (Acts 1:2, KJV). A mere three verses later (v. 5), Luke again points to the powerful and majestic coming of the Holy Spirit, and in verse 8, he alluded to the after math of His coming: "'But ye shall receive power after that the Holy Ghost is come upon you: and ye shall be witnesses unto me both in Jerusalem, and in Judea, and in Samaria, and unto the uttermost part of the earth'"(Acts 1:8). It is safe to say then that with the emphasis on the Holy Spirit, Acts would be better named the Acts of the Holy Spirit. Although the ancient Church Fathers named it the Acts of the Apostles, it is an account of two of the most popular apostles, Peter and Paul.

Luke continues the second volume by explaining that Jesus revealed Himself to the disciples. These actual sightings were the infallible proofs of His resurrection from the dead, the writer referred to in verse 3. His appearances were not a one–time occasion, but they extended over a forty–day stretch. They were also accompanied by preaching and teaching sessions where the Lord divulged to the disciples the things pertaining to the Kingdom of God. The other Gospel writers fill in the details of these resurrected appearances. Luke for an example shows Jesus meeting the disciples on the road to Emmaus and Him opening up the Scriptures to them. He also ate with them which provided assurance to them that He was indeed not an apparition or a ghost, but the risen Savior (see Luke 24:13–53). John's Gospel account of the resurrected Savior shows Him giving the disciples a partial and temporary measure of the Holy Spirit by breathing on them. Furthermore, John's record amplifies that Jesus offers what each individual needs in relationship to faith (see His encounter with Mary and Thomas in John 20:17–29).

Additionally, John shows the resurrected Jesus present at the disciples' last fishing expedition and sharing an intimate breakfast with them, and His restoration of Peter to the fold after being denied by Cephas three times (John 21).

Verse 4 again shows Jesus speaking to His disciples. This time He instructs them to stay in Jerusalem for the coming of the promise of the Father. They had been officially authorized to carry on His work in the Great Commission (Matthew 28:18–20; Mark 16:15–16; Luke 24:49–53; John 21:21–23). Now, he directed them to wait for the promise of the Father, which would empower them to do so. The promise of God always has to do with God's presence, protection, and/or deliverance. Used here it has to do with all three of these things. The Spirit of God was drastically needed to pave the road of evangelistic opportunities for them as they would be pursuing a path never before explored within the confines of salvation history. The one Resource they needed to share His Gospel appropriately and effectively was the Holy Spirit. It would guide their steps, protect them from their Jewish and Roman adversaries, and deliver them from a variety of other challenges and difficulties. In other words, these were things that the disciples were unable to achieve on their own. They needed the power and presence of God to succeed in their mission. Hence, they were reminded to stay in Jerusalem. Jerusalem was the center of Jewish religious culture and experience, and well–known for its significance to the Jewish faith. It would now be the place for the outgrowth of the Christian movement as it pivoted away from Judaism.

II. Jesus' Departure to Heaven and Luke's Allusion to the Work He Left for the Apostles (Acts 1:6–11)

This section of our study focuses on the question/answer session that took place between Jesus and His disciples. Events surrounding the crucifixion show Jesus being conceived as a political figure, who would restore the prestige of Israel and promote her recovery to claim her place among the elite group of nations. This expectation of Jesus to finally accept His role as a political Messiah emerged as two of His disciples requested sacred positions of authority over the other disciples (Mark 10:37). Their perceived misconception of the warrior like Messiah made it difficult for them to conceive of Jesus otherwise. It was this misconception that lay at the root of their question about the Kingdom. Although the Pharisees and some of the other Jewish officials failed to see Jesus was the Messiah, it was clear they perceived Him to be a threat to their religious and political status. His popularity among the people did not escape the long–awaited eyes of the Pharisees, who later commented in the aftermath of the Triumphant Entry into Jerusalem that... "behold, the world is gone after him" (John 12:20, KJV). It was this type of expectation and fear that motivated the disciples to ask the resurrected Jesus of His intentions towards the restoration of the Kingdom to Israel. The resurrection now caused their messianic hopes to re-surge. They felt what Jesus could accomplish in this apocalyptic role was highly possible since he had overcome life's greatest obstacle, death (*Broadman,* p. 19).

It is highly probable that given the circumstances involved, the demonstration of ultimate power that came through the resurrection that Jesus anticipated this question would come to the forefront ... "Lord, wilt thou at this time restore gain the kingdom to Israel (Acts 1:6)?" The disciples were patriotic and desired for the nation to be restored to her former glory. However, Jesus as always did not hesitate to rebuke His disciples for their going off on tandems. This time was no different. Jesus was leaving them physically. They are the ones who must continue to carry out His ministry. It is apparent Jesus' rebuke here is to refocus their attention on the thing they would be responsible for, world–wide evangelism, beginning first in Jerusalem. He instructs them as their Mentor to evangelistic consideration beyond Israel. Sure, they were to begin in Jerusalem, but the capital city would only be the starting point. Their salvific efforts must go beyond it to include, Judea, Samaria, and the uttermost parts of the world. Jesus forbade them from inquiring about the scheduling of the Father's timetable, it was beyond their ability to comprehend it, and according to the Lord's response to Nicodemus, how could they conceive of the heavenly, when they originally could not conceptualize what it meant to be born again (John 3:5–12).

Rather than focus on the things of God, Jesus redirected their attention to their reception of the Holy Spirit. There was no question about whether or not He was coming, their focus was to be on His reception in their hearts. Possession of the Spirit would transform them into viable witnesses to the presence of the living Lord in the areas surrounding Jerusalem and Judea, respectively. From these areas their witness was to cover Samaria, and ultimately encompass the entire world. Both Jews and Gentiles would receive the witness of the apostles. It is a repeat of Matthew 28:18–20, the Great Commission. The world had to be brought into God's plan of salvation. It was not primarily a Jewish event, but it would start in Jerusalem. Even more important is that it fulfills the promise in John's Gospel. In John 14–16, Jesus instructs and alerts the disciples that He is going away, but would send in His place an Advocate, the Comforter. In the Great Commission He promised to be with them always. Here we notice His continuous presence in their reception of the Spirit. As He promised to them possession of the Spirit, He was taken out of their sights as He ascended on a cloud into the heavens. The point is they were never alone. God's promise to them to receive the power of the Spirit was as good as done. Furthermore, Jesus had breathed on them saying … "Receive ye the Holy Ghost" … (John 20:22, KJV).

Clouds were important heavenly objects that denote the presence and power of God. In the Exodus, God revealed Himself in pillars of cloud and of fire. He predicts His return in the Second Coming will be similar to His Ascension into heaven.

Finally, the glory of the moment rested in the amazing feat of Jesus ascending into heaven even as He spoke to them. A couple of angelic figures reinforced Jesus' future return to earth. In between His Ascension and return to earth, the implication is that disciples must be about the business of Christian evangelism.

THE LESSON APPLIED

This passage of Scripture teaches that Jesus placed in the hands of the disciples His ministry of world–wide salvation. After several appearances by the resurrected Lord to His disciples, Jesus finally charged them to wait to be endowed with power from the Holy Ghost. He focuses their attention to share the Gospel message and to emphasize the Father's love for them as expressed in the activities of Jesus Christ.

LET'S TALK ABOUT IT

Why does Scripture often support itself?

The uniqueness of Scripture to support itself is seen in the continuity of its message about Jesus. Paul stated it best when he said that "All scripture is inspired of God, and is profitable for doctrine, for reproof, for correction, for instruction in righteousness. (2 Timothy 3:16). Scripture illuminates Scripture and helps us to determine its meaning more clearly. It also enables us to discover the purpose of our calling..

HOME DAILY DEVOTIONAL READINGS
MAY 1–7, 2023

MONDAY	TUESDAY	WEDNESDAY	THURSDAY	FRIDAY	SATURDAY	SUNDAY
God's Strength Revealed	The Spirit of Truth	The Spirit Testifies of Jesus	The Lord My Chosen Portion	Amazement at the Spirit's Power	The Promise Fulfilled	Receive the Gift of the Spirit
Psalm 68:17–19, 24–35	John 14:15–27	John 16:1–15	Psalm 16	Acts 2:1–13	Acts 2:14–28	Acts 2:29–42

THE BIRTH OF THE CHURCH

ADULT TOPIC: FEAR AND TRUST	BACKGROUND SCRIPTURE: ACTS 2:1–42

ACTS 2:1–8, 14–24, 37–39

King James Version	*New Revised Standard Version*
AND when the day of Pentecost was fully come, they were all with one accord in one place. 2 And suddenly there came a sound from heaven as of a rushing mighty wind, and it filled all the house where they were sitting. 3 And there appeared unto them cloven tongues like as of fire, and it sat upon each of them. 4 And they were all filled with the Holy Ghost, and began to speak with other tongues, as the Spirit gave them utterance. 5 And there were dwelling at Jerusalem Jews, devout men, out of every nation under heaven. 6 Now when this was noised abroad, the multitude came together, and were confounded, because that every man heard them speak in his own language. 7 And they were all amazed and marvelled, saying one to another, Behold, are not all these which speak Galilaeans? 8 And how hear we every man in our own tongue, wherein we were born? • • • • • • 14 But Peter, standing up with the eleven, lifted up his voice, and said unto them, Ye men of Judaea, and all ye that dwell at Jerusalem, be this known unto you, and hearken to my words: 15 For these are not drunken, as ye suppose, seeing it is but the third hour of the day. 16 But this is that which was spoken by the prophet Joel; 17 And it shall come to pass in the last days, saith God, I will pour out of my Spirit upon all flesh: and your sons and your daughters	WHEN the day of Pentecost had come, they were all together in one place. 2 And suddenly from heaven there came a sound like the rush of a violent wind, and it filled the entire house where they were sitting. 3 Divided tongues, as of fire, appeared among them, and a tongue rested on each of them. 4 All of them were filled with the Holy Spirit and began to speak in other languages, as the Spirit gave them ability. 5 Now there were devout Jews from every nation under heaven living in Jerusalem. 6 And at this sound the crowd gathered and was bewildered, because each one heard them speaking in the native language of each. 7 Amazed and astonished, they asked, "Are not all these who are speaking Galileans? 8 And how is it that we hear, each of us, in our own native language? • • • • • • 14 But Peter, standing with the eleven, raised his voice and addressed them, "Men of Judea and all who live in Jerusalem, let this be known to you, and listen to what I say. 15 Indeed, these are not drunk, as you suppose, for it is only nine o'clock in the morning. 16 No, this is what was spoken through the prophet Joel: 17 'In the last days it will be, God declares, that I will pour out my Spirit upon all flesh, and your sons and your daughters shall prophesy,

MAIN THOUGHT: "For the promise is for you, for your children, and for all who are far away, everyone whom the Lord our God calls to him." Acts 2:39

King James Version	New Revised Standard Version
shall prophesy, and your young men shall see visions, and your old men shall dream dreams:	and your young men shall see visions, and your old men shall dream dreams.
18 And on my servants and on my handmaidens I will pour out in those days of my Spirit; and they shall prophesy:	18 Even upon my slaves, both men and women, in those days I will pour out my Spirit; and they shall prophesy.
19 And I will shew wonders in heaven above, and signs in the earth beneath; blood, and fire, and vapour of smoke:	19 And I will show portents in the heaven above and signs on the earth below, blood, and fire, and smoky mist.
20 The sun shall be turned into darkness, and the moon into blood, before the great and notable day of the Lord come:	20 The sun shall be turned to darkness and the moon to blood, before the coming of the Lord's great and glorious day.
21 And it shall come to pass, that whosoever shall call on the name of the Lord shall be saved.	21 Then everyone who calls on the name of the Lord shall be saved.'
22 Ye men of Israel, hear these words; Jesus of Nazareth, a man approved of God among you by miracles and wonders and signs, which God did by him in the midst of you, as ye yourselves also know:	22 "You that are Israelites, listen to what I have to say: Jesus of Nazareth, a man attested to you by God with deeds of power, wonders, and signs that God did through him among you, as you yourselves know—
23 Him, being delivered by the determinate counsel and foreknowledge of God, ye have taken, and by wicked hands have crucified and slain:	23 this man, handed over to you according to the definite plan and foreknowledge of God, you crucified and killed by the hands of those outside the law.
24 Whom God hath raised up, having loosed the pains of death: because it was not possible that he should be holden of it.	24 But God raised him up, having freed him from death, because it was impossible for him to be held in its power.
37 Now when they heard this, they were pricked in their heart, and said unto Peter and to the rest of the apostles, Men and brethren, what shall we do?	37 Now when they heard this, they were cut to the heart and said to Peter and to the other apostles, "Brothers, what should we do?"
38 Then Peter said unto them, Repent, and be baptized every one of you in the name of Jesus Christ for the remission of sins, and ye shall receive the gift of the Holy Ghost.	38 Peter said to them, "Repent, and be baptized every one of you in the name of Jesus Christ so that your sins may be forgiven; and you will receive the gift of the Holy Spirit.
39 For the promise is unto you, and to your children, and to all that are afar off, even as many as the Lord our God shall call.	39 For the promise is for you, for your children, and for all who are far away, everyone whom the Lord our God calls to him."

LESSON SETTING
> **Time:** AD 29/30
> **Place:** Jerusalem

LESSON OUTLINE

I. The Holy Spirit Gives Us a
   Common Language
   (Acts 2:1-8)
II. Peter's First Sermon
   (Acts 2:14-24)

III. Repentance and Baptism
(Acts 2:37-39)

EXPOSITION

I. THE HOLY SPIRIT GIVES US A COMMON LANGUAGE (ACTS 2:1-8)

The book of Acts is about overcoming barriers. Many barriers existed for the apostles, who had been charged with the task of disseminating the Gospel message. They had been advised to wait in Jerusalem until they had been endowed with the power of the Holy Ghost. In John's Gospel account, they had already been given a measure of the Holy Ghost when Jesus breathed on them (John 20). In fact, John 14-16 is an account of Jesus' prophecy of the full coming of the Holy Spirit, who is virtually His other self. As such, the Holy Spirit would be infused in the disciples and activated, even motivated, their living and their divinely assigned tasks. The Greek word for the Holy Spirit *hagios pneuma,* reveals Him as being a part of the Godhead by the use of *hagios,* which usually means "set apart." In this sense, it describes an actual person, especially when connected to the article. The article distinguishes the Holy Spirit as an entity within Himself. That is to say, the article points to the Holy Spirit as a definite and distinguished person. The Holy Spirit encompasses all of the attributes of personhood; He thinks, feels, acts, creates, sustains, and even energizes. In the Johannine text and here in Acts, the Holy Spirit acts like God as He initiates actively with human creatures and fortifies them for divine purpose. The major point in this section of our lesson is that the Holy Spirit is best understood when compared to the backdrop of Genesis 6. In Genesis 6, human beings who, at that time spoke one language, came together to build a name for themselves by constructing a skyscraper that would call attention to their technological ingenuity. Humanity, as depicted in the Genesis account, extended the first parents' indulgence in human pride to the world conglomerate and simultaneously demoted God to a secondary role that denied His divine sovereignty.

As a result of this ungrateful action, God confounded their language, which, in turn, prohibited them from working together to complete their project. Humanity had already suffered estrangement from God because of the first parents' disobedience. The natural conclusion is that estrangement from God results in conflict between members of the human family. Their refusal to acknowledge God as the Sovereign Creator and Ruler of the universe now erupts in total estrangement of the human family and outlines the destructive pattern of human life as it wanders further away from God, into chaos and miscommunication. Acts 2 is the divine reversal of Genesis 6. Luke records nothing short of a phenomenon. During the celebration of Pentecost, Jews, and Proselytes from various ethnic background converge in Jerusalem for the celebration.

Pentecost, originally an Old Testament festival known as the Feast of Weeks, was the second greatest feast of the Jewish year. It was a harvest festival where the first fruits of the wheat harvest were presented to God. The feast was celebrated approximately 50 days after the Passover, symbolizing covenant renewal. The New Testament emphasized it as a common understanding and celebration of the ability of the Spirit of God to overcome human differences and conflict.

The phenomenon occurs precisely at this point when people from all over the world come together at the Jerusalem feast and their language barriers are overcome by the power that accompanies the Spirit of God. It is the direct reversal of what happened at the Tower of Babel. The people who assembled with a goal of oneness and pride without God at Babel left in discord and confusion, but those who assembled for different reasons at Pentecost with their hearts opened toward God actually experienced community, as the Spirit overrode all language, cultural, and social barriers. The outpouring of the Spirit is depicted as a miracle of speaking and hearing that the church uses to format and develop its concept of community.

The Spirit of God not only allows them to overcome barriers of language, culture, and geography, but their common experiences of enthusiasm and achievements are highlighted also. The point of the text is that human togetherness and cooperation can be a blessed and wonderful thing when humanity recognizes and works within the Sovereignty of God and gives Him the praise due His name.

Issues of diversity can also be overcome and used as strengths and propellants for greater accomplishments when given over to the Spirit of God. Diversity can lead to enhanced cooperation between human beings as they compliment the gifts and talents of one another. Acts 2 and Genesis 6 cannot and should not be interpreted without each other. Genesis 6 emphasizes humanity's greatest sin and failure, whereas Acts 2 emphasizes its greatest accomplishment in light of the will and power of the Spirit of God. And as a result, an outstanding community is formed.

II. PETER'S FIRST SERMON (ACTS 2:14-24)

This is Peter's first sermon. His sermon is the first of the missionary addresses of Acts (see Acts 10 and 13). It represents the preaching of the early church, consisting of "scriptural proofs concerning the Messiah (see Joel 2:28-34; Psalms 16:8-11; 110:1) some references to Jesus' ministry, an emphasis on his death and resurrection, and a call to repentance" (see John Polhill's *Acts* in the *New American Commentary: An Exegetical and Theological Exposition of the Holy Scripture.* Broadman Press: Nashville, p. 107). The sermon falls into two parts, It connects Jesus to the event of the Spirit coming in power pointing to His decisive victory in the resurrection, and resulting in a call to repentance. It is quite clear that Peter is the one who wields the authority as the representative of the Twelve. He calls on his fellow Jews to listen attentively to what he has to say.

First, he points out that these men are not drunk with new wine. He references the time of day as the authority. That is to remind them it is only 9:00 a.m. (more commonly known as the morning hour of prayer in the Jewish context). Rather than being drunk, their behavior is the predicted work of the Holy Spirit that the prophet Joel prophesied about years ago. Peter corrected their apparent misunderstanding and used it as an entrance into his sermon. Peter saw the Spirit's coming as an universal gift that came with the messianic age, but also as an indicator of the end of time (notice his inclusion of women and daughters, everyone would receive Him. vv. 17-18). It is a prophetic movement energized by the Spirit of God Himself. It is the New Testament's equivalent to the Old Testament's, the *Day of the Lord* (see Isaiah 7:18-25; 13:19-11; 24:21-22; Jeremiah 46:10; Zephaniah 1:14-18; Amos 5:18-20; Joel 2:31).

Verses nineteen and twenty speak of apocalyptic signs in the heavens and on the earth—signs related to the unveiling or revelation of God's plan for the end of time. The darkened sun and blood-colored moon are the signs in heaven (see Rev. 6:12). These correspond with signs on the earth: blood, fire, and billows of smoke. Ultimately, all these signs and wonders are related to the final cosmic events leading up to the second coming of Jesus.

However, the focus here is not to judge those nations that have abused Israel, rather it is a day wherein the Spirit of God will be poured out as an indicator of His salvific activity. It is a continuation of the church's missionary work that started with Jesus, and that Peter, and Paul later continued (Mark 4:35-5:1-12; Acts 9-11). This salvation is based upon God's willingness to bring the entire world under the umbrella of divine forgiveness as expressed in John 3:16 and Romans 10. It becomes the backdrop of Acts 2:21, "And everyone who calls on the name of the Lord shall be saved" (NRSV). Luke presents Jesus here as Lord. The Greek word *kurios* (kurios) is grouped with the Hebrew *Messiah* (Messiah) to indicate whoever accepts Jesus as Lord must, correspondingly, accept Him as God's Messiah (His anointed One). These activities point to a deeper meaning. Peter bluntly pointed out that this deeper understanding was directed to the Jews. He argued, "You yourselves know these things" (v. 22). The point is Peter creatively and very effectively reports there is an unbreakable link between the Spirit, the ministry of the Church as witnesses, the suffering of Jesus, and His *Parousia* or Second Coming. Yet Peter concluded his message just as Joel concluded his. "And everyone who calls on the name of the Lord will be saved" (Acts 2:21, NIV).

III. REPENTANCE AND BAPTISM (ACTS 2:37-39)

Peter uses the ecstatic occasion to inform them of God's activity in Jesus Christ and calls upon them to repent and believe the Good News that he has just shared with them. Peter's call for repentance and Baptism is reminiscent of Jesus' preaching and Baptism (Mark 1:14-15). The immediate result of Pentecost and of Peter's sermon is the giving of a formula for entrance into the new community. Christianity had not yet emerged from the realm of Judaism, but Peter's call for repentance and Baptism continues the extended extrapolation process of removing the infant religion from its Judaistic envelopment. In this new and developing religion, Jesus Christ is the centerpiece, the focused object of worship and agent of God's fellowship and reconciliation with humanity. Those who accept Peter's sermon posit themselves as members of a new community.

It is worthy to note that repentance and baptism are taken together here. Repent means to turn away from one thing and to turn to something else. In this sense, it has a dual connotation. Peter calls upon his hearers to turn away from their sin and unto God as expressed in the Person and Life of Jesus Christ. Their act of repentance is to be accomplished by Baptism. Baptism is identification with Jesus Christ. It symbolizes and affirms faith in His death, burial, and resurrection. Baptism and repentance are the corresponding responsibilities of all those who are convicted with the truth of God's activity in Jesus. Even though Baptism is primarily symbolic, one must agree to it and accept it as a condition for renewed fellowship with God. Thus, repentance and Baptism are necessary components to human salvation and cannot be muted or diluted. The call of Peter for repentance and subsequent Baptism is none other than the call for human beings to accept what God has done in Jesus. Accepting Jesus Christ through these two acts reveals one's faith in God and becomes the basis by which one receives the gift of the Holy Spirit. Peter's sermon results in about 3,000 persons voluntarily submitting to Jesus as Lord and Savior through repentance and Baptism.

THE LESSON APPLIED

This lesson affirms two things—the Holy Spirit gives us a common language, and that language results in a common experience. The common language is the language of God's love for humanity. When human beings accept God's love and render unto Him due praise, honor, and worship, they can reach their unlimited potential and cross over any barrier that would affect their renewed fellowship with Him. Those who built the Tower of Babel in the name of human pride and human achievement failed to express homage and love to God, their Creator. Whereas at Pentecost, human potential and unity are achieved through proper recognition of God and reaches maximum effectiveness through the divine energy of the Holy Spirit. That is to say, people can only reach their full potential as they worship and praise God properly.

Peter's call on the Day of Pentecost is the same call that comes to us so that we might recognize God as the Sovereign Lord and Creator. Through repentance and Baptism humanity can become a new community of faith in Christ Jesus.

LET'S TALK ABOUT IT
What is sin?

The Greek word for sin is *hamartia*. It means "to miss the mark." Sin is the missing of the mark that God set for humanity in terms of its thoughts, words, and deeds. Sin is the failure to meet God's standard of righteousness. Repentance and Baptism pave the way for us to be saved through faith in the Lord Jesus.

HOME DAILY DEVOTIONAL READINGS
MAY 8–14, 2023

MONDAY	TUESDAY	WEDNESDAY	THURSDAY	FRIDAY	SATURDAY	SUNDAY
Sent to Preach and Heal	Rejoice in Salvation, Not Power	God Protects and Preserves	My Soul Longs for God	Then the Lame Shall Leap	Peter Heals in Jesus' Name	Peter Preaches Salvation through Jesus
Luke 10:1–9	Luke 10:10–24	Psalm 41	Psalm 42	Isaiah 35:1–10	Acts 3:1–11	Acts 3:12–26

JUMPING FOR JOY

ACTS 3:1-11

King James Version

NOW Peter and John went up together into the temple at the hour of prayer, being the ninth hour.

2 And a certain man lame from his mother's womb was carried, whom they laid daily at the gate of the temple which is called Beautiful, to ask alms of them that entered into the temple;

3 Who seeing Peter and John about to go into the temple asked an alms.

4 And Peter, fastening his eyes upon him with John, said, Look on us.

5 And he gave heed unto them, expecting to receive something of them.

6 Then Peter said, Silver and gold have I none; but such as I have give I thee: In the name of Jesus Christ of Nazareth rise up and walk.

7 And he took him by the right hand, and lifted him up: and immediately his feet and ankle bones received strength.

8 And he leaping up stood, and walked, and entered with them into the temple, walking, and leaping, and praising God.

9 And all the people saw him walking and praising God:

10 And they knew that it was he which sat for alms at the Beautiful gate of the temple: and they were filled with wonder and amazement at that which had happened unto him.

11 And as the lame man which was healed held Peter and John, all the people ran together unto them in the porch that is called Solomon's, greatly wondering.

New Revised Standard Version

ONE day Peter and John were going up to the temple at the hour of prayer, at three o'clock in the afternoon.

2 And a man lame from birth was being carried in. People would lay him daily at the gate of the temple called the Beautiful Gate so that he could ask for alms from those entering the temple.

3 When he saw Peter and John about to go into the temple, he asked them for alms.

4 Peter looked intently at him, as did John, and said, "Look at us."

5 And he fixed his attention on them, expecting to receive something from them.

6 But Peter said, "I have no silver or gold, but what I have I give you; in the name of Jesus Christ of Nazareth, stand up and walk."

7 And he took him by the right hand and raised him up; and immediately his feet and ankles were made strong.

8 Jumping up, he stood and began to walk, and he entered the temple with them, walking and leaping and praising God.

9 All the people saw him walking and praising God,

10 and they recognized him as the one who used to sit and ask for alms at the Beautiful Gate of the temple; and they were filled with wonder and amazement at what had happened to him.

11 While he clung to Peter and John, all the people ran together to them in the portico called Solomon's Portico, utterly astonished.

MAIN THOUGHT: Jumping up, he stood and began to walk, and he entered the temple with them, walking and leaping and praising God. Acts 3:8

LESSON SETTING
Time: 30 AD
Place: Jerusalem

LESSON OUTLINE
I. **A Beggar's Common Plea (Acts 3:1–5)**
II. **An Unexpected Response (Acts 3:6–10)**
III. **Confronting the Real Issue (Acts 3:11)**

UNIFYING PRINCIPLE

People often focus on alleviating the consequences of a problem rather than on solving the problem itself. How can we be more open to the latter possibility? When a man who could not walk begs for money, Peter and John respond by healing the man.

INTRODUCTION

The book of Acts shows the continuation of Jesus' ministry through the power of the Holy Spirit. The Holy Spirit energized the disciples to demonstrate to the world why Jesus entered into the human frame of reference.

In Acts, the barriers that prohibited the disciples from sharing the Gospel are eliminated one by one. First, the barrier of selfishness and incompetence is overcome. Under the guidance of the Holy Spirit, the disciples developed courage, which quelled their fear of chastisement by the Jewish religious authorities. Second, the Holy Spirit awakened the disciples' slumbering faith. At Jesus' death, they were a hopeless group of might–have–beens. After being infused by the Spirit, they became confident, articulate, and daring. They had received the message of salvation and were willing to share it at whatever cost. Third,

the Holy Spirit provided them with a common language—the language of love. Gone were the barriers that prohibited them from relating to fellow needy members of God's creation.

Not only could they communicate more effectively because of the pervasiveness of the Spirit, but they also committed their lives to God through sharing their possessions and goods. Fourth, this sense of sharing possessions flowed from a more general concern they had learned from Jesus Himself. The loving compassion for His creation caused God to envelop Himself in human flesh and journey through the centuries to provide hope to humanity. They witnessed Jesus healing the poor, neglected, and rejected subjects of the Decapolis and the area around Galilee. The Holy Spirit had convinced them that continuing Jesus' ministry must be pursued, relentlessly.

As Peter and John prepared to enter the Temple for worship, they encountered a man who lay in dire straits. His request for alms (Acts 3:1-5) demanded their attention and provoked a sympathetic response. But these bold, courageous, compassionate disciples of Jesus empowered by the Holy Spirit saw that the man possessed a greater need than the one he requested from them. This lesson examines the beggar's common plea (Acts 3:1–5), the unexpected response from Peter and John (Acts 3:6–10), and the real issue confronting all people who are often wrapped up in their physical and materialistic concerns (Acts 3:11–16).

The text posits we must request more than the need to be filled. Our physical needs may be more apparent to us and to others, but they must never be allowed to overshadow our spiritual need of God's presence and power in our lives. This man suffered tremendously, not only because of limited mobility, but more so because he displayed an emptiness that left him deplorable and wretched. The apostolic duo saw his greater need and restored him to the Kingdom of righteousness.

EXPOSITION

I. A BEGGAR'S COMMON PLEA (ACTS 3:1–5)

The Jewish people had regular times for worship and prayer. The ninth hour (three o'clock in the afternoon) was a popular time for prayer and ceremonial sacrifices called the evening *Talmud.* During this time people would come to the temple to give thanks for the day's blessings and to invoke God's blessings for the next. Peter and John devout, faithful Jews, committed themselves to this traditional time of prayer.

Jesus had sent out the disciples in pairs on various evangelistic crusades (Luke 9:1–6; 10:1–20). It is quite possible that the paring of Peter and John started during that time. In Acts, the two act as a dynamic duo on several occasions (Acts 3:1, 3:11; 4:13, 19: 8:14). On these occasions, Peter is the primary spokesperson and appears to be fulfilling Jesus' earlier designation of him as leader of the group of disciples. John takes on the role as a silent, but constant supporter. The two exhibit the type of witnessing that the Luke–Acts sequence has become known for. According to Jewish tradition, two witnesses are necessary in order for an event to be valid (2 Cor. 13). Peter and John, as a pair, fulfill that tradition.

Upon entry into the temple complex, Peter and John meet a man who is described as being crippled from birth. The Greek word *cholos* means "lame from the mother's womb." It was not a case of circumstance or some physical mishap that made the man handicapped. The lame man is being carried back and forth to the temple generated sympathy is the hearts of those who passed by. They were compelled to donate alms so he could support himself. His cause was helped by the rabbinic code, which encouraged Jews to observe the three pillars of the Jewish faith—the Law, worship, and charity. Worshipers such as Peter and John would be hard pressed to ignore anyone who pleaded for alms. For Peter and John, the weight rested not on them following the rabbinic code, but on them following the example of compassion exemplified by their Lord.

Verses 3–5 reveal the cripple man's only request. He solicits alms from Peter and John. His request is unlike the requests made by others in the Luke–Acts sequence who ask Jesus directly for restoration (Luke 5:12–16; 6:17–19; 7:1–10; 8:49–56; 9:37–43; 18:35–42).

The path leading to the temple entrance was frequently laden with beggars who knew their proximity to the temple provided them with their best opportunity to receive help. In most cases, contributors did not take the time to converse with beggars, much less give them individual attention—but this occasion would be different. Peter and John's response proved to be a stark contrast to the norm. The man asked for economic support, but received much more than he bargained for. His request for help was met with a non-tangible gift that went beyond anything the man could have imagined or thought.

II. AN UNEXPECTED RESPONSE (ACTS 3:6–10)

The imperative *blepo* (meaning "look") used by Peter captures the seriousness of the situation. The Greek *atenizo* means "to focus intently upon one." Peter and John gave the man undivided attention and demanded his attention in return. Their encounter would not be an everyday occurrence. The man may have thought an extravagant gift would eliminate his need to depend on the generosity of others. In a way, he was on the right track.

The heart of the narrative resides in verse 6. The usual gift was silver or gold; maybe even a loaf or two of bread. Peter's gift did not mislead the man. Peter immediately informed the man not to look for economic assistance. The use of the contrasting conjunction "however" followed to indicate they were mindful of his predicament. The conjunction also points to Peter and John's awareness that the man possessed a deeper need. Nevertheless, they implied that he would not be carried away empty–handed. Peter's subsequent statement, "Such as I have, I give to you," secures the man's hope of receiving something, even though he realized it would not be what he had expected.

The gift the crippled man was about to receive greatly exceeded his expectations and supplied him with hope and enthusiasm that had long since evaporated. Peter invoked the name of Jesus to bring the man to a state of physical health he had never before experienced. Notice, the man had been crippled since birth or infancy. He had known no other way than to be carried back and forth to his destination. Were Peter and John playing a cruel joke on him? And even if he remembered the healing activities of Jesus, did His ministry not end with a shameful and embarrassing death on the cross? These things probably ran though his mind as he listened to Peter's statement of economic poverty. Why had they stopped if they had nothing to give?

The invoking of one's name in Hebrew theology is to call upon authority or power. Peter's use of Jesus' name connects the activity of Jesus' healing ministry and places it on a continuum. It places Jesus' power on a scale equal to God's, while implying Jesus' physical absence is not indicative of his inability to heal. The text implies that faith in Jesus is more than enough to activate the divine force that came with Him.

The handshake of encouragement was the final act that activated the flow of the Holy Spirit's power into the man's body. Immediately, the man jumped to his feet and walked by his own power into the house of worship he had been forced to lie outside of for quite some time. Now his access to the Temple was not limited to the court of the Gentiles, but he could enter into its inner compartments (Lev. 21:17–20; 2 Sam. 5:8). His healing by the Holy Spirit, through the name of Jesus, had removed another barrier that had denied him spiritual acceptance since birth. Whereas Judaism deemed him unfit for worship, the new religion of Jesus Christ extended full personhood and acceptance of him.

The previously crippled beggar had good reason to jump for joy. The Greek word *hallomai,* found in the Septuagint in Isaiah 35:6 and here in a celebrative praise, is carried out in the form of "leaping of joy." The Isaiah text reads, "Then will the lame leap like a deer." The writer's use of this rare Greek word illustrates the intensity of the joy of the healed. Leaping is natural for deer, and it will be a natural reaction for the one who has, since birth, been deprived of the privilege of movement that most people enjoy.

III. CONFRONTING THE REAL ISSUE (ACTS 3:11)

To those who frequented the temple for worship, the vision of the unnamed, crippled man seeking alms was a common sight. They came to know him as a dormant fixture at the temple. The landscape changed; the fixture after his healing moved about, walked, leapt, and praised God loudly and boldly. The transformation is startling. They knew what he had been and watched as he shouted glory to God. His open display of emotion prepared the way for Peter's sermon, which would confront the real issue at hand.

Verse 11 is a transitional verse that links the first 10 verses to the last 15. The first 10 verses deal with the miracle of the lame man being healed, which becomes the backdrop for Peter's preachment in verses 12–16. Across from the Court of the Gentiles in Solomon's Colonnade was the place where Peter gave his second sermon in as many chapters. Acts reveals two sermons by Peter, one delivered earlier at Pentecost, and one given at Solomon's Colonnade. In light of their earlier fear of the Jewish authorities who were partially responsible for the death of Jesus, the disciples' courage is remarkable.

Calling the attention of the people, Peter corrected their assumption that he and John were responsible for the miracle. Peter gave the credit to Jesus. Peter accused the Jewish people of a lack of faith and of crucifying the one God had glorified. Emphasis on glorification of Jesus refers to His resurrection from the dead and denotes God's ability to reverse the worst of evil human maneuvers.

The murder of Jesus allowed murderer Barabbas to be released, despite Pilate's attempt on at least three occasions to let Jesus go. Peter points out the Jews' flagrant denial of the One God sent to bless and redeem them. The other titles Peter used to emphasize Jesus' role as the Messiah include "Righteous One" and "Author of life." The demons in Mark's Gospel recognize Jesus as the "Holy One of God" (Mark 1:24). The terms denoting Jesus as the "Righteous One" and as the "Author of Life" can be found in Mark 1:24; 5:7; Hebrews 2:10, and 12:2, respectively. As such, Christ has come blazing the trail of new life and renewed fellowship with God.

The importance of Jesus' role here is seen in the healing of the lame man. Faith in Jesus causes those who are crippled to be made whole. Thus, Peter called upon the spectators and witnesses of the man's healing to repent so that God would grant them a blessing equal to the one they had just witnessed.

THE LESSON APPLIED

This text is important because it calls people to see the blessings of God that have come in Jesus Christ. First, God entered the human frame of reference in Jesus in order to provide salvation. The resurrection set into motion by the Holy Spirit eradicates barriers between God and humanity as well as barriers between human beings. The healing of the lame man is the prime example of this holy activity in human life. As they enter the temple, Peter and John are confronted by a nameless person, lame from birth, seeking alms. He gets more than what he asked for. The preaching pair gives him Jesus and the full restoration of his limbs.

As Christians, we must be aware that we can give each other Jesus when we have nothing else to give. This miracle provides the Jews with another opportunity to accept Jesus through faith, even though they had already rejected and crucified Him. His sermon points out their great need and God's willingness to restore them.

Essentially, Peter and John replicate the ministry of Jesus under the power of the Holy Spirit. They provide or administer the first healing to take place since the resurrection. The Jewish officials might have found a temporary sense of relief after the crucifixion that Jesus was no longer present to irritate them with His presence and corrective theology and understanding about God. Peter's preaching, along with the duo's healing of the lame man at the gate of the temple more than likely erased any belief that the Jesus' movement had waned. Acts 4:1–22 shows that the name of Jesus continued to provoke fear and anxiety in the Jewish officials as the disciples empowered by the Holy Spirit had become embolden in their faith.

LET'S TALK ABOUT IT

1. Why is Acts 3:1–11 important?

This passage is important because it shows that the healing ministry of Jesus continued after His death. The apostles do not create a new ministry, but gain new courage to continue the one Jesus had called them to participate in. This passage shows that all are empowered by Him as the name of Jesus and His spiritual presence are more than enough to infuse spiritual healing and new life. This first healing miracle noted in Acts sends a signal that Christianity is alive and well, as is its progenitor, Jesus Christ.

2. Why is faith so important in Acts?

Faith is important in the book of Acts, and in all of the other Gospel accounts because it is the activity that connects one to Jesus. In John 20:29-30, the writer announces blessings on those who have not seen but believe. The verses end with a reminder that the materials were written to enhance the readers faith and that the purpose of an enhanced faith is to propagate eternal life. Faith is the conduit that connects us to the Christ as the eternal life giving Resource we need to experience divine salvation.

HOME DAILY DEVOTIONAL READINGS
MAY 15–21, 2023

MONDAY	TUESDAY	WEDNESDAY	THURSDAY	FRIDAY	SATURDAY	SUNDAY
Full of Grace and Power	The First Martyr	The Far Countries Wait for God	Peoples Shall Come to the Lord	God Is Present Everywhere	Samaritans Embrace the Gospel	The Spirit Guides Us
Acts 6:8–15	Acts 7:48—8:2	Isaiah 60:9–14	Zechariah 8:1–8, 20–23	Psalm 139:1–10	Acts 8:4–17	Acts 8:26–40

AN ETHIOPIAN OFFICIAL BAPTIZED

ADULT TOPIC:	BACKGROUND SCRIPTURE:
BREAKING DOWN BARRIERS	ACTS 8:26–40

ACTS 8:29–40

King James Version	*New Revised Standard Version*
THEN the Spirit said unto Philip, Go near, and join thyself to this chariot.	THEN the Spirit said to Philip, "Go over to this chariot and join it."
30 And Philip ran thither to him, and heard him read the prophet Esaias, and said, Understandest thou what thou readest?	30 So Philip ran up to it and heard him reading the prophet Isaiah. He asked, "Do you understand what you are reading?"
31 And he said, How can I, except some man should guide me? And he desired Philip that he would come up and sit with him.	31 He replied, "How can I, unless someone guides me?" And he invited Philip to get in and sit beside him.
32 The place of the scripture which he read was this, He was led as a sheep to the slaughter; and like a lamb dumb before his shearer, so opened he not his mouth:	32 Now the passage of the scripture that he was reading was this: "Like a sheep he was led to the slaughter, and like a lamb silent before its shearer, so he does not open his mouth.
33 In his humiliation his judgment was taken away: and who shall declare his generation? for his life is taken from the earth.	33 In his humiliation justice was denied him. Who can describe his generation? For his life is taken away from the earth."
34 And the eunuch answered Philip, and said, I pray thee, of whom speaketh the prophet this? of himself, or of some other man?	34 The eunuch asked Philip, "About whom, may I ask you, does the prophet say this, about himself or about someone else?"
35 Then Philip opened his mouth, and began at the same scripture, and preached unto him Jesus.	35 Then Philip began to speak, and starting with this scripture, he proclaimed to him the good news about Jesus.
36 And as they went on their way, they came unto a certain water: and the eunuch said, See, here is water; what doth hinder me to be baptized?	36 As they were going along the road, they came to some water; and the eunuch said, "Look, here is water! What is to prevent me from being baptized?"
37 And Philip said, If thou believest with all thine heart, thou mayest. And he answered and said, I believe that Jesus Christ is the Son of God.	
38 And he commanded the chariot to stand still: and they went down both into the water, both Philip and the eunuch; and he baptized him.	38 He commanded the chariot to stop, and both of them, Philip and the eunuch, went down into the water, and Philip baptized him.

MAIN THOUGHT: He commanded the chariot to stop, and both of them, Philip and the eunuch, went down into the water, and Philip baptized him. Acts 8:38

ACTS 8:29—40

King James Version	New Revised Standard Version
39 And when they were come up out of the water, the Spirit of the Lord caught away Philip, that the eunuch saw him no more: and he went on his way rejoicing.	39 When they came up out of the water, the Spirit of the Lord snatched Philip away; the eunuch saw him no more, and went on his way rejoicing.
40 But Philip was found at Azotus: and passing through he preached in all the cities, till he came to Caesarea.	40 But Philip found himself at Azotus, and as he was passing through the region, he proclaimed the good news to all the towns until he came to Caesarea.

LESSON SETTING
Time: AD 30
Place: Jerusalem

LESSON OUTLINE
I. Philip Is Led by the Spirit (Acts 8:29)
II. Philip Expounding the Scriptures (Acts 8:30–35)
III. The Positive Effect of Philip Following the Spirit (Acts 8:36–40)

UNIFYING PRINCIPLE
There are many social conventions that prevent us from interacting with others. How do we move past these social conventions? The Spirit moved Philip to approach the Ethiopian eunuch and guide him in understanding God's Word.

INTRODUCTION
This passage of Scripture is a continuation of the account of Philip's evangelistic efforts, as directed by the Holy Spirit. Acts 8:4–17 describes how the Gospel was brought into Samaria. Jesus had instructed the disciples to spread the Good News in Jerusalem, Judea, Samaria, and to the outermost regions of the world. Philip's encounter with the Ethiopian eunuch fulfills the last of these directives, which the Church would later build upon in order to provide an extended ministry to the Gentiles via the Apostle Paul. Philip's progression from serving on the benevolent ministry team to world-class evangelist is amazing. What provoked his tremendous sense of mission and purpose? What fortified him to maintain an aggressive, evangelistic posture that led to the baptism of people previously rejected by members of the Jewish faith? The prevalence of the Spirit in Philip's ministry illustrates that his evangelistic efforts are part of God's plan to include non-Jewish people in His fellowship, as underscored by Philip's witness to the Ethiopian eunuch. He operates at the bidding of the Spirit. This lesson examines the leadership of the Spirit in Philip's ministry (Acts 8:29), Philip's obedience to the Spirit in approaching the chariot and expounding the Scripture to the eunuch (Acts 8:30–35), and the positive outcome of his obedience (Acts 8:36–40).

EXPOSITION

I. PHILIP IS LED BY THE SPIRIT (ACTS 8:29)
The emphasis in this passage is clearly on the activity of the Spirit. Chapters 8–10

show a dramatic increase in the Spirit's involvement in the mission of Gentile evangelism. Philip has just been involved in the conversation of the Samaritans; now he becomes involved in another conversion that represents the Word of God being preached to the "ends of the earth" (i.e., Africa). The eunuch's conversion is followed by that of Paul and then Cornelius, but it precedes the other two which build off of a more-than-chance encounter .

The narrative begins with the initiative of God. Reminiscent of the angelic appearance to Mary (Luke 1:26–38), Jesus (Matt. 4:11), and the disciples (Matt. 28:5–7), Philip is approached by an unnamed heavenly messenger who directs him to witness in a most unlikely place and to a most unlikely person. He was directed to a deserted road south of Jerusalem leading to Gaza. Philip complied with the divine directive and found himself in the company of an Ethiopian eunuch who was the government treasurer for the queen of Ethiopia. Ethiopia was an ancient nation of Meroe that flourished from the eighth century B.C. to the fourth century A.D. (a period of about 1,200 years). The Old Testament refers to ancient Ethiopia, or Meroe, as the Kingdom of Cush. Situated in northeastern Africa near the current nation of Sudan, Ethiopia was composed primarily of black people.

Once again, the underlying emphasis in Acts is that the Spirit breaks down all barriers to salvation, even racial and ethnic ones. The man that Philip approached was a eunuch. Eunuchs were usually males who were castrated as boys in order to be used as keepers of harems and the treasury. They were found to be extremely trustworthy and loyal to their rulers. So widespread was the practice of placing them over the treasury that the term "eunuch" became a synonym for "treasurer," even when castration was not involved. In our text, both terms "eunuch" and "treasurer" are used, which means the man Philip approached was likely an actual physical eunuch. He was on a pilgrimage to Jerusalem. The pilgrimage to the holy city indicates that he was a "God-fearing Gentile," but was prohibited from full membership into the Jewish faith because he was a eunuch (Deut. 23:1). He could visit the temple, but could not enter it. The man was reading from the scroll of the prophet Isaiah (Isa. 56:3–8). The Spirit directed Philip to stand near the chariot, and he obeyed.

II. PHILIP EXPOUNDING THE SCRIPTURES (ACTS 8:30–35)

The text is clear that both parties, Philip and the eunuch, are not aware of the inner workings of the Spirit of God. The eunuch is reading from the Book of Isaiah. The passage is part of the Servant Songs. It depicts a scene of utter hopelessness, something closely akin to what the eunuch had just experienced with his being denied entrance into the temple. His status as a eunuch was seen as a physical blemish that prohibited him from enjoying the privileges of Judaism. The eunuch identified with the suffering servant in the passage. When Philip approached the carriage at the insistence of the Spirit and heard the Scriptures being read aloud, he inquired if the eunuch comprehended what he was reading. The play on words in the Greek text is interesting. *Ginoskosis* refers to comprehending or understanding, and *anaginoskeis* refers to the reading itself. The use of both words in this context emphasizes the man's inability to understand what he was reading. How then would he come to understand the passage? The Spirit of God was already aware of the eunuch's implied spiritual need and had already taken the steps to fulfill it. The Luke-Acts sequence emphasizes the need for scriptural interpretation and direction. It is not enough for one to desire salvation; he must also understand God's plan of salvation. It is the heart that understands God's Word that will grow spiritually and bear fruit. Recall in Luke 24:45, the disciples received such guidance from Jesus, and later in Acts 9:10–19, the Apostle Paul received similar guidance from Ananias.

The eunuch expressed his inability to understand Scripture on his own and invited Philip to sit with him. The eunuch was reading text that detailed the suffering and humiliation of Christ. Philip was able to illustrate the meaning of the text by comparing the Old Testament image of a slaughtered lamb to Jesus' crucifixion, and the lamb, before it was sheared, represented Jesus' silence before the Sanhedrin. Jesus' conviction on trumped–up charges related to Isaiah's reference to injustice. The reference to "his descendants" meant that his followers would undergo similar persecution and suffering (v. 33).

In the concluding portion of verse 33, Philip saw Jesus' subsequent exaltation in the Resurrection and the Ascension. Philip started with the apparent passage the eunuch was reading from and shared with him the Good News about Jesus. Philip unfolded the mystery of the Gospel of Jesus Christ to the eunuch, and the eunuch was convicted and believed.

III. The Positive Effect of Philip Following the Spirit (Acts 8:36–40)

Philip committed himself to following the movement of the Spirit of God. He circumvented his plans, traveled to the desert road, approached the eunuch's carriage, and interpreted the Scriptures for him. Philip's message was so convicting that the Eunuch wished to be baptized immediately. This is important for two reasons. First, it shows the eunuch's full identification with and acceptance of Philip's preaching and teaching. Second, it denotes his departure from Judaism and acceptance of Christianity. Note that this story has overtones of the Old Testament story of Naaman, the Syrian captain, who was healed from leprosy after he washed in the Jordan River (see 2 Kings 5:1–19).

As the carriage passed a pool of water, the Ethiopian asked, "Is there anything to prevent my being baptized right now?" The verb "prevent" used in verse 36 indicates the removal of barriers hindering the spreading of the Gospel. In this case, a "triple" barrier—race, culture, and physical make-up—was removed. The eunuch was previously restricted from being a full member of Judaism because of his person. Because he was also a Gentile, he would have had to give up his full identity to be a proselyte. Furthermore, he suffered from the stigma of being black, which was prevalent in both Greek and Roman societies. But now, he received full acceptance in the Christian faith. All barriers to full acceptance and personhood had been washed away.

Philip's conversion of the Ethiopian eunuch is also important because it is the precursor of a concentrated Christian movement in North Africa. Many of the Apostolic Father and Bishops of the early church sprang from the African Church in North African (see the Theology of the Apostolic Fathers, *Tertullian, Irenaeus, The School of Alexandria: Clement and Origen* in *A History of Christian Thought* by Justin Gonzalez, Abingdon Press: Nashville, pp. 61-221, 1970).

The Spirit recognized the man's need from the outset and used the events in this passage to fulfill it. Philip's aversion to the Gaza road, the man reading the Scripture without understanding it, and the convenience of passing by a pool of water all came together. The Spirit had carefully orchestrated the events of this passage to lead to the fulfilment of the eunuch's spiritual need. Verse 37 is omitted in most modern translations because it is not found in most early manuscripts. It is considered to be an addition to the request for baptism in terms of a confession of faith. However, the eunuch had actually already asserted his faith by inviting Philip to interpret the Scriptures for him and then by requesting to be baptized. Verse 38 points out the type of baptism that the eunuch experiences. The Greek word that is used here is *baptizo*, which means submersion into. The type of baptism mentioned here is important because it shows that Philip is consistent in carrying out the practices of the mother church. Immediately, Philip, like the prophet Elijah, was snatched up by the Spirit and led to continue spreading the Good News to others who needed it. The Spirit had led him there and now led him elsewhere. The eunuch went home in great joy. God's purpose had been served.

THE LESSON APPLIED

Philip followed the Spirit, which intentionally led him to evangelize the Gospel to a Gentile that had been rejected by Judaism. The pervasiveness of the Spirit in this passage shows us that God is deeply interested in who we are as persons and desires to supply our needs. Physical, cultural, and racial backgrounds are not barriers to being fully accepted by God. Jesus died on the cross for all people. Philip understood this and allowed the Spirit to carry out His most holy purposes through him. Do you allow the Spirit of God to pervade your living, help you make decisions that include the rejected in your circle of friends? God wants to save the world from destruction, sin, and evil, but He desires to use you as the most effective communicator of His message of love. Philip allowed Him to use him. Will you allow the Spirit to use you?

LET'S TALK ABOUT IT

1. What is the major point in the story of Philip and the Ethiopian eunuch?

The major point in this story is that the Spirit of God works through people and uses events to bring awareness of their need for God. Philip was led by the Spirit to the chariot, where a eunuch from Ethiopia was confused about what he was reading. Philip enlightened him, after which the man expressed his desire to accept Jesus as Lord and Savior. The Spirit of God brought the two men together for "salvific" purposes. He also seeks to use one to help others in ways one may not yet know.

2. Why is the story of the Ethiopian eunuch significant?

This story is important because it fulfills Jesus' command to the disciples to take the Gospel to the "ends of the earth." Africa, at that time, was considered by the Greeks and Romans to be on the perimeter of the world. It is also important because it is the first completely non-Jewish instance of conversion to Christianity in Acts. The eunuch could not become a full member of Judaism, but the Spirit intentionally led Philip to share the Gospel with him. Also, the fact that the eunuch is black shows the progressive, inclusive nature of the Scriptures hundreds of years before any of the human rights movements (women's right, workers' rights, civil rights, etc.). Divine salvation requires only faith in Jesus and a willingness to turn to God and away from sin. Physical make-up, cultural inclination, and ethnicity are not, and should never become, prerequisites for gaining God's favor. The story of the Ethiopian eunuch shows that God's favor is neither predicated on outward physical appearance, status, or origin of birth, nor based upon income, education, or preconceived notions of social acceptance. We automatically incur it because of His great love for us and His desire to restore us unto Himself.

3. How can we understand the Word of God unless someone guides us?

"Faith cometh by hearing and hearing by the word of God" (Rom. 10:17, KJV). The Word and the Spirit have the power to radically changed one's life, as is seen in this text. Philip, filled with the Holy Spirit, was a great preacher. He was not concerned with a great cathedral with fabulous design and structure, beautifully stained-glass windows and a big symbol of the cross hanging over the pulpit. What the congregation was wearing, where they lived, or how they looked didn't concern him at all. He was only interested in preaching the Word of God to save souls, and he was willing to allow the Spirit to lead the way. When Philip caught up with the Ethiopian eunuch, he was reading the Scriptures. However, reading is not enough—we must understand what we are reading. The angel that directed Philip to the eunuch could have taught him the Scriptures, but God did not give that commission to angels. God has given the responsibility of spreading His Word to the ends of the earth to His people. Therefore, Philip preached to the eunuch the Word of God and guided him through the Scriptures. The eunuch believed on Jesus and was born again! He insisted on stopping his caravan and being baptized, immediately.

HOME DAILY DEVOTIONAL READINGS
MAY 22–28, 2023

MONDAY	TUESDAY	WEDNESDAY	THURSDAY	FRIDAY	SATURDAY	SUNDAY
The Heavens Tell God's Glory	A Heavenly Gospel	Only Christ Matters	Our Citizenship Is in Heaven	Blinded by the Light	Saul Begins to Preach Jesus	Saul Escapes to Jerusalem
Psalm 19	Galatians 1:10–24	Philippians 3:1–14	Philippians 3:15–21	Acts 9:1–9	Acts 9:10–22	Acts 9:23–31

SAUL OF TARSUS

| ADULT TOPIC:
THE CHALLENGES OF CHANGE | BACKGROUND SCRIPTURE:
ACTS 9:1–31 |

ACTS 9:9–17

King James Version

AND he was three days without sight, and neither did eat nor drink.

10 And there was a certain disciple at Damascus, named Ananias; and to him said the Lord in a vision, Ananias. And he said, Behold, I am here, Lord.

11 And the Lord said unto him, Arise, and go into the street which is called Straight, and enquire in the house of Judas for one called Saul, of Tarsus: for, behold, he prayeth,

12 And hath seen in a vision a man named Ananias coming in, and putting his hand on him, that he might receive his sight.

13 Then Ananias answered, Lord, I have heard by many of this man, how much evil he hath done to thy saints at Jerusalem:

14 And here he hath authority from the chief priests to bind all that call on thy name.

15 But the Lord said unto him, Go thy way: for he is a chosen vessel unto me, to bear my name before the Gentiles, and kings, and the children of Israel:

16 For I will shew him how great things he must suffer for my name's sake.

17 And Ananias went his way, and entered into the house; and putting his hands on him said, Brother Saul, the Lord, even Jesus, that appeared unto thee in the way as thou camest, hath sent me, that thou mightest receive thy sight, and be filled with the Holy Ghost.

New Revised Standard Version

FOR three days he was without sight, and neither ate nor drank.

10 Now there was a disciple in Damascus named Ananias. The Lord said to him in a vision, "Ananias." He answered, "Here I am, Lord."

11 The Lord said to him, "Get up and go to the street called Straight, and at the house of Judas look for a man of Tarsus named Saul. At this moment he is praying,

12 and he has seen in a vision a man named Ananias come in and lay his hands on him so that he might regain his sight."

13 But Ananias answered, "Lord, I have heard from many about this man, how much evil he has done to your saints in Jerusalem;

14 and here he has authority from the chief priests to bind all who invoke your name."

15 But the Lord said to him, "Go, for he is an instrument whom I have chosen to bring my name before Gentiles and kings and before the people of Israel;

16 I myself will show him how much he must suffer for the sake of my name."

17 So Ananias went and entered the house. He laid his hands on Saul and said, "Brother Saul, the Lord Jesus, who appeared to you on your way here, has sent me so that you may regain your sight and be filled with the Holy Spirit."

MAIN THOUGHT: So Ananias went and entered the house. He laid his hands on Saul and said, "Brother Saul, the Lord Jesus, who appeared to you on your way here, has sent me so that you may regain your sight and be filled with the Holy Spirit." Acts 9:17

LESSON OUTLINE
I. **Christ's Appearance to Saul (Acts 9:9)**
II. **The Call To Be Persecuted (Acts 9:10–17)**

UNIFYING PRINCIPLE

Our natural tendency is to hate our enemies. How do we respond when our enemies need our help? God used Ananias to help Saul take his first steps in faith, even though Saul had been an enemy of the early church.

INTRODUCTION

Because of Paul's aggressive missionary efforts and willingness to go against the status quo in Jewish life, the Church was challenged to throw its full efforts behind evangelizing Gentiles. Paul saw the developing potential of the budding Christian community and was equally as aggressive in perpetuating its growth as he was, at first, in destroying it. A zealous Hellenist Jew from Tarsus in Cilicia, Paul is introduced by Luke as a witness to the innocent death of Stephen. Saul encouraged Stephen's stoning and participated in the persecution of the Hellenist (Greek-speaking) Christians that followed. He sincerely believed that Stephen had blasphemed against God.

Paul also studied at the foot of Gamaliel and became a member of the Jewish religious establishment. Yet, his conversion experience implies that the martyrdom of Stephen affects him subconsciously, and he cannot escape the image embedded in his mind of Stephen. Stephen saw Jesus on high at the right hand of God. Interestingly, it is the same Jesus on "high" who confronted Saul on the road to Damascus.

Paul's conversion is the second of three conversions in as many chapters (Acts 8, 9, and 10). The Ethiopian eunuch is converted from a semi-Judaistic "proselyte" to Christianity; Saul is converted from Judaism; and Cornelius and his household become believers through Peter. The significance of the triple conversion narrative suggests that the major thrust of the book will emphasize the conversion of the Gentiles to the Christian faith. Saul's conversion then plays an important role in Luke's development of the history of the Church. If the single most destructive person, in terms of one's negative input into the Christian faith, can be converted to the religion that he once imprisoned others for practicing, then nothing can stop or restrict its growth. And nothing did. The Christian community, once out of the holds of Judaism, truly fulfilled Jesus' commandment to take the Gospel to the ends of the earth.

EXPOSITION

I. SAUL ENCOUNTER WITH ANANIAS (ACTS 9:9)

There are three narratives of Saul's conversion recorded in the Book of Acts. Acts 22:3–21 and 26:12–18 both record Saul's conversion with slightly varying details and emphases. We cannot proceed without considering the events that lead up to Saul's encounter with Ananias. Let's briefly examine Acts 9:1-8.

Acts 9:1-2 focuses on Saul's behavior and evil intent against the people of God. Saul is described by Luke as seeking to destroy people of the Way. The Greek term *O Thos*, interpreted as "The Way," was one of the earliest known self-imposed names for Christians. Paul took offense at this term believing it to be diverting people from Judaism. The prosecutor of Christians is on his way to Damascus to arrest those guilty of carrying out or participating in this blasphemous fraud.

Acts 9:3–6 provides details of Saul's encounter with the glorified Jesus. His journey was suddenly interrupted by an exceptionally intense light. It was so intense that it was more brilliant than the noon day sun (see 26:13). Dazzling light is frequently a component of epiphany scenes—those in which God appears to persons—in the Bible. Saul fell to the ground because he was overwhelmed by the light. The encounter became all the more overwhelming by the solemn repetition of his name by Jesus in verse four. This repetition of a person's name is found in both the Old Testament (see Gen. 22:11; also 1 Sam. 3:10) and the New Testament (see Luke 8:24; 10:41; 22:31). The voice in Saul's ears inquires as to why He was being persecuted. The voice asked, "Saul, Saul, why do you persecute me?"

Saul addressed the voice as *Kurios* (Gk: meaning "lord" or "master"), which could have been the equivalent of "sir" or similar terms of respect at the time. Saul more than likely meant the term in the sense of Lord, recognizing the heavenly origin of the voice. Jesus' question to Paul identifies Jesus with the Church. Thus, Paul cannot ignore the obvious; he had been persecuting the Lord God.

Paul learns quickly who the Lord is. The divine response indicts Paul for his presumptuousness. He had terrorized the Church vehemently because he assumed the believers' claims about Jesus to be blasphemous and ludicrous. Paul believed Christians equivocated Jesus with God; now he beheld the same Jesus with unmistakable proof that He was indeed the Lord of heaven and earth.

Jesus' identification with the Church and with His disciples meant that Saul had been on the "wrong side," promoting the wrong cause, and persecuting the wrong people. Saul discovered he was opposing far more than human beings loyal to the teachings and Lordship of Jesus; he was opposing Jesus Christ directly. This portion of the narrative signals the end of any further comments from Saul.

Jesus now provides Saul directions for the next steps he will take. He was instructed to proceed to Damascus just as he had intended. Upon his arrival in Damascus, Saul would then be supplied with further instructions. No further elaboration of Saul's divine encounter is given. It is enough that he saw the Lord. This experience placed Paul on an equal footing with the Twelve. He later claims it as his selection to divine apostleship (1 Cor. 9:1; 15:8; Gal. 1:16).

Saul's traveling companions were mentioned in the narrative for the first time in verse seven. They, too, were awestruck—so much so they were speechless. They had been direct witnesses to at least a part of Saul's experience. His traveling companions provide evidence that Paul's experience is an objective one. They heard the voices in conversation but did not see the vision of Jesus that Saul had seen. They heard a sound but did not see the vision. A later recollection of the event recorded in Acts 22:9 points out that the companions saw the light but did not hear the voice. Initially, the two accounts appear to be contradictory, but upon closer inspection, the two accounts verify one another. Paul's companions heard a sound and saw a light. They did not participate in the heavenly communication, however, since it was directed to Paul, and they were not privileged to see the vision of Jesus, nor were they allowed to hear the words spoken to Paul. The revelation stunned Paul and left him blind. Blindness here underscores Paul's transformation.

That major detail of the experience was reserved for Saul, exclusively and rightfully so (see 1 Cor. 9:1; 15:8; also Gal. 1:16). It sets the stage for his conversion and validated his apostleship.

The glaring light and vision of Jesus witnessed by Saul were so overwhelming he was stricken blind by them. Acts records an episode in which blindness came as punishment for the irreverent response of Elymas to the work of the Holy Spirit (see Acts 13:6–12). Saul's blindness revealed his brokenness and utter helplessness. This helplessness and bewilderment also find testimony in the fact that Saul avoided food and drink for three days because he was so traumatized by the experience. Polhill says of Saul, "The raging persecutor had been reduced to a shambles" (see John B. Polhill. *The New American Commentary: An Exegetical and Theological Exposition of Holy Scripture. Volume 26. Acts.* Broadman Press: Nashville, P. 236).

Jesus' appearance to Paul is the only account of His reappearing after the Ascension (except in John's vision of the Revelation of the Last Things).

Saul was the Church's number one enemy. Before the vision, he was assertive, forceful, and authoritative. Now, he experienced brokenness and helplessness. Others led him about the city. What a drastic change! Reduced to total powerlessness, Saul did not consume food or drink for three days, which can be observed as an act of penitence as well as an indication of how his world had been turned upside down.

II. THE CALL TO BE PERSECUTED (ACTS 9:10–17)

Verse 10 denotes a scene shift. The movement of the text goes from Paul's seeing Jesus to what this vision means for him. The setting of this part of the narrative takes place in Damascus. It is not to be confused with modern day Syria, whose capital city is called Damascus. Damascus of Paul's day was an ancient city which dated back to 2000 BC Situated on the border of Arabian Desert, it linked Egypt and Mesopotamia with mainstream trade routes. A disciple named Ananias lived there. The Lord appeared to him, and Ananias responded. He received instruction to seek out Paul. Notice the preciseness of the information of Paul's location. Both the house and the street locations were given. God also told Ananias that He had revealed to Paul that Ananias was coming to provide him with divine directions. Corresponding visions were given to both Ananias and to Paul. These visions signaled the divine orchestration of events. The first vision provided Ananias with step-by-step instructions. He was to enter the house of Judas and lay hands upon Saul so that he might recover his sight (v.

12). The laying on of hands here did not signal any special ordination, but served to revealed to Saul the awesome and sovereign power of God. The second vision revealed to Saul that someone was coming to instruct him.

Verses 13–14 emphasize Ananias' reluctance to get involved with Saul. He was well aware of Saul's misdeeds and atrocities on the believers. He even knew Saul had received authorization from the chief priests to arrest Christian fugitives who had fled Damascus to escape his assault against them. Ananias' questioning of God's wisdom is recorded by Luke to show the miraculous contrast involved in Saul's transformation. The Church's number one enemy was now a member of the group of believers that he prosecuted aggressively.

God had plans for the former prosecutor. He would be God's chosen instrument to carry the Gospel to the Gentiles. The use of the word "chosen" here is interesting. He was chosen for a purpose—to carry Jesus' name to Gentiles. Saul was called to bear witness to Jesus to the "ends of the earth." This meant that not only would he embark on missionary journeys to distant lands, but he would also defend the Gospel before political and religious authorities (Acts 24—26). Ananias welcomed Saul as a brother in the faith and carried out his responsibilities as Jesus' agent. Saul's conversion was complete.

After regaining his sight and being baptized by Ananias, Saul spent several days there in Damascus with the disciples. Although he was familiar with the Old Testament Scriptures, Saul needed instruction in how they pertained to the teachings of Christ. He was probably already familiar with many of the Christian teachings since he had been exposed to them through the ministries of Stephen and other Christian Hellenists.

Saul immediately began to witness on his own account. He preached in the Jewish synagogues that "Jesus is the 'Son of God.'" The phrase "Son of God" is only found once in Acts and was the central theme of Saul's preaching. What a stunning reversal! The major thorn in the side of the Christian community was now preaching the resurrection of Jesus with bold confidence. Listeners in the synagogue simply could not believe that the former persecutor had made such a radical about face. His zeal as a persecutor of the Church was out-matched by his zeal for the Gospel. He had seen the Lord and knew what his new purpose was. His in-depth knowledge of the Scriptures, coupled with the personal revelation of Jesus, made him a skillful interpreter of the Gospel message. His hearers inquired. "Isn't this the same man who raised havoc in Jerusalem among those who call on his name?" They were baffled, and rightfully so. For Saul, "old things are passed away; behold, all things are become new" (2 Cor. 5:17–21, KJV).

Acts 9:16 prophesied that Saul would suffer like he caused others to suffer for the sake of the Gospel, first in Damascus (vv. 23–25), and then in Jerusalem (vv. 26–30). The Jews in Damascus became angry and violent when they could not refute his message. He preached in Damascus for approximately three years before departing to Jerusalem (Gal. 1:17–18). The Damascus Jews had developed a plot to take his life. During that short period of time, Saul's preaching was making inroads into the Damascene synagogues.

These disciples in the area discovered the plot to kill him. The city gates were being watched, so they developed an alternate route to get Saul out of the city. They lowered him in a basket through the window of a house built along the city walls (2 Cor. 11:32–33).

THE LESSON APPLIED

This lesson portrays God's initiative to fulfill His own purposes. God called the Church's number one enemy and made him a witness to and for the His truth. God calls people like us to minister and to witness for him. One's past deeds do not prohibit a person from receiving a call from God.

This passage also shows that God can use evil for His own divine purpose. Although the text implies, through Saul's silence, that he was quite remorseful and maybe taken back by guilt, it affirms that he overcame them and used his energies as a springboard for the Christian witness.

God selected Saul for a mission. You will pay a cost for preaching, teaching, and living for God just like Saul paid a price, but rest assured, it is well worth it. Many people will be saved, and you will have fellowship with God also. More importantly, you will fulfill your purpose by carrying out God's will for your life, and consequently enable others to discover their true purpose for living as well.

LET'S TALK ABOUT IT
Why is the ministry of Paul important?

In hindsight, we can see why God called Saul. He ably and willingly shared the Gospel to the ends of the earth. He set up a church hierarchical system for its continued life. He provided the central theology of the relationship between Jesus and the Law and Judaism in general. Saul, later called Paul, (Paul is the Greek version of the name Saul) placed the resurrection of Jesus at center stage. He broke down racial, ethnic, and cultural barriers that would have restricted God's salvation and fellowship with to only a segment of humanity. Paul took the religion of Jesus and opened it up to all who would accept it.

All person who are non-Jewish owe a debt of gratitude to Paul. We are evidence of his commitment to fulfill the divine objective of universal salvation. Even the Jewish people owe Paul a debt of gratitude for helping them to see that they were chosen to remind all people they are of special value to God, that we were created in His image and likeness.

HOME DAILY DEVOTIONAL READINGS
MAY 29–JUNE 4, 2023

MONDAY	TUESDAY	WEDNESDAY	THURSDAY	FRIDAY	SATURDAY	SUNDAY
God's Servant Will Establish Justice	Live by Faith, Not Works	My Servant Shall Restore Israel	God Will Not Forget You	God Desires You Live in Purity	Clothe Yourselves with Love	You Shall Be Redeemed
Isaiah 42:1–7	Galatians 2:16–21	Isaiah 49:1–13	Isaiah 49:14–23	1 Thessalonians 3:11–4:8	Colossians 3:8–17	Isaiah 52:1–12

Fourth Quarter

June

July

August

YOUR GOD REIGNS

ISAIAH 52:7–12

King James Version

HOW beautiful upon the mountains are the feet of him that bringeth good tidings, that publisheth peace; that bringeth good tidings of good, that publisheth salvation; that saith unto Zion, Thy God reigneth!

8 Thy watchmen shall lift up the voice; with the voice together shall they sing: for they shall see eye to eye, when the LORD shall bring again Zion.

9 Break forth into joy, sing together, ye waste places of Jerusalem: for the LORD hath comforted his people, he hath redeemed Jerusalem.

10 The LORD hath made bare his holy arm in the eyes of all the nations; and all the ends of the earth shall see the salvation of our God.

11 Depart ye, depart ye, go ye out from thence, touch no unclean thing; go ye out of the midst of her; be ye clean, that bear the vessels of the LORD.

12 For ye shall not go out with haste, nor go by flight: for the LORD will go before you; and the God of Israel will be your reward.

New Revised Standard Version

HOW beautiful upon the mountains are the feet of the messenger who announces peace, who brings good news, who announces salvation, who says to Zion, "Your God reigns."

8 Listen! Your sentinels lift up their voices, together they sing for joy; for in plain sight they see the return of the LORD to Zion.

9 Break forth together into singing, you ruins of Jerusalem; for the LORD has comforted his people, he has redeemed Jerusalem.

10 The LORD has bared his holy arm before the eyes of all the nations; and all the ends of the earth shall see the salvation of our God.

11 Depart, depart, go out from there! Touch no unclean thing; go out from the midst of it, purify yourselves, you who carry the vessels of the LORD.

12 For you shall not go out in haste, and you shall not go in flight; for the LORD will go before you, and the God of Israel will be your rear guard.

MAIN THOUGHT: How beautiful upon the mountains are the feet of him that bringeth good tidings, that publisheth peace; that bringeth good tidings of good, that publisheth salvation; that saith unto Zion, Thy God reigneth! (Isaiah 52:7, KJV)

LESSON SETTING
Time: 712 BC
Place: Jerusalem

LESSON OUTLINE

UNIFYING PRINCIPLE

Both in our personal lives and in society as a whole there are times of chaos and uncertainty. Is there a reality bigger than the chaos we experience? Even in the midst of exile, Isaiah proclaims, "God reigns."

INTRODUCTION

Isaiah is writing about the joyous good news that Israel will soon be emancipated from her exile in Babylon. The overriding theme here is that although Israel had been conquered by her enemies, such as the Egyptians and Assyrians, *Yahweh* is now going to set these captives free and return them to Zion (Jerusalem). Moreover, the prophet provides a comparison and contrast to the Exodus, the history of which was known by Israel. *Yahweh* issues a plan of action and offers encouragement to the people as He prepares them for their return to the Holy City. A prominent theme here is salvation, which is found in verses seven and ten, as a reflection of the power and majesty of the Lord. Additionally, this exodus is to be visible to all of God's enemies so that they may realize that *Yahweh* will protect His people. The good news is that the God of Israel reigns supreme and will go before His people as He promised.

EXPOSITION

I. ANNOUNCEMENT OF GOOD NEWS (ISAIAH 52:7–8)

The opening of this section describes the mountains as a place of serenity and peace. The terms used to describe the place are "beautiful" (NKJV) and "lovely" (NASB), which provide images of grandeur and splendor. These images set the backdrop for the blessings that *Yahweh* is providing for His people.

Mountains can be places of security from terror, but in the Scriptures, we find comfort that mountains were sacred sites. Abraham was to offer his son Isaac on Moriah, known as "the chosen of Jehovah" until God stayed his hand. This site is where Solomon's temple was later built, which had been the spot that had been the threshing-floor of Araunah the Jebusite (2 Sam. 24:24). Moses was called into the service of the Lord on Horeb, the mountain of God, in front of a "burning bush" (Exodus 3:1–2). In the New Testament, Jesus is associated with mountains in that he used them for acoustical purposes when teaching the people. However, the sacredness of the mountain becomes evident when Jesus sends away the crowds and retreats alone to the hills to pray (Matthew 14:23).

The announcement is that of peace, happiness, and salvation to a people who have had their share of disappointment and despair. However, in this case, the message is that the exiles will be returning to Jerusalem. In this scenario, we find a messenger who is bringing good news. The Hebrew term used here is *basser*, whereas, later, we find this term to denote good news, as in the New Testament, Gospel. The English translation of the Greek *euan-*

gélion, which, in its most general sense, in the New Testament, refers to the word of salvation made available to the world in and through Jesus Christ.

The beauty of the mountain is connected to the messenger who is described as having beautiful feet. This is not to say that the feet of the messenger are attractive but to describe the magnificence of his mission. The description of the messenger is that of respect and prominence, as Paul will later write, "How beautiful are the feet of those who preach the gospel of peace, who bring glad tidings of good things" (Romans 10:15). Interestingly, the Jewish Bible begins verse 7 with, "How welcome on the mountain are the footsteps of the herald" (messenger). The messenger tells Zion that "Your God reigns." The book of Psalms helps us to understand this announcement. The "Enthronement Psalms" (Psalm 93; 97; 99) all begin with the words, "The Lord reigns." These psalms celebrate *Yahweh* as Israel's real king, though the Psalms speak of the king in Jerusalem. However, the good news for the exiles is that if *Yahweh* is their king, then they can be sure of rescue, since he is more powerful than any earthly king.

Isaiah writes that the messenger shouts to the people to listen to the watchmen (on the walls). Recall that Habakkuk stationed himself on the ramparts of Jerusalem and watched (waited) to see what *Yahweh* would say to him (Habakkuk 2:1). Like a sentinel standing in a watchtower to detect the first signs of an approaching enemy, Habakkuk had resolved to position himself so he might obtain the earliest and clearest information and then, like a watchman, inform his waiting brethren. As God's own Presence returns to Jerusalem, like Habakkuk, the prophet imagines that the lookouts in Jerusalem's higher buildings or fortifications will see God's presence as it comes toward the city. They will shout, or interestingly, they will sing together, initially, as the voices of the watchmen of Jerusalem on the city walls, who are at their posts guarding the city. These men are calling out or "lifting their voices" to the people in the city when they see that *Yahweh* (or the messenger) is approaching.

Then the guards are joined by the people shouting joyfully in unison at the news of the Lord's coming. In this case, the watchmen and the people will have the opportunity to see the glory of God. Some commentators render this as their being presented the miracle in a face-to-face encounter with the majesty of the Lord. This passage was composed after some Judeans had already returned to Jerusalem but before the full-fledged redemption that Isaiah anticipated had come to pass. "When the Lord restores Zion" is mostly futuristic prophecy. It is not clear, however, whether the watchmen see the messenger bringing the news that *Yahweh* is coming back to Zion, or whether they actually see *Yahweh* Himself returning to Zion. The idea of *Yahweh* returning to Zion could be expressed by the one crying in the wilderness saying, "Prepare the way of the Lord, make straight in the desert a highway for our God" (Isaiah 40:3). The Lord's return to Jerusalem implies a return of His people to the city.

II. A DAY OF REJOICING (ISAIAH 52:9–10)

This is a day of rejoicing as the messenger encourages the people to "break forth," meaning to spread out throughout the city and region to broadcast the good news of God's coming. The phrase "you waste places of Jerusalem" describes the exiles who are from the city that have been laid waste or have mostly been destroyed during the Babylonian invasion. In July 587 BC (2 Kings 25:2 ff.; Jeremiah 52:5 ff.), just as the city's food supply was exhausted, the Babylonians breached the walls and poured in. A month later (2 Kings 25:8–12; Jeremiah 52:12–16), the Babylonians returned to Jerusalem and, acting on orders, put the city to the torch and leveled its walls. Certain leading citizens were executed (2 Kings 25:18–21; Jeremiah 52:24–27), while a further group of the population was deported to Babylon. Its cities destroyed, its economy ruined, its leading citizens killed or deported, the population consisted chiefly of poor peasants, incapable of making trouble (2 Kings 25:12; Jeremiah 52:16). The state of Judah had ended forever.

However, Jerusalem will be restored. Recall the later account of the rebuilding of the wall of Jerusalem, and of the registry Nehemiah had found of those who had returned from Babylon. The people told Nehemiah, "The survivors who are left from the captivity in the province are there in great distress and reproach. The wall of Jerusalem is also broken down, and its gates are burned with fire" (Nehemiah 1:3). The period of soothing has begun; the Lord has comforted His people, as assigned to the messenger, "Comfort, O comfort My people, says Your God" (Isaiah 40:1). The message here is that Yahweh is restoring the people to the city and also, to their Holy Land, which should result in their emancipation from Babylonia. When the Lord returns, the righteous remnant will sing joyfully because He will have comforted and redeemed His people. However, because of disobedience, Jerusalem will continue to be occupied by foreign powers.

Isaiah uses the metaphor and imagery of God's "holy arm" as a source of strength and power. Perhaps, he may have referred to the prophet's prayer where he pleads for the righteous to be strengthened, asking Yahweh to "awake and put on strength, the arm of the Lord." This is the same arm that cut apart Rahab, a mythical sea monster representing Egypt. The power of the arm of the Lord would rise up again to save His people (Isaiah 51:9). The term used here is hasab, which means to "lay bare" or to "strip off" anything that would impede the use of the arm. As in a fight, a warrior would take off his tunic because he would have greater agility to slay his enemy.

"In the sight of all nations" means "before the eyes of all nations," that would witness the power and majesty of the Lord who loves and protects His people. Recall that David praised God for revealing His power "in the presence of my enemies" (Psalm 23:5), to show the nations that aligning against Yahweh is a serious mistake. This may seem irrational in that the people have been captured and their cities devastated, but the message here is that God is in control, as the hold of the enemies is temporary. All nations, i.e., "the ends of the earth," will see the power of Yahweh and realize their resistance against Him is futile. The salvation of the Lord will be revealed in the sense of God's protection and rescue of His people. The lord will demonstrate His power.

III. Instructions for Departure (Isaiah 52:11–12)

In this scenario, *Yahweh*, through the prophet, is commanding the people to leave Babylon. This is a reminder of the Exodus, when God had Moses prepare the people to leave, "This is how you shall eat it: your loins girded, your sandals on your feet, and your staff in your hand;" (Exodus 12:11). In addition to eating and observing the first Passover, Israel realized that this was the time of God's deliverance, and they were ready to follow His orders.

One misinterpretation of the Exodus is that all of Israel left Egypt with Moses. There were Israelites who did not leave because they either did not believe Moses and his plan of departure, or observe the Passover by placing lamb's blood on their doorposts, or had been elevated to Egyptian positions that they did not want to abandon. In addition, some may have left at a later date, after they witnessed the Exodus actually happen without immediate reprisal. Nonetheless, this exhortation is addressed to those in Babylon who would have to choose between staying in relative security there or risking the long journey back to Palestine.

In some cases, such as in the original Exodus, Israel was allowed to take "spoils" of Egypt. For example, when Israel had completed her preparations for leaving, the people asked for "the Egyptian's articles of silver, articles of gold, and clothing." The Lord had given the people favor in the sight of the Egyptians, so that they granted them what they requested, thus they plundered the Egyptians (Exodus 12:35–36). However, the account of their preparation for departure does not include any mention of plunder or obtaining of spoils. *Yahweh* demanded that Israel not take anything unclean from Babylon, which in this case, was anything Babylonian. Although it may be unclear who the prophet is specifically addressing, he is giving orders about the condition in which people are to leave Babylon, as they have to be ritually clean. It is possible that these orders are not addressed to all the exiles but only to those carrying the sacred vessels during the new Exodus, which would normally be the priests and Levites. It is possible that the first two lines of verse 11 concerned all of the exiles, while the last two were directed to the priests.

"You who carry the vessels of the Lord" are probably the priests, and the vessels spoken of here are most likely the golden vessels and other utensils of value that the Babylonians took as "booty" from the temple in 597 BC (2 Kings 24:13). Moreover, they could also be new sets of vessels (see Ezra 7:15–20; 8:24–30). Additionally, because the vessels will accompany the divine presence along their journey, they must maintain ritual purity. The "midst of her" not only speaks of Babylon but the atmosphere of the land and in this case, the stench of Israel's enemies and her oppression. The people had to cleanse themselves and be ritually clean because they were to be in a position to worship the Lord after leaving the country. The people are not to leave in a hurry this time, but calmly, assured of God's leading them and giving them protection.

Israel will not go out in haste or go out as fugitives. Verse 12 in the NKJV records the line "go by, or in flight". This means that Israel was not to hang its head as if her people were escaping in some sort of clandestine manner because *Yahweh* wants His enemies to see His power and majesty in the protection of Israel. This line tells the exiles not to see themselves as fugitives but as His people who have been rescued from the clutches of the enemy. To leave as fugitives would give credence to Egypt, in that Israel would be ashamed in their emancipation. Israel will rejoice because as in the original Exodus, when He provided a pillar of cloud by day and a pillar of fire by night, their journey will be accompanied by *Yahweh* (Exodus 13:21–22). Isaiah prophesies that *Yahweh* will lead the exiles and provide a rear guard for their overall protection. The earlier Exodus from Egypt is contrasted with the imminent exodus from Babylonia. The former took place in haste and confusion, but the new exodus will be more stately.

THE LESSON APPLIED

This missive is to tell Zion the nightmare is over! The description is yet another account of God's protection over Israel, even under what may be considered horrible circumstances and conditions. One may draw a line from Israel's exodus from Babylon to the return of Nehemiah and Ezra to Jerusalem. The fact that Israel is experiencing a form of slavery again is telling; however, even in her punishment, God never withdraws His love. Judah still belongs to God and there is no impediment to her redemption. Because of her captivity, God's name is reviled among His enemies. God's own reputation is harmed by the Babylonian exile, since people may think that this represents the triumph of the Babylonian gods over the God of Israel, and the reason God is sure to liberate the nation.

LET'S TALK ABOUT IT
Is it possible to maintain peace in the midst of the craziness of life?

Believers praise God for the peace that only God can bring. Pastors, for example, have to reassure members in times of crisis, such as in the death of a loved one. This situation is never easy because believers may agree with the assessment that God is an ever-present help in the time of trouble (Psalm 46:1) only when it is applicable to someone else. When trouble comes close, the misfortune can try their faith. Nonetheless, believers must continue to hold on to their faith, especially when it "hits home." In the "midst of a storm," believers must continue to praise God for the tranquility that only He can provide. The old phrase continues to resound: "He may not come when you want Him, but He's always right on time." That means God will be present when you need Him.

MONDAY	TUESDAY	WEDNESDAY	THURSDAY	FRIDAY	SATURDAY	SUNDAY
The River of Life	Receiving Everlasting Joy	The Right Kind of Spirit	Peace in the Midst of Distress	God Is Our Refuge	Christ Is Our Peace	A New Heaven and Earth
Ezekiel 47:1–13	John 16:20–33	James 3:13–18	Psalm 4	Psalm 46	Ephesians 2:11–22	Isaiah 65:17–25

HOME DAILY DEVOTIONAL READINGS
JUNE 5–11, 2023

GOD'S KINGDOM OF PEACE

ADULT TOPIC:	BACKGROUND SCRIPTURE:
A LIFE OF HOPE AND PEACE	ISAIAH 65:17–25

ISAIAH 65:17–25

King James Version

FOR, behold, I create new heavens and a new earth: and the former shall not be remembered, nor come into mind.

18 But be ye glad and rejoice for ever in that which I create: for, behold, I create Jerusalem a rejoicing, and her people a joy.

19 And I will rejoice in Jerusalem, and joy in my people: and the voice of weeping shall be no more heard in her, nor the voice of crying.

20 There shall be no more thence an infant of days, nor an old man that hath not filled his days: for the child shall die an hundred years old; but the sinner being an hundred years old shall be accursed.

21 And they shall build houses, and inhabit them; and they shall plant vineyards, and eat the fruit of them.

22 They shall not build, and another inhabit; they shall not plant, and another eat: for as the days of a tree are the days of my people, and mine elect shall long enjoy the work of their hands.

23 They shall not labour in vain, nor bring forth for trouble; for they are the seed of the blessed of the LORD, and their offspring with them.

24 And it shall come to pass, that before they call, I will answer; and while they are yet speaking, I will hear.

New Revised Standard Version

FOR I am about to create new heavens and a new earth; the former things shall not be remembered or come to mind.

18 But be glad and rejoice forever in what I am creating; for I am about to create Jerusalem as a joy, and its people as a delight.

19 I will rejoice in Jerusalem, and delight in my people; no more shall the sound of weeping be heard in it, or the cry of distress.

20 No more shall there be in it an infant that lives but a few days, or an old person who does not live out a lifetime; for one who dies at a hundred years will be considered a youth, and one who falls short of a hundred will be considered accursed.

21 They shall build houses and inhabit them; they shall plant vineyards and eat their fruit.

22 They shall not build and another inhabit; they shall not plant and another eat; for like the days of a tree shall the days of my people be, and my chosen shall long enjoy the work of their hands.

23 They shall not labor in vain, or bear children for calamity; for they shall be offspring blessed by the LORD—and their descendants as well.

24 Before they call I will answer, while they are yet speaking I will hear.

MAIN THOUGHT: The wolf and the lamb shall feed together, and the lion shall eat straw like the bullock: and dust shall be the serpent's meat. They shall not hurt nor destroy in all my holy mountain, saith the LORD. (Isaiah 65:25, KJV)

ISAIAH 65:17–25

King James Version	*New Revised Standard Version*
25 The wolf and the lamb shall feed together, and the lion shall eat straw like the bullock: and dust shall be the serpent's meat. They shall not hurt nor destroy in all my holy mountain, saith the LORD.	25 The wolf and the lamb shall feed together, the lion shall eat straw like the ox; but the serpent—its food shall be dust! They shall not hurt or destroy on all my holy mountain, says the Lord.

LESSON SETTING
Time: 712 BC
Place: Jerusalem

LESSON OUTLINE
I. **New Heaven and a New Earth (Isaiah 65:17–20)**
II. **The Lord Will Provide (Isaiah 65:21–23)**
III. **Tranquility in the Land (Isaiah 65:24–25)**

UNIFYING PRINCIPLE
All living creatures long to thrive, but sometimes circumstances cloud our imagination for paths to change. What can remove the "clouds" and open us to new possibilities? Isaiah 65 describes God's new creation in which God will establish perfect peace.

INTRODUCTION
Most Bible scholars are familiar with the prophet Isaiah. He was based in Jerusalem and his prophecy was directed to Judah. It is thought that Isaiah lived approximately 760–673 BC and prophesied for many of those years. This missive, however, is attributed to someone scholars identify as Deutero-Isaiah or "Second Isaiah," who is an anonymous author of chapters 40–55 of Isaiah. In 65:17–25, the summons to faith is recast as a vision of a "new heaven and a new earth," which people can anticipate by their actions in the world. God is assuring the prophet that when the people return to Zion, they will have His blessings of the land and security from their enemies.

EXPOSITION

I. NEW HEAVEN AND A NEW EARTH (ISAIAH 65:17–20)

The topic for this section is a renewal of creation, as the world itself will be transformed in the new age that God brings. God is declaring, "I am creating a new heaven and a new earth," the term for "create" (*bara'*) suggesting future tense; and, the Jewish Bible reads, "I am creating a new heaven and earth," also signifying the creating of a new future. Of course, the language may recall the original "in the beginning, God created the heavens and the earth" account (Genesis 1:1); however, the term *chadash* means new or fresh, which indicates that the imagery is toward a heaven and earth that has not yet come into being. In this case, Isaiah is prophesying about the future, as was later written by John who saw "a new heaven and a new earth, for the first heaven and the first earth had passed away" (Revelation 21:1). Following the thousand-year reign of Christ, this is an "all things made new" heaven and earth – not the present heaven and earth, renovated – which is supported by the additional statement, for the first heaven and the first earth had passed away.

Additionally, the phrase "the first heaven and earth passed away" connects with Isaiah's statement that the former things will not be remembered. It indicates that the conditions and situations that Israel has encountered will be faded from their memories. Their minds will be focused on the rescue and redemption of the Lord. In this case, the good (blessings) will rinse away memories of the bad.

Continuing with the present tense, Israel is to be glad and rejoice "for what I am creating," i.e., Jerusalem, the Holy City. Here, Isaiah is speaking of the renewal of the current Zion, which is in need of restoration that will later be a task for Ezra and Nehemiah; however, it is an amazing prophecy because John will "see" the holy city, New Jerusalem, coming down out of heaven from God (Revelation 21:2). In both situations, *Yahweh* is restoring and creating Jerusalem, and her people, for His glory. *Yahweh* considers His people being in bondage to be offensive because the pagan nations will view *Yahweh*'s sovereignty over the world as suspect. Moreover, the inhabitants of the world will follow the deities that they believe have the power to bless and protect them. Part of God's delight is that Israel will acknowledge *Yahweh* as her God and remain committed to her walk with Him.

God declares that He will rejoice in the restoration of Jerusalem and "delight" (Jewish Study Bible), be glad, or be satisfied in His people. In this case, *Yahweh* will receive satisfaction knowing His people are safe but also, that the people now realize in whom their security lies. Isaiah assures Israel that the sounds of weeping and wailing will be eradicated because God hears their cries. Israel can take comfort in this promise because God had "seen the oppression of His people in Egypt and [had] heard their cry because of their bondage" (Exodus 3:7). In the early days of their return from Babylon, they were distressed to see that their country was still in ruins after the Babylonian invasion. God's promises were not yet fulfilled completely, but in His new creation, joy and happiness will replace their sadness.

Continuing the imagery, premature infant or elderly death will cease to occur. Notice the contrast between the two. The infant dies in childbirth (or soon thereafter), dying too early to have a future, whereas the old man also dies too soon. Although he is old and has reached what may be seen as the end of his days, he may not have reached his goals or completed all of those things assigned to him.

The imagery of a youth living to reach the age of one hundred is a metaphor of the youth living up to his or her potential. The average lifespan of "the days of our life, they contain seventy years, or if due to strength, eighty years" (Psalm 90:10). A 100-year-old man would not be considered a youth; however, in this case, the person who reaches this particular age will retain his or her vitality. The person who reaches an advanced age is considered to be wise and spiritually mature. Unfortunately, the persons who fail to reach this number of years will be thought to have been accursed (*qalal*), which would identify them as detestable or vile people, who were in this situation, doomed to miss the blessings of the New Jerusalem.

II. THE LORD WILL PROVIDE (ISAIAH 65:21–23)

This section is filled with the most descriptive aspects of Israel's coming prosperity. As with the Lord's original gift of the Promised Land, Israel will build houses for themselves and live in them! "They will plant vineyards" imagines that they will plant crops, becoming farmers, but also, that they will become ranchers and shepherds. That they will "eat their fruit" means that the land will be bountiful and prosperous, so that these owners and their families will be well-fed from the crops or meat that the property will yield.

As God created the land, He also owned the land, and this was not to be thought of as a form of reparation for the exiles. For example, following the American Civil War the financial plight of the formerly enslaved would have improved if they had access to ownership of land or property. After all, one of the principal promises of America was the possibility of average people being able to own land and all that such ownership entailed. After the Israelites were subjected to occupation and exile, landownership was a blessing because the land was a gift from the Lord.

In this case, Israel will not build houses for another to forcibly take away. Additionally, they will not be subjected to planting while someone else (their enemies) eat of their yield. Recall in the days of Gideon, the Midianites and Amalekites would raid the lands of the people and leave nothing – no crops, sheep, or other livestock – and force Gideon to thresh wheat in the winepress in order to hide it from the Midianites (Judges 6:3–11). In their return to Zion, Israel will not have to fear invading, marauding bands determined to wreak havoc on Israel.

Here, God compares the lifetime of a tree, devoid of human causation, which can be long and can endure the natural changes that occur in creation. Likewise, the days or period (*yom*) of God's people are measured by a stoic object. This should not be misunderstood as a sign that the people will live as long as a tree (or forever), but that blessed longevity will be granted to them. Additionally, God's chosen ones will "wear out the work of their hands," meaning that their hands will wear out before the land stops producing, as they will be in command of the land.

Moreover, Israel will not find their labors or their living to be in vain, as the work of their hands will be successful. Despite unforeseeable natural occurrences, such as drought and famine (which can discourage farmers and ranchers), the people of God will not see their work unfulfilled. This phrase could also possibly mean that the prophetic work of Isaiah will not be in vain but will be rewarded.

That the women will not "bear children for calamity," or as the Jewish Bible reads, "they shall not bear children for terror," indicates that Israel will not need to produce their offspring and the future of the nation for warfare or strife. In the period of the ancients, police forces were nonexistent; therefore, the young members or warriors of the tribes had to protect their families. In this situation, God reveals that in all things, He will be their protector.

God has previously said that He will bring forth from the descendants of Jacob and Judah an heir of His mountains. His elect or chosen will inherit it, and His servants will live there (Isaiah 65:9). In this case, *Yahweh* is restoring the confidence of Israel in the covenant that has been issued throughout her history. This situation is no different, in that the protection and security of *Yahweh* will occur because of the walk of their fathers that ensured God's blessings. Additionally, the youth, i.e., the offspring of the people, must also develop and have a relationship with the Lord. Moreover, the good fortune of all of the people will be inherited by their descendants who remain loyal to God.

III. TRANQUILITY IN THE LAND (ISAIAH 65:24–25)

Isaiah predicts that the Lord will be so attuned to His people that He will answer before they pray. Normally, people pray to God and wait for His response: however, this pattern changes the manner in which they are to think. God already knows the supplications and needs of His people before their utterances are spoken.

The act of "calling" does not only come from the people calling upon *Yahweh* because *Yahweh* happens to also call on His chosen for ministry and for faithful living. Unfortunately, there exists those who are unfaithful and do not answer when the Lord calls, nor do they listen when He speaks. However, in the new creation, the situation will be entirely different, as *Yahweh* will be so swift that while they are yet still speaking, He will respond.

This section predicts a time when peace and tranquility will be the normal atmosphere. Even the wolf and the lamb will coexist in peace. The beginning of verse 25 is actually a shorter version of 11:6 ff., which includes adversaries, such as the leopard and the young goat and the calf and young lion, laying down together, putting aside natural aggression.

Even eating habits will change, as the lion who is usually a meat eater will be able to ingest straw like an ox – it does not say the ox will eat meat. However, the point here is that the carnivorous animals, such as the lion and bear will not hunt other animals in their quest for food.

Interestingly, there is an emphasis on one of the animals that is not included in this image of peace. Notice that the serpent's food shall be the dust of the earth, which is a continuation of the mandated curse that was pronounced during the conflict in Eden. Recall that after the serpent had deceived Eve, God said to the serpent, "Because you have done this, you are cursed more than all cattle, and more than every beast of the field; On your belly you shall go, and you shall eat dust all the days of your life" (Genesis 3:14). In this case, where other animals seem to represent a pardon of sorts, the serpent is not forgiven for the life-changing deceit that was promulgated upon Eve. This animal will not be let "off the hook" because it symbolizes evil and the evil one.

Another perspective of the continued curse on the serpent can be seen in the term *'aphar*, which is translated as dust. The serpent is to eat the dust of the earth, which includes any recurring debris. Recall that Isaiah commands Israel to "shake yourself from the dust" (Isaiah 52:2), and Jesus tells His disciples to "shake off the dust from under your feet" (Mark 6:11), as a testimony of their being rejected. In Isaiah, its habit of eating dirt is the reason the snake will not be seeking to eat other creatures. However, if the term *'adamah*, which means dirt or earth is used, it could mean that the serpent shall dine off of the people, as in contributing to their misfortunes, as a continuous representative of Satan. In this case, this term must not be mistakenly used, or it will give credence to Satan and denigrate *Yahweh* as the Savior of His people. Nevertheless, the serpent is not given a reprieve in this idyllic scene of peace and tranquility.

Additionally, the "nursing" child will be able to play by the hole of the cobra, and the weaned child will put his hand on the viper's den (Isaiah 11:8). Although it is not part of this segment, this does not abrogate or annul the verdict of the serpent. Instead, it points to the figure of the child (Jesus) who continues to wield power over the serpent and Satan. Moreover, *Yahweh* declares that evil or harm will not occur in His holy mountain, i.e., which is Zion but actually refers to the entire world.

THE LESSON APPLIED

Micah's words could be applicable in this missive as the peace and tranquility that the Lord provides. Recall that the language of "beating their swords into plowshares and their spears into pruning hooks" will allow Israel to be immune to human conflict and "neither shall they learn war any more" (Micah 4:3). However, in this case, it is not because Israel is powerful that they are about to be freed from Babylonian exile; it is because of God's love and protection. Because of the problems and conditions of today's society, e.g., shootings and murders, we as Christian believers live in a period when we could feel as if we are exiled. Nonetheless, we must continue to remain faithful to the promises of the Lord in that He will make all of these crooked places straight. The resolution to our issues is to reside and abide in the love of God.

LET'S TALK ABOUT IT

How might we believe in a Kingdom of peace in a world of violence?

Believers have known sorrow but are secure in their knowing that through the risen Christ, good can be brought out of struggle. In many of our nation's cities, we find an overriding atmosphere of anguish because crime is removing the children. Unfortunately, many of the affected families do not know the Lord and therefore, do not have the faith to place their trust in Him, even if it is simply seeking the solace that only He can provide. Believers, however, realize that in Jesus Christ, we are delivered from all defects of life. As Christians, we must not relinquish our position in the Kingdom because we have a record of God's provisions. Again, a continuing theme is blessings and peace for those who walk with the Lord.

HOME DAILY DEVOTIONAL READINGS						
JUNE 12–18, 2023						
MONDAY	**TUESDAY**	**WEDNESDAY**	**THURSDAY**	**FRIDAY**	**SATURDAY**	**SUNDAY**
The Confidence of God's Servant	God's Servant Will Make Many Righteous	Forsaking All for the Kingdom	The Greatest Must Be a Servant	Who Is Like the Lord?	A Humble Act of Love	God's Servant David Shall Be King
Isaiah 50:4–9	Isaiah 52:13–53:12	Mark 10:17–27	Mark 10:35–45	Psalm 113	Mark 14:1–9	Ezekiel 37:15–28

GOD'S SERVANT-KING

ADULT TOPIC: ALL FOR ONE AND ONE FOR ALL	BACKGROUND SCRIPTURE: EZEKIEL 37:15–28

EZEKIEL 37:21–28

King James Version

AND say unto them, Thus saith the LORD God; Behold, I will take the children of Israel from among the heathen, whither they be gone, and will gather them on every side, and bring them into their own land:

22 And I will make them one nation in the land upon the mountains of Israel; and one king shall be king to them all: and they shall be no more two nations, neither shall they be divided into two kingdoms any more at all.

23 Neither shall they defile themselves any more with their idols, nor with their detestable things, nor with any of their transgressions: but I will save them out of all their dwellingplaces, wherein they have sinned, and will cleanse them: so shall they be my people, and I will be their God.

24 And David my servant shall be king over them; and they all shall have one shepherd: they shall also walk in my judgments, and observe my statutes, and do them.

25 And they shall dwell in the land that I have given unto Jacob my servant, wherein your fathers have dwelt; and they shall dwell therein, even they, and their children, and their children's children for ever: and my servant David shall be their prince for ever.

26 Moreover I will make a covenant of peace with them; it shall be an everlasting covenant with them: and I will place them, and multiply them, and will set my sanctuary in the midst of them for evermore.

New Revised Standard Version

THEN say to them, Thus says the LORD God: I will take the people of Israel from the nations among which they have gone, and will gather them from every quarter, and bring them to their own land.

22 I will make them one nation in the land, on the mountains of Israel; and one king shall be king over them all. Never again shall they be two nations, and never again shall they be divided into two kingdoms.

23 They shall never again defile themselves with their idols and their detestable things, or with any of their transgressions. I will save them from all the apostasies into which they have fallen, and will cleanse them. Then they shall be my people, and I will be their God.

24 My servant David shall be king over them; and they shall all have one shepherd. They shall follow my ordinances and be careful to observe my statutes.

25 They shall live in the land that I gave to my servant Jacob, in which your ancestors lived; they and their children and their children's children shall live there forever; and my servant David shall be their prince forever.

26 I will make a covenant of peace with them; it shall be an everlasting covenant with them; and I will bless them and multiply them, and will set my sanctuary among them forevermore.

MAIN THOUGHT: My tabernacle also shall be with them: yea, I will be their God, and they shall be my people. (Ezekiel 37:27, KJV)

EZEKIEL 37:21—28

King James Version	*New Revised Standard Version*
27 My tabernacle also shall be with them: yea, I will be their God, and they shall be my people. 28 And the heathen shall know that I the Lord do sanctify Israel, when my sanctuary shall be in the midst of them for evermore.	27 My dwelling place shall be with them; and I will be their God, and they shall be my people. 28 Then the nations shall know that I the Lord sanctify Israel, when my sanctuary is among them forevermore.

LESSON SETTING
Time: 594 BC
Place: Babylon

LESSON OUTLINE
I. **Reuniting Israel and Judah (Ezekiel 37:21–23)**
II. **The Davidic Kingdom (Ezekiel 73:24–28)**

UNIFYING PRINCIPLE

To many, the world seems to be in turmoil and disarray. How can life change for people who are scattered, separated, and have little concern for one another? Ezekiel proclaims restoration of relationships under a renewed covenant in which God says, "I will be their God and they will be my people."

INTRODUCTION

Ezekiel, son of a priest named Buzi, was among the leading Judean citizens exiled, with King Jehoiachin, to Babylon in 597 BC His call to be a prophet is dated to about 594, and his last recorded oracle, to around 574. We have little biographical information, and Ezekiel's marriage is only known because of the notice about his wife's death in 24:15–24. A contemporary of the Judean prophet Jeremiah (who he does not mention), Ezekiel's primary period of activity in Babylon was twenty-five years before the writer(s) of Second Isaiah (Isa. 40–55). His knowledge of Jerusalem can be explained either by his own earlier experience there or by reports that reached the exiles in Mesopotamia. Ezekiel is remembered for apocalyptic visions, such as a "wheel in the middle of a wheel" and the "valley of dry bones."

EXPOSITION

I. REUNITING ISRAEL AND JUDAH (EZEKIEL 37:21–23)

Previously in this chapter (vv. 15–17), Ezekiel was given a sign that visualized God's restoration of Israel. In the first set of verses, Ezekiel was told to take two sticks of wood and write on one of them the name of Judah and on the other, the names of Ephraim and Joseph. Judah is the southern kingdom, and Joseph is the father of Ephraim, the central tribe of the northern Kingdom, Israel. Ezekiel was then to hold them together like one stick. In this gathering, *Yahweh* declares that He will "take the sons of Israel from among the nations where they have gone" (or been taken into exile) and "gather them from every side and bring them into their own land." Recalling the command to Moses, in which the Lord said, "Speak to the children of Israel, and get from them a rod from each father's house, all their leaders according to their fathers' houses

– twelve rods and write each man's name on his rod" (Numbers 17:1–2). Just as one gathers sticks for a fire, God will gather the exiles to establish them as one nation, with David as their king, undoing the damage caused after the death of Solomon with the divisions of the monarchy. In the future, from every side, *Yahweh* will bring Israel back into her own land, which includes Jerusalem and surrounding regions.

Verse 22 provides promises for Israel that will be fulfilled at the Second Coming of Christ, which include but are not limited to the unification of the two kingdoms. The kingdoms will be united into a singular entity, as one nation, which is a reflection of the original design of the first kingdom under David. The divisions of the United Kingdom of Israel occurred around 931 BC as Jeroboam, the son of Nebar and a former servant of Solomon (1 Kings 11:26), became the first monarch of the ten tribes in the north, which retained the name "Israel." Following the death of Solomon, his son, Rehoboam, succeeded his father as king of the two southern tribes, which were called Judah. Because of greed and intrigue, the land was split into two factions, and now, *Yahweh* is sending a message to Ezekiel and the people that this split and its causes will be eviscerated. In the repair of this situation, there can be only one solution, as God is not placing His trust in a human king again.

There will not be a priest or prophet anointing another human to be placed in the role of an earthly monarch. The next king will be a king who is dedicated to the lives and prosperity of all of the people, not just a select few. The prophecy given to Ezekiel will be fulfilled by a celestial king whom Israel has been waiting for: Jesus, the Messiah.

In verse 23, *Yahweh* again reveals promises for Israel that will be fulfilled at the Second Coming of Christ, which include purification from all idolatry. Confidentially, *Yahweh* declares that the people will no longer defile themselves with their idols or fetishes (Jewish Bible). The exiles found themselves in this southern Mesopotamian land, whose capital city was Babylon (or *Bab-ilu*, meaning "gate of god"). Babylon had many deities that were in direct opposition to the will of *Yahweh*. Unfortunately, many of the people in this group drifted into the worship of Babylonian gods.

Yahweh will deliver Israel from all detestable things and from her sins, representing the promise of a celestial future. For the nation to bathe in this redemption, they must purify themselves and be cleansed. For a devout Jew, the thought of being unclean is repulsive. However, in this case, Israel will not be able to self-cleanse; the cleansing will occur because of the blood of the Messiah.

Connecting to the Davidic king, *Yahweh* uses language that we find spoken by the great-grandmother of David, Ruth: "Your people shall be my people, and your God, my God" (Ruth 1:16). Here, God declares that "they will be My people and I will be their God." This is a declaration that Israel will forever walk with the Lord.

II. THE DAVIDIC KINGDOM (EZEKIEL 73:24–28)

Ezekiel's prophecy envisions the future kingdom of Israel, which reunifies Israel and Judah under the rule of a Davidic king. At this juncture in history, King

David (ca. 1010–970 BC), the son of Jesse, the second king, and the first king of the United Kingdom, has been dead for some years. Ezekiel (born 621 BC) is writing around 594 BC He speaks of "my servant David," which is not David resurrected but David's greatest descendant: Jesus, the Messiah. Incredibly, David was known as a dedicated shepherd before he gained fame for defeating Goliath and becoming king. In verse 24, however, Ezekiel links the shepherd qualities of David to those of the "Good Shepherd," who "knows My sheep, and am known by My own" (John 10:14). Ezekiel further connects David (the earthly king) to Jesus (the heavenly king), who was also called "King of the Jews" (Matthew 2:2; Mark 15:26; Luke 23:38; John 19:21).

Ezekiel proclaims that "they will walk in God's ordinances and keep His statutes." Paul will later writes that they will observe the new covenant, not the Law, which cannot annul the covenant that was confirmed before by God in Christ (Galatians 3:17). Moreover, "the covenant that I will make with the house of Israel after those days, I will put my laws in their mind and write them on their hearts; and I will be their God, and they shall be my people" (Hebrews 8:10) is a signal that the new covenant will be honored under one shepherd or king.

A king is not only the leader of a people but is also the protector of his nation. For the nation to live "on and off" the land, the days must be times of peace, in absence of war, which is destructive to crops and the people. That "they will live on the land that God gave to Jacob" identifies the land as the Promised Land, Canaan, or Palestine.

The land was not new land but the lands previously settled by Israel. These lands were snatched away by foreign invaders; however, the restoration of these lands by the Servant-King will ensure that Israel and all of her descendants will live on and off the land, as it would be passed down to successive generations. Even though Ezekiel speaks of Israel's return to the land, history reveals that the land will be later controlled and occupied by the Seleucids and Romans. After the return of the exiles, the land would be known as the "Land of the Jews." Since most of the Israelites who returned from the exile were from the tribe of Judah, they were called Jews and their land, Judea. At some point in history, Israel would no longer be a national entity, nor one coterminous (coexisting) group with the descendants of the Israelite tribes, or the inhabitants of the old national territory – not even a community of those who in some way, acknowledged *Yahweh* as God, offered Him worship, and rallied around the Law. This is a futuristic vision of the Promised Land as being perfected in Heaven. As in chapter 34, King David, however, is clearly subservient to God. He is God's servant (v. 24) and is called a prince (v. 25) rather than a full-fledged king.

Ezekiel declares that *Yahweh* "will make a covenant of peace with them and it will be everlasting." This description by Ezekiel is futuristic. Ezekiel draws on the tradition of permanent Davidic rule, where God tells David, "Your house and your kingdom shall be established forever before you. Your throne shall be established forever" (2 Samuel 7:16). This is considered as an eternal covenant, literally, the "covenant of peace," concentrating on the role of the temple as the center of both Israel and the nations.

Israel, however, has been guilty of breaking covenants. How can Ezekiel see Israel maintaining the integrity of a new agreement between the nation and *Yahweh*? It is because *Yahweh* promises that this covenant will be everlasting, and Israel will be multiplied and become prosperous, which is not relegated to the bounty of the land but denotes the prosperity of their relationship with the Lord. This time, Israel will be guaranteed success because of His presence and sanctuary, which will be filled with only those who wish to worship in it and are dedicated to the Lord.

God declares, "My dwelling place will be with them." The identification of this place is understood by the definition of the term *mishkan*, which here, means "dwelling place" but also means tabernacle, as the dwelling place of God. Recall that the tabernacle was the portable sanctuary said to have been built at Mt. Sinai in the time of Moses and used until Solomon built the first temple. The tabernacle is also called the "tent of the testimony" (Numbers 9:15), the "tabernacle of the meeting" (2 Chronicles 5:5, NKJV), or the "Tent of the meeting" (2 Chronicles 5:5, NASB). This was the pre-defined worship place that housed the ark of the covenant, which was a box made of acacia wood overlaid with gold, in which the tablets inscribed with the Ten Commandments were kept. The tabernacle would later give way to the temple, and the implements and the ark would be placed in its Holy of Holies.

The Jewish Bible quotes *Yahweh* saying, "My presence shall rest over them" (v.

27), revealing another perspective of His protection and guidance. In the image of a reconnaissance satellite hovering above the troops, *Yahweh* is able to see the dangers and the entire circumferential scope of Israel's movements. Here, the Lord is dedicated to the future of His people, and the manifestation of His simply "being there" is to serve as a comfort to Israel. Not only does *Yahweh* declare that His *mishkan* will be with his people; it indicates that the Lord will also live in the people.

The first line of "I will be their God again" is being told from God's perspective. It means more than *Yahweh* being their deity but indicates that He will be accepted by the people, and they will freely appreciate the Lord in their lives. In this situation, the people have been separated from the Lord because of their exiled state and in some cases, their being attracted to and worshiping the idols of their land of deportation. That "I will be their God" is a reminder of God's love for Israel and a promise that He made His tabernacle among the people, that "My soul will not reject you" (Leviticus 26:11).

The second part of the phrase is from the perspective of the people, as "they will be my people." Heaven is rejoicing in the fact that another covenant is in the making with the people, who should be overjoyed that God is guaranteeing their rescue from exile and a return to their former lands. Although Ezekiel is projecting a future promise of God, the people are to simply joyfully embrace *Yahweh* as their God.

Ezekiel, however, is projecting from God's language, not expressing the language of the people. It is the blissful prediction of what God sees, even if it has to happen as a vision of heaven, where perfection is finally reached. Here, *Yahweh* rejoices in the promise of the people loving and being faithful to Him again!

Concluding this section, Ezekiel declares that "when the sanctuary of the Lord abides among Israel forever, the nations shall know that I the Lord do sanctify Israel." In verse 28, the term *miqdash* means temple (sanctuary) or holy place. It means that when *Yahweh* is saturated in the midst of Israel – not simply in the land but in their hearts and minds – the power that will emanate from this union is that the pagan nations (who do not know the Lord) will know that "I am their God." Other nations will not cross God, and God will not be embarrassed before idol nations because His people refuse to follow His mandate, as His sanctuary will be with them forever.

THE LESSON APPLIED

The lesson of this writing may serve as a thoughtful excursion into the future where God's people live "happily ever after." The premise of the prophecy is that Israel will be returned to her lands and will forever enjoy the grace of the Lord. What may not be clear in the flowery declarations is that the people coming out of Babylonian exile will not totally remain faithful to *Yahweh*; they will not live this idyllic scenario in their return to Zion. As Christians who

God has prospered, we must not make the mistake of believing that we only see *Yahweh* as a God of an eschatological future, while neglecting to honor and serve Him today. If we disregard our walk with Him, we will not be included in any prophetic vision for the future Kingdom. Contemporary Christians must not lose the perspective of beautiful biblical stories.

LET'S TALK ABOUT IT

How should these promises to Israel impact our understanding of the Israeli and Palestinian impasse?

Christians from diverse backgrounds have differing views on the complexity of the Israeli/Palestinian conflict. Unfortunately, many Christians do not connect the Scriptures with the present reality of the political ramifications of the holy land. Christians who read the Scriptures seem to dismiss the events, such as the destruction of the temple (AD 66-70) or the domination of the Roman Empire and its implications. In many of our churches, we do not explain the presence of the modern state of Israel that was formed in 1948 by the Allied Powers as an answer to the horrors of the Holocaust. Many of our churches cannot explain the tension between the Palestinians and the Jews, Let us work to resolve these conflicts and help put the pieces together for others.

HOME DAILY DEVOTIONAL READINGS						
JUNE 19–25, 2023						
MONDAY	**TUESDAY**	**WEDNESDAY**	**THURSDAY**	**FRIDAY**	**SATURDAY**	**SUNDAY**
Love with an Everlasting Love	A New Covenant	We Walk by Faith	Renewed in Christ	God Abounds in Steadfast Love	Love Is the Greatest	The Lord Is in Your Midst
Jeremiah 31:1–9	Jeremiah 31:27–34	2 Corinthians 5:1–11	2 Corinthians 5:12–21	Psalm 86:1–7, 9–16	1 Corinthians 13	Zephaniah 3:14–20

RENEWED IN GOD'S LOVE

ZEPHANIAH 3:14—20

King James Version

SING, O daughter of Zion; shout, O Israel; be glad and rejoice with all the heart, O daughter of Jerusalem.

15 The LORD hath taken away thy judgments, he hath cast out thine enemy: the king of Israel, even the LORD, is in the midst of thee: thou shalt not see evil any more.

16 In that day it shall be said to Jerusalem, Fear thou not: and to Zion, Let not thine hands be slack.

17 The LORD thy God in the midst of thee is mighty; he will save, he will rejoice over thee with joy; he will rest in his love, he will joy over thee with singing.

18 I will gather them that are sorrowful for the solemn assembly, who are of thee, to whom the reproach of it was a burden.

19 Behold, at that time I will undo all that afflict thee: and I will save her that halteth, and gather her that was driven out; and I will get them praise and fame in every land where they have been put to shame.

20 At that time will I bring you again, even in the time that I gather you: for I will make you a name and a praise among all people of the earth, when I turn back your captivity before your eyes, saith the LORD.

New Revised Standard Version

SING aloud, O daughter Zion; shout, O Israel! Rejoice and exult with all your heart, O daughter Jerusalem!

15 The LORD has taken away the judgments against you, he has turned away your enemies. The king of Israel, the LORD, is in your midst; you shall fear disaster no more.

16 On that day it shall be said to Jerusalem: Do not fear, O Zion; do not let your hands grow weak.

17 The LORD, your God, is in your midst, a warrior who gives victory; he will rejoice over you with gladness, he will renew you in his love; he will exult over you with loud singing

18 as on a day of festival. I will remove disaster from you, so that you will not bear reproach for it.

19 I will deal with all your oppressors at that time. And I will save the lame and gather the outcast, and I will change their shame into praise and renown in all the earth.

20 At that time I will bring you home, at the time when I gather you; for I will make you renowned and praised among all the peoples of the earth, when I restore your fortunes before your eyes, says the LORD.

MAIN THOUGHT: The LORD thy God in the midst of thee is mighty; he will save, he will rejoice over thee with joy; he will rest in his love, he will joy over thee with singing. (Zephaniah 3:17, KJV)

LESSON SETTING

> Time: 640–610 BC
> Place: Judah

LESSON OUTLINE

I. The Joy to Jerusalem (Zephaniah 3:14–17)
II. Yahweh Gathers Israel in Triumph (Zephaniah 3:18–20)

UNIFYING PRINCIPLE

People can suffer consequences for the poor choices of a previous generation. Where or in whom can a new generation find a fresh start? Zephaniah 3 promises that God takes away judgement and brings renewal fashioned out of love.

INTRODUCTION

Zephaniah, whose name means "Jehovah has concealed," or "Jehovah of darkness," was the son of Cushi and the great-grandson of Hezekiah. Ninth in order of the minor prophets, he prophesied in the days of Josiah, king of Judah, and was a contemporary of Jeremiah. In this passage, Zephaniah introduces prophecy and judgment to motivate repentance that results in a promise of restoration. Additionally, Zephaniah reflects on the millennial age and some of its blessings: pure worship (v. 9, i.e., the meaning of purified lips, in contrast to the blasphemy of idolatrous worship); the Jews being regathered and purified (vv. 10–13); Christ personally reigning in your midst (v. 15); security (v. 16); enemies punished (v. 19); and Israel restored to her land (v. 20).

EXPOSITION

I. THE JOY TO JERUSALEM (ZEPHANIAH 3:14–17)

The prophet Zephaniah proclaims good news for the people of Judah in the face of impending doom. He encourages the people to shout for joy, but how can they cry aloud for joy when they have seen the northern kingdom conquered by the powerful forces of the Assyrian Empire? Zephaniah realizes that *Yahweh* has placed judgment on Judah because of their unfaithfulness and rejection to adhere to His edicts. Yet, they are being encouraged to show gladness at a chaotic time.

Zephaniah has predicted in his message that their goods and houses will be plundered. In this case, the houses that they build will be a waste of time because they will not be able to live in them, nor enjoy the produce of their fields (1:13). Zechariah promises that the Lord will stretch out His hand against the north, destroying Assyria and Nineveh (2:13).

The direct message here is to the "Daughter of Zion" or "Fair Zion" (Jewish Study Bible), who are identified as the people in Jerusalem that have remained faithful to the Lord, even in the face of this impending disaster. The hope for Zephaniah is that their faithfulness will be pleasing to the Lord, and they will be able to trust God for their eventual deliverance.

In this case, the prophet proclaims that the Lord has removed or annulled His judgments. However, this must not be viewed as a renouncement of the current situation, Judah is going into exile. In a prediction that foresees the future, all of the wrongs that have been perpetrated against *Yahweh* will be forgiven. Judah's enemies will be swept away and were of both foreign and domestic lineage. In this case, the particular sins were religious against which Zephaniah inveighed. Behind the prophet's attacks on the infiltration of foreign religions into Judah lies the first commandment: "You shall have no other gods before me" (Ex. 20:3). The worship of Israel's God was exclusive and binding. Therefore, the enemy must not solely be viewed as the invading infidels but also the arrogant members of the Judean community who were "fair weather" adherents in their commitment to the Lord.

Jerusalem is being encouraged not to be afraid. However, the people realize that their forces will not be powerful enough to ward off the invaders. Judah weathered previous invasions. The people had every reason to be afraid, but Zephaniah encourages them not to be fearful or to let their hands fall limp. The imagery of limp or drooping hands (Jewish Study Bible) promotes a state of insecurity, as the term used here is *rph*, translated as weak, feeble, or inactive. Weak hands cannot withstand the power of the enemy, as the warrior will not be ready for battle. However, another metaphor is that the hands of the people would be inactive, in that they would not be ready for any instructions that the Lord would provide – such as the instructions He gave to Moses for the Exodus – or that their hands (and hearts) would be inactive in their prayers to Jehovah.

In verse 17, Zephaniah describes *Yahweh* as a "victorious warrior" who is a constant presence in the midst of Israel. In this period, a mighty warrior was a known valuable asset. Persian conquest is key to the emancipation of the people from Babylonia. Zephaniah is injecting that it is actually the Lord who is the power behind their freedom, not the Persians. Although the physical battles between Persia and Babylon had economic and political results, it is actually *Yahweh* who is orchestrating the events. Since *Yahweh* is a constant presence, Israel needed to be reminded of the language of "God is our refuge and strength, a very present help in the time of trouble" (Psalm 46:1). In the imagery of contests or free "give-a-ways," where you must be present to win, the presence of *Yahweh* makes Israel a "winner" in their return to Zion.

The second clause says, "He will be silent in his love," which can be problematic because the mention of silence here clashes with the loud singing or "shouting aloud" in verse 14 and the shouts of joy at the end of verse 17. *Yahweh* being quiet in His love indicates that God lovingly created the events of Israel's emancipation behind the scenes, while not allowing the people to know His intentions.

In this rescue, there should be shouting and exultation in the land. *Yahweh* is a victorious warrior with these enemies; however, the image is to be understood that He is a triumphant warrior who brings victory (Jewish Study Bible), as, in general, one that neither "slumbers nor sleeps." Unfortunately, in their defeat and subsequent exile, there will be segments of the people who will believe that God has abandoned them; yet, they are mistaken, as their punishment occurs because *Yahweh* willed it. Now that the chastisement is over, the people are to rejoice because of the soothing calm of the love of the Lord.

II. YAHWEH GATHERS ISRAEL IN TRIUMPH (ZEPHANIAH 3:18–20)

Zephaniah declares that the Lord will gather those who grieve about the appointed feasts. The people of Israel looked forward to celebrating their feasts because of both the communal aspects and the religious observances of the events. However, many Jews, scattered from their homeland, had sorrows because they were unable to take part in these appointed feasts.

The obvious danger is that God announced, "I hate and despise your feast days, and I do not savor your sacred assemblies" (Amos 5:21). Here, Amos declares that God's disdain for the celebration of their feasts is because of Israel's religious hypocrisy, and that the "Day of the Lord" would be a day of exile rather than exaltation, although repentant individuals could escape this disaster (Amos 5:18–27).

To those who are "long disconsolate (Jewish Study Bible) that came from you" – that originate from Judah (especially Jerusalem) – the reproach (*cherpah*) or shame of being exiled shall be relieved. *Yahweh* promises that He will lift their heads during their most excruciating times, in the midst of economic and political losses, suffered because of a lack of faithfulness to the Lord and their embrace of foreign idols. The rest of the world must be laughing at the shame of the mighty kingdoms of God being taken by countries that worship and align themselves to lesser gods! However, Israel (Judah) is to lift their heads. The reproach will not have to be endured.

In this prediction, all of Israel's oppressors are going to have to face the might of Israel's God. The Jewish Study Bible is quite explicit as it renders this phrase, "At that time I will make an [end]" to or completely cease the roving nations' aggressions. Moreover, these wayward nations will be punished by *Yahweh* for their transgressions against His people. If the people repent and understand the prophecy, Israel will prosper in the face of those who formerly tormented her and purged her of both inhabitants and lands. Since *Yahweh* is a God for all of the people, He declares that He will look out for the weak and those who are unable to defend themselves. "I will save the lame", who are imagined as those that are infirmed and walk with a limp, and the "sheep" of the land who may not understand the danger of their opponents.

Furthermore, *Yahweh* will gather all of those that have been scattered by the invaders, who forced people into hiding for self-preservation, which would have uprooted Israel from their lands and holdings. The people who have dispersed are identified as those who were also incapable of resisting the invasion of the enemy forces; still, the outcasts present another vivid image of the actual conditions of the people.

Usually, the portrait of the outcasts are those that are repudiated by their own. God will bring together the masses of His lost and all who are subject to His will. Micah echoes Zephaniah 3:19 in an eerily parallel fashion, saying, "The Lord GOD, who gathers the outcasts of Israel, says …" *Yahweh* will not only restore the scattered, the outcast, and the rejected-unto-Him; He will reverse their shame into praise before the "eyes of the entire earth."

The book concludes with a strong announcement of hope for its readers; such positive conclusions typify prophetic books. The fortunes of Israel/Judah will be restored, and this restoration includes the gathering of the exiles. In this concluding verse, the Lord is telling Israel that the people of the earth will have praise for them. That "I will give you renown and praise among all the peoples of the earth" is a sign that *Yahweh* is satisfied with seeing the inhabitants of all lands, especially those who oppressed Israel, witness her vindication as a restored people who belong to the Lord. As aforementioned, the image of a rejected and scorned Israel would have been an embarrassment to *Yahweh*. Another perspective is that the Lord is saying to the faithful that He has praise for them for holding on to what is true in His earthly Kingdom and standing strong – not renouncing Him – in the time of trouble, as others may have done. This is another image of the pride *Yahweh* can have in His people. Today's English Version expresses the wider meaning, with the Lord saying, "I will make you prosperous once again" and "restore your fortunes," "even before your eyes" (Zephaniah 2:17). The image of restoration will be realized by an ever-loving, everlasting God, whose rule and mercy is supreme, ending with the words, "The Lord has spoken."

THE LESSON APPLIED

Zephaniah 3:12–13 identify the remnant of Israel as a humble and lowly people; yet, they are not to be thought of as poor or weak. Israel will be uplifted and take its refuge in the name of the Lord. Additionally, her people will repent of their former deceitful nature. Moreover, *Yahweh* will protect them, and they will not have to cower over the fear of being bullied or subjected to foreign rulers. In our schools, streets, and neighborhoods, there exists an underlying fear in our youth of being perceived as weak, which causes many to portray a false sense of bravado and courage. A message that needs to resound is that the Lord continues to look out for His youth, even when the world is full of bullies.

LET'S TALK ABOUT IT

Do you believe that God wants justice and mercy to rule?

Believers are thankful that God wills justice and mercy, and that God's will is being done wherever there is justice and mercy. In the midst of the many horrors that this life can conjure, believers have a sincere knowledge and understanding that we are kept by the power of the Lord. "His will be done" must not simply be reduced to materials from a prayer or a sermon; it must become an integral component of our belief system, which allows us to be confident in our walk with the Lord. God is a God of justice and mercy, and where He wills, justice and mercy will be the rule, rather than the exception.

HOME DAILY DEVOTIONAL READINGS
JUNE 26–JULY 2, 2023

MONDAY	TUESDAY	WEDNESDAY	THURSDAY	FRIDAY	SATURDAY	SUNDAY
The Redeemed from Every Nation	God's Invitation to Peace and Care	Dreams and Visions Revealed	God's Peace Will Be with You	God Makes All Things New	Glory and Honor of the Nations	Rejoice! The King Is Coming!
Revelation 7:4–17	Isaiah 55	Daniel 7:1–14	Philippians 4:4–9	Revelation 21:1–14	Revelation 21:15–27	Zechariah 9:9–17

PEACE TO THE NATIONS

ADULT TOPIC: WORLD PEACE	BACKGROUND SCRIPTURE: ZECHARIAH 9:9–17

ZECHARIAH 9:9–13, 16–17

King James Version

REJOICE greatly, O daughter of Zion; shout, O daughter of Jerusalem: behold, thy King cometh unto thee: he is just, and having salvation; lowly, and riding upon an ass, and upon a colt the foal of an ass.

10 And I will cut off the chariot from Ephraim, and the horse from Jerusalem, and the battle bow shall be cut off: and he shall speak peace unto the heathen: and his dominion shall be from sea even to sea, and from the river even to the ends of the earth.

11 As for thee also, by the blood of thy covenant I have sent forth thy prisoners out of the pit wherein is no water.

12 Turn you to the strong hold, ye prisoners of hope: even to day do I declare that I will render double unto thee;

13 When I have bent Judah for me, filled the bow with Ephraim, and raised up thy sons, O Zion, against thy sons, O Greece, and made thee as the sword of a mighty man.

• • • • • •

16 And the LORD their God shall save them in that day as the flock of his people: for they shall be as the stones of a crown, lifted up as an ensign upon his land.

17 For how great is his goodness, and how great is his beauty! corn shall make the young men cheerful, and new wine the maids.

New Revised Standard Version

REJOICE greatly, O daughter Zion! Shout aloud, O daughter Jerusalem! Lo, your king comes to you; triumphant and victorious is he, humble and riding on a donkey, on a colt, the foal of a donkey.

10 He will cut off the chariot from Ephraim and the war-horse from Jerusalem; and the battle bow shall be cut off, and he shall command peace to the nations; his dominion shall be from sea to sea, and from the River to the ends of the earth.

11 As for you also, because of the blood of my covenant with you, I will set your prisoners free from the waterless pit.

12 Return to your stronghold, O prisoners of hope; today I declare that I will restore to you double.

13 For I have bent Judah as my bow; I have made Ephraim its arrow. I will arouse your sons, O Zion, against your sons, O Greece, and wield you like a warrior's sword.

• • • • • •

16 On that day the LORD their God will save them for they are the flock of his people; for like the jewels of a crown they shall shine on his land.

17 For what goodness and beauty are his! Grain shall make the young men flourish, and new wine the young women.

MAIN THOUGHT: And the LORD their God shall save them in that day as the flock of his people: for they shall be as the stones of a crown, lifted up as an ensign upon his land. (Zechariah 9:16, KJV)

LESSON SETTING
Time: 494 BC
Place: Zion/Jerusalem

LESSON OUTLINE
I. The Coming Messiah
(Zechariah 9:9–10)
II. Deliverance of Judah and Ephraim
(Zechariah 9:11–13)
III. God Restores His People
(Zechariah 9:16–17)

UNIFYING PRINCIPLE
People are frustrated and discouraged under oppressive rule. What can put an end to corrupt leadership? Zechariah 9 envisions a day when God brings down all earthly powers and initiates an eternal reign of peace.

INTRODUCTION
This lesson is an examination of prophecy by the prophet Zechariah, whose name means "Jehovah is renowned or remembered." In the first eight verses of chapter 9, Zechariah details prophecies against Israel's neighboring nations that culminate in verse 8 with a declaration of God's protection of His people. In the following verses of the lesson, *Yahweh* encourages the returning exiles to rejoice in the announcement that the Messiah is coming, while describing the blessings that the people will experience. This prophecy will be fulfilled during the triumphal entry into Jerusalem (Palm Sunday), when He presents Himself to Israel as the undisputed king. A humble king, the coming Messiah will bring salvation and redemption to Israel and humankind.

EXPOSITION
I. THE COMING MESSIAH (ZECHARIAH 9:9–10)
God commands the citizens of Jerusalem to rejoice greatly, indicating that they are not to be restrained by their expressions of joy and happiness. His command does not seem to limit their worship in the temple but should be understood as corporate worship throughout the land. Verse 9 does not directly mention that the speaker is the Lord; however, because the personal pronoun "I" appears in verse 10, it serves as evidence that it is God. Although His command is directed to the "Daughter of Zion" and the "Daughter of Jerusalem," it does not refer to a single individual born in or living in Zion/Jerusalem but rather, to the city itself, addressed as a female figure, because the Hebrew word for "city" is grammatically feminine. This phrase indicates a term of endearment, since God lovingly refers to Jerusalem as His female child (devoid of any sexual identification), as all of Israel, including the returning exiles, are known as God's children. They are to shout in triumph because the Lord has a plan to destroy the oppressors and protect His people. Moreover, promises of restoration are now presented to the people who have recently returned from Babylonian exile and are now wondering what their future holds. That He has "seen with His own eyes" (v. 8) recalls the language when Moses has an encounter with God, who is in the form of the "Burning Bush," and God tells Moses, "I have surely seen the oppression of My people who are in Egypt, and have heard their cry because of their taskmasters, for I know their sorrows" (Exodus 3:7). As

Israel receives the news of this prophecy, the people have reasons to celebrate with joyous celebrations. God tells Israel, "… behold, your king is coming to you" (v. 9); however, the Hebrew word may be better understood as "look" or "look out for," in the essence of commanding Israel to watch, wait, and be ready to receive the coming king (Messiah). At this juncture, Israel may have a difficult time with the concept of having a king. Their history has been plagued by bad kings, as well as oppressive foreign monarchs. However, the coming king that God is speaking of is a better gift than any earthly ruler and will provide more than earthly aspirations because His mission is salvific and eternal. The people of Zechariah's era will not witness the arrival of the king; however, the prophecy is revealed by these signs that the new king will be humble, as opposed to the haughty and arrogant rulers of Israel's past. For some, there are problems with the word "humble," as it is often understood as someone who is oppressed, weak, or poor. In His mission, the Messiah does, however, reflect the attribute of "lowly," as He declares that He is gentle and lowly in heart (Matthew 11:29). This concept does not refute His power but indicates that the Messiah has chosen to direct His ministry and mission to the marginalized, the poor in spirit, and those who desperately need a Savior. However, in the eyes of the worldly (the "rich and famous"), it would be absurd and beneath a king's status to ride a donkey. The Messiah was not to be an earthly king, riding on a horse into the stronghold of another oppressive regime (the Roman Empire), for this would have sent the wrong message to Rome, and to Israel. The mission of this new king will not be the acquisition of earthly kingdoms but the redemption of God's children into His heavenly Kingdom. As the Messiah will say, "Tell the Daughter of Zion, behold, your king is coming to you, lowly, and sitting on a donkey, a colt, the foal of a donkey" (Matthew 21:5).

Yahweh promises a series of aggressive actions that He will formulate against the enemies of Israel. That He will "cut off" indicates that God will remove the offending entity from any source of power; and in His speaking of a person, the one who is "cut off" will be removed from any type of relationship with the Lord. First, He will cut off the chariot of Ephraim, then, the horse from Jerusalem, followed by the "bow of war." The statement, "I will cut off the chariot from Ephraim and the war horse from Jerusalem," speaks of the total removal of any military action from the borders of the land, Ephraim on the north and Jerusalem on the southern regions of the Promised Land. There will be no need for the implements of war, as the messiah will unite and protect Israel while safeguarding her borders. The coming king will have the power to be mighty in war but gentle in peace. Additionally, His dominion or influence will be to all nations inside the boundaries of the expanse of the universe. Although filled with power, the goal of the coming king will not be to promote war but to establish peace. This prophecy provides a glimpse into the future, as the image of God's destruction of war instruments – removing the chariots, the war horses, and the battle bow. The peaceful rule of this coming messianic king will extend from sea to sea and from the River – the Euphrates (cf. Micah 7:12; Isa. 7:20) – to the ends of the earth. These expressions clearly indicate the worldwide extent of the messianic Kingdom.

II. DELIVERANCE OF JUDAH AND EPHRAIM (ZECHARIAH 9:11–13)

Continuing with His discourse on both Judah and Ephraim, *Yahweh* reminds them that He favors the tribes because of the covenant that has been sealed with them. Additionally, *Yahweh* promises restoration and blessings for those who remain in Babylon. God remains faithful to His promises and reminds them of the "blood of My covenant" between God and Abraham, which was ratified by an oath and the spilled blood of several animals. In this solemn ceremony, during which the Lord made a binding agreement with Abraham, God assured him of the ultimate fulfillment of His promises. "I have set your prisoners free" means that God had provided the release of Israel from Babylon, who was conquered by the Persians. Through *Yahweh*'s intervention and influence, the Persian king, Cyrus, issued a decree of liberation to the Jews (Ezra 1:1–2). The people who were held captive in Babylon are the "Daughters of Jerusalem" (v. 11). In bringing a remnant back to Zion, it is the Lord who is responsible for their emancipation. Recall, it was the Lord who allowed Jerusalem to be captured by the Babylonians because of their turning away from the Lord and their rejection of Him. Nonetheless, God promised Jeremiah that He would return His people back to Zion (Jeremiah 3:14). The imagery here is that these remnants have been rescued from a forsaken place, the waterless cistern, which symbolizes a dungeon or the place of exile. Verse 11 of the Jewish Study Bible begins with, "You, for your part, have released Your prisoners from the dry pit." Based on this translation, *Yahweh* is speaking of Himself, saying that He has accomplished His part of the prophecy and promise, allowing the return of the exiles. Now, these former prisoners may return to the fortress of Zion. Recall that the Lord is also referred to as a rock, fortress, and deliverer, in whom the Psalmist placed his trust because he considered God as His stronghold (Psalm 18:2). These former captives are blessed with hope that better days are ahead, especially with the promise of the coming Messiah. Israel will be restored to Jerusalem/Zion, which will allow resettlement and a rebuilding of the city and the temple. Additionally, the restoration of their faith and religious practices will be returned to the Holy City. Moreover, if the remnants will honor the covenant, they are promised a double portion of blessings, which is a myriad of items that are too numerous to be itemized. "For I will bend Judah as My bow" and "I will fill the bow with Ephraim" means that God will use Judah as His bow, and Ephraim, as His arrows! These two statements add something to each other and need to be understood together. Just as both a bow and an arrow are needed to form an effective weapon, so the Lord would use both the people of the south (Judah) and the people of the north (Ephraim) to form an effective instrument for carrying out his purposes. Recall that the once United Kingdom of Israel split into two factions: the Northern, which was destroyed by the Assyrians (722 BC) and the Southern Kingdom, taken by Babylon in 586 BC On the surface, the breakup of the kingdom may seem to have occurred because of political differences and jealousies; however, the actual reason for their destruction was spiritual, in their rejection of *Yahweh* and devotion to idol worship.

Additionally, God promises to stir up the sons of Zion against the sons of Greece. Some scholars consider that the mention of Greece means that this passage comes from the time after the conquests of Alexander the Great, who died in 323 BC The Greeks could not have been unknown to the other nations of western Asia after they had defeated the Persian armies of King Darius at the battle of Marathon in 490 BC The Hebrew word for Greece is *yawan*. This name is also found as "Javan" in Genesis 10:2, 4 and in other places in the Old Testament, such as Isaiah 66:19, where it appears, in general, as a part of a list of foreigners. These verses predict the defeat of Greece.

III. GOD RESTORES HIS PEOPLE (ZECHARIAH 9:16–17)

However, to show that the Lord is in control of her destiny, *Yahweh* assures Israel that her God will save her in the day of promise. Although Israel's enemies may seem powerful and invincible, they are no match for God's supremacy, as the "Lord Almighty will protect his people like a shield." Israel will withstand and conquer those who attack her by "slinging stones" (v. 15). Verse 16, however, moves the image to a military victory although, through the intervention of *Yahweh*. Israel's military efforts will be successful, yet, this verse redirects the image to God in a protective role as a shepherd, who will protect His flock from the wolves and other carnivorous creatures that lie in wait to devour the animals. This imagery presents *Yahweh* as the supreme protector against the wiles of Satan who wishes to consume Israel and all believers while removing them from the pastoral settings of God. Moreover, God has to protect His flock from human thieves, who would steal the animals for their own personal gain. In this image, *Yahweh* is the supreme defender and enforcer of salvation and the right to the "tree of life."

The historical record is devoid of Israel's conquering of lands; and the armies of the Maccabees seem to resemble a militia that has gathered to defend its homeland, rather than a standing army, aggressive in nature and function. In general, Israel (or later, Judah) will be a country occupied by foreign empires. Therefore, as it was following the Exodus, when Moses and the people needed food and God supplied quail and manna, Israel would be forced to totally depend upon God as they awaited the coming Messiah. Here is a direct connection to the role of Jesus, not as a military commander, but as the One who comes to redeem His people to the Lord. He is not an earthly king but is king of the universe. This verse is eschatological in nature, pointing to the judgment, the final destiny of the soul, and the redemption or rescue of humanity.

Several translators and theologians interpret the comeliness and beauty of verse 17 as a reference to the attractiveness of the people; however, it is probable that the beauty actually describes the Lord in His splendor. The NKJV declares, "For how great is its goodness and how great its beauty," which must recall that the goodness and beauty of God are clearly His. Moreover, *Yahweh* describes how the yield of the land will bless Israel, as "grain shall make the young men flourish, and new wine will foster the maidens." This is traditional language to describe the fruitfulness of the age when the Messiah rules the earth. Grain and wine are staple products in the holy land. We are not to understand that the young men will eat all the bread, and the maidens (or "young women," NIV) will drink all the new wine. Rather, the two statements should be taken together as indicating plenty of both for everybody. "The young men and women will grow strong [or flourish/thrive] on the grain [or bread] and wine."

THE LESSON APPLIED

Following the exile, with the exception of the Maccabean Period, Israel will not be a military nation, as she was during the time of David and Solomon. This is important because *Yahweh* has shifted her position to a greater dependence on the Lord for her survival. The role of Israel (as her not being a military power) provides the context for the Messiah as king, whose "kingdom is not of this world" (John 18:36). *Yahweh* encourages the people to rejoice and celebrate in victory, although they will not physically touch the Messiah, audibly hear His preaching, or be able to touch the "hem of His garment." Nonetheless, the prophetic promise is that He is coming; and the people of Zechariah's era, although devoid of the physical Messiah, will receive the blessings of the spiritual Messiah.

LET'S TALK ABOUT IT

How does the coming of the Messiah effect our position as those who believe in freedom and Christ?

Believers put their faith in Christ as their ultimate leader and guide. As the United States prepares to celebrate another Independence Day, believers must see the promises that far exceeded, the imaginations of some of the founders such as the declaration that "all men are created equal." The Declaration of Independence is filled with lofty ideals of Enlightenment, in which men, in their revolutionary spirit, believed in the rights and freedom of men. Sadly, these supposedly upstanding idealogues only believed in the rights and liberty of men. From this period, believers have prayed to the Lord to make the ideals of this covenant apply to all people, which demands that faith in Christ is a must and recognition of Christ as King is undeniable.

HOME DAILY DEVOTIONAL READINGS
JULY 3–9, 2023

MONDAY	TUESDAY	WEDNESDAY	THURSDAY	FRIDAY	SATURDAY	SUNDAY
Teach Us to Pray	Your Kingdom Come	The Lord Is King!	Shout to God, the King	The Lord of the Sabbath	God's Gentle Servant	The Kingdom of God Has Come
Luke 11:1–13	Matthew 6:5–15	Psalm 97	Psalm 47	Matthew 12:1–13	Matthew 12:14–21	Matthew 12:22–32

THE KINGDOM HAS COME UPON YOU

ADULT TOPIC:
A DEMONSTRATION OF POWER

BACKGROUND SCRIPTURE:
MATTHEW 12:1–32

MATTHEW 12:22–32

King James Version

THEN was brought unto him one possessed with a devil, blind, and dumb: and he healed him, insomuch that the blind and dumb both spake and saw.

23 And all the people were amazed, and said, Is not this the son of David?

24 But when the Pharisees heard it, they said, This fellow doth not cast out devils, but by Beelzebub the prince of the devils.

25 And Jesus knew their thoughts, and said unto them, Every kingdom divided against itself is brought to desolation; and every city or house divided against itself shall not stand:

26 And if Satan cast out Satan, he is divided against himself; how shall then his kingdom stand?

27 And if I by Beelzebub cast out devils, by whom do your children cast them out? therefore they shall be your judges.

28 But if I cast out devils by the Spirit of God, then the kingdom of God is come unto you.

29 Or else how can one enter into a strong man's house, and spoil his goods, except he first bind the strong man? and then he will spoil his house.

30 He that is not with me is against me; and he that gathereth not with me scattereth abroad.

31 Wherefore I say unto you, All manner of sin and blasphemy shall be forgiven unto men: but the blasphemy against the Holy Ghost shall not be forgiven unto men.

New Revised Standard Version

THEN they brought to him a demoniac who was blind and mute; and he cured him, so that the one who had been mute could speak and see.

23 All the crowds were amazed and said, "Can this be the Son of David?"

24 But when the Pharisees heard it, they said, "It is only by Beelzebul, the ruler of the demons, that this fellow casts out the demons."

25 He knew what they were thinking and said to them, "Every kingdom divided against itself is laid waste, and no city or house divided against itself will stand.

26 If Satan casts out Satan, he is divided against himself; how then will his kingdom stand?

27 If I cast out demons by Beelzebul, by whom do your own exorcists cast them out? Therefore they will be your judges.

28 But if it is by the Spirit of God that I cast out demons, then the kingdom of God has come to you.

29 Or how can one enter a strong man's house and plunder his property, without first tying up the strong man? Then indeed the house can be plundered.

30 Whoever is not with me is against me, and whoever does not gather with me scatters.

31 Therefore I tell you, people will be forgiven for every sin and blasphemy, but blasphemy against the Spirit will not be forgiven.

MAIN THOUGHT: But if I cast out devils by the Spirit of God, then the kingdom of God is come unto you. (Matthew 12:28, KJV)

King James Version	*New Revised Standard Version*
32 And whosoever speaketh a word against the Son of man, it shall be forgiven him: but whosoever speaketh against the Holy Ghost, it shall not be forgiven him, neither in this world, neither in the world to come.	32 Whoever speaks a word against the Son of Man will be forgiven, but whoever speaks against the Holy Spirit will not be forgiven, either in this age or in the age to come.

LESSON SETTING
Time: AD 27
Place: Galilee

LESSON OUTLINE
 I. **Jesus Rebukes the Pharisees (Matthew 12:22–24)**
 II. **A House Divided Cannot Stand (Matthew 12:25–27)**
 III. **Jesus' Authority Versus Satan's Weakness (Matthew 12:28–29)**
 IV. **The Unpardonable Sin (Matthew 12:30–32)**

UNIFYING PRINCIPLE
People suffer from various afflictions. Where can we look for the deliverance we need to be made whole? Jesus' power to deliver people from any affliction, including demon possession, was a sign of the arrival of God's Kingdom.

INTRODUCTION
Jesus had been accused of breaking Sabbath laws by eating (plucking) grain and healing a man with a withered hand. It seems that some local Pharisees had heard about what they considered to be Jesus' disregard for the Sabbath laws, and their bitterness overcame their need to be rational. Therefore, the local group invited some Pharisees from Jerusalem (with the assistance of some Herodians) to plot against Jesus, as to how they might destroy Him (Mark 3:6). A man who needed healing and an exorcism was brought to Jesus. It is here that the Pharisees accused Him of being in the employ of Beelzeboul, another name for Satan. Jesus rejected their statements and reveals who is actually Satan's employ.

EXPOSITION

I. JESUS REBUKES THE PHARISEES (MATTHEW 12:22–24)
Jesus has been presented with a man who has several issues, as he is demon-possessed, blind, and mute. The text does not state who brought this demon-possessed man to Jesus, "they", could refer to nearly anyone (v. 22). His demon possession was not so much an illness in itself but a cause or contributor to the man's blindness and inability to speak. Here, the Greek term *kophos* is softened, as it can mean blunted, dull, or even dumb. In what seems to be a quick response, Jesus healed the man, who began to have the use of his voice (he could speak) and the use of his eyes (he could see). However, this description provides a resolution to only the first two issues that the man suffered. What is not detailed in verse 22 is how Jesus exorcised the demons from the man.

As the restored man responded to his good fortune and refurbished body, the people who were present rejoiced at the miracle. Although Matthew specifies neither the number of years the man had suffered or the crowd size, it is apparent that the people rejoiced because they knew the man and had observed his illness. As they witnessed a miracle, their reaction was to ask if Jesus was the son of David. The faithful of Judah would be looking for the Messiah. Because of their knowledge of prophecy, a sizable segment of the people, including the Pharisees, would have connected David to the Messiah as a well-known component of their faith. The healing and exorcism of this man invigorated the crowds. The Greek term used here is *existemi*, meaning amazed or astonished; however, in this case, it reveals that the people were quite beside themselves, as if they had "lost their minds." Since it was Jesus who healed the man, the people knew Jesus was special, and many understood that this form of healing could only come from heaven.

In verse 24, there is a question of whether or not the Pharisees were present for the healing and exorcism. Several scholars believe that because the Pharisees heard about the curing, it indicates they were not present and only came to confront Jesus after the actual event. In their confrontation with Jesus, they acknowledged the restored condition of the man; however, that is not their issue. Seething with jealousy and fearing the loss of face, the Pharisees accused Jesus of being a pawn of Satan. They refused to acknowledge that the power to heal and to exorcise demons comes from God.

II. A HOUSE DIVIDED CANNOT STAND (MATTHEW 12:25–27)

Jesus reminded the Pharisees that "any kingdom divided against itself is laid waste" because it will deteriorate and be conquered from the inside, while the enemy troops stand back and watch the implosion. Additionally, internal strife causes erosion, which is usually understood as a physical malady but is more often a result of spiritual impotence. In this case, Israel, who was once a United Kingdom, knew firsthand the sting of a first-divided, then-destroyed kingdom. The Greek term *oikia* means house but also, building or dwelling. Here, "house" also represents the family, dynasty, or lineage of the tribes of Israel. In this imagery, Jesus presents a scenario where father is pitted against son, mother against daughter, and faction against faction, where no one is in a position to stem the divisions or chasms.

Jesus, however, has come to unite the competing factions and restore Israel to the kingdom of God. The Pharisees knew Israelite history, but could not understand His metaphor.

Continuing the metaphor of a divided house and kingdom, Jesus links a connection to Satan and asks, "How can he divide himself?" If Satan casts out Satan, he erodes from within. If Satan removes himself from the life of someone he delights in destroying, Satan will fight against himself and his own objective to sow discord and terror. Satan is not in the position of restoring a person's fortune unless he benefits and the person "sells his/her soul," being ultimately destroyed and relinquishing the opportunity for salvation. It is necessary that readers understand that the "Satan" of this verse is the same as Beelzeboul of verses 24 and 27.

Verse 27 provides insight into the

groups who occupy Satan's kingdom. Here, Jesus turns the Pharisees' argument against themselves as He connects these Pharisees to their being used in Satan's employ, i.e., "Your sons cast them out." The Pharisees' claim that Jesus' work of casting out demons is done in the power of Satan; but the Pharisees' own followers also cast out demons, and so, Jesus asks from where their power to do this comes. This is a question that they cannot answer without condemning themselves, which simultaneously proves that they are wrong in their conclusions about the source of Jesus' power.

III. JESUS' AUTHORITY VERSUS SATAN'S WEAKNESS (MATTHEW 12:28–29)

"No, it is not Beelzeboul who is casting out the demons." Jesus' response is swift and intense because these Pharisees do not wish to acknowledge that Jesus is the Messiah, and that He has the authority and power to eradicate the demons who are tormenting this man. That He casts out the demons in the "Spirit of God" could also be understood that He casts out demons in the name of God. Jesus has the will of His Father to perform miracles, especially relating to those who represent Satan and the dark powers of the earth. Jesus demonstrates the actual weakness of Satan and the omnipotence of heaven.

Jesus illustrates an example of God's authority and power by presenting a rhetorical question of breaking into the house of a strong man. A strong man's house would be protected by the owner and, because of his strength and reputation, no one would generally be foolish enough to invade the domain of the strong man unless there was

some way to neutralize him. The materials used to bind the strong man had to be adequate, for the strong man could destroy inferior materials used to subdue him. If the strong man is to be bound, the fetters and rope must be of such quality that it is beyond the power of the strong man to overcome. In this case, the alleged "strong man" is an example of the deception that much of the world embraces; Satan's will cannot overcome God's power. Since Jesus had been granted authorization, with his act of driving out demons, He is proving He is greater than Satan, as He is able to go into Satan's realm and come away with the spoils of victory. Since He can do this, He is able to institute the Kingdom of God among them (v. 28). If He were driving out demons by Satan's power, He certainly could not be offering the people God's Kingdom. That would be contradictory; the fact that He was coming to establish the kingdom clearly showed that He worked by the power of the Spirit of God, not by Satan's power.

IV. THE UNPARDONABLE SIN (MATTHEW 12:30–32)

Jesus moves to comment on the dedication and reliability of those who wish to follow Him. As Jesus' reputation grows because of His preaching, teaching, and healing, He will draw tremendous crowds who will seek Him for various reasons. If in the case of the people who seek Jesus because they want to be healed (and not saved), if the healing does not come, it is probable that they will disassociate themselves from His movement. Although Jesus' words, "He who is not with Me is against Me," may seem harsh, they describe two divergent camps of thought.

As previously mentioned, these Pharisees and their followers were in Satan's camp, which excluded them from the Kingdom. Jesus gives a strong warning to those moving away from Him, although some would not fully comprehend who He is. Still yet, while Jesus was not completely understood, the power evidenced through Him should never have been misunderstood, especially by the religious leaders.

However, Jesus reveals the depth of God's love and the propensity of His forgiveness. In verse 31, Jesus declares that "sin and blasphemy committed against God will be forgiven, although blasphemy against the Spirit shall not be forgiven." Describing His love for humanity, God will forgive the evil things that people do to one another, and He is also willing to forgive the evil things that they say against Him. Therefore, anyone who criticizes Jesus (God) may not understand His mission and power; however, His presence should not have been misunderstood by the religious leaders of the period because their resistance to Jesus proved sustainable.

THE LESSON APPLIED

Blasphemy is not always understood in the world today. For the non-believer, the term does not make sense because part of the definition requires that it contain an expletive that dishonors God, as the older generation would say, "using the Lord's name in vain." However, in the era of Jesus, blasphemy was real and a crime against the Holy Spirit. Additionally, this specific sin cannot be reproduced today, for it required Jesus' presence on earth, with His performing miracles through the Spirit's power. Nonetheless, many believers have reduced themselves to a position of committing modern-day blasphemy through the usage of such expletives and refusing to acknowledge the ramifications for the generations that follow.

LET'S TALK ABOUT IT
Does God still bring about healing?

Believers trust that healing comes from God, even if the healing doesn't look the way they thought it would. When a loved one is hospitalized, people pray for God's healing and subsequent restoration. However, if the sought-after healing does not occur, many feel that God has not heard or denied their prayers. God heals in many ways beyond our sensibilities. Healing through surgery may allow the patient to live but carry a "thorn in the flesh". Sometimes a person succumbs to his or her illness but is granted a heavenly reward. God heals Christians, and we have to be ready by faith in whatever form He chooses. Count it as a blessing that He heals us in the way that seems best to Him.

HOME DAILY DEVOTIONAL READINGS
JULY 10–16, 2023

MONDAY	TUESDAY	WEDNESDAY	THURSDAY	FRIDAY	SATURDAY	SUNDAY
The Kingdom's Small Beginnings	The Wind and Sea Obey Jesus	Listen to God's Voice	God's Wisdom Is Unconventional	The Spirit Reveals God's Ways	God's Harvest of Righteousness	Receiving and Understanding the Word
Mark 4:21–32	Mark 4:33–41	Psalm 95	1 Corinthians 2:1–8	1 Corinthians 2:9–16	Isaiah 61	Matthew 13:1–9, 18–23

THE SOWER AND THE SEED

ADULT TOPIC:	BACKGROUND SCRIPTURE:
GROWING STRONG	MATTHEW 13:1–23; MARK 4; LUKE 8:5–15

MATTHEW 13:1–9, 18–23

King James Version

THE same day went Jesus out of the house, and sat by the sea side.

2 And great multitudes were gathered together unto him, so that he went into a ship, and sat; and the whole multitude stood on the shore.

3 And he spake many things unto them in parables, saying, Behold, a sower went forth to sow;

4 And when he sowed, some seeds fell by the way side, and the fowls came and devoured them up:

5 Some fell upon stony places, where they had not much earth: and forthwith they sprung up, because they had no deepness of earth:

6 And when the sun was up, they were scorched; and because they had no root, they withered away.

7 And some fell among thorns; and the thorns sprung up, and choked them:

8 But other fell into good ground, and brought forth fruit, some an hundredfold, some sixtyfold, some thirtyfold.

9 Who hath ears to hear, let him hear.

• • • • • •

18 Hear ye therefore the parable of the sower.

19 When any one heareth the word of the kingdom, and understandeth it not, then cometh the wicked one, and catcheth away that which was sown in his heart. This is he which received seed by the way side.

New Revised Standard Version

THAT same day Jesus went out of the house and sat beside the sea.

2 Such great crowds gathered around him that he got into a boat and sat there, while the whole crowd stood on the beach.

3 And he told them many things in parables, saying: "Listen! A sower went out to sow.

4 And as he sowed, some seeds fell on the path, and the birds came and ate them up.

5 Other seeds fell on rocky ground, where they did not have much soil, and they sprang up quickly, since they had no depth of soil.

6 But when the sun rose, they were scorched; and since they had no root, they withered away.

7 Other seeds fell among thorns, and the thorns grew up and choked them.

8 Other seeds fell on good soil and brought forth grain, some a hundredfold, some sixty, some thirty.

9 Let anyone with ears listen!"

• • • • • •

18 "Hear then the parable of the sower.

19 When anyone hears the word of the kingdom and does not understand it, the evil one comes and snatches away what is sown in the heart; this is what was sown on the path.

MAIN THOUGHT: But he that received seed into the good ground is he that heareth the word, and understandeth it; which also beareth fruit, and bringeth forth, some an hundredfold, some sixty, some thirty. (Matthew 13:23, KJV)

King James Version	*New Revised Standard Version*
20 But he that received the seed into stony places, the same is he that heareth the word, and anon with joy receiveth it;	20 As for what was sown on rocky ground, this is the one who hears the word and immediately receives it with joy;
21 Yet hath he not root in himself, but dureth for a while: for when tribulation or persecution ariseth because of the word, by and by he is offended.	21 yet such a person has no root, but endures only for a while, and when trouble or persecution arises on account of the word, that person immediately falls away.
22 He also that received seed among the thorns is he that heareth the word; and the care of this world, and the deceitfulness of riches, choke the word, and he becometh unfruitful.	22 As for what was sown among thorns, this is the one who hears the word, but the cares of the world and the lure of wealth choke the word, and it yields nothing.
23 But he that received seed into the good ground is he that heareth the word, and understandeth it; which also beareth fruit, and bringeth forth, some an hundredfold, some sixty, some thirty.	23 But as for what was sown on good soil, this is the one who hears the word and understands it, who indeed bears fruit and yields, in one case a hundredfold, in another sixty, and in another thirty."

LESSON SETTING
Time: AD 27
Place: Sea of Galilee or Lake Gennesaret

LESSON OUTLINE
I. Jesus Teaches in Parables (Matthew 13:1–9)
II. Jesus Explains the Role of the Sower (Matthew 13:18–23)

UNIFYING PRINCIPLE
Human endeavors have no guarantee of success. Why do our efforts sometimes seem to fail? Jesus' parable of the sower reminds us that the success of what we do is not entirely dependent on us.

INTRODUCTION
Previously, Jesus had been in a house, probably, in Capernaum, which served as Jesus' base of operations in Galilee. While speaking to the crowds that were present, an interesting occurrence developed.

Someone mentioned that His family (His mother, brothers, and sisters) were outside, which led Him to say that "whoever does the will of My Father who is in Heaven is My mother, brother, and sister (Matthew 12:46–50). Concluding, Jesus will leave the house and retreat to the lake front, where He will teach the parable of the sower, directing the crowd to an awareness of their relationship to the Kingdom and teaching the disciples that understanding the complexities of heaven is a continuation of constant learning. Additionally, the parable examines the totality of humankind, who either rejects or accepts Jesus and has a commitment to the Lord. In this parable, Jesus provides several examples of how man aligns with God.

EXPOSITION

I. JESUS TEACHES IN PARABLES (MATTHEW 13:1–9)
As Jesus left the house where He was

previously teaching and walked down to the banks of the lake, it seems that He was preparing to rest after the discourse that He had provided, which Matthew records in chapter 12. Jesus' respite, however, was brief, as large crowds came upon Him, including many of those who were gathered outside of the house. Although probably fatigued, Jesus responded to the people who wished to hear His words. He decided to get into a boat to instruct the crowd because while He was on the beach, the people would have pressed Him and jostled for a position to be close to Him. It was also easier to get into a smaller boat and anchor in the shallows, yet close enough to be heard by all of the people who were standing on the shoreline. It was imperative that the people would be able to hear Jesus' teaching. The fact that Jesus "sat down" should not be a cause for concern, it was customary for teachers to sit as opposed to standing, while instructing.

Jesus' method of instruction was in the form of a parable because Jesus knew His audience. A parable is a figure of speech in which a moral or spiritual truth is illustrated by an analogy drawn from everyday experiences. Jesus began his parable with an account of a person who decided to sow some seeds. He identifies the sower as a farmer, i.e., "a farmer went out to sow his seed" (NIV), as he would when planting his garden or sowing in his field. Nevertheless, as the man sowed, some of the seeds fell beside the road, away from the intended area. A better understanding here is to use "path" (v. 4) instead of "road," which implies a larger area, as a grain field would often have a path going alongside it or even through it.

Nonetheless, Jesus mentions that some birds happened to see the bare seeds lying in view of this unobstructed pathway. The unprotected seeds are food for these hungry birds, so, driven by their instincts, they "swoop down" on the seeds and consume them in a matter of seconds. Jesus notes that some other seeds fell on rocks, but they did sprout up. The meaning here is not to celebrate this group of seeds because the rocks were probably covered with a thin layer of soil, which allowed them to extend their roots. The image here is that Jesus is warning against having a shallow religion, commitment, and understanding of the faith. Although these seeds would sprout, their growth would be stunted, and they would be incapable of bearing good fruit because their root system would never develop – they would wither away and die. Believers must have a proper connection with the Lord that allows continuous blessings, not a representative of shallow faith that lacks depth, such as this group of seeds represents. The agrarian residents of the area would have a personal understanding of and inherently respond to the examples of sowing seed and the possible outcomes of these practices.

In this section, the sun, although valuable and necessary, is viewed as a destructive element on the development of the seeds, which in this case, were left defenseless because they were lying on top of the soil and not embedded in the ground. The overpowering rays of the sun did not spare the seeds that could not be protected; they dried up because they did not develop a root system that allowed water and nutrients to protect them from the sun.

Here, the sun represents pressure and

various sorts of evil that place a strain on the lives of the believer. Although the sun is necessary for the development of the seeds, too much sun will destroy them because their core cannot withstand the rays. The spiritual implication here is that the Holy Spirit acts as a modifier that allows Christians to live with the pressures of this world. In this image, these seeds represent people who have potential but wither or fall away because they are not anchored in the Lord and are thereby, removed from His support system.

Jesus notes that there were other seeds that did extend their roots and were initially able to anchor in the ground; however, their issue was where these seeds were located, as they tried to develop among weeds or thorns, whose roots choked them. Christians cannot allow themselves to live in spiritual practice and spaces with the human "thorns of Satan," who by their sheer numbers and influences, will have the ability to eradicate the believer.

Thankfully, some seeds did fall on the proper ground and were able to yield a crop according to their germination. In this case, it is the dedicated disciple to which Jesus is referring. Additionally, Jesus emphasizes that the crowds should take heed to this parable and His declaration of "he who has ears, let him hear" as a quasi-rebuke. However, in our modern culture, we might say, "Pay attention to what I am saying," or "Does this make sense?" or "Do you understand?" The Scriptures are filled with commands for the people to hear the Word, and probably one of the more familiar statements is the Shema (Deuteronomy 6:4), signifying the most basic confession of faith in Judaism. The verse means that the Lord (*Yahweh*) is totally unique, and He alone is God. Therefore, believers, like the Israelites, could have a sense of security that was totally impossible for their polytheistic neighbors because their gods could never act in harmony due to their unpredictability, lack of morality, and commitment to their subjects. Hearing leads to understanding, which then leads to action, such as doing. It is important that the crowds understand the parable and be in a position to design a component of their lives according to the moral of this story. Nonetheless, Jesus is insisting that this multitude not miss out on the lesson because of its deep spiritual implications.

II. JESUS EXPLAINS THE ROLE OF THE SOWER (MATTHEW 13:18–23)

Previously, Jesus told the disciples that they were blessed because they were privileged to see (understand) and hear these truths (v. 16). Jesus' disciples heard the same truths as the leaders, but their response was entirely different. The disciples saw and believed; the leaders saw and rejected. Since the leaders turned from the light they had been given, God gave them no additional light.

In this section (vv. 18–23), Jesus explains to His disciples the meaning of the Parable of the Sower. The disciples asked Jesus why He taught the crowd using the parable style (what modernists would call allegories). Guiding the disciples to the spiritual implications, Jesus taught them that these accounts were filled with hidden aspects that were understood by the faithful but not comprehended by the unbeliever. The parables would also reach into the future, as these parables presented truths about the Kingdom in the current day. These truths are called "mysteries" (v. 11) because they were not revealed in the Old Testament and are revealed by Christ only to those who are properly related to Him (vv. 11–13; Mark 4:11–12). Again, insisting that the crowd is indeed paying attention, Jesus tells them to hear this parable of the sower. He reveals the meaning of the parable in that "when anyone hears the word of the kingdom and does not understand it, the evil one [Satan] comes and snatches away what has been sown in his heart." Additionally, Jesus identifies the one who has been snatched away by Satan as the seed that was sown and fell by the roadside.

Jesus identifies the seed that was sown on rocky ground as a man who hears the Word and initially receives it with joy, although his life may be in a rocky place. In this image, the sprouting of the seed invokes a time for celebration; however, this man is being lulled into a false state of happiness because his situation is tenuous. He has no firm root or commitment to himself or to the Lord, his situation is temporary; and when trouble comes he runs or turns away from what should be the source of his strength. This man is not stable or dependable in his commitment and faithfulness to the Lord. This man also represents those who wish to get close to Jesus in order to obtain the benefits (such as healing and blessings) but do not wish to become authentic disciples. Unfortunately, in our modern-day culture, we are witnesses to many pseudo-Christians who may derisively be thought of as "wanna-be" members of the Kingdom but lack the allegiance to remain in the Kingdom.

Continuing, the man who is represented by the seed that fell among the thorns is the man who hears the Word but rejects it outright. This is the person who does not believe in the salvation of the Lord, and for this reason, the Word of God does not have a purpose in his life. The image here is the multitude of the unsaved who find religion and a Christian lifestyle a waste of time. The persons represented here are consumed with their small-sphere world and its worries that affect only their needs and desires. Among the entities that would filter out a desire to align oneself with Christ is the deceitfulness of wealth. It represents a focus on the obtaining and retaining of one's treasure at the expense of being part of the kingdom and having received salvation. As in the legendary account of the rich young ruler, the man who is so focused on his wealth that he is blinded by its allure and is, therefore, choked or suffocated from receiving or "doing" the work of the Lord. In this situation, the image is that the crop becomes useless, with its only value assigned to the fire and garbage heap.

Jesus reaches the apex of the story by highlighting the man who is represented by the seed that fell on good soil. As with humans, crops need major nutrients, such as nitrogen, phosphorus, and potassium, among others. These minerals strengthen the crops and have a direct effect on their bloom and the quality of the fruit they bear. The quality of the fruit owes itself to many factors, as does the quality of the Christian experience. Jesus' objective here is not simply the quality of the good soil but the end result, i.e., the sweet and magnificent fruit that becomes the end product. The lesson here is to understand that the Word is represented by the seed, and if it is sown among people of good will (good soil), the result will be a blossoming of disciples who will advance God's Kingdom on earth. Jesus will declare that the seeds that fell on good ground are those who, having heard the Word with a good and noble heart, keep it and bear fruit with patience (Luke 8:15).

Another perspective could be that people are represented by the seed that falls on good ground, which is "good people." Authentic Christians, aided by the nutrients of the Spirit, will reciprocate the growth and flourish of other true disciples that are planted among them. Moreover, the fruits are multiplied, which is also a metaphor reflecting that this man's family and his descendants are in a continuous position, in the manner that is the cycle of perennials, to bear good fruit. This is the explanation of the good fruit resulting in a crop of a hundred-, sixty-, and thirty-fold yield, as it will be passed throughout successive generations.

THE LESSON APPLIED

Jesus taught in parables for several reasons, all of which were filled with implications for their apostolic future. Jesus' teachings were designed to undergird these men for the period when they would be "on their own," as He returned to heaven. Jesus taught in parable-style to reveal the truth to His followers, while fulfilling prophecy, especially that of Isaiah who believed that his service to the Lord would result in the nation's healing. However, the people had not listened, nor would they begin listening; in fact, their hearts became even more hardened against the Lord. Jesus' emphasis on the "eyes" is to explain that Israel, in His day, could not believe because they would not believe.

LET'S TALK ABOUT IT

Jesus gives four different reactions to the Word. Should we all have the same one?

People can have different responses to the same events, depending upon their context. One of the most notable examples can be found in the church, where the motivation for worshipers should be similar, if not the same. However, the reasons for church attendance vary among people and are driven by context. Unfortunately, this example magnifies the problems that occur because people may attend the same worship service and hear the same music, same prayers, and same preaching but become affected by these elements in a vastly divergent manner. This is but one example of why Jesus must be the center of our rationale for worship.

HOME DAILY DEVOTIONAL READINGS
JULY 17–23, 2023

MONDAY	TUESDAY	WEDNESDAY	THURSDAY	FRIDAY	SATURDAY	SUNDAY
Preparing for God's Harvest	The Righteous Yield Their Fruit	Examine the State of Your Faith	Search Me, O God	God Brings Every Deed into Judgment	God Will Deal with the Weeds	The Righteous Will Shine
Matthew 3:1–12	Psalm 1	2 Corinthians 13:1–10	Psalm 139:11–18, 23–24	Ecclesiastes 12	Matthew 13:24–33	Matthew 13:34–43

WEEDS AMONG THE WHEAT

ADULT TOPIC:
GROWING TOGETHER

BACKGROUND SCRIPTURE:
MATTHEW 13:24–30, 36–43

MATTHEW 13:24–30, 36–43

King James Version

ANOTHER parable put he forth unto them, saying, The kingdom of heaven is likened unto a man which sowed good seed in his field:

25 But while men slept, his enemy came and sowed tares among the wheat, and went his way.

26 But when the blade was sprung up, and brought forth fruit, then appeared the tares also.

27 So the servants of the householder came and said unto him, Sir, didst not thou sow good seed in thy field? from whence then hath it tares?

28 He said unto them, An enemy hath done this. The servants said unto him, Wilt thou then that we go and gather them up?

29 But he said, Nay; lest while ye gather up the tares, ye root up also the wheat with them.

30 Let both grow together until the harvest: and in the time of harvest I will say to the reapers, Gather ye together first the tares, and bind them in bundles to burn them: but gather the wheat into my barn.

• • • • • •

THEN Jesus sent the multitude away, and went into the house: and his disciples came unto him, saying, Declare unto us the parable of the tares of the field.

37 He answered and said unto them, He that soweth the good seed is the Son of man;

New Revised Standard Version

HE put before them another parable: "The kingdom of heaven may be compared to someone who sowed good seed in his field;

25 but while everybody was asleep, an enemy came and sowed weeds among the wheat, and then went away.

26 So when the plants came up and bore grain, then the weeds appeared as well.

27 And the slaves of the householder came and said to him, 'Master, did you not sow good seed in your field? Where, then, did these weeds come from?'

28 He answered, 'An enemy has done this.' The slaves said to him, 'Then do you want us to go and gather them?'

29 But he replied, 'No; for in gathering the weeds you would uproot the wheat along with them.

30 Let both of them grow together until the harvest; and at harvest time I will tell the reapers, Collect the weeds first and bind them in bundles to be burned, but gather the wheat into my barn.'"

• • • • • •

THEN he left the crowds and went into the house. And his disciples approached him, saying, "Explain to us the parable of the weeds of the field."

37 He answered, "The one who sows the good seed is the Son of Man;

MAIN THOUGHT: Let both grow together until the harvest: and in the time of harvest I will say to the reapers, Gather ye together first the tares, and bind them in bundles to burn them: but gather the wheat into my barn. (Matthew 13:30, KJV)

MATTHEW 13:24–30, 36–43

King James Version

38 The field is the world; the good seed are the children of the kingdom; but the tares are the children of the wicked one;

39 The enemy that sowed them is the devil; the harvest is the end of the world; and the reapers are the angels.

40 As therefore the tares are gathered and burned in the fire; so shall it be in the end of this world.

41 The Son of man shall send forth his angels, and they shall gather out of his kingdom all things that offend, and them which do iniquity;

42 And shall cast them into a furnace of fire: there shall be wailing and gnashing of teeth.

43 Then shall the righteous shine forth as the sun in the kingdom of their Father. Who hath ears to hear, let him hear.

New Revised Standard Version

38 the field is the world, and the good seed are the children of the kingdom; the weeds are the children of the evil one,

39 and the enemy who sowed them is the devil; the harvest is the end of the age, and the reapers are angels.

40 Just as the weeds are collected and burned up with fire, so will it be at the end of the age.

41 The Son of Man will send his angels, and they will collect out of his kingdom all causes of sin and all evildoers,

42 and they will throw them into the furnace of fire, where there will be weeping and gnashing of teeth.

43 Then the righteous will shine like the sun in the kingdom of their Father. Let anyone with ears listen!

LESSON SETTING
Time: AD 27
Place: Sea of Galilee

LESSON OUTLINE
I. The Wheat and the Tares (Matthew 13:24–30)
II. The Fate of the Tares (Matthew 13:36–43)

UNIFYING PRINCIPLE
The world is a spectrum of good and evil. How will people be recompensed? Jesus' parable of the weeds teaches that the Son of Man will distinguish between evil and righteous people.

INTRODUCTION
Jesus is continuing to teach the crowds that have gathered along the seashore in the form of parables. Remember that these parables are provided to the believers, such as His disciples, to explain that there are mysteries of heaven that will be revealed at the proper time. In this lesson, Jesus illustrates the comparison of the wheat and the tares, or as it has been called, "The Parable of the Weeds." Additionally, there has been a shift from the examination of "good soil" in the last lesson to the implications of "good seed." This lesson begins with the wheat and tares, skips the account of the mustard seed, and the leaven, then returns to the wheat and tares, as Jesus moves into a house for the final part of this discourse.

EXPOSITION

I. THE WHEAT AND THE TARES (MATTHEW 13:24–30)
Our lesson begins with Jesus introducing another parable, that of the wheat and the tares. Jesus will present additional parables that offer a picture of the Kingdom of heaven, saying it is "like..." (Matthew

13:44 ff., Mark 4:30 ff., and Luke 13:20 ff.), to gain the attention of the people. He starts by stating that the "kingdom of heaven may be compared to a man who sowed good seed in his field." Wheat is a common grain that is primarily used in bread; however, many non-agrarian people are unfamiliar with the term "tares." Tares are plants that resemble wheat, having the same stalk and greenness until the ear appears, and only then is the difference noticed. Tares are mentioned only in Matt. 13:25–30 and will not produce any fruit that is worthwhile. This species of ryegrass produces seeds that are a strong soporific poison, and it grows plentifully in Syria and Palestine. The grains of the tares resemble those of wheat so that it is very difficult to separate them by sifting; so, as a result, tares are often sown together with the wheat, growing along with it in the field. Darnel flour is poisonous and gives a bitter taste when mixed into bread dough. No farmer would ever consciously sow tares in his field.

At a certain time during the night, when the shadows could conceal them – and while the men who tended to the fields were asleep – the enemy comes and purposely sows tares among the wheat seed. With this unscrupulous act occurring at night, it is probable that these renegades sowed the tares wildly. Nonetheless, the tares fell among the wheat seeds, beginning the cycle of destruction.

In this case, the wheat represents all of God's children. Additionally, the time at which the tares appeared must not be taken to imply that the weeds suddenly shot up after the wheat had matured. The meaning is that the distinction between the weeds and the wheat was not evident until heads of grain began to form on the wheat. As a result, the wheat and the weeds grew together and would continue to do so until the time of harvest, removing the weeds early would result in destroying the wheat (vv. 28–29). Therefore, the two (the wheat and the tares) must grow together until the harvest when the weeds would be pulled out and destroyed.

The servants of the landowner were probably horrified when they realized that tares were growing among the wheat, leading them to question the landowner by asking if he had sown only good wheat seeds in his field. In this case, the owner may have acquired the seeds, but it would have been the servants who had done the majority of the work in sowing the seeds. It would seem that the servants should have known what type of seeds were sown. However, the seeds of wheat and tares are almost identical, and neither would have been suspected to be the wrong seeds. Not wishing to be blamed for this situation, the servants would definitely want to clear themselves of this error.

The landowner, however, replied that the sown tares were an act of deliberate sabotage and that "an enemy" had committed this crime. At this point, the landowner may not have had any idea of the identity of the enemy. Their immediate reply was to ask if they (the servants) could go and capture them, which indicates that there was a person (but most likely, a group) that they wished to target. However, this act could have led to a serious confrontation and possible bloodshed, which the landowner did not want to envision.

Instructing his servants to "stand down,"

the landowner shifted his attention to the salvaging of his crop because it could mean the difference between feeding his household, making a profit or being financially ruined by a worthless harvest. The servants wanted to uproot the tares, believing they could isolate them from the wheat plants. However, the landowner disagreed. He forbade his servants to uproot the invasive tares while attempting to leave the immature wheat among the weeds. He knew that if they pulled up the tares (weeds), they might accidentally also uproot the wheat plants with them, thus, destroying the crop.

The landowner instructed the servants to "allow them both [the wheat and tares] to grow together until the harvest." The servants would first gather the tares, which indicates that the tares were easily recognizable. Continuing, the landowner instructed the servants to bind the worthless tares and tie them into bundles, which would be thrown into a fire to be burned. Several scholars believe that this action may reflect the custom of using dried weeds for fuel when there was a shortage of wood. However, in the context of the parable, the implication is that these weeds are burned immediately because they are useless. This is probably because the parable is an allegory of the final judgment.

II. THE FATE OF THE TARES (MATTHEW 13:36–43)

After an interlude, Jesus leaves the boat and the crowds and goes into a house. In what seems to be a more intimate setting, the disciples ask Jesus to explain the moral and significance of the aforementioned parable. Although the disciples were primarily fishermen, they probably knew the difference between the wheat plants and the vicious weeds, which are identified as tares. In this case, the disciples would suspect that Jesus was teaching the crowd a narrative that had deeper implications than the misfortunes of a targeted landowner.

Jesus explains to His disciples that the sower of the good seed, as the Son of Man, is Himself, Jesus. The title Son of Man was frequently given to the prophet Ezekiel, probably to remind him of his human weakness; and in the Old Testament, it is used only in Psalm 80:17 and Daniel 7:13. However, in the New Testament, it is used forty-three times as a distinctive title of the Savior, noting the true humanity of our Lord. Ironically, Jesus never refers to Himself as the Messiah. Jesus refer to Himself as the Son of Man (Matthew 26:62–64). Incredibly, the forces of the dark family of Satan recognized Jesus as the Son of God during His exorcism of the man who lived in the cemetery of the Gadarenes, crying out, "What have we to do with You, Jesus, You Son of God, have You come to torment us before the time?" (Matthew 8:28–29). Unfortunately, many humans continue to deny Jesus as the Messiah, Savior, Redeemer, and Son of God.

Continuing, in verse 38, Jesus identifies five distinct entities: (1) the field, which represents the world, (2) the good seed, identified as Christians or believers who are committed to the mission of the Lord, (3) the tares, as the sons or pawns of the evil one, (4) the harvest, as the end of the age, and (5) the reapers, as angels. Jesus teaches that the world is fertile and is filled with promise for the expansion of the Gospel, which in turn, leads to the salvation of all humankind. In this imagery, the field (the world) is rich with good soil and filled with the aforementioned nutrients that would allow anyone who is "in Jesus" to develop and produce "good fruit." In God's creation, the field was perfect and (although, spoiled by sin), through the intervention of Jesus, had returned to its place of prominence.

The good seed (i.e., Christians and faithful believers) has been planted in the rich soil of the world to assist in the growth of the fruitful seeds into plants that bear the "good fruit" of the Lord. Although the "harvest is plentiful while the laborers are few" (Matthew 9:37), the mission is to continue to expand the Kingdom with those who wish to be a part of eternity.

The harvest, being the end of the age, is the period that will be reserved for the gathering of the faithful who have lived their lives for Jesus and with Jesus. This statement represents a Jewish and early-Christian thought that time is divided into two ages: the present evil age and the future glorious age. Therefore, "the end of the age" is equivalent to "the end of the world" or "the end of time."

The fact that the reapers are identified as angels (and not Jesus, personally) must not be confused. Jesus dispatches these beings to assist Him in leading the produce of the good seed. The angels by themselves do not have the authority to initiate the beginning of the new age. They will continue to serve as messengers but, in this case, as guides to the designated meeting place.

Using the example of the fate of the tares, Jesus explains that although they have to be gathered during the harvest, they will be assigned to the bonfires used for the destruction of useless materials. They are disposed of because of being non-contributors to the bounty of the farm. "Burned with fire" signifies the burning fires of hell that will happen at the end of the world when those who are corrupt are assigned to live with Satan. Jesus paints the image of the end of the world and the people who have followed Satan as non-contributors to the mission of Christ; therefore, their assignment to the rubbish heap of eternity becomes a sobering reality.

Jesus concludes with a ray of hope based on the faith of the believer, declaring that the Son of Man will dispatch His angels who will remove all stumbling blocks and obstacles to the Kingdom. These angels will eliminate or "weed out" all items, physical and spiritual, that impede the progress of the believer in his/her progression towards Jesus and the Kingdom.

The Greek term *anomia* is translated as "lawlessness;" however, a more lucid understanding of how it is referenced in the New Testament is not highlighting the absence of the Law but the deliberate violation of the Law. The phrase "coupled with sin" (*hamartia*) represents missing the mark that is ordained by God. God has placed in our hearts an innate knowledge of what is good and evil. Furthermore, John will declare that "everyone who practices sin also practices lawlessness; and therefore, sin is lawlessness" (1 John 3:4)!

In this case, "these are they" are remanded to the eternal fires of hell, and it will be too late for these, who rejected Jesus and the promise of the Kingdom. This group will be found lamenting that they did not recognize Jesus as Savior and Redeemer, as they are now crying (weeping) and "gnashing" their teeth (Matthew

8:12; 22:13; Luke 13:28). This group will not have blessings and protection because the fires of the end of the age will be continuous. John will later confirm that "in those days, men will seek death and will not find it; they will desire to die, and death will flee from them" (Revelation 9:6). The writer of 2nd Esdras, a non-biblical but important Jewish text, provides a clear warning that "the pit of torment shall appear, and opposite it shall be the place of rest; and the furnace of hell shall be disclosed, and opposite it the paradise of delight" (2 Esdras 7:36).

Coming forth from the separation will be believers, as the righteous will evolve and shine as bright as the sun in the Kingdom of the Lord. The faithful will be those who are the recipients of the blessings of their heavenly Father who kept them from stumbling, as Christians are presented "faultless" before the throne (Jude 24). Again, the instruction of "He who has ears must listen" is appropriate.

THE LESSON APPLIED

In this discourse, Jesus illustrates a simple lesson in the midst of a complex world. Humans have been granted the freedom to make the choice of either living with the Lord, according to His standards, or selecting a lifestyle advertised by the dark powers of Satan, which results in eternal death.

Although the examples were designed for the people of the period, the tutorial also serves as a warning for the contemporary world. We, as Christians, may feel marginalized (and often brutalized) by society-at-large; however, we receive protection and blessings, seen and unseen, and must continue to cling to the promise of hope that our eternal future is secure and that we will live with Jesus forever!

LET'S TALK ABOUT IT

In what sense do our choices determine in which pile we will land?

Most folks understand that good people can make bad choices and vice versa. However, many adults often refuse to accept the consequences of choices, especially when bad choices impact them in a negative manner. Humans tend to make excuses for such behavior or choices, e.g., poverty, lack of education, or the absence of "good" parenting. While these issues may factor into community problems, a personal lack of commitment to the Lord has more of an impact than people want to give it credit. Remember that sin is separation from God, no matter how it functions; and bad choices are much easier overcome when one adheres to the lifestyle of the Lord requires of us. Let each one of us live for Him, and He will empower us to succeed, and bring glory to His name.

HOME DAILY DEVOTIONAL READINGS
JULY 24–30, 2023

MONDAY	TUESDAY	WEDNESDAY	THURSDAY	FRIDAY	SATURDAY	SUNDAY
Wisdom Is Better than Jewels	Where Shall Wisdom Be Found?	A Miraculous Catch of Fish	Praise the Lord from the Heavens	Store Up Treasures in Heaven	God's Word Is Great Treasure	Heaven's Hidden Treasures
Proverbs 8:1–12	Job 28:1–2, 12–19	Luke 5:1–11	Psalm 148	Matthew 6:19–33	Psalm 119:161–176	Matthew 13:44–52

FINDING AND GATHERING

ADULT TOPIC:	BACKGROUND SCRIPTURE:
SEARCHING FOR BURIED TREASURE	MATTHEW 13:44–52

MATTHEW 13:44–52

King James Version	New Revised Standard Version
AGAIN, the kingdom of heaven is like unto treasure hid in a field; the which when a man hath found, he hideth, and for joy thereof goeth and selleth all that he hath, and buyeth that field.	"THE kingdom of heaven is like treasure hidden in a field, which someone found and hid; then in his joy he goes and sells all that he has and buys that field.
45 Again, the kingdom of heaven is like unto a merchant man, seeking goodly pearls:	45 "Again, the kingdom of heaven is like a merchant in search of fine pearls;
46 Who, when he had found one pearl of great price, went and sold all that he had, and bought it.	46 on finding one pearl of great value, he went and sold all that he had and bought it.
47 Again, the kingdom of heaven is like unto a net, that was cast into the sea, and gathered of every kind:	47 "Again, the kingdom of heaven is like a net that was thrown into the sea and caught fish of every kind;
48 Which, when it was full, they drew to shore, and sat down, and gathered the good into vessels, but cast the bad away.	48 when it was full, they drew it ashore, sat down, and put the good into baskets but threw out the bad.
49 So shall it be at the end of the world: the angels shall come forth, and sever the wicked from among the just,	49 So it will be at the end of the age. The angels will come out and separate the evil from the righteous
50 And shall cast them into the furnace of fire: there shall be wailing and gnashing of teeth.	50 and throw them into the furnace of fire, where there will be weeping and gnashing of teeth.
51 Jesus saith unto them, Have ye understood all these things? They say unto him, Yea, Lord.	51 "Have you understood all this?" They answered, "Yes."
52 Then said he unto them, Therefore every scribe which is instructed unto the kingdom of heaven is like unto a man that is an householder, which bringeth forth out of his treasure things new and old.	52 And he said to them, "Therefore every scribe who has been trained for the kingdom of heaven is like the master of a household who brings out of his treasure what is new and what is old."

MAIN THOUGHT: Then said he unto them, Therefore every scribe which is instructed unto the kingdom of heaven is like unto a man that is an householder, which bringeth forth out of his treasure things new and old. (Matthew 13:52, KJV)

LESSON OUTLINE
  I. **Hidden Treasure**
     (Matthew 13:44–46)
 II. **The Net is Cast**
     (Matthew 13:47–52)

Unifying Principle

People express a desire for some wisdom to direct their lives. What inspires clarity when choosing between traditional paths and new teaching? Jesus' parables about the Kingdom of heaven offer a connection between the old (wisdom of ancient of Israel) and the new (Jesus' fresh understanding of spiritual things).

Introduction

The phrase "The kingdom of heaven is like" is mentioned four times in the verses that encompass our lesson. In this imagery, Jesus continues to teach in a parabolic, metaphorical style that reflects simple approaches to everyday life skills but also, mysteries that foretell the manner in which believers will be included in the Kingdom, at the exclusion of the non-believer. As a preview, Jesus portrays fish as the people of the world, the Gospel as a net, and the separation of the unregenerate who continuously reject Jesus and God. The key here, however, is whether Jesus' pupils, His disciples, understand the meaning of these parables and if they will dedicate their lives to their truths and meanings.

Exposition

I. Hidden Treasure
(Matthew 13:44–46)

Jesus compares the Kingdom of heaven to several concepts. These accounts are designed to encourage the audience to move beyond the normal acquisitions of the world and start to imagine how to reach the rewards of eternity.

The Greek word for treasure is *thesauros*. However, in this case, "treasure" will serve as a metaphorical reference to the mind, body, or soul. The idea in this image is that treasure is connected to eternal life. In our current society, people play the lottery hoping they will become instant winners and cash in on what could be perceived as "treasure."

Jesus portrays the "find" as accidental, i.e., the man finds this treasure in someone else's field. His implications are clear. In the account, the man is overcome with joy over his find and, in his need to secure the field and his treasure, he sells all of his possessions and purchases the field. However, in the spiritual imagery of this missive, this field does not belong to the man but belongs to God. The lesson is not to imply that we can buy God or items that belong to Him but that the man sacrifices in order to acquire the things of God.

While Jesus is sharing several of the mysteries of heaven, His desire is to develop disciples and believers who may obtain what might be thought of as unobtainable. The message here is clear: Those who seek and find the Kingdom of heaven discover something that is so valuable that they fear they will lose it or someone will rob them of it. Therefore, resorting to human instincts, they hide it or (in this case) bury it in a field.

Another perspective is to realize that we, the Christian believers, are the treasure that is buried in the field, and we are priceless to the man (Jesus) who claims us, as Jesus, who sacrificed His life by giving up His position (and possessions) in heaven to purchase the field – the "purchase," representing Jesus' crucifixion. Although the field was originally owned by God (and Jesus) since the formation of the world, the field has lapsed into a state of dis-ownership and detachment from heaven because of the human rejection of God by His creation. Therefore, Jesus had to reclaim what was originally His, thus bringing about a restoration to both the land and its treasure. Otherwise, the fact that the treasure was buried again is not to be taken in a negative connotation, as if the believers are dead or need to be removed from the scene. Instead, this may metaphorically demonstrate that Jesus has re-buried Christians in Him and placed them in a protective place until the time of His coming.

The next section starts with "again" to signal a continuation of the account. However, Jesus uses an example of the search for and "find" of a precious pearl. The use of this participle supports the conclusion that the two parables are intended to convey the same point, and most commentators interpret them in this light.

No one can say who 'discovered' pearls – they were probably first found by ancient peoples searching the shores for food. Pearls are known as the 'Queen of Gems,' and were once the exclusive property of the rich and powerful. The Romans and Egyptians prized pearls and used them as decorative items as far back as the 5th Century BC Pearls have a place in Hindu, Islamic, and Christian traditions, often to symbolize purity and perfection.

The value of pearls can be found in the New Testament, especially in the Apocalypse, as John chronicles (1) the woman who was arrayed in purple and scarlet and adorned with gold, precious stones, and pearls (Revelation 17:4), (2) where an inventory of the merchants of the earth revealed them having gold, silver, precious stone, and pearls (Revelation 18:12), and (3) the Twelve Gates in the New Jerusalem were adorned with twelve pearls (Revelation 21:21).

In this case, Jesus presents a merchant who is seeking fine pearls. This merchant, we assume, is well-trained, experienced in his craft, and knows exactly for what he is looking. This merchant has a keen eye and is able to spot a pearl worthy of examination because he knows the value of the pearl. The pearl of great value may represent the Church, the bride of Jesus Christ. Pearls are uniquely formed. "Its formation occurs because of an irritation in the tender side of an oyster. There is a sense in which the Church was formed out of the wounds of Christ and has been made possible by His death and sacrifice" (John F. Walvoord, Matthew: Thy Kingdom Come, p. 105).

All oysters do not necessarily produce fine pearls. This can be used as an analogy because some people reject Jesus, they will not produce good fruit (in this case, a precious pearl). In nature, the pearl is produced under uncomfortable circumstances, equating to the pathway of the Christian, which is not always comfortable or easy. Nonetheless, through the fires and mine fields of life, Christians endure the obstacles, and because of the faithful commitment of the believers, they emerge as a valuable asset in the Kingdom. When they are tried in the fire of oppression, God blesses them to come out as pure as gold.

II. THE NET IS CAST (MATTHEW 13:47–52)

Jesus switches imagery for this next parable and because His disciples are fishermen the examples He uses are close to their hearts. Jesus begins with the illustration of a dragnet being cast out or thrown into the sea. In most cases, this net would be thrown from one of the types of fishing crafts used by the men who plied their trade in the waters of the region, especially on the industrious Sea of Galilee. It is clear several of His disciples were fishermen, including Peter, James, and John. Remember, at the ordination of their discipleship, Jesus' invitation to "follow Him" would result in their becoming "fishers of men" (Mark 1:17). The *net* was a large dragnet with floats at the top to keep it from sinking, and weights at the bottom. It was often dragged ashore in a large semicircle by several men. In this case, the fishermen had to work together, with their boats being strategically placed so that the entire group could prosper by catching a large number of fish. This would be in contrast to the individual fisherman, who could not maneuver a larger net and therefore, get a smaller catch. Regardless of the size of the catch, the net would contain a variety of fish, species of all types that were native to these waters.

When the nets were filled, the catch would be taken to the beach, where the "good fish" would be separated from *the bad*. The "good fish" refers to fish that are edible, while the bad refers to fish that cannot be eaten, which may indicate that they were rotten, although that is not the meaning here. In a Jewish context bad fish would be those that were specifically forbidden by their Law for consumption. In the imagery of the wheat and tares account, the good fish are put into a type of vessel or container that could be used for solid substances, such as fish, or liquids, such as oil (Matt. 25:4). The vessel was made of any number of possible materials: wood, clay, shell, gold, silver, or copper.

In our context, we often find fishermen who release the small fish back into the water; however, in this case, the nondesirable fish will not be returned but will be destroyed. Jesus said this sorting represents the angelic separation of the wicked from the righteous at the end of the age (v. 49; vv. 37–43). This separation will occur when Jesus Christ returns to establish His Kingdom on earth (25:30).

Jesus' references to the "end of the age" are a reminder of the end times, which include all aspects of the end of physical life as well as Jesus' second coming. Theologians refer to the term eschatology, which comes from a combination of Greek words meaning the study of the "last things" or "last days." Unfortunately, many people in contemporary society derisively reject this thought and do not believe in either heaven or hell. Yet, the Scriptures are filled with predictions of the end days, such as reported that "the day of the Lord will come like a thief, in which the heavens will pass away with a roar and the elements will be destroyed with intense heat, and the earth and its works will be burned up" (2 Peter 2:9, 10). Moreover, the end of the age will witness acts that seem unnatural to the ravenous nature of our competitive world, as was prophesied that "the wolf will dwell with the lamb, the leopard will lie down with the young goat, the calf and the young lion and the fatling together, and a little boy will lead them" (Isaiah 11:6).

In what is a fitting recapitulation, Jesus reminds His disciples that the angels will continue with their duty of assisting with the separation, and there will be continuous consternation and discomfort shown by weeping and the gnashing of teeth. The rotten or decayed fish represent the worthless, who have nothing to contribute and by their outright rejection of Jesus, have relinquished their rights and privileges as inheritors of the Kingdom. Like the bundles of tares, this group of "bad fish" have been remanded to the furnace (fire) of hell and its accompanying torments.

The disciples have been given several portrayals of the Kingdom of heaven. When Jesus asked if they understood, they replied in the affirmative, saying that they did. However, did they really understand these parables, or did they react as a school child who does not want to seem lost when the teacher asks if the class understands the homework? What will determine this will not be the disciples' immediate grasp on the intellectual side of the paradigm but that which will be revealed by their actions. They would have to seek the truths and develop their ministries within these concepts. These parables are dominated by warnings about the separation of those who are not worthy to become a part of God's domain. What seems to be left out is the imagery of the beauty of the Kingdom of heaven, such as its nature, scenery, and atmosphere. In this case, the objective is to impress upon the people and the disciples that one has to be worthy to enjoy the fruits of their labors, as the rewards will be present for only those who place themselves in a position to be selected for entry. The Kingdom of heaven is like a few things that are everyday observances of what is given by God, but if it is only approached by the simplicity of the situation – not understanding the spiritual concepts of the Kingdom – the disciples and the remainder of the world will be forever lost.

Usually, when we read or hear about a scribe (a teacher of the Law) in the New Testament, especially in the Gospels, the very mention conjures up negative notions because of their participation on the Sanhedrin Council and their accompanying conspiracies with the Pharisees who continually attempted to discredit Jesus. However, in this case, Jesus is speaking of scribes who have become disciples of the Kingdom. Although "scribe" is used in this Gospel 23 times, this is the only place where it is used of a believer. In this case, Jesus is revealing that the position of a man in society does not determine the position of his heart, and this/these scribe(s) have the ability to deliver the greatest things of the Kingdom, in the manner of their Christian lifestyles and belief systems. These scribes or teachers of the Law will actually interpret the Law according to the will of God and will be more in tune with the differences between the "Letter of the Law" and the "Spirit of the Law." Although these scribes are trained men of the Scriptures, they will become disciples of the rule of the Lord. In this case, these men will serve as proper conduits between the prophesy and promise of what we know as the Old Testament and the fulfillment of the promise of the new, as in the coming of the Messiah (Jesus Christ). The treasures of God, both old and new, are represented in His blessings of the past, and the grace of the present and future.

THE LESSON APPLIED

Jesus uses these different parables to illustrate the simplicity of understanding the basic concepts of the Kingdom, while at the same time, escalating the mysteries that are found within these hidden truths. The value of Jesus' redeeming the lost and escorting the believers to heaven is reality in the midst of unbelief. The agnostics and atheists of our society, those who in their ill-conceived sanctuaries, worship Satan and Norse mythological gods, have been warned throughout the centuries as the Gospel has been preached all over the world. The message of Jesus is clear; those who wish to live in an eternal state of salvific existence have the opportunity to do so, even though we live in a society that is anti-church and anti-religion. The message remains simple: Come to Jesus while you have time! It is important to remember that even as at times it appears that some of us are out of time, as long as we draw breath, it is not too late. He beckons us to come. The invitation to come is His gift of life to us.

LET'S TALK ABOUT IT

Is there anything that you are willing to give up everything to obtain?

In the first verse of our lesson Jesus compares the Kingdom to a man who finds a treasure in a field and sells everything to obtain the field. The treasure that was found was apparently so valuable and so able to change the trajectory of his life that he counted everything he held as being without merit in comparison. In as much as this parable is about the Kingdom of God there are also other practical applications for modern believers. For some, this parable may be applicable to a calling. Consider Abraham, who left everything to follow God's call. Another appropriate example is the disciples, Peter asks the Lord, "Look, we have left everything and followed you" (Mark 10:28). God's calling and purpose may very well place demands on us in which we would willingly give up everything to pursue. For some, that will be a vocation of ministry, but for others it will look different. It could be that one is called to return to school and leave behind a lucrative career. For another, it may be to start a new business, finish the prototype on an invention, or author a book. For still another it may be to answer the call to minister to others whereever you are. What is it? What is it that you must pursue at all costs? Pursue it!

HOME DAILY DEVOTIONAL READINGS
JULY 31–AUGUST 6, 2023

MONDAY	TUESDAY	WEDNESDAY	THURSDAY	FRIDAY	SATURDAY	SUNDAY
You Must Be Born Again	God Loves the World	Take Up Your Cross	God Sweeps Away Our Sins	God's Spirit and Words Remain	Rebirth and Renewal through the Spirit	Called to Freedom
John 3:1–9	John 3:10–21	Matthew 16:21–28	Isaiah 44:21–28	Isaiah 59:1–8, 16–21	Titus 3:1–8	Galatians 5:13–26

INHERITING THE KINGDOM

ADULT TOPIC: INNER STRUGGLES	BACKGROUND SCRIPTURE: GALATIANS 5:13–26

GALATIANS 5:13–26

King James Version

FOR, brethren, ye have been called unto liberty; only use not liberty for an occasion to the flesh, but by love serve one another.

14 For all the law is fulfilled in one word, even in this; Thou shalt love thy neighbour as thyself.

15 But if ye bite and devour one another, take heed that ye be not consumed one of another.

16 This I say then, Walk in the Spirit, and ye shall not fulfil the lust of the flesh.

17 For the flesh lusteth against the Spirit, and the Spirit against the flesh: and these are contrary the one to the other: so that ye cannot do the things that ye would.

18 But if ye be led of the Spirit, ye are not under the law.

19 Now the works of the flesh are manifest, which are these; Adultery, fornication, uncleanness, lasciviousness,

20 Idolatry, witchcraft, hatred, variance, emulations, wrath, strife, seditions, heresies,

21 Envyings, murders, drunkenness, revellings, and such like: of the which I tell you before, as I have also told you in time past, that they which do such things shall not inherit the kingdom of God.

22 But the fruit of the Spirit is love, joy, peace, longsuffering, gentleness, goodness, faith,

23 Meekness, temperance: against such there is no law.

New Revised Standard Version

FOR you were called to freedom, brothers and sisters; only do not use your freedom as an opportunity for self-indulgence, but through love become slaves to one another.

14 For the whole law is summed up in a single commandment, "You shall love your neighbor as yourself."

15 If, however, you bite and devour one another, take care that you are not consumed by one another.

16 Live by the Spirit, I say, and do not gratify the desires of the flesh.

17 For what the flesh desires is opposed to the Spirit, and what the Spirit desires is opposed to the flesh; for these are opposed to each other, to prevent you from doing what you want.

18 But if you are led by the Spirit, you are not subject to the law.

19 Now the works of the flesh are obvious: fornication, impurity, licentiousness,

20 idolatry, sorcery, enmities, strife, jealousy, anger, quarrels, dissensions, factions,

21 envy, drunkenness, carousing, and things like these. I am warning you, as I warned you before: those who do such things will not inherit the kingdom of God.

22 By contrast, the fruit of the Spirit is love, joy, peace, patience, kindness, generosity, faithfulness,

23 gentleness, and self-control. There is no law against such things.

MAIN THOUGHT: For, brethren, ye have been called unto liberty; only use not liberty for an occasion to the flesh, but by love serve one another. (Galatians 5:13, KJV)

GALATIANS 5:13–26

LESSON SETTING
Time: AD 57–58
Place: Corinth

LESSON OUTLINE
I. **A License to Love (Galatians 5:13–15)**
II. **The Relation of the Flesh and the Spirit (Galatians 5:16–21)**
III. **Fruit of the Spirit (Galatians 5:22–26)**

UNIFYING PRINCIPLE

People may experience conflict in their decision-making. What moves people toward life-giving choices? Galatians contrasts the healthy fruit of choices guided by the Holy Spirit, with the unhealthy consequences of choices that oppose the Spirit.

INTRODUCTION

Evidence suggests that the church in Galatia was founded by Paul on a second visit to the region during his Third Missionary Journey (Acts 18:23). The church seems to have been composed mainly of converts from idolatry (4:8) but also, of Jewish converts, who under the influence of Judaizing teachers, probably sought to incorporate the rites of Judaism with Christianity and were succeeding in dividing the church. This epistle was written for the purpose of counteracting this Judaizing tendency and recalling the Galatians to the simplicity of the gospel, while also, vindicating Paul's claim as a divinely commissioned apostle. The concepts of the guidance of the Spirit and the powerful emotion of genuine love are examined in this passage.

EXPOSITION

I. A LICENSE TO LOVE (GALATIANS 5:13–15)

Paul begins this section by referring to his opening statement, "It was for freedom that Christ set us free; therefore, keep standing firm and do not be subject again to a yoke of slavery" (Galatians 5:1). His emphasis is that we were called to freedom and provided an opportunity not to simply be emancipated from oppressive nations and regimes but free from any demonic forces that shackle and confine the Christian believer. Israel should inherently remember her history of enslavement to the Egyptians. Throughout the Scriptures, we find God constantly reminding Israel that it was His benevolence and mercy that resulted in her being set free from the yoke of slavery. Paul reminds the Christian that the yoke of oppression continues to exist. Paul's argument rests on the liberty that is based on spiritual redemption and the grace of God.

Therefore, freedom in the Lord carries with it many responsibilities and challenges. This freedom must reflect the values of the Kingdom and cannot be subject to the temptations of society and the world. As we are called to be witnesses to the goodness of the Lord and the mission of Jesus, the call to freedom must serve as a witness that Christians can indeed withstand the enticements and call of popular society that are not compatible with the direction of the Lord. Herein lies the conflict: Freedom does not provide a license to abscond Christian principles in order to satisfy our physical and psychological desires. In many cases, there remains a distinct difference between desires and needs. Christians must resist the physical and psychological pull of our bodies and minds into the abyss of unhealthy cravings. Paul denounces the negative aspects of the freedom of the flesh, or the physical freedoms that are misused by humanity.

Freedom comes with responsibilities, in that Christians must not allow it to harm or conflict with their relationship with the Lord. Christian freedom provides a license to serve humanity in both a *philos* and *agape* capacity – that is, brotherly love and sacrificial love, respectively. Paul's message here addresses many of the issues of the Galatians. They loved being part of the Church but because of their background and culture they believed they could also enjoy the world and remain in the camp of the Christian mission. Paul is correctly defining Christian freedom and channels it into the objective of service.

The license of Christian freedom is not to abuse its attributes or properties but is given so that we might love one another.

Unfortunately, contemporary society has diluted and devalued love with its usage in so many shallow ways. Love has been substituted by human desires and promises that do not allow for the purity of love to be practiced. Paul defines love for the Galatians by quoting Jesus, who when asked, "What is the greatest commandment," said, "You shall love the Lord your God with all your heart, and with all your soul, and with all your mind." Continuing, Jesus added that "you shall love your neighbor as yourself" (Matthew 22:37–39). Jesus quoted this phrase from Leviticus 19:18, as these two commandments serve as a foundation for the Law and the Prophets. The idea of loving one's neighbor as oneself is an act of agape or sacrificial love that was realized in God's "loving the world that He gave His only Son;" an act that humans could not repay. The gift of Jesus is everlasting and eternal. The license to love is a gift that can only come from heaven to those who have the faith to believe in its power.

Paul warns that if believers devour one another the results will be destructive for all parties. The Greek term *dáknō* provides a more descriptive image beyond the physical act of "biting" and can be used metaphorically, meaning to thwart, irritate, or sting. Like the bite of a venomous snake the poison that enters the bloodstream can be painful and deadly. These are some of the effects that humans feel when resorting to animalistic behavior. Paul warns that if these aggressions are practiced, all parties will be destroyed or devoured, as with the nature of wild animals who stalk their targets and devour their prey. That such love needed to be mutually expressed in the Galatian churches is made clear here. As a result of the inroads of false teachers, the church was divided and engaged in bitter strife. The Galatians were encouraged to keep the church safe from destructive elements.

II. THE RELATION OF THE FLESH AND THE SPIRIT (GALATIANS 5:16–21)

As a counter to verse 15, Paul declares that if one walks by the Spirit, His companionship will serve as a buffer to the desires of the flesh. For Paul, walking by and with the Spirit greatly improves one's chances that he or she will not fall victim to the wiles and temptations of Satan. For the believer, that action must be perpetual and consistent – as the Greek verb *peripateo* is literally translated, "keep on walking," as if each step in the life of the Christian depends upon the Spirit – which will result in victory over the negative impulses of human desires.

Moreover, the issue is that the needs or wants of the flesh within our *human* spirit continually fight against the will of God. Temptations are constantly present in our daily lives; however, in the words of a sage, "All things that look good to you are not necessarily good for you." Even the strongest believer faces enticements that are legal in the society in which we live but are contrary to the edicts of the Gospel and that of the Lord. The flesh and the Spirit live on "opposite ends of the street," and these opposites do not meet. Because of the gift of the Spirit, there is a battle, as the Spirit fights back against the wants of believers to satisfy these seemingly-uncontrollable impulses that, in many cases, provide only a temporary sense of satisfaction. Since the two are in opposition with one another, it creates a conflict within us; however, Christians who walk in the Spirit must not do as they please when it conflicts with God's law.

The Christian who is led by the Spirit is not under the Law. For Paul, a former Pharisaic Jew, the "whole Law" may be rendered as "all the laws" or "all the laws given through Moses," and an equivalent for "summed up in one commandment" may be "equal to just one commandment" or "to one law." In this example, there is no conflict because Jesus has come *after* the Law was given to fulfill the Mosaic edicts and restore humans back to the Lord, which the Law was incapable of completing. In this case, "the laws do not command you" or "do not have authority over you" because it is the Spirit, not the Law, that sanctifies us. Being under the Spirit is not only a call to obedience but also lends a person to their adhering to the moral obligation that is a requirement for being a disciple of Christ and receiving eternal life.

Paul lists items that he calls "deeds of the flesh," which are human actions and attitudes that are not pleasing to God. Paul highlights fornication and/or adultery (KJV) The word that is used here in the Greek is *porneia*. It looks familiar as its English cognate is pornography which most would consider to be immoral. This term is somewhat ambiguous as it has a range of meanings but all point to deviant sexual mores. Secondly, impurity, refers to the uncleanliness that comes from a life that is not lived in accordance with the kind of moral code befitting a Christian. Third, licentiousness is viewing sexual behavior that has no restrictions and is uncontrolled. Lastly, *idolatry* is a direct affront to the Lord, as these practitioners embrace other "gods" who believers have been commanded to avoid. Continuing, Paul provides an additional eleven sins to an extensive list, warning the promising Galatian church to live according to the characteristics of Heaven.

III. FRUIT OF THE SPIRIT (GALATIANS 5:22–26)

Paul now lists nine attributes that are the fruit of the Spirit, which serve as a rebuttal to the negative articles and behavioral shortcomings that were previously listed (see verses 19–21). The list begins with love and is followed by those things that emanate from the reservoir of love, which is the foundation of God's gift of Jesus. Notice that the word "fruit" (*karpos*) is singular and not plural as in "fruits." The reason is that fruit of the same kind from the same parent are listed singularly, they are part of the same crop. Keeping with this imagery, Paul likens "fruit" to the behavior of the Christian, whose deeds and conduct come from the same parent, the Spirit.

Paul is not condemning the Law, but he is saying that the Law by itself cannot control or produce these qualities. The Law supports all of these virtues; however, it is only through the Spirit that these merits are actionable. Human nature, because of our free will, can embrace love, joy, peace, and the remainder; however, it is the conviction of the individual to live according to the mandates of the Spirit. Nonetheless, if the Holy Spirit is actively at work in the lives of believers, the evidence will be apparent, strengthening the Christian with the knowledge that he/she is a product of the fruit of the Spirit.

Nonetheless, those who belong to Jesus Christ – Who is not mentioned in this segment until now – have crucified their flesh that possesses these passions and desires. In this portion, Paul applauds the believer who has turned away from the temptations that serve to entice him/her from a walk with the Lord. Interestingly, Paul uses the image of the crucifixion in describing the method by which the Christian has been able to overcome his/her weaknesses. The connection is obvious: Jesus was crucified but was not destroyed in the method He chose to provide our redemption. Therefore, the concept is clear: Believers allow the Spirit to serve as the agent that enables Christians to reject the lifestyles of their former lusts. In the act of His crucifixion, all the barriers to heaven were removed, and as such, the Christian who "crucifies" his/her flesh has buried the items that served to lure the believer from the Lord. Being born again is an image of new life; therefore, the crucifixion of the flesh is equated to the gift of new life. Still, Paul realizes that the Christian must be vigilant and in constant spiritual warfare to remain above the negative desires of the human body and spirit.

It is in this manner that Christians must live and walk by the Spirit in constant warfare for our souls. Paul poses these phrases as a conditional directive that is meant to bring a sense of balance to the life of the believer. As an "if-then" statement, where the first proposition leads to an affirmative conclusion, Paul is stating that we are able to walk by the Spirit because we live by the Spirit. Living and walking in the Spirit is a visible manifestation of the Christian lifestyle. Believers may occasionally ponder our sense of security in the Spirit; however, Paul reassures the believer that living by the Spirit allows the Spirit to control the flow of our emotions, thoughts, and therefore, deeds. Through our faith in Jesus, we are able to confidently embrace the gift of the Spirit.

However, herein lies a warning. Paul remonstrates with the believer not to become haughty or arrogant because we have the blessings of the Spirit. He discourages the Christian from becoming "boastful" (*kenodóxos*), meaning empty or vain, as it denotes a person who is void of real worth but wants to be admired by others (See Gal. 5:26). Christian behavior is to lead the non-saved to the Lord, not to the anything or anyone else.

THE LESSON APPLIED

Paul provides a list of emotions and actions that denigrate the principles of a Christian lifestyle and warns the believer to avoid at all costs the influences of these selfish tendencies. However, Paul also provides several positive countermeasures to encourage the Galatians and the faithful that there is a respite for the seemingly obvious, overwhelming negatives of the human spirit. In this series of options, Paul lists several positive attributes that can be obtained by humans in their lifestyle of embracing the power of the Spirit. The motive here is that the faithful can control human impulses that would naturally veer toward evil through the intervention of the Spirit that is a constant in the everyday lives of the Christian disciple.

LET'S TALK ABOUT IT

Is it possible to "walk" in the Spirit only when one chooses? Or is it possible to do so on a daily basis alone?

Believers walk with Christ every day, not just in moments of moral crisis. It is disconcerting for pastors to witness people request prayer only when something bad or stressful is taking place in their lives. In many cases, this group may only come to church when there is a family or financial emergency that needs to be publicly shared. Whether this is for sympathy or the need for commiseration, churches do their best to empathize with these subjects, while not approving of their actions. Believers, however, realize that our security is in a daily walk with the Lord because our walk with Him is not based on what He does for us but upon the joy of a relationship with our Savior, whether it is during a crisis or a period of celebration. Our relationship with Him honors God first for who He is. He alone is the Lord God of heaven and earth. We should strive to serve Him daily.

HOME DAILY DEVOTIONAL READINGS
AUGUST 7–13, 2023

MONDAY	TUESDAY	WEDNESDAY	THURSDAY	FRIDAY	SATURDAY	SUNDAY
God Guards the Paths of Justice	Hunger and Thirst for Righteousness	Righteousness in God's Kingdom	God Keeps the Steadfast in Peace	Rejoice in God's Word	Rejoice in Hope	Righteousness, Peace, and Joy
Proverbs 2:1–11	Matthew 5:3–12	Matthew 5:13–20	Isaiah 26:1–11	Nehemiah 7:73–8:3, 5–6, 9–12	Romans 12:9–21	Romans 14:10–23

THE NATURE OF THE KINGDOM

ADULT TOPIC:	BACKGROUND SCRIPTURE:
BUILD UP ONE ANOTHER	ROMANS 14:10–23

ROMANS 14:10–23

King James Version	New Revised Standard Version
BUT why dost thou judge thy brother? or why dost thou set at nought thy brother? for we shall all stand before the judgment seat of Christ.	WHY do you pass judgment on your brother or sister? Or you, why do you despise your brother or sister? For we will all stand before the judgment seat of God.
11 For it is written, As I live, saith the Lord, every knee shall bow to me, and every tongue shall confess to God.	11 11 For it is written, "As I live, says the Lord, every knee shall bow to me, and every tongue shall give praise to God."
12 So then every one of us shall give account of himself to God.	12 So then, each of us will be accountable to God.
13 Let us not therefore judge one another any more: but judge this rather, that no man put a stumblingblock or an occasion to fall in his brother's way.	13 Let us therefore no longer pass judgment on one another, but resolve instead never to put a stumbling block or hindrance in the way of another.
14 I know, and am persuaded by the Lord Jesus, that there is nothing unclean of itself: but to him that esteemeth any thing to be unclean, to him it is unclean.	14 I know and am persuaded in the Lord Jesus that nothing is unclean in itself; but it is unclean for anyone who thinks it unclean.
15 But if thy brother be grieved with thy meat, now walkest thou not charitably. Destroy not him with thy meat, for whom Christ died.	15 If your brother or sister is being injured by what you eat, you are no longer walking in love. Do not let what you eat cause the ruin of one for whom Christ died.
16 Let not then your good be evil spoken of:	16 So do not let your good be spoken of as evil.
17 For the kingdom of God is not meat and drink; but righteousness, and peace, and joy in the Holy Ghost.	17 For the kingdom of God is not food and drink but righteousness and peace and joy in the Holy Spirit.
18 For he that in these things serveth Christ is acceptable to God, and approved of men.	18 The one who thus serves Christ is acceptable to God and has human approval.
19 Let us therefore follow after the things which make for peace, and things wherewith one may edify another.	19 Let us then pursue what makes for peace and for mutual upbuilding.
20 For meat destroy not the work of God. All things indeed are pure; but it is evil for that man who eateth with offence.	20 Do not, for the sake of food, destroy the work of God. Everything is indeed clean, but it is wrong for you to make others fall by what you eat;

MAIN THOUGHT: Let us therefore follow after the things which make for peace, and things wherewith one may edify another. (Romans 14:19, KJV)

King James Version

21 It is good neither to eat flesh, nor to drink wine, nor any thing whereby thy brother stumbleth, or is offended, or is made weak.
22 Hast thou faith? have it to thyself before God. Happy is he that condemneth not himself in that thing which he alloweth.

23 And he that doubteth is damned if he eat, because he eateth not of faith: for whatsoever is not of faith is sin.

New Revised Standard Version

21 it is good not to eat meat or drink wine or do anything that makes your brother or sister stumble.
22 The faith that you have, have as your own conviction before God. Blessed are those who have no reason to condemn themselves because of what they approve.
23 But those who have doubts are condemned if they eat, because they do not act from faith; for whatever does not proceed from faith is sin.

LESSON SETTING
> **Time:** AD 57–58
> **Place:** Corinth

LESSON OUTLINE
   I. **Do Not Judge (Romans 14:10–13)**
   II. **Being Acceptable to God and Humans (Romans 14:14–18)**
   III. **Christian Convictions (Romans 14:19–23)**

UNIFYING PRINCIPLE
People sometimes judge the flaws and faults of others rather than focusing on their own shortcomings. What is it people hope to prove when passing judgment on others? Romans 14 offers an alternative to passing judgment on one another, suggesting that we resolve instead to pursue what makes for peace and for mutual upbuilding.

INTRODUCTION
The previous nine verses use the image of eating and not eating as a method of comparing people and their ways. "One who eats" is not better than "one who does not eat" are examples. The climax of these verses ends with "For not one of us lives for himself, and not one dies for himself; for if we live, we live for the Lord, or if we die, we die for the Lord; therefore, whether we live or die, we are the Lord's. For to this end Christ died and lived again, that He might be Lord both of the dead and of the living" (Romans 14:1–9). Paul presents these images of food, where any item can be substituted, which can either enlighten or destroy a person or those brothers and sisters around him. This missive to the Christian church at Rome is aimed at the believer who must understand the metaphors that are intended to teach the believer to keep the faith, be respectful of others, and allow the Holy Spirit to guide their walk with God.

EXPOSITION

I. DO NOT JUDGE (ROMANS 14:10–13)
Humans tend to judge our brothers and sisters because of the deep-seated idea that we must be better than someone else. Social stratification and the need to be valued, even at the expense of those less fortunate, drive the human experience. No one has been able to solve this issue,

which has caused wars, the loss of friendships, and created interpersonal strife. In this case, Paul asks this question from the standpoint of the lifestyle of the Christian believer in our walk with the Lord.

Paul asks why we hold our brothers and sisters in contempt? The definition of contempt is the feeling that a person or a thing is beneath consideration, worthless, or deserving scorn. When we "look down" on our brothers and sisters we usually treat them badly.

We cannot act in the manner of the average person who is not serious about a walk with God. Jesus has warned to "judge not lest you be judged" (Matthew 7:1) because our perspective is biased and based on human perspective. The worthiness of all humankind, including Christian believers, will be judged of the kingdom. All of us are going to stand before the *bema*, the judgment-seat of Christ. All believers must know and understand that God has given Jesus the authority to execute judgment.

It is written that "every knee shall bow to Me," which indicates that no one has the authority that would enable them to marginalize or brutalize our brothers and sisters. When we hold each other contemptuously, we place people in a position where we expect them to "bow down" to us, as in words that are reminiscent to Paul's Letter to the Philippians where he declares that "at the name of Jesus every knee shall bow, and every tongue confess" (Philippians 2:10–11). Nonetheless, Paul may have recalled Isaiah, where it is written that "to Me every knee will bow, and every tongue shall swear allegiance," (Isaiah 45:23) to support his argument. However, the content of this phrase in Old Testament contexts is often "to acknowledge that God is God" (NEB, "acknowledge God"), and so, the TEV translates this phrase by everyone will confess that I am God. Paul's language here indicates that the act of bowing and confessing can only be ascribed to the One who is worthy of our praise, which is Jesus the Lord. Only God has the honor of being worshiped.

In this case, each person will give an account to God of the summation of his/her life. In our explanation to God about what we have done and why, Christian believers should have lived a lifestyle that would not render us embarrassed to be "presented before the throne." When judgment comes, it will not be the responsibility of humans to judge, but the final verdict will be from the Lord. Therefore, we are to stop judging each other. Paul is speaking about a form of judgment that restricts the growth of a fellow believer. Paul warns about using judgments as a form of creating obstacles or a "stumbling block" that would cause our brother or sister to fall. These obstacles are not limited to erecting barriers that are insurmountable but are also the presenting of tempting situations that will cause our brothers and sisters to be drawn into sin and separation from God. The church must be determined not to become a stumbling block, to accomplish this, we must be very deliberate in realizing what these "stumbling blocks" look like.

II. Being Acceptable to God and Humans (Romans 14:14–18)

Shifting his imagery, Paul continues his message. Paul uses the imagery of food and reflects on the prohibitions that are based in the Law. Jewish Christians would understand or at least be familiar with these edicts when determining what was clean or unclean. An honorable Jew would observe all food laws.

Although Paul is convinced that all things are clean through Jesus, he does not say it. Paul means that even though something may not be wrong in itself, if a person believes it is wrong and does it, then, that person commits a sin against his/her conscience. Therefore, what is considered clean becomes unclean for this person. So, if a new Jewish believer feels that certain meats are unclean and should not be eaten, they are truly unclean to him/her, and would sin by partaking.

In this case, Paul is asking the believers to understand what a barrier is, using the concept of ceremonial cleansing. What is spoken can become obstacles for others. Paul is simply saying that when a person is convinced that he/she is right, they believe it unto themselves whether anyone else believes it or not. When used in a positive manner, such as "no one can separate me from the Lord," this is totally acceptable, if not admirable; but when used in a pompous and negative manner, this scenario reeks of arrogance.

Food serves as a metaphor for anything that can be used to cause division. It could have said, "because of money (or lack thereof) your brother is hurt." Food, in this case, can be substituted with anything that can be negatively used for destruction. When your brother or sister is hurt, we are no longer walking in love or by the Spirit because the Spirit will not allow this type of behavior or thought. This next phrase is awkward: "Do not destroy with your food-him for who Christ died." The phrase means that we are not to hurt or spiritually destroy (*apóllumi*) your brother with food, allow our actions to taint another's spiritual walk. We cannot permit our spiritual freedom to demolish others in the process.

Actually, it is not the food that one eats that ruins the person for whom Christ died, but it is eating certain foods that causes such a person's ruin. Here again, food is a metaphor as Christ did not die for food but died to save all people.

The kingdom of God is not eating and drinking. It is possible that Paul was warning the members of the church to avoid being part of the pagan Roman bacchanalia, which were festivals of Bacchus, the Greco-Roman god of wine, freedom, intoxication, and ecstasy, which emanated from an Epicureanism philosophy which argued that pleasure was the chief good in life. Christians must recognize that the kingdom is about righteousness, peace, and joy in the Holy Spirit. The person who serves God in the manner of seeking the kingdom and all of its righteousness will find peace and joy.

III. CHRISTIAN CONVICTIONS (ROMANS 14:19–23)

Therefore, the Christian believer who is determined to walk in the ways of the Lord must be concerned that it is one of edification and encouragement. This walk with God must be deliberate and purposeful, in that we are sensitive to the needs and feelings of others. Paul speaks of being dedicated to a lifestyle that creates peace and harmony. "To pursue peace" is a Semitic idiom which means "to try to live in peace with one's fellow-man." In the totality of world history, all of the wars that have been fought were destructive and costly, as lives have been lost and people forever changed. Peace, in all cases, becomes a precious commodity and must be actively pursued if humankind is to survive.

Referring to verses 16–17, then, do not destroy what is God's or His workmanship for the sake of the imagery of food. All things created by God are clean, but they become evil when used by evil persons. Whatever a person consumes or lifestyle he/she lives, he/she must not use it to create an obstacle or do anything to erect a "stumbling block" for another. Our faith reflects our personal relationship with God. Faith is a standard in our walk with God. However, every believer should have standards and principles but should see that they are used to help others, never to hinder them. Christians find joy in what we know is right; therefore, do not condemn yourself because other men may doubt your relationship with the Lord.

THE LESSON APPLIED

Christian conscience is a large component in the Christian walk with the Lord. There are many opportunities and temptations for the believer to "backslide" or live a hypocritical lifestyle. Christians must be strong in the faith and realize that our language can affect the lives of the non-believer but can especially influence fellow Christians. People watch the Christian who is faithful to his/her church, who tithes, who is not ashamed to praise and worship the Lord. When believers do not act accordingly, whether in church settings or outside, the power of the Lord vested in the Christians is diluted instead of illuminated. Therefore, the Christian conscience or guidance of the Holy Spirit must be nurtured and not ignored.

LET'S TALK ABOUT IT

How can I best help and support the ministry of my local church and pastor?

Believers care about the well-being and faith journeys of others. Christians who are committed and love their churches are constantly inviting potential new members to attend services and meet their pastors. What is sad is when other members of the church refuse to evangelize and criticize those that do. Moreover, it is not solely the pastor's role to bring others into the church. If people are not proud of the church they attend or are a member of, then, what does that say about their membership? We must bring people to Christ because among many things, the well-being of others, which includes their faith journeys, can only occur when one's life is based in the faith. Faith is the one ingredient we need to assure we are pleasing to the Lord our God Through faith we are blessed to enjoy an the presence of God.

HOME DAILY DEVOTIONAL READINGS
AUGUST 14–20, 2023

MONDAY	TUESDAY	WEDNESDAY	THURSDAY	FRIDAY	SATURDAY	SUNDAY
Fear Not; God Is with You	No More Condemnation	Wait for Redemption with Patience	The Spirit Helps in Our Weakness	Rescue the Weak and Needy	Stewards of God's Mysteries	God's Power Exhibited in Weakness
Isaiah 41:1–14	Romans 8:1–15	Romans 8:16–25	Romans 8:26–39	Psalm 82	1 Corinthians 4:1–6	1 Corinthians 4:7–21

JUDGMENT IN THE KINGDOM

ADULT TOPIC:	BACKGROUND SCRIPTURE:
GOD'S COMMENDATION	1 CORINTHIANS 4:1–21

1 CORINTHIANS 4:1–6, 17–21

King James Version	*New Revised Standard Version*
LET a man so account of us, as of the ministers of Christ, and stewards of the mysteries of God.	THINK of us in this way, as servants of Christ and stewards of God's mysteries.
2 Moreover it is required in stewards, that a man be found faithful.	2 Moreover, it is required of stewards that they be found trustworthy.
3 But with me it is a very small thing that I should be judged of you, or of man's judgment: yea, I judge not mine own self.	3 But with me it is a very small thing that I should be judged by you or by any human court. I do not even judge myself.
4 For I know nothing by myself; yet am I not hereby justified: but he that judgeth me is the Lord.	4 I am not aware of anything against myself, but I am not thereby acquitted. It is the Lord who judges me.
5 Therefore judge nothing before the time, until the Lord come, who both will bring to light the hidden things of darkness, and will make manifest the counsels of the hearts: and then shall every man have praise of God.	5 Therefore do not pronounce judgment before the time, before the Lord comes, who will bring to light the things now hidden in darkness and will disclose the purposes of the heart. Then each one will receive commendation from God.
6 And these things, brethren, I have in a figure transferred to myself and to Apollos for your sakes; that ye might learn in us not to think of men above that which is written, that no one of you be puffed up for one against another.	6 I have applied all this to Apollos and myself for your benefit, brothers and sisters, so that you may learn through us the meaning of the saying, "Nothing beyond what is written," so that none of you will be puffed up in favor of one against another.
• • • • • •	• • • • • •
17 For this cause have I sent unto you Timotheus, who is my beloved son, and faithful in the Lord, who shall bring you into remembrance of my ways which be in Christ, as I teach every where in every church.	17 For this reason I sent you Timothy, who is my beloved and faithful child in the Lord, to remind you of my ways in Christ Jesus, as I teach them everywhere in every church.

MAIN THOUGHT: Therefore judge nothing before the time, until the Lord come, who both will bring to light the hidden things of darkness, and will make manifest the counsels of the hearts: and then shall every man have praise of God. (1 Corinthians 4:5, KJV)

1 CORINTHIANS 4:1–6, 17–21

King James Version	*New Revised Standard Version*
18 Now some are puffed up, as though I would not come to you.	18 But some of you, thinking that I am not coming to you, have become arrogant.
19 But I will come to you shortly, if the Lord will, and will know, not the speech of them which are puffed up, but the power.	19 But I will come to you soon, if the Lord wills, and I will find out not the talk of these arrogant people but their power.
20 For the kingdom of God is not in word, but in power.	20 For the kingdom of God depends not on talk but on power.
21 What will ye? shall I come unto you with a rod, or in love, and in the spirit of meekness?	21 What would you prefer? Am I to come to you with a stick, or with love in a spirit of gentleness?

LESSON SETTING
Time: AD 57
Place: Ephesus

LESSON OUTLINE
I. Servants of Christ
(1 Corinthians 4:1–6)
II. Correction Through Love
(1 Corinthians 4:17–21)

UNIFYING PRINCIPLE
It is easier for us to pronounce judgment on the wrongs of others than to make our own wise choices. How can we remain focused on the right things? The First Letter to the Corinthians indicates that God's people are subject to the same judgment and discipline as everyone else.

INTRODUCTION
Writing from Ephesus, Paul is addressing the church at Corinth where divisions and strife are tearing the church apart. In the church, there are self-appointed leaders who are not under the authority of the Lord and are refusing to acknowledge Paul's apostolic status. In this case, these renegades are questioning Paul's authority, leadership, and judgement. However, Paul seeks to instill discipline in the church and restore its discord and strife. Paul writes this letter during a period of pain as he realizes that the work in the church is being compromised by people who want to be in charge, at the expense of the people and the vulnerable believers who could lose their faith. Paul could easily have become angered and succumbed to the emotion of hatred; however, he depends upon his walk with the Lord to control his response to the challenges of the Corinthian church.

EXPOSITION
I. SERVANTS OF CHRIST (1 CORINTHIANS 4:1-6)
Paul understands that servants of God should be seen by others in a positive light because of their walk with the Lord and the Holy Spirit. As servants of the Christ, we must also be good stewards of the Christian lifestyle and keepers of the mysteries that God has revealed to us, which the unchurched will not understand. Here, Paul uses the term "servants" (*hupērétēs*), which is defined as subordinate. This must not be confused with the term *doúlos*, which represents a slave, i.e., one who is in a state of servitude or bondage.

Christians are stewards of the mysteries of God, which we did not receive until we were redeemed into the body of Christ. This concept is directed to the believer because the non-believer is not given revelation to the kingdom when they do not believe it exists. Believers do not know all of the mysteries of the Lord, but God gives required revelation at required times. Old Testament prophecy and New Testament revelation are examples of mysteries that come to fruition. When the disciples asked Jesus why He taught in parables, He answered, "Because it has been given to you to know the mysteries of the kingdom of heaven, but to *them* it has not been given" (Matthew 13:10–11).

Paul states that it is required of Christians to be excellent stewards. Christians who are trustworthy in their stewardship usually exude confidence in all other matters because it is a component of their walk with the Lord. Therefore, for Paul, those who serve in an apostolic calling must project confidence in appointed stewards.

Paul declares that it is a small thing to be examined by "you." This "you" happens to be his accusers who he collectively refers to as a human court. Paul deflects their self-imposed importance, stating that, "Whatever happens here in earthly law courts, I am subject, not to this kind of judgment, but to the higher judgment of Christ." This verse is about Paul's real status as someone who is responsible to Christ. It is believed that this is a metaphor for the accusation of Paul misusing the Gospel in his position as an apostle. In this case, Paul is not being accused by an established ecclesiastical body or civil assembly but by the "court of opinion" that has been conjured by his detractors. In keeping with his commitment to Christ, Paul declares that he does not examine himself. Paul is confident of his innocence in these matters. Noting that he has not been acquitted of these charges, Paul must realize that it is possible that his accusers do not want to find him innocent in this situation. He does not believe that others are capable of casting judgment upon him because, as a servant of Christ, they were not competent to judge him or the quality of his service. Therefore, he is not discouraged in his ministry.

In this case, Paul is saying that his accusers should not continue to pass judgment on him because they are in error in their accusations. Paul loves the church and is warning his accusers against aligning themselves with rumors and innuendoes. Instead, they should wait for a proper time to reach their conclusions about his authenticity and calling from the Lord. For Paul, the right time is God's timing, and they should wait on the Lord to reveal any questions or issues that are the source of the controversy. When Paul speaks of the hidden things, in darkness, he is speaking of what is unknown, not what is being purposely concealed. In our contemporary age, transparency has become a buzzword; however, here, Paul is not attempting some cover up but is asking these disgruntled members of the church to allow the Lord to adjudicate this issue. In contrast to verses 3–4, the verb for pronounce judgment is the simple form *krinō*, referring not to an examination by a judge but to the verdict at the end of the trial (as in Matt. 7:1). The Lord's revelation will also disclose the motives of the hearts of his accusers, as well as the heart of Paul! When God's disclosure happens, all people will praise God because He will give to every person what is deserved praise. In this case, Paul is encouraging the people to wait on the Lord to reveal the answers to their questions.

Apollos met Paul in Corinth and was useful in "watering the good seed" Paul had planted, but the disciples of Apollos segregated themselves into his camp, creating further divisions (1 Corinthians 1:12–13). When Paul writes that he has figuratively applied, he is referring to himself and Apollos, although it is important to understand that others, whom he did not name, were the real culprits.

It is in this case that Paul uses his example with Apollos to warn the people not to exceed what is written, i.e., you might learn by us to live faithfully according to the Scriptures. Paul and Apollos would serve as curative examples of men under authority who did not go beyond what was written. They obeyed the Word of God, not their own inclinations or worldly opinions. Therefore, no one should become arrogant and look down on others with contempt, disdain, or disrespect. Paul wanted the Corinthian church to align themselves with the humility of Jesus.

II. Correction Through Love (1 Corinthians 4:17–21)

Timothy serves as a lieutenant to Paul as well as a disciple, and Paul refers to him as his "own son in the faith" (1 Timothy 1:2). Paul recommends that the Corinthians receive Timothy (and the letter) because his demeanor and commitment will remind them of Paul's walk in Christ. Paul notes that his encouragement to the church is not selective because it is Paul's pedagogy to instruct all churches in this manner. Timothy serves as a personal example of the faith and of someone who is worthy of bringing the letter to Corinth.

Sadly, Paul concedes that some members of the Corinthian church do not believe that he will visit. Moreover, this group probably does not care whether Paul comes to Corinth because his presence would usurp their authority. Their arrogance also reveals that they are acting out because they do not believe he will come. Paul anticipated that not all would be moved by his appeal. Some, probably the unnamed party leaders (v. 5) or guardians (v. 15), were arrogant, which was the major cause of the Corinthians' division problem. In this case, they might not be swayed by his exhortation but would only be moved through some sort of action.

However, Paul reminds them that he will visit them soon, "if the Lord wills." Paul has already decided in obedience to God and in fulfillment of his apostolic office to visit the Corinthians. He is speaking rather of God's secret will, his hidden plan for the future, which is unknown to Paul, and which will be known only as it comes to pass. For Paul, "if the Lord wills" means that Paul has to be guided by and protected by the Lord. When he visits, Paul will find out who his detractors are and will not listen to the words of the false leaders of the church.

Paul now takes a softer tone, a reconciliatory approach as in that of a teacher or father. Referring to verse 19, Paul does not believe that his teaching will sway the obstinate members of the church, he calls for action because the Kingdom does not consist of words but of power.

Concluding this missive, Paul asks what the church desires. The word "rod" in the phrase, "Shall I come to you with a rod?" represents a form of chastisement. However, in this case, the rod does not invoke a physical form of punishment but one who has the authority to remove those self-imposed members that (without the authority to be in positions of leadership) are guilty of dividing the church. He is speaking of a staff of righteousness that promotes the love of God. In his quest to promote peace and demonstrate love, Paul speaks as a loving father that has to instill discipline. For Paul, the church will be saved through the spirit of gentleness, which is not to be confused with the Holy Spirit but with the inner graciousness that we possess in our walk with the Lord.

THE LESSON APPLIED

In this lesson, Paul demonstrates that there is a proper manner to address church strife and divisions within the body. In the modern age, most people have known about a church that has spilt, not because of doctrinal issues but issues as to who is in power (and the way that power is defined). For Paul, the lack of discipline in this situation reflected the knowledge that some members will not submit to the will and authority of the Lord. Today, we must be careful not to allow that which is defined as "new approaches" to destroy the foundational integrity of the church. That which Jesus created when He told Peter that He would build His church must not be lost through a disconnection from our foundational traditions, and not given over to those who would use the church for their own purposes.

LET'S TALK ABOUT IT

Can believers find a sense of security in anything other than the Gospel?

Believers find spiritual and eternal security not in money, politics, possessions, or influence, but in God's love and service. In this case, we are not speaking of church members who seek money and power in the same manner as the non-believers, who pursue "things" and possessions to gratify the ego of their being accepted into a modern caste system.

Authentic believers are committed Christians who may obtain what may be viewed as worldly possessions but in reality, are gifts and blessings from God. That which provides authentic Christian joy is the emotion and gratification that comes from our love and service to others. In our walk with the Lord, authentic believers realize that through Him, we can experience a combination: worldly possessions, positions, and power. God blesses us to enjoy life in its fullness.

HOME DAILY DEVOTIONAL READINGS
AUGUST 21–27, 2023

MONDAY	TUESDAY	WEDNESDAY	THURSDAY	FRIDAY	SATURDAY	SUNDAY
Earth Is Full of God's Glory	In Him We Have Our Being	Many Will Go to God's House	Jesus Is Able to Save Forever	Awake and Sing for Joy!	The Most Important Message	The First Fruits of the Dead
Isaiah 6:1–8	Acts 17:22–31	Micah 4:1–7	Hebrews 7:11–25	Isaiah 26:12–21	1 Corinthians 15:1–14	1 Corinthians 15:15–28

GOD'S KINGDOM WILL BE ALL IN ALL

ADULT TOPIC:	BACKGROUND SCRIPTURE:
GOD'S AUTHORITY AND POWER	1 CORINTHIANS 15:1–28; EPHESIANS 1:15–23

1 CORINTHIANS 15:20–28

King James Version

BUT now is Christ risen from the dead, and become the firstfruits of them that slept.

21 For since by man came death, by man came also the resurrection of the dead.

22 For as in Adam all die, even so in Christ shall all be made alive.

23 But every man in his own order: Christ the firstfruits; afterward they that are Christ's at his coming.

24 Then cometh the end, when he shall have delivered up the kingdom to God, even the Father; when he shall have put down all rule and all authority and power.

25 For he must reign, till he hath put all enemies under his feet.

26 The last enemy that shall be destroyed is death.

27 For he hath put all things under his feet. But when he saith all things are put under him, it is manifest that he is excepted, which did put all things under him.

28 And when all things shall be subdued unto him, then shall the Son also himself be subject unto him that put all things under him, that God may be all in all.

New Revised Standard Version

BUT in fact Christ has been raised from the dead, the first fruits of those who have died.

21 For since death came through a human being, the resurrection of the dead has also come through a human being;

22 for as all die in Adam, so all will be made alive in Christ.

23 But each in his own order: Christ the first fruits, then at his coming those who belong to Christ.

24 Then comes the end, when he hands over the kingdom to God the Father, after he has destroyed every ruler and every authority and power.

25 For he must reign until he has put all his enemies under his feet.

26 The last enemy to be destroyed is death.

27 For "God has put all things in subjection under his feet." But when it says, "All things are put in subjection," it is plain that this does not include the one who put all things in subjection under him.

28 When all things are subjected to him, then the Son himself will also be subjected to the one who put all things in subjection under him, so that God may be all in all.

MAIN THOUGHT: And when all things shall be subdued unto him, then shall the Son also himself be subject unto him that put all things under him, that God may be all in all. (1 Corinthians 15:28, KJV

UNIFYING PRINCIPLE

People frequently question the order of power in the world. Where can we find an authority whom we can trust to control the universe? The letter to the Corinthians declares that through the death and resurrection of Jesus Christ, all creation is ultimately subjected under God.

INTRODUCTION

This section of Paul's analysis on the importance of the resurrection is to note that there is an orderly process as to who will be transformed first and why. There are scoffers and unbelievers that will never accept the resurrection as fact; yet, belief in the resurrection is based on the faith Christians have in the mission of Jesus. For many (even believers) who view the resurrection as a nice novelty, Paul makes it clear that the resurrection has a deeper meaning beyond the mystery and majesty of Jesus simply defeating the specter of the cross. The resurrection of Jesus is actually the key to the redemption of humanity, and Paul is declaring that Christians must embrace the resurrection because it is our entry into eternal life with the Lord. The death and resurrection of Jesus Christ is the central point of the Christian faith.

EXPOSITION

I. CHRIST, THE FIRST FRUITS (1 CORINTHIANS 15:20–22)

Paul begins this section with a declaration as a refutation to those who have said that the resurrection was false and that God played no role in it. Paul argues that if there was no resurrection of the dead, then Christ could not have been raised, making his preaching a lie and his faith worthless (1 Corinthians 15:12–19). However, Paul declares that Christ has been raised from the dead and serves as a standard of God's plan for the reclamation of fallen humanity. Jesus' resurrection is considered to be the first fruits of those who have died.

As the plan for the existence of believers in eternity, Jesus' resurrection is also part of the gift that was returned to God. Jesus must be considered a "first," as He was present during creation. Jesus also serves as a prototype. In the Old Testament, the Hebrew words translated "first fruits" refer either to the portion of the crop that is the first to be ripe or to the part that is best. Here, Paul utilizes the metaphor of first fruit to speak of the relationship between the resurrection of Christ and the resurrection of the dead. Christ's resurrection is the "first fruit of those who have fallen asleep," and like the first fruits of the harvest, it is a taste and guarantee of the full harvest of resurrection yet to come.

Adam's death was due to the sin of disobedience. As the first couple realized their mistake, God pronounced specific judgments on them stating that Adam would have to live by the "sweat of his brow" until he returned to the ground from which he was taken, saying, "For dust you are" (Genesis 3:19). There is a bond between Adam and the earth (*ʾăḏāmâ*), and it is from this *ʾăḏāmâ* that Adam gets his name (Genesis 2:7). Additionally, in the curses pronounced by God, the earth is cursed because of Adam (Genesis 3:17).

Paul notes that this is the reality, that humans came by death according to his bad choices, but also, that humanity, through the resurrection, has a gift from God. In Adam, all people die, but Jesus, who is also known as the "Second Adam," defies death and is a pathway to be restored to life. The resurrection is dedicated to believers who dedicate their lives to their walk with the Lord.

II. ORDER OF THE RESURRECTION (1 CORINTHIANS 15:23–26)

Paul is focused on the order of the resurrection that has been decided by God. The resurrection is not a haphazard event but was part of the plan of redemption.

There is a ranking for the resurrection at the Second Coming of Jesus, which is first, Christ, and then, those who are present at His coming. However, Paul later identifies a third group in the account. He writes that "we shall not all sleep, but we shall all be changed." Again, referring to death as applied to one who "sleeps with his fathers," believers will not be incarcerated by the power of death but will be restored *for* everlasting life. Noting that flesh and blood cannot inherit the Kingdom (1 Corinthians 15:50–52), Christians will be presented faultless before the throne of God (Jude 24). For Christians, it will be our turn to have earned the right to be called unto Jesus at His coming.

Then comes the end, which is actually the beginning of our reigning with Him in heaven. This signals the end of the world or the end of the age, as Jesus will hand over the Kingdom to God when He has abolished all rule, authority, and power. In the realms of heaven, the celestial methods that were formerly used will not be necessary. That Jesus seems to give over all authority and power does not mean that He abdicates His dominion; instead, the need for this type of authority that had been focused on an earthly existence will not be needed in the heavenly Kingdom. He has accomplished His mission of redemption and now gives (or *hands over*) all things back to God, His Father.

For Paul, the last enemy is death. Paul exults in his knowledge that Christ has defeated death, which is the ultimate sin because it can mean permanent rather than temporary separation from God. Later in the larger passage, Paul mockingly says that death is swallowed up in victory. Paul uses the term *katapinō*, i.e., swallowed up, whereas, a better meaning here is that Christ devoured or destroyed the specter of death in His conquest of the cross. As if he were taunting Satan and the unbelievers of the world, Paul asks "O death, where is your victory, O death, where is your sting?" (1 Corinthians 15:54–55). Moreover, Christ has taken away the pain of the grave, which was introduced at the first murder, and the Adamic curse, thus, removing the pain of death.

III. ALL THINGS SUBJECTED TO CHRIST (1 CORINTHIANS 15:27–28)

When Paul writes that He has put all things in subjection under His feet, it means that God is in control of all things in this world, including historical events, natural disasters, and the future of His people that He places under the feet of Jesus. The identification of whose feet Paul is speaking of can be confusing. An example of placing all things (made) under His feet can be understood as the dominion that God initially gave to Adam (humans). That "You have made him to have dominion over the works of Your hands and have put all things under his feet" (Psalm 8:6), in this case, is the feet of a human representative of the Kingdom. However, the identity changes as God speaks to Jesus, where it is written, "The LORD said to my Lord, 'Sit at My right hand, till I make Your enemies Your footstool'" (Psalm 110:1). Additionally, the writer of Hebrews clarifies the identification that is used here stating, "You have put all things in subjection under His feet," noting that "He left nothing that is not put under Him" (Hebrews 2:8). The clause *who puts all things under him* may be rendered as "who causes Christ to rule over all things." All things are subjected to Jesus because He is the power behind having everything subjected to His supremacy.

However, the scriptural interpretation of subjection is *hupotássō*, which means to place in order or to place under, in an orderly fashion. God, as Creator, has established dominion over the earth. "In the beginning, God created the heavens and the earth" (Genesis 1:1), which means that the Master Creator is automatically the dominant One in the forming of the universe. In the creation account, there is order and clarity as God creates deliberate concepts of the world on each of the first six days. The word "dominion" first appears when God said, "Then God said, "Let us make humankind in our image,

according to our likeness; and let them have dominion over the fish of the sea, and over the birds of the air, and over the cattle, and over all the wild animals of the earth, and over every creeping thing that creeps upon the earth."" (Genesis 1:26).

The need for this type of order is to reject worldly and celestial chaos while redeeming humanity from the act of Adam eating from the "tree of the knowledge of good and evil," which was the cause of the "fall" (Genesis 2:17). Unfortunately, humanity did not believe God's threatened judgment of death as a consequence of his disobedience, which God has to address. Because God alone can give true meaning and lasting purpose to life, humanity is separated from God in death. Moreover, we are left to define and give purpose to our existence, a task at which we have dismally failed, because apart from God, we have a meaningless existence.

Therefore, order is foundational in this sense in the act of subjection, as submission is first given to Jesus, then, given to God. This requires the understanding of "but when God has subjected everything to Himself, then the Son Himself will also be subjected to God who subjected all things to Him." Another method of understanding the concept is expressed in this manner: "When God has put all things under the Son, he will also subject the Son to Himself, he who put all things under." This speaks of Christ (15:24) when in the end, He will hand over the Kingdom to God, the Father. After Christ "has put all things under His feet," He then, submits Himself to the Father as the Messiah, having accomplished His task of redemption. This is not to imply that the Son is inferior to the Father but, when death is conquered at the end of the Millennium, then, all things will be under the administration of the triune God. It is important not to miss that God is ultimately in control of the entire submission process and guarantees that it is a methodical and orderly affair.

Paul concludes by declaring that when all is subjected to God, He becomes the "all-in-all." God as the all-in-all means that He is everything to all people; however, humankind has to allow God to be the entirety of our existence. God has allowed us to exist in a "free will" society where we have the freedom to choose to live with or without Him in our lives. Paul's message here is to the believer who has the experience and faith of walking in the "ways of the Lord." Only the Christian believer who utilizes the power of prayer and the quest to follow the steps that God creates can trust God with every segment and totality of our lives.

THE LESSON APPLIED

Many "church folk" have reduced the resurrection to the ending of a story where they "lived happily ever after." Sadly, the most affirming of Paul's verses that ask, "Death, where is your sting or victory?" are only taken seriously during a funeral and at a graveside committal. Believers must not dilute the reality of the resurrec-

tion of the believers, and the damnation of those who choose to follow the evil one, because knowledge of these future events will shape our lives and determine our destiny in the Lord. Believers cannot ignore the mandates of God, especially the method by which He sent His Son to die on the cross for our sin. However, we must remember that the story does not end with the cross, nor the resurrection, which holds the greater importance because of its determination of eternal life.

LET'S TALK ABOUT IT

If we can confirm Jesus is returning, how do we hold to the faith?

People often doubt that which cannot be experienced with the senses or understood with logic and reason. Unfortunately, many will openly state that "if I don't see it, I don't believe it." One of the most used words in the Gospel of John is "believe." Jesus knew that one's belief system is based on one's faith. An example is Jesus' words to Thomas following the resurrection, when He said, "Blessed are those who have not seen and yet believed" (John 20:29). Many who profess to be Christians will never be able to receive blessings because these mysteries defy logic and reason in our modern sensibilities. Faith is the conviction that God is real whether we can see Him or not.

HOME DAILY DEVOTIONAL READINGS
AUGUST 28–SEPTEMBER 3, 2023

MONDAY	TUESDAY	WEDNESDAY	THURSDAY	FRIDAY	SATURDAY	SUNDAY
Follow God, Not Human Traditions	Obedience, Not Sacrifice	Be Gracious to Me, O Lord	Jesus, a Friend of Sinners	Humility Before God and Others	Come to God in Cleanliness and Holiness	Be Cleansed Inside and Out
Mark 7:1–8	1 Samuel 1:19–23	Psalm 6	Luke 7:24–34	Luke 14:7–14	Exodus 30:17–21	Luke 11:37–44

*PARTIAL BIBLIOGRAPHY

FIRST QUARTER

Brueggemann, Walter. 1986. Genesis: Interpretation: A Bible Commentary for Teaching and Preaching. Westminster: John Knox Press.

Brueggemann, Walter. 2011. First and Second Samuel: Interpretation: A Bible Commentary for Teaching and Preaching. Westminster: John Knox Press.

Carter, Walter, and Amy-Jill Levine. 2013. The New Testament: Methods and Meanings. Abingdon Press.

Collins, John. 2018. A Short Introduction to the Hebrew Bible. Third. Fortress Press.

Kaiser, Walter C. 2012. The Expositor's Bible Commentary: Exodus. Edited by Frank Gaebelein. Zondervan.

Kalland, Earl S. 2012. The Expositor's Bible Commentary: Deuteronomy. Edited by Frank Gaebelein. Zondervan.

Lockyer, Herbert, FF Bruce, and R.K. Harrison, eds. 1986. Illustrated Dictionary of the Bible. Thomas Nelson.

Marbury, Herbert Robinson. 2015. Pillars of Cloud and Fire: The Politics of Exodus in African American Biblical Interpretation. New York University Press.

Martin, Ralph P. 1992. Ephesians, Colossians and Philemon: Interpretation: A Bible Commenatry for Teaching and Preaching. Westminster: John Knox Press.

Mathews, Kenneth A. 2005. Genesis 11:27-50:26: An Exegetical and Theological Exposition of Holy Scripture. Vol. 1. The New American Commentary 1B. Nashville, Tenn: Broadman & Holman.

McCann, J. Clinton. 2011. Judges: Interpretation: A Bible Commentary for Teaching and Preaching. Westminster: John Knox Press.

Miller, Patrick D. 1990. Deuteronomy: Interpretation: A Bible Commentary for Teaching and Preaching. Westminster: John Knox Press.

Sailhamer, John H. 2012. The Expositor's Bible Commentary: Genesis. Edited by Frank Gaebelein. Zondervan.

Wilder, Terry. 2005. The New American Commentary: Ephesians: An Exegetical and Theological Exposition of Holy Scripture. Vol. 31. Holman Reference.

Wolf, Herbert. 2012. The Expositor's Bible Commentary: Judges. Edited by Frank Gaebelein. Zondervan.

Youngblood, Ronald F. 2012. The Expositor's Bible Commentary: 1 & 2 Samuel. Edited by Frank Gaebelein. Zondervan.

SECOND QUARTER

Achtemeier, Paul J., Harper & Row, Publishers, and Society of Biblical Literature, eds. 1985. Harper's Bible Dictionary. 1st ed. San Francisco: Harper & Row.

Barclay, William. 1976. The Daily Study Bible: The Letters of James and Peter. Edinburgh: St Andrew Press.

Brown, Raymond E., Joseph A. Fitzmyer, and Roland E. Murphy, eds. 1990. The New Jerome Biblical Commentary. Englewood Cliffs, N.J: Prentice-Hall.

Brueggemann, Walter. 1977. Land: Place As Gift, Promise, and Challenge in Biblical Faith. Overtures to Biblical Theology 1. Philadelphia: Fortress Press. 1997. Cadences of Home: Preaching Among Exiles. 1st ed. Louisville, Ky: Westminster John Knox Press.

Davids, Peter H. 2009. The First Epistle of Peter. Repr. The New International Commentary on the New Testament. Grand Rapids, Mich: Eerdmans.

Gaventa, Beverly Roberts, and David L. Petersen, eds. 2010. The New Interpreter's Bible One-Volume Commentary. Nashville: Abingdon Press.

Gorman, Michael J. 2004. Apostle of the Crucified Lord: A Theological Introduction to Paul and His Letters. Grand Rapids, Mich: Eerdmans.

Hanson, Anthony Tyrrell. 1982. New Century Bible Commentary: The Pastoral Epistles. Grand Rapids : London: Wm.B. Eerdmans Pub. Co. ; Marshall, Morgan & Scott Pub. Ltd.

Keil, Carl Friedrich, and Franz Delitzsch. 1989. Commentary on the Old Testament. Vol. 10.

May, Herbert G., and Bruce M. Metzger, eds. 1977. The New Oxford Annotated Bible with the Apocrypha, Revised Standard Version. New York: Oxford University Press.

Moo, Douglas J. 2007. James: An Introduction and Commentary. Tyndale New Testament Commentaries. Downers Grove, IL: IVP Academic.

Noth, Martin. 1960. The History of Israel. New York, N.Y.: Harper and Row.

Pleins, J. David. 2000. The Social Visions of the Hebrew Bible: A Theological Introduction. 1st ed. Louisville, Ky: Westminster John Knox.

Provan, Iain W., V. Philips Long, and Tremper Longman. 2015. A Biblical History of Israel. Second Edition. Louisville, Kentucky: Westminster John Knox Press.

Rad, Gerhard von. 1972. The Message of the Prophets. New York: Harper & Row.

Stein, Robert H. 1992. Luke. The New American Commentary, v. 24. Nashville, Tenn: Broadman Press.

The Interpreter's Bible: Ecclesiastes, Song of Songs, Isaiah, Jeremiah. 1987. 48. print. Vol. 5. Nashville, TN: Abingdon Press.

The New Interpreter's Bible Commentary. 2015. Vol. 3. Nashville: Abingdon Press.

Wall, Robert W, N. T Wright, J. Paul Sampley, and Richard B Hays. 2015. The New Interpreter's Bible Commentary: Introduction to Epistolary Literature ; Romans; 1 & 2 Corinthians; Galatians. Vol. 9.

Westermann, Claus. 1969. Isaiah 40-66: A Commentary. The Old Testament Library. Philadelphia: Westminster Press.

Westermann, Claus, and Robert Henry Boyd. 1976. Handbook to the Old Testament. Minneapolis: Augsburg Pub. House.

Willmington, H. L. 2011. Willmington's Guide to the Bible. 30th anniversary ed. Carol Stream, Ill: Tyndale House Publishers.

Winter, Bruce W. 2001. After Paul Left Corinth: The Influence of Secular Ethics and Social Change. Grand Rapids, Mich: W.B. Eerdmans.

THIRD QUARTER

Word Pictures in the New Testament by Archibald Thomas Robertson. Volume II. The Gospel According to Luke. Nashville: Broadman Press.

Alan Culpepper, in The New Interpreter's Bible: A Commentary in Twelve Volume. Luke/John. Abingdon Press; Nashville.

Genesis 10:15; 22:21; 37:22; 43:33; 44: 12; Exodus 6:14; Numbers 3:2; Deuteronomy 21:17; I Samuel 17:28; First–Born by V. H. Kooy, in The Interpreter's Dictionary of the Bible E–J, Vol. 2. Abingdon Press: Nashville.

*PARTIAL BIBLIOGRAPHY

Robertson, Word Pictures in the New Testament.

Robertson, Word Pictures in the New Testament.

Eugene Boring. The Gospel of Matthew, Introduction, in The New Interpreter's Bible. Vol. VIII. Abingdon Press: Nashville..

Boring, The New Interpreter's Bible.

Gail R. O'Day, The Gospel of John in The New Interpreter's Bible. Volume 9. Abingdon Press: Nashville, p. 565; John 3:14, 30; 9:4.

Mark by Pheme Perkins in The New Interpreter's Bible: A Commentary in Twelve Volumes. Matthew and Mark. Volume VIII. Abingdon Press: Nashville.

James Brooks, Mark in the New American Commentary: An Exegetical and Theological Exposition of the Holy Scripture NIV Text. Broadman Press: Nashville, p. 89; see also The Broadman Commentary. Vol. 8: General Articles Matthew, Mark. Broadman Press: Nashville, p. 307; see also, Archibald Thomas Robertson, Word Pictures in the New Testament, Vol. 1. The Gospel According to Mark. Broadman Press: Nashville.

Robertson, Word Pictures.

The New Interpreter's, Mark.

Robertson, Word Pictures.

Matthew 12:43-45, Also, The Interpreters Bible.

The Gospel of Luke: A Commentary on the Greek Text Carlisle: Paternoster Press, 1978.

John A. T. Robertson. Word Pictures in the New Testament. Volume II, The Gospel According to Luke. Broadman Press: Nashville.

E. W. Clark in the The Interpreter's Dictionary of the Bible: An Illustrated Encyclopedia. Emmaus. Abingdon Press: Nashville p. 98; see also, R. Alan Culpepper. The New Interpreter's Bible: A Commentary in Twelve Volumes. Volume IX Luke-John.

John A. T. Robertson. Word Pictures in the New Testament. Volume II. Luke. Broadman Press: Nashville.

O 'Day. The New Interpreter's Bible. Luke.

Robertson. Word Pictures in the New Testament. Volume II. Luke.

Word Pictures.

Gail O'Day, John. The Interpreters' Bible. Volume IX. Luke-John. Abingdon Press: Nashville.

O'Day, The New Interpreters' Bible Ibid.

O'Day, John, The Interpreters' Bible.

George Beasley-Murray, The Word Biblical Commentary Volume 36. John. Word Book, Publisher: Waco.

Murray, The Word Biblical Ibid.x.

Gail O'Day, John. New Interpreters' Bible: A Commentary in Twelve Volumes, Abingdon Press: Nashville.

(O'Day, New Interpreters' John.

John Beasley Murray. Word Biblical Commentary. Volume 36. John. Word Books, Publisher: Waco.

John A. T. Robertson, Word Pictures in the New Testament. Volume 5. John. Broadman Press, 1932.

Acts, Broadman Commentary, Nashville.

John Polhill's Acts in the New American Commentary: An Exegetical and Theological Exposition of the Holy Scripture. Broadman Press: Nashville..

The Theology of the Apostolic Fathers, Tertullian, Irenaeus, The School of Alexandria: Clement and Origen in A History of Christian Thought by Justin Gonzalez, Abingdon Press: Nashville, 1970.

FOURTH QUARTER

"2 Esdras." In The Oxford Encyclopedia of the Books of the Bible. , edited by Lorenzo DiTommaso. Oxford Biblical Studies Online, http://www.oxfordbiblicalcstudies.com/article/opr/t280/e61 (accessed Apr 8, 2022)

Blue, J. R. (1985). Habakkuk. In J. F. Walvoord & R. B. Zuck (Eds.), *The Bible Knowledge Commentary: An Exposition of the Scriptures* (Vol. 1). Wheaton, IL: Victor Books.

Bright, J. *A History of Israel*, second edition, Philadelphia: The Westminster Press, 1972.

Dictionary of Biblical Imagery, edited by Leland Ryken, James C. Wilhoit, and Tremper Longman III, Downers Grove, Illinois: InterVarsity Press, 1998.

Dyer, C. H. (1985). Ezekiel. In J. F. Walvoord & R. B. Zuck (Eds.), *The Bible Knowledge Commentary: An Exposition of the Scriptures* (Vol. 1). Wheaton, IL: Victor Books.

Easton, M. G. (1893). In *Illustrated Bible Dictionary and Treasury of Biblical History, Biography, Geography, Doctrine, and Literature.* New York: Harper & Brothers.

Elwell, W. A., & Beitzel, B. J. (1988). *Babylon, Babylonia.* In Baker encyclopedia of the Bible (Vol. 1). Grand Rapids, MI: Baker Book House.

Everson, A. J. (2000). Isaiah, Book of. In D. N. Freedman, A. C. Myers, & A. B. Beck (Eds.), *Eerdmans dictionary of the Bible.* Grand Rapids, MI: W.B. Eerdmans.

Goldingay, J. (2014). *A Critical and Exegetical Commentary on Isaiah 56–66.* (G. I. Davies & C. M. Tuckett, Eds.). London; New Delhi; New York; Sydney: Bloomsbury.

Halpern, B. (2000). David. In D. N. Freedman, A. C. Myers, & A. B. Beck (Eds.), *Eerdmans dictionary of the Bible.* Grand Rapids, MI: W.B. Eerdmans.

Klein, R. W. (2000). Ezekiel, Book of. In D. N. Freedman, A. C. Myers, & A. B. Beck (Eds.), *Eerdmans dictionary of the Bible.* Grand Rapids, MI: W.B. Eerdmans.

Koester, C. R. (2000). Tabernacle. In D. N. Freedman, A. C. Myers, & A. B. Beck (Eds.), Eerdmans dictionary of the Bible. Grand Rapids, MI: W.B. Eerdmans.

Martin, J. A. (1985). Isaiah. In J. F. Walvoord & R. B. Zuck (Eds.), *The Bible Knowledge Commentary: An Exposition of the Scriptures* (Vol. 1). Wheaton, IL: Victor Books.

McNicol, A. J. (2000). Gospel, Good News. In D. N. Freedman, A. C. Myers, & A. B. Beck (Eds.), *Eerdmans dictionary of the Bible.* Grand Rapids, MI: W.B. Eerdmans.

Ogden, G. S., & Sterk, J. (2011). *A Handbook on Isaiah.* (P. Clarke, S. Brown, L. Dorn, & D. Slager, Eds.) (Vol. 1 & 2). Reading, UK: United Bible Societies.

Ryrie, Charles, New American Standard Study Bible, (Chicago: Moody Press, 1995).

The Jewish Study Bible, second edition, edited by, Adele Berlin and Marc Zvi Brettler, New York: Oxford University Press, 2014.

Walvoord, J. F. (1985). Revelation. In J. F. Walvoord & R. B. Zuck (Eds.), *The Bible Knowledge Commentary: An Exposition of the Scriptures* (Vol. 2). Wheaton, IL: Victor Books.

https://www.pbs.org/wnet/african-americans-many-rivers-to-cross/history/the-truth-behind-40-acres-and-a-mule/

* See Full Bibliography online at rhboyd.com.